Be All You Can Be

From a Hitler Youth in World War II
to a
US Army Green Beret

An Immigrant's Memoirs

Written in his own words
by
Major Dieter H.B. Protsch
US Army Special Forces, Retired

Note for Librarians: a cataloguing record for this book that includes Dewey Decimal
Classification and US Library of Congress numbers is available from the Library and
Archives of Canada. The complete cataloguing record can be obtained from their online
database at:
www.collectionscanada.ca/amicus/index-e.html
ISBN 1-4120-3674-7
Printed in Victoria, BC, Canada

TRAFFORD

Offices in Canada, USA, Ireland, UK and Spain
This book was published *on-demand* in cooperation with Trafford Publishing. On-demand
publishing is a unique process and service of making a book available for retail sale to the
public taking advantage of on-demand manufacturing and Internet marketing. On-demand
publishing includes promotions, retail sales, manufacturing, order fulfilment, accounting and
collecting royalties on behalf of the author.
Book sales for North America and international:
Trafford Publishing, 6E–2333 Government St.,
Victoria, BC V8T 4P4 CANADA
phone 250 383 6864 (toll-free 1 888 232 4444)
fax 250 383 6804; email to orders@trafford.com
Book sales in Europe:
Trafford Publishing (UK) Ltd., Enterprise House, Wistaston Road Business Centre,
Wistaston Road, Crewe, Cheshire CW2 7RP UNITED KINGDOM
phone 01270 251 396 (local rate 0845 230 9601)
facsimile 01270 254 983; orders.uk@trafford.com
Order online at:
www.trafford.com/robots/04-1502.html

10 9 8 7 6 5 4 3

Foreword

The title of the book "Be All You Can Be" is the old Army slogan, which was not just a phrase to me. I firmly believed in this statement and it was to become the driving force in my entire life, not just a military career.

I had never dreamed of writing a book, especially not my own memoirs. Talking to my children, grandchildren and friends who often queried me about my past, I was strongly encouraged to put down in black on white my experiences of a rather challenging life.

I recalled my early youth in Germany, growing up during the Third Reich and World War II and combat in Berlin following a disastrous trek from the Polish Border after having bombed out earlier by allied air raids. My experiences living under the Soviet occupation in 1945, including several days as a POW and our family's survival are all brought back to life in my memoirs.

And so are my experiences following a flight from Berlin through the Soviet Zone in Germany, joining a Para-military US Army organization, my eventual immigration to the United States and a fulfilling 20-year military career from serving as an enlisted soldier to becoming and retiring as a commissioned officer. My military training included Officer Candidate School, Ranger, Airborne, Jungle Warfare and eventually Unconventional Warfare Training. I retired from the Green Berets, the elite United States Army Special Forces, having served several tours overseas in Germany, Korea and Viet-Nam.

I must express my appreciation to all those close friends who continuously prompted me to finish my book. I am indebted to those special friends, who selflessly offered their expertise in editing and providing the final design of the cover. Persuaded by many who knew me closer not to use a co-writer, I decided to write the book "In my own words". All those people who knew me closer will undoubtedly hear me speak as my expressions in the text still reflect my German heritage and may even suggest a German accent.

Acknowledgements

A special thanks to my dedicated friends who helped me overcome technical difficulties:

Cover Design
Susan Gauntlett

Editing
Susan Wilson Younkins
Marlena Gudz

Needless to say, my sincere and heartfelt thanks go to my wife and lifelong partner, Christine, who always stood by me in many tough and challenging times. It was extremely difficult for both of us to build a new life in a foreign country, but even in my absence, while I was in the service, she handled all difficulties as a stay-home mother without complaints. Totally dedicated to our children and me, she mastered to provide our family with a beautiful home and a friendly atmosphere by being a true partner, a friend and excellent mother. I know in my heart, that I could never have succeeded and accomplished the things I did without her backing and support.

Contents

Chapter III
Reaching Adulthood – Yearning for Independence

Chapter IV
A Dream Fulfilled - America

Chapter V
Back to the Old Country

Chapter VI
My First Taste of the Orient

Chapter VII
After a Brief Stay Home, the Far East Beckons Again

Chapter VIII
Europe Once More

Chapter IX
Back in the USA

Chapter X
Permanent Retirement Not in My Cards

Chapter I

My Youth in the Third Reich

Parents' History

One of the greatest regrets I have is the fact that I never really questioned my parents about their past, their childhood and my great-grandparents. Only rarely did they talk about their earlier life. What I did find out was only sketchy and did not help me much in trying to understand their convictions, their desires in life and their goals.

Now, when my children ask me about their great-grandparents, I must admit to them that I was never close enough with my parents that they willingly laid their past open to me. As the oldest of three children, my sister being four years and my brother six years younger, I should have been more inquisitive.

Only two of my grandparents were still alive. Both were well-educated and considered well-to-do middle class. I was not too fond of my father's mother, but adored my mother's father, who was a well respected precision engineer working on optical instruments. While my grandfather hailed from Koenigsberg in East Prussia, my grandmother came from Breslau, Upper Silesia, now Poland but once part of the German Empire. Unfortunately, my grandfather died in 1947 of malnutrition. Living under the Soviet occupation with limited food resources, he consumed excessive amounts of a salad dressing he believed to have beneficial nutrients and vitamins. Apparently he damaged his stomach causing his death. The night he died in the hospital we could hear him knocking his pipe on the stove, as he usually did when he was visiting.

I saw my grandmother quite frequently after the war until she died at a good age of 94. One of the reasons my parents never offered to explain their past is probably the fact that I was born in one of the more turbulent times in the history of Germany. My father, Willy Protsch, was born in 1898 and served in the Kaiser's infantry France during World War I until the surrender in 1918. He was wounded twice and received the silver German badge for combat wounds. It was a severe blow for him experiencing the loss of the war as a young soldier. During the turbulent years in the 20's and the Weimar Republic, he apparently became enthused with the idea of a new and revitalized Germany.

The communist party was growing rapidly in Germany, but the majority of his generation rejected the idea of communism then growing strong in Russia. He was excited about restoring Germany to its old glory. As the son of middle class parents in Germany, he had finished high school before his military service and after the war he began his apprenticeship working for an insurance company. At that same time he became interested in one of the nationalist parties, later to be called National Socialist German Workers Party (Nationalsozialistische Deutsche Arbeiter Partei). The NSDAP or Nazis, were the devout opponents and sworn enemies of the Communists, the Spartakists. I do remember him recalling some of his battles with the "reds", similar to our present turf battles among the various gangs in the states. My mother, Margarete Protsch, a secretary at his insurance company, later relayed to me how she was called upon to mend his wounds received during many fistfights and brawls. He often had to fight his way through their territory on the way to party meetings on his motorcycle with a comrade in his sidecar.

As the party grew, he became more actively involved, and so did my mother. They both became charter members and as such recipients of the golden party insignia during the late 1920's. Over the years my father became a '*Standartenführer*' (Colonel) of the Standarte IV of the SA (Sturmabteilung), Hitler's "Stormtroopers" in one of Berlin's larger districts. SA men were members of a para-military unit, which was formed to protect political leaders of the party. His closest friend and comrade-in-arms was one of Kaiser Wilhelm's sons, the Prince August Wilhelm, also called "AUWI" by close friends. Among my prized possessions are copies of personal letters written by Prince August Wilhelm to my father from his American internment camp in Ludwigshafen in February 1947. When I was born in April 1932, after the party and Hitler came to power in 1931, my parents were honored to have the party chief in Berlin, '*Gauleiter*'

Dr. Joseph Goebbels, become my godfather at the baptism. Little did Dr. Goebbels know that I was not too fond of the cold water dripping on my head. As he was holding me and to everybody's embarrassment I wetted his uniform jacket and pants.

My parents envisioned a great future for me, their first son; I was not to be the only child, as Hitler strongly supported motherhood to provide for a growing nation of dedicated Germans and my mother was not about to disappoint him. After a third child was born, my mother was awarded the '*Mutterkreuz*' (Cross of Motherhood) for her efforts in building a strong nation. As the party movement grew in the early 30's, my parents found themselves involved in several internal fights for supremacy within the party structure. When the leader of the SA Röhm, was killed by members of the rivaling '*Schutz-Staffel*', SS in 1934, my parents became disgruntled with the new leadership. My father's open criticism apparently presented a threat to the party. He was strongly advised to give up his position and consequently they both did relinquish their active support of the NSDAP.

Still a very dedicated German, my father instead joined the growing German Air Force as an officer of the 1st Airborne Division in Diepholz near Hannover in western Germany. This was also the place where my sister Ute was born. Assigned to the Aviation Ministry in Berlin, our family returned to the Capital, where my young brother Reiner was later born. We had settled down and began enjoying our new home, but little did we realize that Germany was making serious war plans. Germany had begun to expand its territory lost after WWI, by moving into the Rhineland and claiming Austria, Hitler's native country, as part of the Reich. In September 1939 German forces suddenly invaded Poland, thereby entering us into another war, which developed into World War II, making Great Britain one of our adversaries.

While my mother was strictly caring for us children, my father, unfortunately, was constantly gone as a result of his active duty assignments during World War II. On 20 May 1941 he successfully parachuted onto the Island of Crete, which Germany then occupied until the end of 1941. When Field Marshall Erwin Rommel was getting short of personnel battling American and British forces, my father was flown into Africa and assigned to Rommel's General Staff. After the retreat of the German '*Afrika Korps*' from Africa in 1943 he was transferred with Rommel to the Atlantic Wall, near Cherbourg, France. While they prepared for the anticipated allied invasion, the rest of our family was subjected to daily allied air raids in Berlin. It was in late 1943 when a bomb landed in our backyard, destroying our house. Evacuated from Berlin to safety near the Polish border we later had to escape from there back to Berlin during the Russian advance. For over two years we did not hear from my father until after the war in 1947 from his '*Internierungslager*' (POW internment camp) Darmstadt in western Germany. Following his release from the POW camp, my parents and our family was finally reunited again in 1950 in Heidelberg, then the US Zone, Germany.

My Early Youth and Education

I entered grammar school in Zehlendorf in May 1938, a suburb for the middle class of Berlin. There is not much I remember from that period, except for a few pictures we recovered from other relatives. One was showing me at age 6, beaming and carrying a huge '*Zuckertüte*'. This traditional sugar cone is given to all first day students as a present for starting in the school education system. Our residential area in Berlin was a quiet neighborhood of mostly 3-4 story buildings surrounded by trees, parks and lakes. It was quite idyllic and my daily walks to school with fellow students in my block were a lot of fun. When our apartment became too small for our family my parents decided to move into a larger two-story row house in Berlin-Britz, a more suburban district of Berlin. We even had a backyard for planting vegetables. The surrounding area was predominantly agricultural and a lot quieter. I did not have any difficulties finding and making new friends. Strangely enough though something else and unique was introduced into our lives. Air raid sirens. We never comprehended the seriousness of the sirens but considered those practice drill fun since we never expected any enemy planes ever to reach Berlin.

How wrong we were. I had just turned ten years when the war caught up with us in Berlin. Although they had practice air raid siren off and on, that one day in May of 1942 we typically disregarded the sound of the sirens. Suddenly the air seemed filled with howling, whistling sounds, followed by an explosion and a feeling of the air being pressurized. As instructed we ran to the nearest apartment house that displayed the air raid shelter symbol. We sought shelter in the basement. When no other bombs fell, we assumed that the air raid was over and we left the shelter of the building and ran home. From that day on, the air raids increased and became a nightly recurrence.

My father as a young Infantry soldier of the Kaiser's Army during WW I at age 18 in 1917

Our mother with her traditional German hairdo.

Father in his SA "Standarten-Führer" uniform in Berlin, Germany.

First Family portrait of my parents and I at age 2

My first school day in Berlin-Britz, holding the customary candy-filled "Zuckertüte".

My father as Oberleutnant (1st Lt) of the Luftwaffe (German Air Force)

Mother with her three children. Reiner, Ute and I.

The re-united family in 1948 at Heidelberg in West-Germany.

Although a fear never really developed, a lot of people living in single homes in the suburbs began building their own separate bomb shelters in their backyards. So did our family, but we never used it except for storing canned food and water just in case our house was ever hit. But the government wanted to make sure that an ample supply of water was available and one day they built a swimming pool in our yard. Not for swimming, however, but for emergencies such as putting out fires caused by bombardments in the immediate neighborhood.

Induction into the Jungvolk – A Life with Air Raids

At the age of ten years, all of my class mates and I were inducted into the '*Jungvolk*' (young folk) of the 'Hitler Jugend' (Hitler's Youth). All boys ten years to thirteen years old in the *Jungvolk* later graduated into Hitler Youth at age fourteen to eighteen.

This was in those times one of my proudest days. The *Jungvolk* could be compared to the Cub Scouts of the Boy Scouts as our guidelines and laws were similar to those of the Scouts. We always compared ourselves with them except instead of being internationally oriented we were strictly a national organization. We also had a counterpart in the young girls. They were called '*BdM*' or '*Bund Deutscher Mädchen*', the association of German Girls. Our mission was to serve the fatherland. For all of us boys it was a great day when we were given our uniforms. It consisted of a brown shirt, black corduroy shorts with belt and brass buckle, a scarf and cap. The most precious item of course was the side arm, a bayonet with the inscription '*Blut und Ehre*' (Blood and Honor). My assignment to an actual unit, the '*Fähnlein*' 14, '*Bann*' 61, (Company 14, Battalion 61), gave me the proud feeling of being an important part of a great rising nation and a defender against Germany's enemies. The greatest surprise and most memorable experience was the day when '*der Führer*', the leader Adolph Hitler visited our unit shaking our hands.

Having just started learning English in school, it was now being expanded to include military terminology. We were excited to be shown actual war material found at downed aircrafts and bomb fragments. In order to get a better picture of our military branches of the '*Wehrmacht*' (defense forces), we were also invited for vacations to various military installations such as the naval facilities at Penemünde and Heringsdorf, on the shores of the Baltic Sea. These visits were always very impressive. As guests of the soldiers and seamen and the future defenders of the German Reich, we were always given excellent treatment. Many of us were swayed to join either the Navy or one of the other services once we reached the appropriate age for enlistment. Even though I was almost persuaded to join the Army, I was still more impressed with the *'Luftwaffe'*, Germany's Air Force of which my father was a proud officer. After about a week in a HJ campsite on the beach we were all ready to go back home. As big city guys, these little coastal towns were nice to visit but did not have much more to offer to us young boys. We were always looking forward to returning home, even though it meant going back to the air raids.

With the increase of bombardments, school attendance was reduced but our training by the Hitler Youth was increased in the area of recognizing Anglo-American air-dropped munitions. Instructions included locating, collecting and deactivating *'Phosphor Bomben'* (incendiary bombs), which smashed through house roofs and failed to explode. Although my mother felt that I was too young to be involved in such dangerous work, I felt differently. It was probably the fact that I was wearing a uniform, which gave me the false feeling of being older. It took us several hours each time after the nightly bombing to look for and find holes in the roofs. The customary stone shingle roofs usually leave pretty large holes that were easily noticed and replaced. Once identified, we proceeded to the attics to locate the "stick" phosphor bombs. We then tried to deactivate them unless they were badly damaged and too difficult to dismantle. This type of munitions was approximately 35-40 cm long and 12 cm in diameter with an octagon shaped one half of brittle cast iron. This part contained the liquid phosphorous and the other consisting of aluminum sheeting with a small igniter button for the fuse. The munitions' main purpose was to cause fires in the attics. A soon as they were rendered harmless, we transported them to a special destination for destruction. Fortunately, we found many duds, which did not break apart upon impact.

Among us boys our favorite interests were the collection and trading of bomb fragments at school. It was always a challenge to find the biggest piece of shrapnel and be able to identify it properly. This did not, however, compare to the excitement we experienced when our troop was given the task to search for downed allied pilots and crew after they had been shot down over Berlin. I was only once involved in the capture of an American. Two *'Luftschutzwärte'* (Air Defense wardens) and about ten of us boys found him hanging in a tree on his parachute, seemingly dazed and unable to cut himself loose. After some confusion and several attempts on our part, we finally cut him down and captured him. For an enemy he seemed quite a nice guy. Especially, after he slowly lowered his hand into his flight suit and pulled out some of chocolate, which he offered to us boys and the air warden. We didn't believe one boy's suspicion that it might be poisoned. We gladly accepted the offer and smilingly enjoyed the gift. Of course the expected resistance and firefight with the downed pilot never materialized since he did not even carry a weapon.

Upon the order of the air warden, who, by the way, had the only weapon, we escorted the pilot to the nearest police station. There he was turned over to a German Air Force Officer since he was also an officer. According to our enemy uniform recognition training, he was an American Lieutenant and was subsequently shipped to a *'Gefangenenlager'*, a POW camp outside Berlin. This was the first time we could actually practice our English, and were proud to show off what we had learned in school.

After several months, I lost interest in collecting *'Granatsplitter'* (grenade shrapnel), especially following the loss of our home by bombs in October 1943. It was around midnight, when the sirens went off as usual. Turning on the radio, we heard the dreaded announcement that a fleet of enemy aircraft has reached the cities of Hannover-Braunschweig on a course to the capital, Berlin. This generally activated the air raid sirens and gave us about 5-10 minutes to seek shelter. We would then go to a clearly marked air raid bunker, should we be away from home, or to get down into our basement. These locations were considered relatively safe unless subjected to a direct hit by a bomb.

One day, hearing the sirens my mother awakened my brother, sister and me after which we grabbed our clothes and proceeded to go downstairs to the basement. It was a habitual procedure after all these months, except this night was to be different. As we huddled in the various corners of the basement, the sound of impacts drew closer and closer. Suddenly our basement shook, blue sparks crackled along the water pipes and mortar drifted from the basement ceiling. After that, total silence. For what seemed to be hours, nobody spoke. We had the distinct feeling either we got bombed or a bomb hit very close by. Everything was very quiet around us. After a very long time had passed, my mother finally got up and walked up the stairs to open the basement door to see what had happened. When she could not budge the door, I got up to help her. When, after many frantic attempts, we finally opened it, we saw a star-filled blue sky with searchlights criss-crossing the sky. Several 88mm antiaircraft guns still firing in the distance at aircrafts, which reflected like shiny silver in the searchlight's beam.

Our house, or what used to be our house, was reduced to a roofless building. The adjacent residences did not fare much better. Looking up to the sky in total amazement, we saw little what looked like '*Weihnachst-bäume*' lighted Christmas trees, floating down to earth. There was a huge bomb crater in our backyard right where the pool used to be, which was to serve as an emergency water supply in case of fires. Our yard was also littered with small strips of aluminum. We found out later on, that these were dropped by the bombers to confuse our radar and air defense system.

Luckily, we did not have any fire but the air pressure caused enough damage to make it uninhabitable and severely damaged our neighbors' homes. Even our rabbits, which we raised for food in our bathtub on the second floor, were apparently killed by the blast, as we could not locate them anywhere. We were stunned and in tears and returned to our basement, the only shelter we had left. After a while, the air raid warden checking for damages located us and offered to help. Being at a momentary loss, we assured him that we would be all right until daylight.

After the loss of our home we knew that we would probably be placed with another family as was usually done. My mother chose another option open to families who had lost their home through bombing. It was the '*Evakuierung*', an evacuation to a remote area, where we would be relatively safe from aerial bombings. This was a common practice especially for those families of party officials and dependents of the high-ranking military officers at the frontline. We heard that my father had a short tour on the Eastern front, before he parachuted onto Crete. He was subsequently transferred as a first lieutenant to serve with Field Marshal Erwin Rommel's Afrika Korps at Tobruk and Tripoli in Afrika. But before we could leave Berlin, the outbreak of diphtheria in our school forced the government to relocate affected families to a quarantine area in western Germany. Our family was shipped to a castle in Rieneck, near the town of Gemünden. Our stay there was to last several weeks before returning to Berlin.

During the Third Reich, it seemed to me, religion was not that prevalent or important and I cannot remember when our family had ever attended any church services. My grandmother on my father's side was a devout Catholic like Hitler. My parents, one Catholic and the other a Lutheran, decided to be just '*Gottgläubig*', believers without an affiliation to any organized church. They let us children decide for ourselves which belief or ideology to choose for our happiness. I found myself totally involved in my youth activities, which kept me busy each entire weekend. With my father gone most of the time, we never had any memorable family events. I usually had my weekends filled with exciting and productive youth activities, while our mother was usually home teaching my brother and sister. German schools had a requirement for serious homework. In our family it was naturally my mother, who was always available to assist in one's homework while my father was serving at the front.

Evacuation from Berlin – Training for War

Because we did not have any relatives outside Berlin, who could take us in, our family was evacuated to Meseritz, a small border town along the Polish border. After our arrival, I was assigned to a new Jungvolk unit and High School. The whole family was quartered on a 'Rittergut', a knight's manor, owned by a higher-ranking SS official, who was somewhere on the Eastern front as were most able men. But life on the farm there was not too pleasant, since the owners were Catholics and we were considered "only" Protestants. During meal times, we found that our family was only given meager, meatless meals. The host family in turn ate the better cuisine with an abundance of meat. It was a rare addition if we ever got any. This was noticed by the seven French POWs, who were assigned to the farm as laborers under the watchful eye of the guard. He was an older German soldier, who never carried his weapon, but had it locked up somewhere in his room. The prisoners I found were the friendliest group of POWs I had ever met. Two of them Papa and Pierre will always be remembered as genuinely compassionate. They had as much liberty as any German in the area and were well-liked, especially by us.

In general, Germans did not like the French very much, which may have been as the result of World War I. The French were usually portrayed as lovers rather than fighters and they only won the last war with the help of the Americans. That, of course, was also the picture our parents painted of our enemies. I personally found them all to be very polite and particularly hardworking. Their care for the farm and the animals was outstanding and appreciated. Many German farmers would not have been able to handle some of these chores, considering the majority of men were either fighting a war or were physically unable to do such work. Off and on, we could find our POWs working at the local state hospital for the 'Hei-

lanstalt" a medical facility for the mentally handicapped and insane at the suburb of Obrawalde. They were helping out because of manpower short-ages, like our HJ group was tasked to do every once in awhile. Nobody enjoyed that task. We were made to understand that this treatment program was established to prevent the sicknesses from spreading and maintain healthy population.

The mentally insane we saw and pitied, were generally kept in prison-like cells to prevent injuries of the not-so-violent persons. Some were apparently euthanized following permission by immediate relatives and two competent doctors. I guess our exposure to this problem was meant to instill in us young people that in every healthy body lives a healthy mind and that this type of cleansing will maintain a healthy strong nation in the future. This system was generally accepted not only in Germany, but in many countries in Europe. We thought of it as nothing unusual until after the war, when the Russian Army claimed and depicted Obrawalde as a concentration camp. When we saw dead bodies lined up in front of the crematorium we considered a normal occurrence at this institution.

Returning to a more pleasant matter regarding our French POWs, I don't think it was my mother's good looks that prompted them to gladly share their Red Cross "CARE" packages and chocolates with us. It must have been obvious to them that our family was not being treated as ex-pected among Germans. I remember Pierre, the "leader" of the group fre-quently whistling outside our 2d floor window. He was asking my mother to lower a basket, which they then filled with food and delicacies for our family. Needless to say we were grateful to all of them. Watching them walk away laughing and giggling after their delivery, I had the distinct feeling they enjoyed helping us despite our host's hostility towards us.

Not being considered real enemies by many Germans our French friends even had the opportunity to go downtown to see movies although accompanied by the guard. Remembering some unusual eating habits of our POWs, my sister Ute still recalls how they hung up frog legs on the clothesline before preparing them for a meal, which they frequently shared with us.

Our friendship with the POWs was not sitting too well with our hosts. After several very unpleasant arguments with the wife of the manor's owner my mother finally decided to move downtown to eliminate the tension. I just regretted to lose my friends and not being able to ride the horses and cool off in the nearby Obra River. While the school time was rather uneventful, Jungvolk was getting a lot more interesting. It was a requirement at that time that every German know how to swim and I shall never forget my first experience in that sport. One beautiful sunny day our troop was marched onto a bridge over my favorite river and told to strip and jump into the water about 10 meters below. All of us had some basic instructions on swimming and techniques to stay afloat. We all knew roughly what to do. I had often been fishing in the river before and was hoping, that those big fish one could clearly see would get out of the way when we hit the water. Troop leaders lining the banks were some reassurance to us, but overcoming the feeling of fear and proving you have the necessary courage was still quite a challenge. Once I hit the cold water everything seems to fall into place. To my surprise I learned rather quickly and qualified as a swimmer.

Following this type of survival training, we were given more serious training, primarily in small arms by the 'Volkssturm' (folk storm) men. These were members of the auxiliary People's Defense Force, created to supplement and support the regular military with personnel. They were either too young or too old to be drafted and included members of the Hitler Youth aged 14-18 and later even younger as well as older men over 60. Since the standard German rifle K98, issued to the Volkssturm, was generally too heavy for most young boys to handle and carry. Therefore our training for the 10-14 olds was limited to lighter weapons such as the P-38 Pistol, and the 'Panzerfaust' (Tank Fist) or the 'Panzerschreck' (Armour/ Tank Terror). These were the standard lightweight antitank weapon of the German Army. The 'Panzerschreck' was a lot heavier because of its shield up front to protect the face from the back blast of the projectile.

Another rather interesting anti-tank weapon we were trained on was the 'Haftmine', a flat magnetic mine. When placed on a tank between the turret and main body it would explode after a certain amount of friction or pressure was applied to the mine. Placement of this mine was rather dangerous. One would have to move quickly not to get blown up while placing the demolition on the tank. Although many of us were dreaming of killing a big tank, such as the Russian T-34, I was not too enthused to expose myself to that kind of high risk. Not that I was cowardly; I was just cautious and not ready to risk my life at such a young age.

One of the more exciting anti-tank and bunker buster weapon was the 'Goliath'. It was a miniature tank that looked more like an oversized toy than a deadly weapon. Its interior was filled with explosives. In the hands of a well-trained soldier it could be electrically manipulated by wire from behind a fortified position by steering it toward and under a tank or a bunker. The Goliaths were usually distributed to anti-tank units. I was fortunate enough to see one placed into action later during the Battle of Berlin. It was truly exciting to watch it move toward a T-34, hit the tracks and blow them apart. Undoubtedly the Russians must have wondered what hit them.

Most of us young boys were quite enthusiastic about the training. At the same time we wondered though why Germany had to go so far and ask old men, most of whom had already seen combat in World War I to fight another war against the Bolsheviks. Most radio reports from the front lines only told us about victories and some occasional 'tactical withdrawals' to defeat the enemy on a different front. It was apparent even to some of us younger guys, that Germany may be in trouble.

Meeting the First Russians

I had my first taste of the Volkssturm activities during the last months of 1944. Following our disastrous setback and losses at Stalingrad in the Soviet Union news reached us that the Soviet Army was advancing toward Germany. The French POWs were not the only captured enemies in Meseritz we found out. The first obvious signs of the close proximity of combat were the arrival of Russian POWs, which seemed to tell us that we were winning again through our counteroffensives. The captured 'Ruskies', also called 'Iwan', were placed in an old school complex next to the house where we were living. Of course, our curiosity led us to the school to find out what we were fighting against. After watching them for a while in their ragged uniforms, I almost began to feel sorry for them. One young soldier in particular looked starved and tired as he tried to talk to me and make me understand Russian. The one predominant word accompanied by the gesture of putting fingers into his the mouth was "cleb". I only later found out that they were usually asking for bread. Bread, of course, was one of the commodities in Germany also rationed and not that plentiful around. I "talked" and gestured with the young 'Iwan' under the watchful eyes of a Volkssturm guard for a while and decided to find some bread somewhere.

My mother had been told that the Russians were predominantly Ukrainians or "white" Russians, most of whom were sympathetic to Germans. As a matter of fact, some Ukrainian volunteers had even formed an SS

Division, commanded by the Ukrainian General Vlassov to fight against the Soviets. I was made to understand that they did not like Hitler but definitely hated the communists. Short of ration stamps, but still wanting to help, my mother decided to bake her own bread from scratch. Returning with a piece of it, I asked and received permission from the guard to give the Russian boy soldier some bread. Why were the communists putting those young boys into the Army? I was not much later to learn as to why. He expressed his thanks by giving me a beautiful, hand-carved replica of a German Tiger tank. I had to admire his talent in woodcarving. The toy tank had a moving turret and made a sound of a gun, when pushed.

A few days later I was quite surprised, when another Russian joined me along the fence and addressed me in a "broken" German dialect. He told me his name, which I vaguely remember to be German and he relayed to me some his background and talked about his parents. They apparently had migrated to the Ukraine as technicians during the regime of the Czar.

Suddenly the Russians did not seem to be that dangerous anymore, a belief I would rapidly change later during the war, when we were confronted with some of their Mongol frontline shock troops. One of the SS Signal men stationed in our basement explained to me that most of the POWs were conscripts from the Ukraine, who were happy to be prisoners with absolutely no desire to return to the front lines and rejoin the Russian Army. From that day on I made several visits to the POW compound, returning with more different pieces of beautiful handmade toys. My younger sister Ute still remembers the wood carvings they made. Some pieces of art were depicting little chickens pecking at food on a ping-pong paddle type plate. When moved circularly it caused strings under the plate, attached to a weight, to move the chickens.

Although we lost all of them during the following upheavals I can still picture those pieces quite vividly. I have not seen anything like it again except for the traditional Russian wood crafted painted dolls. Each little doll contained up to about five smaller dolls inside one of the other. The outside and largest doll being approximately five inches high. It usually depicted a well-known personality or political figurehead.

The Great Trek

The brief quiet along the Russian front was not to last for very long. We received the bad news that the POW compound was being shipped out toward Berlin. The SS 'Funker', signal men in our basement relayed to us that the Russian Army has broken through several positions along the frontline and was spearheading toward Meseritz. Our city was to be a major *'Auffangslinie'*, a blocking line. Shortly thereafter, block wardens notified the population that in order stop the advance of the enemy, emergency fortifications in the form of *'Panzergräben'*, anti-tank ditches, needed to be dug. Generally, the *'Reichs-Arbeitsdienst'*, the Reich's Labor Service was created and became responsible for building special fortifications and roads. We found out that they were over-committed and were building bunkers, such as three 'Flak Bunkers' in central Berlin. Since no additional troops were available to construct the ditches, we needed to help our soldiers and, of course, ourselves. The military, convinced that we can stop the advancing enemy, asked us to volunteer and to report to certain areas for further instructions.

While my mother immediately joined the call-up, I reported to my troop unit for whatever assignment they had in store for us. After receiving our special instructions we went to a designated area to the east of the town, where I was hoping to find my mother. I could not believe my own eyes what I saw at our rendezvous point. Thousands of people were lined up as far as my eyes could see digging a long ditch under the guidance and help of members of some German *'Pioniere'*, Army Engineers and the Volkssturm. I immediately realized that it was impossible to find my mother among those thousands of workers. The view reminded me of pictures I had in my mind depicting Chinese labor constructing the Wall of China. I remember working every day on the ditch for about a week with only short breaks for army lunch at a *'Feldküche'*, the field mess. The ditch was so designed to let the tank enter it, but then preventing it to get up the steep slope on the other side. We were proud of our work and hoped that it would stop the advance, and if not, at least slow them down.

It was the 31st of January 1944, I believe. One of the SS men woke us up in the middle of the night to tell us that the Russian tanks will soon be getting into firing range of Meseritz. They told us that they had just received orders to withdraw toward the west. Looking out of the window we noticed most of the neighbors had already packed their valuables and started fleeing the area. With the exception of some military vehicles, we spotted many horse-drawn carts and trailers, many of them overloaded, with people walking alongside. We immediately took the few valuables we had and, with a brief look back, left the last "home" we were to have for a long time.

Mother, the kids and I proceeded on foot along a slow moving column towards the West. We were hoping to find and join some friends. Realizing that it was going to be a long trek we needed to find some type of transportation. Picking up a train ride somewhere along the way was our hope. In the interim, we fortunately found a former worker from the farm where we used to stay. He had always liked us when we lived at the farm and willingly made room on his horse-drawn wagon for our few bags and a small suitcase. Apparently our former host had already fled the area by car, leaving the workers to their fate. The guard had also released the French POWs to fend for themselves. He told us that they were somewhere in the trek helping other refugees. Naturally they had no desire to be "liberated" by the Soviet Army. They also realized that they needed some sympathetic Germans to get them through military check points. As young as they were they could otherwise be likely to get shot as deserters, partisans or spies.

The convoy along the road to Berlin was an unusual mix of civilian German refugees, foreigners and military personnel on foot and on vehicles. The Army, we heard, was trying to reestablish a foothold and form a new line of defense. When we got word along the column that a control point was nearby, male civilians usually disappeared to rejoin us past the check point. These were manned by *'Kettenhunde'*, the German Army military police. They were called 'chain dogs', because of their large metal plate hung on a chain around the chest and neck. Besides general traffic control, it was their function to collect and direct personnel for further service in military units. Luckily for us, our farmhand was combat-wounded and one-armed.

It was a depressing site and an unbelievable mess, especially during darkness. It was easy to lose one's sense of direction and get separated from friends and family. The greatest help moving in the dark were our indestructible dynamos. They were small handheld flashlights, which did not need any batteries. A small built-in generator was activated by a light push on a pressure lever, which produced enough light to view the immediate area for about 10 meters. Movement during nighttime was scary. Off and on we observed the flashes of guns and impacting rounds coming closer from the rear. The sight and sound passing us on either side made us wonder when the Russians might catch up with us. This dreadful thought alone gave us the will to continue without much rest. I had never experienced such a feeling of total loss before in my life. Watching my mother with her expression of despair in her eyes made me feel even worse. I had always known her to be a proud and caring mother. Her experience of helpless-ness made me realize that she was devastated not being able to change our situation into which we were placed through no fault of our own.

Noticing her desperation, I suddenly realized that, as the oldest of us three kids, I had to assume the role of the family protector and provider. With all the chaos around us, I did not even know where to start. Looking at my younger sister I sensed that she had the same feeling and that she understood the situation. She agreed to watch my mother and her younger brother from now on, while I made plans to canvass the area ahead of us to find food and drinking water. Those items were not only essential for our own personal survival but also the survival of the horse pulling our wagon. Without the horse and the wagon our travel would have been a tremendous torture.

From day to day the situation began looking more and more hopeless. My greatest fear was the possibility of getting lost so far from Berlin. Our biggest problem was the slow progress of the column, especially after a strafing run of Soviet *'JaBo's'* or *'Jagdbomber'* aircraft over the convoy. Those 'chase' bombers were constantly looking to hit and destroy military formations on roads leading to or coming from Berlin. It took a long time to clear the road of damaged equipment and the dead and wounded and it was clear that the refugees were also becoming a serious obstacle to our troops trying to re-supply and relocate. As soon as we heard or saw an enemy plane approach, we all jumped off the road seeking cover in the ditches, behind trees and destroyed vehicles. When under attack we were of course always hoping nothing would happen to our horse, which was generally exposed, unless we were going through a wooded area. After we scrambled back, we continued the trek. Passing burning destroyed mili-tary vehicles and dead soldiers along other unfortunate refugees, who met the same fate, it made us wonder if we would be next. The smell of dead people and animals was sickening. Many people that could or would not get out of the way were run over by tanks and other tracked vehicles try-ing to take up defensive position along the route. What remained of their bodies was usually unrecognizable.

Wearing a uniform, by now quite dirty and smelly, was sometimes a great help while it also presented a disadvantage. As a member of the Jungvolk and HJ, like a good Boy Scout, you were required to dutifully assist those in need. And the need was great. Occasionally, I was able to do both when the situation presented itself and I could help out some wounded soldiers waiting for transport along the roadside. Picking up food and water for them from Army *Feldküchen,* the mobile German field kitchen, I was at the same time able to provide some food items for the family. It was often difficult to locate the family again after my runs and I made it a point to always move ahead, so I could spot them come up from the rear. The German Army gasmask containers, a round metal tube, of which I carried two, was the ideal carrying case for food items. Not designed for that purpose, and a left-over from WWI, it became a customary food container. Nobody worried about gas warfare in those days.

It was to be a grueling trip with our hope to safely reach Berlin becoming more doubtful day by day. I hated to watch my mother suffer as she tried to calm down my brother and sister, repeatedly telling them that we would soon be home, even though we had no home as such to return to. Although Ute was a little older, she could not quite comprehend what was happening. Both my little brother and Ute frequently asked for my father, whenever they saw a man from the *Luftwaffe* passing by or lying by the roadside.

The road traffic finally opened up a little after we reached the halfway mark about 80 kilometers (50 miles) east of Berlin, near Frankfurt/Oder. Most of the military had left the main road probably to establish a new line of defense, as we had previously been told. It took us nearly five weeks of continuous walking before we finally reached the outskirts of Berlin. At a nearby 'S-Bahn' rapid transit station we left our faithful horse and wagon and said our goodbyes to our friend, the old farmhand. He had his hands full fending for the horse's welfare. He was a quiet companion and great helper. I noticed that my mother had tears running down her cheeks when she shook his hand for a final farewell. Although my mother got to know him well, I do not even remember his name.

The railroad station was crowded with hundreds of people. After hours waiting we were finally able to take the elevator train to go to one of our relatives. It was an aunt living in the northern section of Berlin, in Charlottenburg, where we hoped to be able to stay for a while, get organized and to plan our next move. Needless to say, I now smelled very bad. I was still wearing the same uniform since our departure from Meseritz and the Polish border. I was looking forward to my first bath in a long while. Our arrival was welcomed by our relatives on my mother's side, but I was ashamed that I had never previously tried to get to know them better. Living in the opposite end of Berlin seemed a lousy excuse. Nevertheless, they treated us like good relatives and the older folks could not stop talking while I was genuinely happy to finally have something to eat and drink. My cousin was watching me intensely as I was very slowly chewing this most welcome meal. I was grateful that water, even though rationed, was still available. So was a clean set of oversized underwear, which just happened to show up.

Return to Berlin and the Air Raids

It only took my mother a few days to reestablish contact with some other relatives and my grandmother. We noticed that, if you found a working telephone, the connections were rare and often interrupted. I am sure that my mother pulled some strings because she got us an apartment in a residential complex in the North-Western district. It was reserved for mostly government personnel, ironically called '*Dr. Goebbels Siedlung*' (Estate), named after my Godfather, whom I had not seen since my baptism. It was a beautiful area that fortunately had not yet been hit by allied bombings; at least not until we got there. This was to change not very long after our arrival. As soon as we had settled in, my new Jungvolk unit welcomed me. At age 13, I was one of the youngest among 13 and 14 year olds in my troop, but I felt equal because I was already told that I was selected to attend the *NAPOLA* (*National Politische Erziehungs-Anstalt*). This school was the equivalent of a military prep school, a national political leadership academy. Our mother still firmly believed that once the war is won, I would attend the academy and after graduation at a proper age become one of the governors of an eastern region. I was always embarrassed when she mentioned it to others, but I guess mothers are usually proud of their older offspring. After what I had seen and experienced on the trek, I did not have much hope of that ever happening. How right I was going to be.

Having had a few quiet weeks, we were welcomed again to our customary '*Luftangriffe*', the air raids. It seemed that the allies had concentrated their efforts primarily on targets of more military importance, such as manufacturing plants for war machinery. Berlin did not have much of that, except for some assembly plants for the new ME-262 jet fighter aircraft outside Berlin. There were apparently several atomic research facilities in the southern sector, while in the northern Spandau research in chemicals was being done. This M-262 '*Düsenjäger*', a Jet Fighter, and the V-2 '*Abwehrraketen*', defense rockets were supposed to change the tide in the war and most Germans were still confident that it would.

Returning to Berlin, we found that school instruction was almost non-existent, as many buildings were destroyed. Many teachers were either called up to serve, were displaced or killed and the students were involved in cleanup and other details such as assisting in some kind of war effort. This usually involved collecting recyclable material, including hair, mostly from women, to be used for insulation in clothing and other wear. Besides being *'Klamotten-Sammler'*, the Berliner term for clothing and rubbish collector, we found ourselves handing out propaganda posters and leaflets or helping with the air defense effort. One of our troop's tasks was to help moving and maintaining different ammunition stocks in an 88mm anti-aircraft *'Flakbunker'* bunker. One of three large towering bunkers around the center of Berlin was located in the *Friedrichshain* Park next to our residential area. This bunker was about four stories high and its top platform with the AA guns was just clearing the tops of trees in the park. Looking at the solid concrete walls it looked like it was indestructible and would withstand any type of bombardment. Adjacent to those AA bunkers were *'Scheinwerfer'*, searchlight batteries, which had survived the air raids without any significant damage.

Not so our residences, as we were soon to find out. Not lacking any excitement I found myself in a rather eerie situation after one of those air raids. Following the siren's sounding of the cessation of an alert, we left the basement shelter across from our apartment. Leaving the building in near total darkness I carried a small suitcase. Our family had to walk across the small park in the middle of the horseshoe shaped complex. Reaching the front of our building I set down my suitcase in the street to look for the keys. When I tried to pick it up again I could not find it. Feeling around, I suddenly lost my balance and fell into a shallow hole. I knew it had not been there before. I found that I had landed on top of my suitcase about two feet down. Apparently I had placed the suitcase on the edge of the hole from where it dropped down. When my mother shined the flashlight towards me, I looked up and saw that I had landed in a hole made by a larger sized bomb lying on its side, still intact. My heart almost stopped and I froze up, not daring to move.

One of the ever-present air raid wardens was called over to my location. He carefully lifted me with my suitcase out of the hole after he had alerted the surrounding people to vacate the immediate area. We had no idea whether this bomb was a dud or on a time delay device, both types we had encountered before. Needless to say, we moved away rather fast to a safer area. When bomb experts determined it to be a dud, we returned to our apartment. Following this shock, I was not able to sleep until the sun came up and the bomb was removed. Looking at the filled crater later that day, I thanked my lucky stars.

As the weeks went by, we were always hoping to hear from my father. News in the radio never mentioned any specific operations or units probably for security reasons. The infrequent mail we did receive always listed another different *'Feldpostnummer'*, the equivalent of an American Army Post Office (APO) number. Since our own address had changed frequently it would make it understandably difficult for my father to contact us. Fortunately, my grandmother received mail more often. She had never moved since the war began and my father being very close to her received letters on a somewhat regular basis. She, therefore, became our sole source of information regarding my father's latest whereabouts. Since our return to Berlin we were finally able to write him again and bring him up-to-date. Even though we had an extended family in my father's sister and her children in Berlin, we rarely communicated with them. There was a deep-rooted rivalry among the families, which I could never understand in my younger years. My mother felt that our immediate family was always shortchanged by grandmother, who favored her daughter, my father's sister. I was just hoping that the war would heal all wounds and they would get along better. They never did.

While the daily air raids by the *'Amis'* and *'Tommy's'* Air Forces continued, we heard only fractions of news from the eastern front and the continued Soviet advances toward Berlin. Our own propaganda seemed fairly upbeat. The leadership in Berlin was even talking about moving additional troops from the western front to the more menacing danger coming from the east. Everybody, it sounded, seemed confident that our military, the *Wehrmacht*, would be successful in turning the war around to bring about a final German victory. It would not be long, we were told, and the third Reich would use its *'Wunderwaffen'*, the secret wonder weapons to defeat our enemies. In the meantime our Hitler Youth and Jungvolk members continued to disseminate propaganda leaflets in the neighborhood. They were designed to convince people not to loose confidence and to continue donating scrap metal, old clothes and other material for our defense industry. Our troop members were also advised to be especially watchful for strangers in our neighborhood and to report unusual and suspicious occurrences.

After having done my share of duties I usually liked to surprise my mother with little gifts. The best gift one could bring or give in those days was food since it was very scarce. Practically everything was being rationed. Although the ration cards showed butter or meat, these items were usually unavailable. Instead, those items were usually substituted in the stores with margarine. If unavailable, it could again be substituted with '*Schmalz*', the animal fat, if one is lucky. Smoked fish and Herring were usually issued in lieu of meat. Bread was still available but it was heavily mixed with various kinds of fiber, looking very close to saw dust. A so-called '*Dauerbrot*', a life-time bread, was the latest development. Remembering an old school friend, Ernst Richter, whose father had a little farm, I got the idea to visit him. He was living about ten kilometers, or six miles from us. I thought I could maybe help out on the farm in exchange for some food. Our reunion was a total surprise. Ernst was glad to see me; to have the company by an old school friend.

Returning home, off course, I usually brought home some goodies in the form of fresh meat, sausage and wheat. Our mother would then grind the wheat in our coffee mill, which had not seen a coffee bean for years. The resulting fresh cream of wheat with plenty of fiber and some fresh whole milk was always a treat. While Ernst was happy to provide me with foodstuff, his father felt quite the opposite. After he noticed that I had been given too much from his son for my help, he admonished him. Ernst however was determined to help as much as possible. He decided to be more creative and devise different ways to smuggle the stuff past his father, including filling an old pair of my mother's "nylon" stockings with wheat and wrapping it around my waistline. It worked and after a while we created and found new and better ways of smuggling.

In contrast to his son Ernst, Dad was not presenting the image of a good and patriotic German at all. He did everything he could not serve in the war like many others did. For us two boys it was now a challenge to get more food out without his knowledge. The weather still giving us a winter with snow on the ground, it made it even harder for us. Our movements left too many obvious tracks behind. I often asked him to be more cautious because I did not want to get a friend into trouble. Vigilance usually paid off and, by not overdoing it, I continued to occasionally provide my family with some welcomed fresh food. My mother was even willing to sacrifice some of her jewelry as a trade and to barter, but my friend would not hear of it. Many German farmers did take advantage of this situation and became quite wealthy through the '*Schwarzmarkt*', the German black market. It was not unusual to find many farmers with oriental rugs in their farmhouses. '*Hamstern*' as the Germans called the way of scrounging, became a basic way of life in all of Germany, especially in the Eastern part.

The Soviet Army Siege of Berlin

I don't quite remember the dates but the allied air raids slowed down significantly around Berlin. We almost missed the usual bombardments. Something was in the making and we all hoped that our troops were making progress. News reached us however that cities like Dresden were still hit hard by air raids, as were some of the coastal towns from where the V2s were being launched against the British island. Around the middle of April 1945 an unusual quiet settled over the entire area of Berlin. Occasionally some Russian bombers started showing up to harass the outskirts of Berlin. Rumors circulated that the Russian Army had broken through several defense lines not too far from our city. We also heard that the Western front along the Rhine River had weakened and that we were placed in a very vulnerable situation.

Some soldiers who had returned from the Western Front stated that our Divisions were standing by to negotiate a peace. Unconfirmed sources even spoke of a plan where our forces would join the American and British forces and move towards Berlin, which some of the allied generals, who did not trust the Soviets, were proposing. This unbelievable plan was to prevent the Russians from proceeding further into Germany or even take Berlin, including some highly important German research facilities. Official statements and news on the radio were often contradictory and left all of us wondering and waiting. There was definitely a great disparity between German broadcasts and BBC, the British Broadcasting Corporation radio station, some of us were tuning in to, to satisfy our hunger for accurate information. Realizing that this could also be mere enemy propaganda, we were still listening to those transmissions. The reception could generally be found to be loud and clear. Our own stations on the other hand were often disrupted through air raids or other enemy action.

Listening to enemy radio stations was, of course, considered treasonous, but with time we overcame any fear of possible punishment. Among us boys, we did not feel unpatriotic at all, but justified to find out what the enemy is saying about us. Some of the British statements seemed so ridiculous they even prompted us to laugh. Nevertheless, it gave us some different information we could evaluate and even strengthened our resolve to continue our struggle. There was no doubt in our minds that the "Tommy", as we called the British, was operating a very effective propaganda machine. Their occasional drop of leaflets showed their efficiency in psychological warfare. Still, their efforts did not appear to have much effect on the population in general, aside from creating a certain uneasiness and apprehension. Our own propaganda was also increasingly busy, reminding us constantly through large posters depicting a shadowy spy and the words, *'Psst! - Der Feind Hört Mit!'* that 'the enemy is listening in' during conversations.

The lull in fighting and the suspense did not last too long. Suddenly, one morning early, in the last week of April and only about four to five days from my birthday, ground fire could be heard in the distance. The word got out that the Red Army had reached the outer perimeter of Berlin and is preparing to encircle the city for a final assault. All male personnel of Hitler Youth age and those able to fight with the Volkssturm were told to report to their respective units. My mother heard the reports and broke into tears. Being without a husband and the oldest son being asked to leave for whatever undertaking, our mother was on the verge of breaking down. My grandmother tried to calm her down, assuring her that she should not worry. Hitler would soon show the Russians what the Germans were made of. Well, I was hopeful but not so sure after the most recent developments. I was still duty bound to follow the directives and somehow felt proud to be asked by the leadership to come to Germany's defense.

The political leadership was constantly talking about our final victory. After all, like our minister of propaganda Dr. Goebbels had repeatedly said about the Germans: *'Wir wollen den totalen Krieg'*, "We want the total war". No matter how bleak it seemed, all of us Jungvolk and Hitler Youth were proud of our role. We still firmly believed in our leaders and our nation. We realized it was not going to be that easy, but we would succeed and emerge the victors once we use our secret weapons, which the government was holding in reserve. Several of us had seen those new rocket planes near Berlin. All we needed was patience until our relief forces arrived from the south and west.

When suddenly, the enemy artillery fire, especially their *'Katyusha Granatwerfer'*, the Russian multi rocket launcher, nicknamed by Berliners *'Stalin-Orgel'* or 'Stalin Pipe Organ' began impacting in several areas of Berlin proper, a general sense of confusion and anguish set in.

Hitler Youth digging trenches to stop advancing Russian tanks.

Wounded Hitler Youth Motorcycle messenger

The last Newspaper for the Berlin defenders on my birthday!

Hitler congratulates and decorates 12-year olds.

10-year old HJ getting "drilled" by older Volkssturm member

After allied bombing and Russian artillery fire most of the City lay
in ruins. Many cellars became the only shelter.

Commonplace sight
of women doing
forced labor under
Russian occupation.

The fate of those who deserted:
Hanged with a sign stating
"I'm a coward"

Lucky remnants of young Hitler youth
surrendering to the allies.

In its flight the rockets created an unusual and rather strange howling sound causing many civilians, unfamiliar with this weapon, to panic. The populace was used to many things, like the whistling of bombs descending on us but not this sound. This was quite different and devastating and was yet another new threat, one we would have to get used to as the war went on.

To our surprise, German Army units and the Volkssturm began moving through our district towards an adjacent district. Many already displaced civilians retreated with them into what they believed to be a safer area. From day to day our Hitler Youth units seemed to have been reduced to smaller groups joining various military units and moving with them. Lacking proper communication means, I had lost contact with my own unit and had no idea where my troop was. I did not see any of my fellow members anywhere nearby. Were they somewhere already fighting or had they left Berlin? Feeling somewhat lost, I remained close to my family. Our mother felt very strongly about my staying with the family. We sometimes saw tanks and heavy equipment moving through the area and for the first time I saw a very young soldier sitting on top of the tower of a tank passing by. Although wearing a tanker's uniform he must have been a HJ member because he could not have been older than eighteen. Mother noticed him too and started crying while she was looking down at me. A couple HJ boys armed with bazookas on bicycles were following the tank. What a depressing sight.

Without a telephone and having lost my personal contact with my own troop I somehow felt left behind, something I did not want to tell my mother. Maybe our mother felt the same way being in limbo and had the urge to move to a safer area. Talking to several neighbors, who claimed that the Russians had not yet completely closed the circle to the west, she also found out that more and more refugees were collecting in the city hindering the military to freely move and fight. The military command responsible for the defense of Berlin had planned to get the refugees and those Berliners who had lost their homes out of Berlin. One very good reason was the fact that we experienced a critical shortage of food supplies and the government was unable to feed us all.

Our mother quickly reached a decision. She asked me to help her grab a couple small bags with whatever valuable possessions we had left. It became clear to me that she was determined to leave for our safety again especially when she found a leaflet stating '*Die Vergeltung kommt*', telling us that "revenge is coming." It was obvious that the Soviet Army wanted to remind us of atrocities committed by German troops against the Russian populace to justify their own criminal acts. Together with my brother and sister, both of whom were completely confused and lost, we locked the door from our appartment and departed. Meeting a few other residents, we joined them and other Berliners marching toward Spandau, a district adjacent to ours in the West. I remember only that the defense forces were to maintain open an area from Berlin toward the West to safely evacuate non-combatants from Berlin. A friend of mine, we called him *'Icke'*, and his mother, joined us on this move during the night, a night, which I was to remember throughout my life.

The district of Spandau-West had seen some heavy fighting during the last few days. The Russians had penetrated that sector to get to the headquarters of the German Army High Command and the bunker from where the defense of the capital was directed. The German defenders of the so-called *'Festung Berlin'* (Fortress Berlin) had successfully repulsed the Russians and we found ourselves right in the middle of some reinforcements arriving to strengthen the breach. With gunfire in the far distance, surrounded by hundreds of people, both military and civilian, we walked to a destination unknown to all of us. We only had one thought in mind. To reach the open gap in the encirclement and get to a safe area outside Berlin, which was only another five miles away. Word had spread, that although the Russian army had surrounded Berlin, the encirclement had been breached and opened enough to allow the huge number of civilians to leave Berlin and escape toward the West. They all hoped they could eventually link up with the Americans; finding food and water was the primary objective.

Viewing the destruction so far from bombings and artillery fire, most of the inner part of Berlin consisted of a mass of tall 'skeletons' of what used to be buildings. The inner city of Berlin lay in ruins, with its population barely surviving in basements. The lack of electricity and running water in most parts of the city created severe, primitive conditions. It was no longer a secret that many starving mothers were unable to feed their babies. Considering the ever-increasing danger of being overrun by hordes of Russians, leaving the city sounded like the best idea. Leaflets dropped by the Russians' Red Army stated that Berlin was surrounded not by divisions but by several armies. This thought and the threat of massive rapes, as they had occurred in already occupied territories, frightened the women, young and old.

Carrying our rather meager personal possessions, which he had left in a few bags, I vividly remember we were walking on a small residential road with one-family homes on both sides. On our feet for hours with only brief breaks to readjust clothing and bags, we hoped to be able to leave the city intact. Strangely enough, every so often we could hear a single shot fired along the column, some distant, some close to us.. Repeatedly, the sky on the horizon would be lit up from flashes followed by rumbling sounds. Counting the seconds from the flash to hearing the sound we could estimate the distance to the impact. It was an eerie march of straggling, tired people.

With the first sign of the sun coming up over the horizon, we could see a strangely quiet column of a mixed group of exhausted people. We all realized now that the previously mentioned five mile distance to the reach the breach was totally wrong. It had to be a lot farther. Vehicles were almost nonexistent on this road and it seemed everybody was cautious not to make a noise that could alert the enemy of our whereabouts. But suddenly the calm was disrupted by another cracking shot from close by. My friend Icke walking next to me, carrying a bag with his mother, was abruptly pulled away from my side. Turning my head toward him, I saw my friend and a German Air force officer next to his mother bending over to help her up. A silent column of people continued bypassing us without paying any attention. My friend's mother was lying on the ground, not moving. Icke tried to lift her head and noticed a large hole in the back of her head. She had been shot. The officer only removed his hat, shook his head and expressed his sorrow. He briefly confirmed that his mother was dead, probably shot by a Russian sniper, probably from a distant tree. When the enemy was forced to evacuate the area, some of them had remained behind in ambush to pick out and shoot higher-ranking military personnel. It was a known technique of the Russians. This sniper however must have missed his primary target. A feeling of despair and rage came over me, as I watched my friend crouch over his mother's body and cry.

I was totally unprepared for what I had witnessed and did not know what to do. I could not imagine what I would have done, had I been in his place. To lose a mother at the age of about ten years this way and just leave her behind, dead in the ditch without a chance to ever see her again, was utterly cruel and hard to comprehend. It was hard for me to understand why an enemy would kill a good woman like her, but it dawned on me that he was probably aiming for the officer, since they were walking side by side. After what seemed to be hours, we finally convinced him to stay with us until we could find some relative of his in the future. We gently laid her down in the ditch off the road, covered her up and rejoined the moving column. Icke did not speak for hours, frequently turning his head in the direction where he left his mother. All we could hear was his sobbing while he was clutching his mother's bag. He was the same age as my sister, but conducted himself like a much older boy, a grown up adult, hardened by the war.

My sister and brother were very quiet and probably did not quite comprehend what had happened. I felt that I understood better, but was still wondering what I would have done if it had it been our mother. We walked all day until darkness set in and then took shelter inside a stranded truck, assuring ourselves that there were no bodies inside. After I made sure I would find the location again in the darkness, I told my family that I was going to find some food.

Crossing the yard of a nearby residence I tripped over a couple of bodies, stumbled and fell flat on my face. Although it was a no-no to use flashlights outside for fear of getting shot at, I took my dynamo flashlight out my pocket. Shining the light across the immediate area, I was stunned to stare into the bluish/white face of a dead Russian soldier still clinching a round hand grenade. Afraid that the grenade could still go off if disturbed it, I carefully moved away from the body. Slowly calming down, I listened for noises and was relieved to hear some German language spoken close by. Following the sound, I found it came from the building close to my location. After I cautiously approached the house, I noticed a dim light in what appeared to be a basement. Looking through the dirty window I saw several SS men sitting next to a field radio. Upon slowly entering the house trying to get downstairs I was spotted and ordered to halt, prompting me to raise my hands in a reflex. After I identified myself I was told to enter their room.

My dirty clothing and face must have giving the impression that I was hungry, which prompted them to offer me something to eat. The bread they had showed some mildew on it, but the 'Scho-Ka-Kola' the hard dark German pilot chocolate was a delicious treat. This chocolate, consisting of a concentration of cocoa, coffee and cola nuts, immediately restores energy and alertness. I was happy when they gave me one of those well-known little round metal containers with chocolate. After some small talk about the family, they suddenly stopped talking when the radio operator raised his hand to demand quiet. The '*Funker*' (radio operator), wearing a headset, started smiling and stated that '*der Führer*' got his belated birthday present. He explained further that he made it safely out of Berlin, flown out by his personal pilot Hanna Reitsch, Germany's best female test-pilot. The report stated that she was flying a small one engine two or three-seater plane, a so-called '*Fieseler Storch*'. One story relayed weeks later told of the heroic flight of hers, landing and taking off from '*Sieges-Allee*' the wide open avenue, leading to the '*Brandenburger Tor*', Berlin's Arc dé Triomphe. The signal men also mentioned that Hitler had appointed *Admiral Dönitz* as the Führer of the Third Reich, who was apparently located along the Western front, hundreds of miles from Berlin.

Not keeping up with days or dates in this turbulent time I suddenly realized that it was only a few days past the 20th April, which was his birthday, with my own coming up on the 29th of April. I was suddenly worried, because I could not understand why he would leave Berlin and let us fend for ourselves. Maybe he had planned to negotiate with the western allies, like recent rumors mentioned. During their casual conversations I heard that the morale among the military was low but the discipline was still high. Many soldiers tired of constant fighting were found wounding themselves to be admitted to a medical facility in a safe area. Increasingly, uniformed personnel found running away from a defensive position were shot on the spot. This was well known to us as being a typical Soviet action in handling deserters among their troops. Hearing all this was very upsetting to me and prompted me to leave the safety of their basement position.

After I said my goodbye to the soldiers I received a larger piece of *Dauerbrot* and some cheese with their best wishes and hopes for a quick victory and went on my way. Avoiding the dead Russians near the house I eventually made it back to my anxious family. My friend was tight asleep. I gave my mother the bounty and relayed my story to her, but she did not show any excitement. She had only one thing in mind: get out of Berlin alive and quickly. But our hopes of making it out of the city diminished from day to day.

Our only newspaper left, called the '*Panzerbär*', or Tank Bear (armor bear) was a special printing for the defenders of Berlin. The paper's heading and logo depicted the city's emblem, a black bear carrying a *Panzerfaust*. This freely distributed small paper reported of great successes and heroic battles of the defenders. It hardly mentioned any setbacks, although we lived them personally. The last issues stressed that efforts were being made to get relief to Berlin. Rumors had it, that spearheads of American troops were only 50 miles from the outskirts of Berlin. The Americans now seemed more like saviors than enemies.

My last copy I received was dated the 29th April 1945, my birthday and a day I will not so soon forget. We all wanted to believe our political leaders and hoped. What else could we do? Talking to military officers though, the outlook was quite different and was in total conflict with the political scenario. It became clear that it did not look good for us along the eastern front. Gradually we began to doubt most official reports, considering them propaganda, especially when we heard about heroic fighting in the streets of many suburbs, where the losses in life on both sides were constantly increasing.

Scrounging Food for Survival – A Taste of Close Combat

The sun finally came up again and shed light over an absolutely horrible scene. We didn't see the whole picture when we arrived at our overnight stop, since it had been relatively dark. Combat dead and wounded could be seen everywhere along the roadside. People were sitting among them attending to their own wounds. Some of them, like us, had stopped to rest and to eat whatever they still had. There just were no food resources in sight. My mother looked desperate and mentioned that she was running out of food again asking me to try and find some food and water.

Desperate people were seen doing desperate things. I also had learned not be picky or timid. Even objectionable situations would not hold me back from getting what I needed to help my family survive. Initially, I found it despicable to search a dead body for food, but the necessity to sustain life helped me overcome any apprehension I used to have before. Searching, I finally found a gas mask container on a dead soldier with some bread and cheese inside. The glove compartment in one of the stranded trucks also produced a large pack of crackers. The rather repulsive condition did not matter anymore. It was still food, which would sustain us for at least a little while until we hopefully find a German mobile kitchen, which became more of a rarity every day during our moves. Although they were strictly serving uniformed personnel and the medical staffs, tending to an overwhelming number of wounded, one could often scrape out some foodstuff from empty containers.

Drinking water was the most difficult to find, but if I did find a source, I had only one canteen to fill for the whole family. If lucky, and if it had rained recently, I would find some dirty water in rain barrels in the gardens of some homes. I made it a point to refill mine, whether it was half full or not, since I could not find another canteen anywhere. I was clear to me that everybody along the route was looking for containers, which were still intact, because most of them were damaged.

On the way back to my family's rest area, I noticed a young but pale looking officer leaning against a tree who seemed to be changing his socks. As I was approaching him from the side I asked him if there was a kitchen nearby, but received no answer. I noticed that he did not move either. As I was about to lean over and touch the shoulder to get his attention, I spotted a small hole over his eyebrow. When I looked closer, I noticed something strange in the back of the head. The picture I saw will forever be another unforgettable experience locked in my memory. I felt sick and had the urge to vomit, but could not. I could only cover him up with an overcoat lying next to him, wondering why nobody was around to take care of his body and all those other dead. Remembering my friend's mother, I was hoping somebody living nearby would have buried her. They may not even have her name, because Icke took her purse and bag. Suddenly I found myself with tears in my eyes, mourning the death of a complete stranger, wondering if he had a family. Relatives, waiting for him to return home some day. And how about all the other dead ? The foul smell of death and destruction was everywhere, mixed in with the drifting smoke from burning vehicles and houses.

Deep in thought I returned to my family and, after a bite to eat, we continued on our way, guided by the stream of people in front of us. We were no longer sure where we were going. We just straggled along in silence, like zombies. I was determined not to relate my experience either to my mother, or brother and sister, especially not to my friend. One thing I still cannot understand to this date is how we were able to feed ourselves without any regular meals available anywhere. The only prospect of getting food was our chance to get out of Berlin and into the countryside. It seemed to be a continuous scrounging for scraps here and there, one day after the other with no end in sight.

. We had not made much headway to get out of Berlin, when we noticed people coming back our way from the front. We were told that the Russians had sealed the gap again and that we better turn around. My mother later found out, talking to an officer, that the Russians had not sealed the gap, but that the route was sealed off by some unit from the *GESTAPO* and the *SA*, who wanted to keep the refugees in the city to help build barricades. Mother swore, that she never wanted to hear the name Goebbels mentioned again. It was his irresponsible doing as a leader in the defense of Fortress Berlin, which had put us into this position. Only roughly three kilometers from the city line and safety, our flight was suddenly cut off.

We realized that we would never have a chance to make it out alive and that we desperately needed to return to a more familiar territory, where we could also find foodstuff and maybe family support again. Considering the devastating experience we had with Icke's mother, our mother was determined to choose a different route. It was wise to travel on a less crowded road. Mother also felt that we should find one of Icke's relatives, who he hoped were still living in the area he remembered. It seemed like an impossible undertaking. The inner city of Berlin lay in ruins, where familiar sights were now unrecognizable. The last allied air raid and the following artillery barrages made a recognition of former structures and areas impossible. Street signs were a rarity.

My suggestion to my mother to temporarily adopt him was considered not practical. He had his own roots somewhere she stated. I had never felt so lost in all my life; no home, no father around and no apparent protection from whatever was going to happen to us in the future. I wondered how my friend felt...

After several days of zigzagging through devastated areas we finally made it back to the more built-up but severely destroyed part of the inner city finding shelter in the underground tunnel of the '*U-Bahn*', Berlin's Subway system. The subway stations had the big advantage of providing shelter from the artillery and small arms fire. It seemed that many subway stations and connecting tunnels had become the refuge centers and shelter, especially for the thousands of wounded, civilian and military. Most wagons were strictly for wounded. While there was a conspicuous absence of food sources, there were a lot of first aid stations, since the city had an enormous number of wounded. I understood that in some areas trains were still running, but only intermittently. Traffic was very limited as electricity was totally unreliable and Russian troops had been found penetrating our perimeter by using the underground tunnels. Expecting subway transportation in that district seemed unrealistic and a waste of time.

Resting for a day, mother decided we should return to the Charlot-

tenburg district, which was only about twelve kilometers from Spandau
and adjacent to where we were. Since my friend, as well as our family
had some distant relatives there, it was the only practical choice we could
make. Besides, once on familiar turf, we would wait for further developments in the war, depending on the tactical situation we hoped would
improve in our favor.

We left the U-Bahn station the following day and emerged from
underground to make our way along some avenues flanked by 4-6 story
buildings. Most of them were only empty shells with bricks and mortar
strewn all over the street, making normal walking difficult. We did not
see many people walking about, as the more fortunate ones were living
and hiding in their basements. We were in the middle of one of the blocks,
when about three or four blocks behind us an artillery round hit the side
of the building with a second one impacting right next to it closer to us.
When a third one hit in a row, I knew it was a Stalin Organ rocket launcher
firing, which meant in a few more seconds the rounds would catch up with
us. We all dashed toward the next building entrance hoping for and finding
an open door to a cellar. But before we all could get inside, the rounds had
caught up with us.

A rocket impacted somewhere across the street, with shrapnel flying
around. With the howling rockets coming in and an earth shattering blast,
I suddenly felt a painful sting behind my right ear. Within the protective
walls, we checked each other out. My sister found a shrapnel in her knee
and my brother covered his one eye because of pain. A small shrapnel
had penetrated the bone below his eye, while my mother had a few minor
scratches. Our bags did not fare to well but we realized that they undoubtedly had somewhat protected us from being hurt badly. My friend Icke
came through without a scratch. The deafening noise and surprising impact shocked all of the family in such a way that they did not even feel any
great pain or reason to cry.

When we found a door and entered a basement where we found several people huddled in the corners, waving us to come in and sit down.
We noticed several families with small children and what appeared to be
an older looking soldier, at least he was in my eyes. Several of the people
asked us what was going on outside. They were afraid to venture outside
themselves, just waiting it out. They had not idea whether we still held
the territory or the Red Army had finally come in since they heard the
heavy artillery impacting. We explained the situation, as we knew it, and

expressed our hopes that we can continue our journey to Charlottenburg the next day. One of the women volunteered to look at our wounds and was nice enough to treat and bandage them. They did not have any great first aid material available, but I remember her removing a tube with some black cream from a wall locker and applying it to our wounds. Even to this day I can remember the peculiar smell of the Ichtolan Salbe, a disinfecting cream, usually applied to boils.

She had hardly finished fixing us up, when several girls in uniform, aged about 16-18 entered the basement. Their ranking member asked all of us, who had hoisted the white flag outside the building. When everyone denied having done this they kept looking around and found what they were apparently looking for. Under a table in the corner the older man was crouched down, half covered up, but his uniform pants and boots were exposed. The leader aimed her pistol at the soldier and ordered him to get up and follow them outside. He was looking around at all of us, as if he was expecting some kind of help, but when nobody interfered or spoke up, he finally got up and left with them. One of the women in the cellar mentioned that she thought he was a deserter, but did not want to say anything. A long quiet set in.

Everybody seems to wonder what would happen to the alleged deserter. My mother carefully closed my jacket and that made me realize that I still had my uniform on. It was only covered by an old civilian style jacket I had found somewhere along the trek, because in April we usually had to wear either jackets or light sweaters. The jacket not only covered my uniform shirt and HJ scarf but also hid my uniform dagger from sight. Although there were older looking boys and girls in the cellar, my mother, it seemed, felt the need to protect us from any unknown dangers

After this incident I decided to find me another weapon, such as a pistol, because armed people were less likely being considered deserters. Discarded guns were plentiful, as there were many weapons still on the dead and wounded in the streets. One also just had to ask any one of the men behind the barricades, fortifications or bunkers for one. The only problem was that they might at the same time assign you to a defensive position. I was not willing to do that just then. I had a strong desire to protect and support my family. Therefore I had no intention of leaving them at that time until they were safe at a home of relatives, wherever that was. That thought prompted me to ask my mother what we were doing there in the cellar waiting. Waiting for what? I asked her, if it was not time to get our things and try to make it to wherever we needed to go. I was not even sure where we were, since this part of Berlin was completely unfamiliar to me and I had not seen a map for weeks to find out what our precise location was. It was obvious that my sister and brother were not too keen to leave and walk again, but we decided to leave and departed after saying brief goodbyes.

When we emerged from the cellar and entered the street again, my mother immediately tried to cover the kids' eyes, because we found the answer as to what could have happened to our soldier. About 100 meters from us, the body of a man was seen hanging from one of the few remaining street lamp with a large hand painted sign around his neck stating '*Ich bin ein Feigling*', (I am a coward). And this was not to be the only man hung from the lampposts as we made our way through obstacles and past manned defensive positions. Reaching a bridge spanning the River Havel, we spotted a large crowd of people in the middle of the bridge. When we had reached the group we saw about twenty people leaning over a dead horse, still hitched to a wagon. Armed with a multitude of knives, women and men were eagerly stripping the horse of any meat left on the bones. While I was reaching for my bayonet, tempted to join in to get some food, my mother forcefully pulled me forward. Firing in the distance probably scared her, but it did not bother the people going after the meat. Their hunger was undoubtedly greater than any fear.

I was very disappointed in my mother. This was a rare chance to get some fresh meat, but she would not hear of it. After hours of straggling along in relative quiet with only distant firing and an occasional Tiger tank with troops following them crossing some intersections in front and behind us, we finally recognized some familiar street names. We spotted one of the well-known symbols of Berlin, the '*Funkturm*', Berlin's radio transmission tower, which was next to the Olympic Stadium, only a short distance from the '*Kurfürstendamm*', Berlin's the 5th Avenue. The now ugly facades of some previously architecturally beautiful buildings showed the devastating scars of the war. There seemed to be no life visible except for a few large tanks around the intersections waiting for an assault. Not knowing where to go from our position, scanning the other side, we noticed a former Hotel, not too badly damaged on the lower two floors. It looked like a prospective temporary shelter and we decided to carefully cross the street to find a place to stay. Running, we learned, will attract attention and cause soldiers to open fire.

Making it to the other side, I spotted an entrance and carefully entered. It was overwhelming what we saw. There were a lot of people, packed among wounded, on the entire floor. When we were about to leave again, someone mentioned that there was still some space in the basement, if we didn't mind. We did not mind. I just wanted to eat something, lie down and sleep. The basement did not have much room either but had several locked storage sections, with what appeared to be canned stuff. Picking a more isolated spot to sleep I noticed that stacked large cans showed that they indeed contained syrups, to include chocolate for making ice cream. We could not believe our eyes. Hungry as we were, this stock presented us with the opportunity to obtain some food, no matter what it was. When my mother checked the lock, someone told her that they were informed that this was hotel property and that access to it was prohibited.

My mother told us kids to stay while she was going to check something out. She returned with a decorated wounded Air Force Officer, who plainly stated that he was taking possession of the food storage items in the name of the "Reich". It did not take long and the lock was removed. After he checked the room, he also found other food items such as nuts, sugar, butter and cookies. It was a gold mine in food. To prevent a panic run on the supplies, he posted some old Volkssturm-man on the door with special instructions. After he had left, several mothers with their children came down to receive some of the items. Before he left he instructed me to get some food for us and then take a larger box upstairs. Had I known better, I would have stayed where I was, but dutifully I followed orders.

Defense of Berlin – Chaos, Destruction and Death

Once upstairs I found a group of maybe 8-10 Hitler Jugend, with a senior leader, being issued German bazookas, the *'Panzer Faust'* and hand grenades. Before I could even say one word, I was sized up and asked if I was familiar with the weapon. I answered him in the affirmative and suddenly found myself being a proud owner of a Panzerfaust. What a difference from my earlier days in the Jungvolk, when I played the fanfare and was a drummer in our battalion's band. Some of the boys were encouraging each other, promising that they were ready to show those Bolsheviks what they were made of.

Well, looking at those excited guys, it seemed to rub off on me too. I was given an oversized jacket, army field gray with long sleeves, which could have fit my father better, and was told to get another box of foodstuff. That was my chance to tell my mother that I was leaving briefly to have some fun with the Ruskies and to please wait and not to move until I got back. I must admit that I was scared and should have known then to quit the war. It was not a game. Our group, with boys ranging from twelve to about sixteen years old, left the building for the next intersection, where we dropped off a box of food to a crew of a tank. The tank, previously disabled, had been pushed into a crater at the intersection in the street. It only exposed its turret above the ground, with the crew operating inside. The idea was to re-use an immobilized tank and at the same time present less of a target.

We entered a building near the tank and received our specific instructions. The group was split up in teams of two and assigned to some basements in the immediate area, which had small windows, level with the street and with a view of the sidewalk. The leader explained to us that they expected the Russians to send patrols into our area and that we could kill them without being in danger ourselves. He also relayed to us that Russians had penetrated the subway system and used the tunnels to bypass the German lines and attack us from the rear. Hitler had thereafter given orders to flood some of the subway system, killing thousands of the enemy. Strangely enough we had heard stories of Russians doing the same thing. Having just been in the subway, I was wondering if our own wounded and refugees were drowned at the same time when they demolished the tunnel walls and flooded some tunnels. Casting those thoughts aside, I believed that we would not sacrifice our own to drown the enemy. I quickly squelched my fears to return to the task at hand.

After a brief search, my comrade and I found an appropriate basement without any people hiding in it. The idea was that we would crouch behind the basement windows, watch and listen. Whenever we would see a Russian, usually only his boots, or hear Russian spoken, we pull the pin, count to three and throw the grenade in their direction. It sounded relatively easy and we could hardly wait to put the idea into practice. We had waited almost the whole day with our stomachs making themselves known, when we finally heard someone approaching. They were not German boots we noticed, but neither one of us found the courage to pull the pins. It was a difficult decision to make because we knew that several units of the Baltic and Russian SS divisions fighting on our side, had also retreated from the approaching Red Army and were involved in the defense of *'Festung Berlin'*.

We wanted to be careful not to kill any of our own. Several hours had passed before we got another chance. Hugging close to the building, we noticed several soldiers passing by the basement window, wearing Russian boots. This time we threw a grenade. The tremendous explosion that followed nearly deafened us. We had a few more chances after a long pause. Covering our ears tightly each time, we expended all of our hand grenades. Without any grenades we suddenly felt naked. Armed with only our two Bazookas, we carefully left the building. Looking around the area to see if it was safe to cross the road back to the hotel, we noticed five dead bodies spread out near our window. Four were Russians, while one appeared to be a German soldier, but wearing Russian style boots. Not seeing any weapon on him, he could have been captured by the Russians. We both felt sick to our stomachs seeing one of our own people killed. It seemed strange that some casualties have a greater effect on a person than others. I was afraid to check if they were all dead. Since none of them moved, I assumed they were.

While trying to make our way back to the hotel, we spotted someone nearby firing from a 4th or 5th floor balcony down into the road at some of our troops, who were seeking cover behind a burned out tank. The shooter could clearly be seen from our position and he had not spotted us yet. It would have been quite easy to fire at him if we had a rifle. When my buddy mentioned that we have something even better, he patted his tank killer. First I thought it to be a waste but then I agreed to fire, since we could not dare to move from our position with the Russian being there. I aimed, shaking and trying to steady myself. With my new comrade coaching me, I removed the safety and fired. It was a beautiful shot I thought, but I hit too high only causing a lot of bricks to fall down on the sniper. Seemingly unimpressed, the Russian continued his firing. Quickly responding, my sidekick fired and the round took the entire balcony down with the Russian on it. We dashed out of our position and ran toward the hotel, hoping nobody else would fire at us. Luck was with us. We made it back to the hotel and found that the troops we had left behind had relocated already. They had left instructions, where we could find them and make contact with them again. But there was no great desire on my part at that time to make contact with that group. The general confusion and serious lack of organization made me wonder, if there was anybody still in overall charge. There was a serious lack of food, ammunition, vehicles and overall control. It was chaotic.

I checked the basement and was relieved to find my family intact. They were worried about me and glad that I had made it back. My young friend Icke, my mother told me, had met someone in the group of combatants, who had relocated during my absence. It was an older Boy, who was willing to take him along to find some of his relatives in the area. I told my comrade, that, rather then trying to find the others I would continue my travel to my planned destination. Being without family or other friends he could go to, he decided to try to find the others. Before leaving from this fairly safe haven, our mother had asked some of the people present where the front lines were. As expected she could not get any reliable information. Nobody was sure as to the location of our own troops or the Russians. Our family decided to take the chance and left the hotel to continue our trip to our relatives, zigzagging through areas that reverberated with gunfire. Hearing sporadic tank and artillery firing to our rear coming closer it inducing us to move as fast as we could, not knowing whether we were running from one danger into another in front of us.

Our little bags, now a little heavier with some organized food stuff, slowed us down significantly. I never liked rain, but a sudden downpour was an answer to our hopes as our canteen was near empty. Disregarding the rain and the firing, we continued our walk, passing through many manned barricades, grateful that nobody mistook us for the enemy. After several hours, we spotted several puddles in various areas which gave us a chance to get some water and quell our thirsts. There just were no other sources of drinking water readily available anywhere along the route, unless we detoured, which we definitely did not want to do. We were exhausted. Wherever we looked, chaos and destruction. The nearly insurmountable piles of rubble presented us with one obstacle after another. There were hardly any buildings left intact and only a few people could be seen occasionally hurrying from one area to another. There was hardly any vehicular traffic on the streets, except for an occasional Mercedes staff car on a major road. They looked very strange, as it had a smoke stack sticking out of the trunk. Only later did I find out that the gasoline shortage was so critical that they had somehow converted the gasoline engines to run on coal and wood. The system was a *'Holzvergaser'* a charcoal carburetor. I realized then that our military really was in a bad shape.

While hurrying toward the inner city, which we believed was still in our hands, we noted thousands of hand written notes on demolished buildings. There were no telephones to be found anywhere. All of our means of communication were reduced to leaving crude messages on the walls, doors and other flat surfaces. Written with chalk and crayons, messages informed others about whereabouts of relatives and friends. Several areas we passed revealed piles of dead, civilians and military. The bodies were not even covered up making me wonder, who placed them there, when were they were going to be buried and by whom? The overall picture was depressing and gave me a deep sense of loss.

What ever happened to our great nation? I was always thinking back to those days, when we had those great parades, which gave us all the great feeling of indestructibility. Speaking to people we met, soldiers and civilians, with the exception of some diehard fanatics, we found that the majority's belief in the Reich's leadership was totally destroyed. The only reason they still fought on was out of fear from the Russians. At this venture, you would be wise not to mention your party affiliation or relationship with any of the *"Partei bonzen"* (Party Big Shots). How could Germany still win the war?

Fear of Losing the War – Rapes by Troops

Exhausted, dirty with blisters on our feet we arrived at our aunt's apartment house hours later and were happy to find their residence still standing. It was a building located to the rear of a high-rise apartment complex. While the front of the complex along the street was just a skeleton of a building, the rear still had survived. Our families had not seen each other for years because we had never been that close. Nevertheless, since we were still relatives, we were welcomed, fed and given a bed to sleep in. This was by no means pleasant, but I was eventually getting used to sleeping with three and four people in one bed. It was also a pleasure to meet my redhead cousin, who I had not seen for years and hardly recognized. She was only a year or two younger than I was.

It must have been the first week of May. We had only stayed there for about two days when we heard heavy firing in the neighborhood. The front lines seemed to have caught up with us again, as we saw several Russian planes passing over our building. There was no sign of our own air force, suggesting those airfields around the capitol had been overrun. From what we heard, territories had changed hands between occupiers and defenders several times. Listening for the sounds of gunfire nearby, a woman suddenly burst into our apartment. She was hysterical, yelling *"Sie sind hier!"* (they are here), while trying to mess up her hair and her looks. I didn't know what to make of her strange behavior. All the women present in the apartment seemed to know what she worried about. Suddenly, they all made themselves busy taking ashes out of the stove and smearing it in their faces. And bodies. It only took a few minutes and I was surrounded by a group of despicable looking women. It was almost comical. The woman who had just burst into the apartment uttered that those Mongol troops take great joy in raping German women.

Embarrassed to watch them change I took the kids and went into an adjacent room. After a few minutes a woman came to our room and I was shocked to finally recognize her by her dress as our own mother. I had never seen such a transformation before in my life. Only a short time later, the kids and I returned to the living room, when we heard Russian voices coming up the stairway and doors being kicked in. I felt at a loss for a moment, but then realized that my uniform could possibly mean a bullet for me. Removing my jacket and uniform shirt I shoved them under a couch. Finding an old blanket, I wrapped it around me and sat down next to my brother and sister, who were huddled in the corner of the room. About four or five women stayed in the living room with some younger girls.

When the door to our apartment was kicked open, I could see a rather disgusting and dirty looking Russian with Mongolian features entering the apartment firing a burst of his submachine gun into the ceiling. When he checked the other rooms, he must have been satisfied that neither soldiers nor any armed Germans were in the apartment. He did not seem to be bothered by me holding the small offspring and returned to the other room. I saw him walking over to the women, who were now all crouching in the corner of the room. Pointing to his wrist and two watches he yelled '*Uri, Uri*'. When nobody moved, just fearfully stared at him, he grabbed the arm of the closest women and forcefully removed her '*Uhr*', the watch. Finally understanding what the Russian wanted, those women, who had watches quickly removed theirs and handed them to him, prompting him to grin and laugh.

But that was not all that he was interested in. After he pocketed the timepieces, he handed his submachine gun to another Russian in the doorway and grabbed a woman next to him, ripped her clothes off and raped her on the floor with everybody silently watching. After he got through, he traded places with the other soldier and grabbed another women, fortunately not my mother, who was holding someone's little kid in her arms.

After the second Russian finished, they both broke out in laughter and left, firing another gun burst in the staircase.

All I could do during this event is cover our kids' eyes, so that they would not have to witness this. I just wished then that I should have had a gun to been able to protect the women. But then again, I realized that I would not have been able to mess with those two Russians. It took quite a while for everybody to regain posture. Almost all of the women cried, with the kids sobbing loud. The two rape victims seemed in pain and obviously ashamed. My own feelings were those of embarrassment of a male having witnessed brutality done by another male to a female without being able to prevent this. I just sat there, unable to say a word to those women. Only later did we find out that many women and young girls, were repeatedly raped, some of them many times by large gangs of soldiers.

Many women could not handle this abuse and as a result they killed themselves and their children. Other young mothers, starving from the lack of food and unable to breastfeed their babies also committed suicide after killing their babies. Quite often they so carefully selected their sites to terminate their lives, that their bodies were often found only weeks afterwards. Many of those casualties were accidentally located by the first groups of 'Trümmerfrauen' (rubble women), which were organized and ordered to work by the occupying Soviet Army to clear and clean up the roads and buildings.

Taken POW

Without any radios or other means of communication, we were in the dark as to the tactical situation in Berlin. Another boy about my age, hungry and tired of hanging around the apartment decided to venture outside and I agreed to join him. Our mothers protested of course, since they did not want us to run into trouble, as if we had not been in trouble before. We used the good excuse to check out the immediate neighborhood to find some food. Women on the other hand would be in immediate danger, if they go out in the open. There used to be a bakery in the same block, I was told, which still had some rationed bread days before the Russians started the assault. The baker told the people before that he would continue to bake until they ran out of flour. Besides, I felt like leaving the women alone for a while and agreed to go with him. Being overanxious to get out, one my age usually neglects to think things through. That would prove to be a big mistake.

As it was cold outside, I put my uniform shirt back on and covered it with my army gray jacket. As we left the building complex, we were surprised to see several Russian soldiers across the street leaning against a disabled German Tiger tank, drinking. It looked like the war was over and they were taking a break. We were both at a loss, having believed that the incident with the raping group before was an isolated incident and the German Army was still in control. Apparently not.

They must have spotted us, because some of them raised their guns at us and one yelled '*stoi*'. My buddy immediately raised his hands. Not knowing what "stoi" meant, I promptly followed suit. We were motioned to come to them and not wanting to get shot, we knew that we had no other choice. We walked over to their side. Suddenly I realized that I had my uniform still on underneath my jacket. I could feel my blood racing to my head and wished that I had taken it off before and to found something else to wear. But that was too late. With a rotten smell on his breath and dirty hands, one of the *Iwans* frisked us both. When he opened my jacked he noticed my uniform and my bayonet I habitually wore. He pulled it out of the sheath and pointed it at my throat. Breaking out into a laugh he suddenly threw it onto a pile of rubble.

I was relieved and thought we could then leave. I should have realized that they would not let us go that easily. Even though my friend did not have any uniform item on him we were both ordered to sit down against the wall. I was hoping that we would find a way to leave, if those guys continued to drink some more. It definitely reeked of alcohol. They seemed to be without any supervision or maybe their officers were busy looking for women. They seemed quite relaxed, what I could not say of ourselves. We didn't even know if the war was over or not. Neither one of us could remember what day or date it was, except that it must have been the first week of May. Only a week or so ago I read the last '*Panzerbär*', newspaper, dated the 29th of April, when I realized then that I had passed and totally forgotten my 13th birthday.

After about an hour of just anxiously waiting, a few more Russians approached our position accompanying several unarmed German soldiers they had probably captured. Both my friend and I suddenly realized that we had been taken prisoner, too. My fear was confirmed, when we were ordered to line up to be marched off. One of the Russians, looked my friend over and unexpectedly kicked him in his butt and pointed with his hand away from group. With a big smile on his face and a quick glance at me, he ran off as fast as he could. Naturally, I tried to follow him but was given a stern '*stoi*' again. Instead, I was pushed into the group of POWs. Looking around, I found myself surrounded by a collection of soldiers, airmen, sailors, Volksturm and Hitler Youth. All of them appeared dirty and rundown, many showing wounds covered with bloody bandages. They undoubtedly represented the remnants of a once proud German military.

I wished I were in my buddy's shoes, wondering what would happen to me and who was going to take care of my family. There was no reason I thought, that they would keep me in the end, because I was not a regular soldier and neither did I look like one. How wrong I was, as I noticed several other boys my age in uniform, even wearing a helmet, being taking in. Wearing a piece of German uniform just like they did probably made me look like a combatant. As we marched off, not much was spoken, except a few asking each other where they were from. Our group was growing larger as we continued to move through the streets, to a destination unknown. Although most of them appeared demoralized, some were considering themselves lucky to be alive, while others wished they could have died with their comrades. I certainly did not think it was funny hearing some of guys talking about our certain destination, the great Russian 'vacation' land of Siberia. Historically, the Soviets shipped their dissidents and prisoners to Siberia for slave work in their '*Gulags*'. Everyone knew that this area was so isolated and remote, that an escape from there was nearly impossible.

While marching through a totally devastated area, filled with rubble, destroyed military equipment and dead bodies, I was constantly hoping for a miracle that would give me a chance to escape. Our group finally reached a walled-in compound, which may have been barracks at one time. Herded into a partly demolished, large open building, we were ordered to sit down and I took my place near a large door opening. At least I could see the outside surrounding area. Not too far from us was a big gap in the wall surrounding the entire compound. Undoubtedly, this was once the main entrance with a road leading into the compound. It was guarded by a lone guard, who walked from one side to the other of the gap. POWs were sitting everywhere, exhausted and hungry, waiting for food.

It was unbelievable, but there was plenty of talk of heavy fighting still going on within Berlin. Some people even mentioned that several German divisions in the West were hoping to join the Americans, who were at Magdeburg, only 100 kilometers from Berlin. We could be liberated again by our own or maybe by the Americans, which were expected to take Berlin instead of the Russians. Propaganda was still alive, doing its best to give us hope in this seemingly totally hopeless situation. It was clear that most of the captured could no longer be persuaded by the NAZI ideology. The promise and belief in a final victory was now replace by the shear will to survive. There was not much left of Berlin. The city was now usually referred to as the *'Reichsscheiterhaufen'*, the Reich's Pyre, with thousands of dead bodies waiting for a decent burial.

Still somewhat hopeful before, after two days my hopes were dwindling. One meal a day of *'Borscht'*, a Russian vegetable soup, was not enough for most of us younger guys. Several groups started plotting a breakout, considering there were only a few Russians guarding us. As the evening approached it was getting darker and I was again feeling starved. The searchlight covering the area had not been turned on as yet. The female guard, an unusual sight, with a Kalashnikov assault rifle around her neck was slowly walking back and forth at the gate. She was smoking a bad smelling 'Makhorka' cigarette and chewing on some food. The objectionable tobacco smell slowly drifted into my direction

It is still unclear what really prompted me, but remembering the Russian POW in Meseritz asking me for bread, I just decided to try the same. Walking up to her from behind. I uttered *'cleb'* tapping her on the shoulder to get her attention. She must have been deep in thought and dazzled, when she turned around pointing her submachine gun into my face. With my hands open, stretched out toward her I mumbled and stuttered "cleb". To my surprise she waved and motioned his weapon toward the outside the gate raising her foot as if to kick me out. My heart almost jumped for joy, as I realized the female guard must have thought I came from the outside looking for food. I didn't think twice. I was only too happy to oblige her in doing her job guarding POWs and keeping beggars out. Maybe my looks convinced her, that I was just a hungry kid from the neighborhood begging for food. I was not about to question her reasoning or action. Maybe it was her motherly instinct. I forced myself to slowly walk toward the outside and turning a corner across the street, I ran as fast as my feet would carry me over the rubble in the road. I was free again...

The Loss of the Battle – Final Surrender of Germany

Not to meet with the same fate again, I turned my uniform jacket inside out to hide the appearance of a uniform, which could have provoked another capture. Strangely enough, I did not encounter too many Russians, but many German civilians searching for relatives. There were many people reading posted papers and notes, advising them where a relative or friend could be found. Eager to get home again, I walked as fast as I could in a pair of shoes that showed signs of falling apart. I tried hard to remember the route that our column had taken to return to where we had come from, but a total darkness that had fallen over the area made it nearly impossible.

It was quite a long way home and too dangerous to travel at night. I still didn't know, whether the war was still going. Finding a covered doorway, I decided to crouch down for a nap from which I did not wake up until early morning, when a Russian convoy rumbled by. I didn't make a move, rather playing dead so not give them any reason to check me out. They finally faded behind some collapsed building and I ventured out to find some people and ask for directions. After I got an idea about the general area, I started my hike back.

I don't remember how many hours it took, wishing I would have had a watch, but the only people owning watches now were the Russians. It was a depressing sight to see all this destruction and its associated smell of decay. All by myself, I was left to my thoughts, wondering what was the present situation and what the future had in store for Germany, my family and me. Have we really lost the war? Is the German Army still fighting? On my way I asked several people, who were cleaning up, what the present status was, but all I would get is a shrug. Nobody was too talkative and I gradually gathered that the worst had happened and the Russians had taken Berlin.

My fears were confirmed when I noticed a long line of people in the distance and at its end a Russian truck with soldiers handing out bread. Nearby a female Russian soldier sitting on a '*Panje Wagen*', a horse drawn wagon, was distributing German chocolate to little kids. It surprised me to see little kids suddenly appearing from nowhere. The picture was truly strange. She had a PPSh-41 submachine gun strapped to her back, holding a young baby in one of her arms while handing out the chocolate with the other. It was obvious that the large box came from Berlin's chocolate factory. Hungry as I was, only one thought crossed my mind and that was to get out of this area and back to my family as fast as possible. Waiting in line for some bread was not worth delaying it. I was used to get along without solid food for a day or two. A badly dented German army water canteen I found with some remaining water helped me to get over the thirst while walking. After my capture I naturally had no extra baggage or comfort items to carry.

I don't remember how long it took me to get back to my aunt's place, but it was late that night. My mother was overjoyed seeing me back again. She had heard from my friend, that the Russians had taken me away and had feared the worst. I finally got the word, that Berlin had surrendered to the Russians on the 2nd or 3rd of May 1945, but the German Army was still fighting in northern and southern Germany and the allies were in the process of occupying all of Germany. It was often hard to tell what the true situation was. The enemy distributed propaganda calling for the cessation of fighting while the German propaganda encouraged us to fight on for a final victory. This, of course, was hard to believe in after the obvious Russian victory. Besides, Germany had run out of soldiers, fuel, food and a clean water supply. Our ration cards were worthless, if anyone still had some. We did not have any for several weeks. Besides, there was no food available for purchase. I cannot even remember seeing one German with any money. Scrounging and bartering was in.

During the last few months before the fall, there was no work for civilians, unless they worked for the war industry. To make matters even worse, Berlin fell into the hands of the Russians, while the Western part of the Reich was occupied by the British, French and Americans. Some of their territory was even promised to be turned over to the Soviets according to an agreement made with Stalin, who we knew to be shrewd and no match for the western allies.

It was the 8th of May 1945, when we heard that Germany had unconditionally surrendered to the Western allies on the 7th May at Reims, France, while Field Marshal Keitel formally signed the ratification in Berlin with the Russians. Following the establishment of four occupation zones many Germans within the Soviet zone decided to choose life under the Western Allies and quietly moved to the West. Although our family would have loved to move to the West, we had no means to do so and mother considered a later relocation. It became clear, the Western Allies appeared to be more tolerant toward Germans. There were clear signs that they were willing to assist the Germans in the rebuilding of the country. In addition, they also began to provide limited food supplies to those in need, except in the Soviet Zone.

Soviet troops raising
their "Hammer & Sickle"
flag over the ruins of a
government building on
5 may 1945.

School children from
Berlin on top of "Mount
Rubble" welcoming the
US Air Force transport
aircraft during the Allied
airlift in 1948.

Pilots and crews of airlift planes are
jubilant about blockade's end.

The Airlift Memorial in Tempelhof
honoring those who lost their lives.

Erecting quonset huts among the ruins.
Although primitive, it was a beginning.
The American Marshall Plan was
instrumental in rebuilding Berlin in the
West in coming years.

"Normal life" returns among the ruins for tempory shelter.
Berliners travelling across borders between the West and the East Sector.

After the construction of "the wall" under the
watchful eyes of border guards in late 1961,
the wall came down on 9 November 1989.

Chapter II

Life in an Occupied Germany

Surviving and Resisting Soviet Occupation

One would expect the victors to try to return the country back to normal after the disarmament.. Not so under Soviet occupation. The loss of the war was a disaster, with many Germans mourning either the loss of loved ones or the capture and transport to Russia's Siberia of parents and young fighters. Many also had their homes destroyed. Most Germans, except the Communist's, were unable to accept the defeat and still believed in fighting the Soviets, the hated Bolshevics. In several areas of Germany, especially the Soviet Zone the *'Wehrwolf'*, the German resistance, emerged in several areas and received quite a bit of quiet support. This could probably be attributed to the criminal treatment of the Germans, especially women, following the Soviet victory. In German folklore the *Werwolf* was a man who could transform himself into a wolf and as such cause damage and kill. The Hitler Youth changed *"wer"*, the man, to *"wehr"*, meaning defense.

I was not aware of any wehrwolf groups in our area, but friends told me that they are actively working in certain areas and were looking for members to conduct operations against the occupation troops. Although enthusiastic about the idea, I was advised not to show my support openly, unless among good friends. Many youths had been turned in by others and arrested for their open support or operations with them. The German population was swiftly introduced to a highly professional and vicious Soviet Secret Police, the NKVD. This branch of the Red Army had divisions in the field and was thorough and ruthless in executing enemies of the state. Germans living under the Soviet occupation were to experience this first-hand, as former political leaders still living in the East were rapidly rounded up and deported to Siberia.

My mother realized that we could no longer stay with my relatives because of the lack of space. We had to find some other shelter back in the district, where we used to live before we were evacuated after the allied air raids and having been bombed out. I didn't like the idea too much, since I grew fond of my cousin Regine, but Berlin was not that big that we could not see each other off and on later. First we had to try to get back to a more normal life, which included finding shelter and food for the family. The Russians, through their newly established Communist Party apparatus, had encouraged food shop owners to return to work and to open their stores if they had not been destroyed.

The nearby bakery was the first one to open and saw a huge mob lining up after the first bread became available. People emerged from the rubble and basements like ants from an anthill. To our surprise, we saw a big Russian truck parked in front of the bakery. Approaching the store, we observed the Russian soldiers lining up people and witnessed something never seen before. Each person, prior to entering the shop, had to let the soldiers shove a long hose under the women's blouses and into the pants and shirts of men. With the help of a compressor, a white powder was then blown into the clothing and finally into the hair of the people. Welcome to Russia. We had experienced our first treatment in a de-liceing station of the Red Army. We questioned ourselves if they wanted to make sure that they are protected from our lice or the other way around. At least they seemed concerned about our health. After standing in line a couple times for several hours to get bread, which was an obvious mix of 50/50 wheat and saw dust, we desperately hoped that we would eventually also see meat stores open up.

Not so surprising, the new military government made a serious effort to control the population and also create living space for those without a home. We hoped to return to Berlin-Britz, our former residential area. Because we had lived there before, the new government assigned us to an apartment, which we had to share with another family. We got one room in a three-room apartment, with the use of a common kitchen. Needless to say, it was not a happy situation for either family, but due to the destruction and shortage of housing, homeowners were forced to accept homeless families. My mother was determined to make this arrangement a temporary one. She wanted to work hard to enable us to eventually move into a place of our own. Once Berlin was cleaned up and gradually rebuilt, as the new leadership had promised, the situation would hopefully improve. Work was slowly becoming available in Berlin, but it proved to be quite different from what my mother expected. Almost every day I was wondering about my father's fate, hoping that he was still alive and somewhere in the West. Knowing him, he would never be able to accept life under the communist system.

Mother as a Slave Laborer for the Russians

Of course, we had our traditional block wardens again to control the people, only this time we found they were all Communists or their sympathizers. Where they all came from so suddenly was surprising, as I always believed we had only National Socialists living in Germany. It did not take the warden long to find out what party affiliation my parents had. As a result, my mother was immediately assigned to work for the Soviet Army in a marble crushing plant nearby. Most others were assigned to a '*Trümmerfrauen Brigade*', (rubble women brigade) to salvage, clean and stack bricks from demolished buildings. The kids and I had to stay home with the other family since schools were not operating yet.

After a couple weeks, and for some unknown reason, our mother was reassigned to harder work in an old oil refinery plant, converting coal into oil. The German industry had developed a technique during the war to convert coal into oil to provide fuel for the industry and automobiles. Their largest production facilities were at Leuna and Buna, as I recall, because they were prime targets for allied bombing raids during the war. This "job" gave her the opportunity to "appropriate" a few coal bricks occasionally to help out feeding our cooking stove in the kitchen and the oven in our room. Every little bit helped, because wood had become very scarce, as many ruins had been stripped of such material during the colder months for firewood.

The new government realized that the populace needed to be re-indoctrinated and educated in line with the communist doctrine. The opening of schools was clearly one of their priorities and local administrators were busy to find appropriate buildings and retrain new teachers. In the meantime, being restless and always hungry, I felt the need to continue scrounging for food. And I was not the only one. Soon I found several boys in my age group, who searched for old stashes of supplies left behind or stored away by the German Army. And that is where I met the Wehrwolf. It was hard to believe, that after several months of occupation, Germany still had some fanatics left trying to defeat the Red Army. It reminded me of the French resistance activities under the German occupation.

During the last days of fighting, members of the Wehrwolf had prepared for the eventuality that Soviets might only temporarily occupy Germany. A strong resistance and acts of sabotage would then be essential for our country to be liberated. The German Wehrmacht had learned from bitter experiences in several countries and found that the resistance is an important factor in regaining a country's control from an occupying force. The leaders, mostly older Hitler Youth members, had developed plans to sabotage trains carrying confiscated supplies out of Germany to Russia. The Soviet Government was determined to remove entire factories and related industrial equipment from Germany.

I recalled incidents from the first days of occupation when common soldiers, many of them apparently uneducated, were also doing their own thing trying to take items back to Mother Russia. Some Mongol soldiers had been found breaking off faucets from the walls to take home. Apparently, they believed that they could have running water, if they just stuck the faucets into a wall. It must have been extremely hard for their officers to explain to the soldiers the basic features of our civilization. Bands of *Kossacks* were often observed roaming the liberated areas with booty hanging from their saddles. It was typical to see Russians carrying four or five "liberated" watches on their wrists. Off and on they could be seen shaking their watches or knocking on them, when they had stopped running. When they could not make them run again they took the watch off and threw it away instead of rewinding them. Asking a Mongol why he did it, the answer would usually be shrugging of his shoulders, stating *'machinist kaput'*, the engineer was dead. Did they believe someone was inside the watch running it? We were in disbelief about the intelligence of some troops, but had to admit that they knew their weapons well and were good fighters. Mostly probably because they did not dare to retreat and face a bullet from their commanders.

One day I saw a soldier occupying a home with several others, washing potatoes in the toilet bowl. Hoping to maybe scrounge some I watched him from nearby. I could not believe my eyes, when he tried to rinse them off by pulling the chain for flushing the toilet. Watching the potatoes disappear, he grabbed his submachine gun and shot at the toilet bowl and water reservoir mounted above near the ceiling. We all knew that the majority of the Red Army was not that ignorant, but it demonstrated that they must have drafted just about every man and women they could find from all walks of life to fight the German Army.

Following the onslaught by the shock troops initially, more civilized troops succeeded them later on. We noticed, on several occasions, that many common Russians often showed compassion and kindness, when alone with Germans, out of sight from their political counterparts. But that did not change our general misery we felt from day to day.

Since I was looking for food supplies, like a few newly found friends in the neighborhood, I joined the Wehrwolf, hoping to obtain edible supplies that way. One of our primary objectives was trying to sabotage trains loaded with potatoes and other food goods or plunder some of the Army warehouses. During the night, even during the posted curfew, we searched the areas around a railroad yard. We targeted some wagons and succeeded in removing boards from the floor. If we could not get enough out of the wagon, we were often causing some of the foods, especially potatoes and sugar beets, to fall onto the tracks. Uneven tracks and gaps often shook the wagon enough to make them lose some of the cargo. It worked fairly well, but was too slow for us. We did succeed once with derailing several wagons of a train by blocking or dismantling some of the rail switches. The Soviets soon realized that the accidents had to be acts of sabotage and placed more guards along the tracks preventing us from continuing those operations.

Switching tactics, we selected harvest collection points of the Russian Army, where people working in the fields turned in their sugar beets in exchange for the processed syrup. We carefully penetrated the storage area at the rear of one facility and removed some beets from some ten feet high mounds. Filled in old burlap bags or boxes, we then turned them in for processed syrup at the front entrance. Of course these actions would neither help to liberate us nor defeat the enemy, except it provided our families with other staples and different food items, which we could also use for bartering. Most of us finally realized that the risks were definitely not worth it.

There was an obvious absence of any political or military leadership and it became evident that this type of national fanaticism had come to an end in Germany. Undoubtedly we saw the end of the so-called Wehrwolf resistance, at least in Berlin. It had outlived its usefulness and the occasional symbol showing up on walls did not phase any body.

Aside from food another shortage among the population was clothing. Most of our clothing was old and worn and had not seen any soap and water for a long time. When almost new German uniform articles showed up at some bartering spots, many women with sewing talents were quick to modify these items into something more resembling civilian garments. Gradually, more and more small food stores reopened. To our surprise the old German currency, the *'Reichsmark'* was still the official tender. Foodstuff was still very limited and rationed, so that all the money did not help those that just happened to have some left over. Jewelry and gold was still the best tender and everybody was wondering how and when normalcy would return in our lives. We were all hoping that our mother would soon be released from her work detail so that she may do some work for better pay. Iwan hardly paid anything for her forced labor, just enough to cover the essential nourishments.

Getting Food under Fire

Our mother did not want to stand by idle on Sundays and asked me on several occasions to help her to get some fresh vegetables like *'kohlrabi'* and cabbage directly from the fields. The only trouble was, that several farms had been confiscated by the Russian Army, became "People's" property and were therefore guarded by troops. I remember one day, after several hours of walking, we approached a red cabbage field in the open beyond a field of *'Rhabarber'* (rhubarb). We noticed a soldier guarding the field, but mother told me to just get down on my belly and we started crawling along the rows of rhubarb plants pushing empty burlap sacks in front of us. The large leaves provided us with enough overhead protection up to a cabbage field about 200 meters beyond the rhubarb. I was looking at the empty sack in front of me imagining it already filled with the expected harvest.

Impatient and curious to know how much further we had to crawl, I lifted my head to check. My mistake! The Russian must have been looking in our direction when I popped my head up and he opened fire with his rifle. The round impacted nearby and too close for comfort. I was glad he was not firing a submachine gun at us. We both froze and then mother whispered to me to crawl backwards. It was quite clear, that we could not turn around without exposing ourselves, because the depth and width of the row was too small. We finally made it back to where we had started from without getting fired on. We were lucky that the soldier was out of sight or we would have had to wait for hours until dark. Although desperate for food, we decided not to try that field again.

After several months, we finally located my grandfather, my mother's father, living in Northern Berlin, who paid us a visit in our one room apartment. He was able to use a newly opened subway line. Following the war he was, like most of the Germans, without work. He was an optical engineer, who used to make precision optical instruments. Always hungry, and too old and weak to fend for himself, he began visiting us about once a week, primarily to have a meager meal with us. He used to smoke his *'Meerschaumpfeife'* (a Turkish tobacco pipe), leaning against a ceramic oven, the only heat source in our room. *Opa*, as we lovingly called him, was bearing a full beard. It was obvious to all of us that he was not in the best of health. Obsessed with eating only the healthiest food, he told us that he is drinking a lot of vinegar salad dressing, which contained a good amount of herbs. This concoction was available in one of the first food stores which opened in his area. My mother advised him against drinking it, but father always knew best. It was not too long thereafter, that he stopped visiting.

We did not think of anything bad until one night. We were suddenly awakened by a familiar knocking sound against the ceramic oven; it was the same sound Opa used to make when he knocked his pipe against the oven, cleaning it. It seemed a bad omen. Several more weeks went by before we received an official letter. It was the first mail we had received after the war had ended, informing us that our Opa had died at home of malnutrition. Strangely enough we recalled the ominous knocking having been on the same evening he died. Unfortunately, the delay in the newly established mail service and the lack of any telephone service at that time, prevented us from attending his funeral. We never found out, where he was buried and assumed that he was cremated like the majority of Berliners. Considering the catastrophic amount of dead still being found in the rubble everywhere during cleanup, we were sure that he was probably one of hundreds of bodies cremated at the time somewhere in Berlin.

In our continued search for edibles and firewood, our small clique of neighborhood youths started to go through old bunkers in hopes to find anything of value. We often found items where we didn't even know what they were. Most of the stuff was ammunition and some weapons, which we retrieved and buried. The last people we wanted to have those items

were the Russians. Among some of the weapons we located were some
Panzerfaust parts, some of which supposedly contained lighter flints in the
warhead. It was not easy to dismantle some of the ammunition, since we
just did not have any adequate tools. But we succeeded collecting some
of the flints. We knew they were quite valuable for our trading and swap-
ping efforts. The black market was blossoming. Gradually, life seemed
to improve, but the continued shortage of food, clean running water and
sporadic electric power made life quite miserable and primitive. At least
we didn't have to worry about bombardments and combat anymore.

The Soviets had a great difficulty to provide the population with the
necessary daily items. Shops or stores were naturally scarce. Adequate
resources were just not available. Their troops, of course, came first and
most of the farms under the Communists were controlled by the Soviets.
The future looked very bleak, even though the propaganda promised us
a great recovery. The Berliners were flooded with Soviet films, shown
in refurbished *'Kinos'*, the German movie theaters. Following the end of
the war, we were shown movies glorifying the great strides the Russians
made following the Bolshevik revolution. As part of our indoctrination to
communism, we were repeatedly told of the victories achieved by the Red
Army and the "outstanding" accomplishments of their state-run factories
and farms. We were to believe that the state did everything for the benefit
of all the people living under communism and under the great leadership
of father Joseph Stalin. For months our population was required to watch
films about the great heroes of the Bolshevik revolution.

In contrast, they followed up presenting us specials, showing the bru-
talities carried out by German troops against the Russian people. This was
hard to swallow, especially after we had all personally witnessed the atrocities executed by the Soviets against the German people. They constantly
emphasized that we should consider ourselves fortunate, finally being liberated from the *'Faschisten'*, as they called the NAZI's. Fortunately, our
family was destined to soon experience a different form of liberation. But
until then I was forced to continue to live under Soviet occupation.

Liberation by US Troops – Establishment of Allied Sectors

The 4th of July shall always have a special meaning to me, probably more
so than to many born Americans. It was a beautiful sunny day when we
received word that the Americans were finally coming to Berlin. We were
pleasantly surprised, because we had no idea that the City of Berlin was

to be partitioned off into four sectors. Each sector was to be occupied by one of the four allied forces, in exchange for the US troops withdrawing from other areas of Germany, which they had actually taken during the war ahead of the Russians. The Red Army would move into and begin to occupy designated German territory previously held by the Americans. This was of course to the dismay of those Germans, who lived there, as they would consequently be living under the Soviets.

It was a great victory for the Communists, who retained half of Berlin while the other Western half was divided into an American, British and French sector. Berlin had 'de facto' become an island within the Soviet Zone of occupation, governed by an allied '*Kommandatura*', a joint command made up of the four commanders of the allied forces. Stalin had pulled off a great coup. With the withdrawal of the Western allies, especially the US Army, the Soviet Union gained vast industrial complexes including the German scientists and their knowledge of advanced technologies, especially in rocket research. Unbeknownst to the United States, they also dismantled and removed vital parts of a nuclear research complex from Western Berlin before the US moved into that area in Berlin. Berliners could not have cared less at that stage. The one good thing that happened to our family was the release of our mother from her forced labor at the refinery, when the Soviets pulled out of our area, as usual leaving hardly anything worthwhile behind.

With a media almost non-existent in Berlin, and the people being sick and tired of propaganda, we all had our doubts about this new development until the 4th of July in 1945. I can't remember how I found out, but the word had spread that the Americans would also take over our sector of Berlin-Britz, where we lived. It did not take long for the Berliners to find out where the US troops would come in and groups of people started assembling in that particular area in Berlin-Zehlendorf, where the US Army Headquarters of Berlin Command was later to be established.

After many hours of patiently waiting along a clean residential avenue, we finally spotted some type of military formation in the distance. Strangely enough, our family and thousands of other Berliners were ready to welcome our former enemies. We all had to admit, the Americans did it in style. The parade was led by a US Army Band, followed by what appeared to be thousands of clean cut, well-dressed soldiers being greeted by an increasing applause from the Berliners lining the street. As a young

German, still a teenager, I was deeply impressed and could not hold back tears when the American Army Band marched by.

It was rather strange and hard to believe how Germans could welcome the most recent enemy of theirs, who had bombed them for years, unless you personally experienced a life under the Soviet regime. What seemed even more surprising was the willingness and the efforts by the allies, especially the Americans, to help us rebuild and revitalize the City, which they had promised. Within a few weeks the US military overwhelmed the population not only with a new culture. New political parties and the establishment of an educational system and free enterprise in commerce began to develop everywhere in our sector. As far as most parents were concerned, the children and our youth needed desperately to return back to school. It was something most of us young children had not even thought of, as we were still trying to survive from day to day.

Gradually, though, things appeared to be looking up and, whether I liked it or not, I was about to be reintroduced to school after a long disruption of well over a year. Fortunately, we were living in our old suburb and found my old elementary school not too badly damaged. Our old home nearby and had been repaired. It now had new tenants living in it, apparently people with communist ties, as I found out from friends, who still lived in the same area. Former members of the NAZI party did not dare to lay claim and retrieve some of their property. In many cases, the Russians not only confiscated the property, but also tried the owners on trumped up charges for a multitude of war crimes. Still, with Russians around, living under US control was no guarantee for one's absolute safety. My mother of course was disappointed but had no desire to even go near our former home and their new residents.

Several months into 1946, I had my first classroom instruction in the old school but now with mostly new teachers. Many of the previous teachers had either been killed, became prisoners of war or had decided to move to the West like an overwhelming number of refugees from the East. It was not easy to catch up with regular school education. Most of us had lost at least two years of regular teaching. It was the result of an evacuation from Berlin, sporadic attendance because of bombings, and finally the battle of Berlin resulting in the destruction of the schools and the political system. In addition, many children and adolescents were so malnourished that they could not attend classes. Both, my sister Ute and I were so anemic and malnourished that we had to walk together to school to make sure we could help each other should any one of us pass out.

The new military government realized the children's dilemma and the American sector commander instituted the so-called *'Quaker-Speisung'*, a US government sponsored lunch program for school children. In addition, families with children were later treated to and received *'CARE'* packages of basic food supplements. Although run by a Catholic Relief agency, the food was distributed regardless of our religious affiliation. Considering our family's scarce income of a few Reichsmark (we still used the old money), the food program was a welcome treat. We were both given *'Biomalz'*, a type of malt concentrate, similar to sugar beet syrup and together with beer yeast, we gradually corrected our shortcomings, regaining better health.

Until the later monetary conversion, bartering was still the only way to obtain extra needed goods. The American troops had their own military scrip, we called it "funny money", which civilians were not permitted to hold or own. In order to stimulate the economy and political recovery, the Allied foreign ministers met in 1947 in Europe to discuss our reconstruction. This was met with firm Soviet resistance. They were not in the least interested in the recovery of a strong Germany. At least not under a system hostile to theirs, as the next years would clearly show. Never before really interested in political developments, our young people seemed to become more and more involved.

A Prelude to Isolation

The first meeting of the four allied Commanders of the Kommandatura in July 1945 was uneventful. The following year the first free election was held on October 1946. The Soviets and their communist friends in Berlin were promoting their agenda for a strong communist dominance in Greater Berlin. The election results, however, were disastrous for their cause. We were all convinced that the communists could never win an election, but we were fearful that they would try anything to somehow gain control of Berlin in its entirety and somehow remove the Allies. For their purposes, the Western powers were getting too strong, economically and politically. We sensed something was brewing, but were confident that the problems would be resolved. It was not going to be that easy.

When the Allies established a new currency, the *'Deutsche Mark'* in West Germany, the Russians went their separate way and instituted their own East Mark, which they demanded to be also valid in all sectors of

Berlin. Fortunately, the Allies insisted on their own currency in Western Berlin, just like in West Germany. This immediately prompted restrictions of free flow of traffic into Berlin from the West by the Soviets. Based upon the immense difference between the economies, the D-Mark value continuously rose until the currency exchange rate reached the ratio of 1:5. While a loaf of bread costs 1 Mark in the West, it was 5 Marks in the East and many items such as oranges or bananas were not even available.

I remember my 14th birthday under the American occupation quite well. Considering the food shortages in those days, although steadily improving, a real birthday party was out of the question. Yet, I was happy when, in lieu of a cake, I received a small bowl of powdered milk, mixed with sugar, in lieu of candy. Instead of a bicycle, which was a dream for most young teenagers, I was given a little Boy Scout pendant to be mounted on a future bike. Considering it a kind of down payment, I was quite content and was looking forward to the day I would get and ride my first bike.

Since I was too young to participate in political activities, which had been a great disappointment so far, I was looking more for comradeship with other boys my age, who had the same interests. Being used to self-discipline and the desire to help others I found my answer in the newly founded '*Pfadfinder*' organization. This pathfinder group represented the new German Boy Scouts, modeled after the British Lord Baden-Powell's international scouting movement. To my surprise, and strangely enough, the German Scouts had adopted the same uniforms as the HJ, probably because those items were common and still available. Only the insignia had changed to the fleur-de-lis. Even the dagger remaining the same.

Of course our rules, regulations and the oath were those of the international movement, but being members of the Pfadfinder unit, it gave us again pride, hope, new directions and a definite purpose in life. The adults on the other hand now had a chance again to become active politically. They could lend their support to one of the two major political adversaries at large in Berlin, referring to the Western allies and their democracies and the Soviets pushing communism. Politically we, the Scouts, were equally challenged by a counterpart in the Eastern sector, the FDJ, the '*Freie Deutsche Jugend*' (Free German Youth), which was anything but free.

As members of the German Communist Party of East Germany they were instrumental in indoctrinating young people in the ideology of their founders, Marx and Lenin. Our primary goal as Scouts was to defend our newly found freedom under democracy and prevent the FDJ to establish themselves in the Western sector of Berlin. While the Americans, the British and to some extent the French supported us, since those countries all had Scouts, the Soviets naturally propped up the FDJ. This East German organization was modeled strictly after the so-called 'Rote Pioniere', the communist Red Pioneers, which was the only youth organization in the Soviet Union. Fierce fistfights became a common occurrence when our groups met in the West sector. As a result, I frequently came home with a bloody nose. Nevertheless, we eventually succeeded in making their operations in our sector very difficult. They soon gave up and preferred to remain in safety within their own jurisdiction. The Western territory had eventually been 'liberated' from them. We were finally free and secure again to 'skinny dip' in our Grunewald Lake, without worrying about those guys and girls stealing our uniforms, which was one of the more devious acts they occasionally resorted to during the summer months.

More and more we all felt the apparent goal of the Soviets; to totally incorporate all of Berlin into their occupation zone under total communist control. Those Communists living in the West sector of Berlin on the other hand had no intention of leaving for their own sector. Instead they were quite content working as moles towards their objective, the eventual reunification.

I recall for instance my mother and other relatives, who we gradually got a hold of, suggesting that I should get confirmed by the Lutheran church. This was previously impossible under the Soviet occupation. Having reached the proper age, I was obligated to go to church three or four times a month to prepare for my confirmation. Right from the beginning I became troubled, when I felt the pastor was discussing the communist manifesto rather than the commandments. He openly glorified Karl Marx, Engels and Lenin in his religious/political comparisons and tried to convince us of the true and real benefits from believing in the peasants' struggles and the achievements of the workers' class. He made blatant statements that the socialist camp is the only true force striving for world-wide peace, freedom and equality.

To drive home his points, he also stated that, in contrast, all the various religions try to dominate people by forcing them to abide by their rules and laws, thereby restricting individual freedoms. Citing factual historical events and wars of past centuries, the pastor appeared, to some, quite convincing. He had obvious difficulties to make any of us believe in his ideal world of socialism. Apparently other parents felt the same way as my mother did when I told her about our classes. It did not take long before he was quietly removed. Had my father known about this incident, I can well imagine how he would have handled this unusual man of the church.

A new pastor was shortly thereafter introduced to perform the confirmation. I didn't really feel like attending the services anymore but did anyway, since my mother had, with a lot of difficulties, converted an old black sweat suit into a dress suit with pleats for this occasion. I could not disappoint her at this stage and felt obligated to go through with the ceremony.

The East German Communists, supported by the Soviets, knew quite well that the outcome of any election would be disastrous for them. In a bold move the German government within the Soviet Occupied Zone created a new party, the '*Sozialistische Einheits-Partei Deutschlands*' (SED). This new Socialist Unity Party of Germany was constituted through a compulsory merger of socialists, communists, Christian democrats and other political orientations into one party under the communist banner. Attempts by the Soviets to also establish this party in Western Germany failed, after the Soviet Administration refused to permit parties from the West to operate freely in East Germany.

This serious conflict threatened to endanger the future existence of the Allied Control Council for Germany. The City of Berlin, being a separate entity in Germany, had its very own temporary constitution and was run by a city government, a Magistrate. It was established in August 1946 and operated with the concurrence of the allied Kommandantura. The Western allies insisted on their guaranteed rights and the rights of all Berliners to political freedoms. The Soviets in turn attempted to limit political freedoms of the Germans and especially of Berliners. This dispute finally prompted the Soviets to walk out of the Allied Control Council and the Allied Kommandantura in 1948.

One primary reason for their walk-out was the dispute over the new German currency. Had East German currency also been decreed throughout Berlin, as demanded by the Russians, it would have been disastrous for all Berliners. The dispute over the two separate new currencies was to mark the beginning of a blockade of Berlin.

Normalcy seemed to return to the three Western military occupation zones as well as the Western sectors in Berlin. With a limited employment being offered, other than the most prevailing jobs of cleaning up and rebuilding the country, Germans could look forward to a better life. The Americans had developed the Marshall Plan, which later greatly invigorated the Western Sectors of Berlin and visually showed a rebirth of the city, a 'Phoenix rising from the ashes'. The West German D-mark and its buying power got significantly stronger. And so was the economy. It was amazing to watch people improvise and devise new articles, when even the common items, such as matches, were very hard to find.

Mother was offered a job working at home, producing a substitute for matches. This product consisted of a small glass vile, filled with glass wool and a chemical liquid and closed with a rubber stopper. A small extra-long matchstick, its end covered with another chemical compound would ignite after a brief insertion into the vile's liquid. Although primitive, it worked and for several months, until the real matches came back on the market, our family assembled and packaged thousands of these "matches" in our one room home. Life for us really began to improve after our mother found another job working in her old field as a secretary. Regular attendance of school for my sister and me helped us to return to a more civilized life and productive existence.

Very few people in Berlin still owned a radio, because they had either lost it during the war or the old tubes had just quit working. Listening to the airwaves, regardless where the stations were located, was always exciting. With the rather slim chance of obtaining a radio on the market, we were challenged to start with the basics. A simple radio receiver. Give the Scouts a challenge and they will accept it. I had never experienced so much fun than to work with my friends at school and the Scouts to "build" our first radio receiver, with which we could receive radio transmissions from England and West Germany. The only local station was Soviet controlled and was strictly a propaganda station.

Having learned the basics, I sat in my corner at home, with an old German Army headset on, poking around a little "lead crystal", made in our chemical class. It required a lot of persistence until I found the right spot of a frequency and strong station. My first "radio receiver" was the size of a mousetrap and needed neither tubes, power hookup nor difficult wiring schematics. Just a headset, the crystal and a lot of patience. I often wished I still had that strange looking but effective means of communication, the simple wire probe and a crystal. A few months later however, I wanted to listen to more than communist propaganda of the only station in Berlin. After a lot of scrounging and determination I finally graduated to a more sophisticated "audio" with several tubes and a loudspeaker mounted on a wooden board. Experiencing a lot of mishaps, failures and electrical shocks of 220 Volts, I was finally lucky and happy to receive English language programs. Most of them were from BBC, the British Broadcasting Corporation and suddenly also AFN, the American Forces Network and "*Die Stimme Amerikas*", the Voice of America. German radio stations in the West were still in the coming, but eventually blocked by powerful signals of interference from the Russians.

Following my graduation from elementary school after five years and the transfer to a High School, I was exposed to a larger curriculum. Fascinated by chemistry, I also played around making small fireworks pieces with red phosphorus and other elements, the exact components I can't remember. These experiments however were abruptly halted when the glass of our apartment window was blown out, while I was preparing a little firecracker on the windowsill. The family did not at all appreciate my enthusiasm for chemistry regardless of my getting a school grade of a '1', the equivalent of an 'A'.

Although my School, the Albrecht-Duerer High School, was about 10 miles away, I did not mind riding the subway every day to get there. I had a great time trying to catch up with our instructions, the amount of which was more than I had expected. The curriculum was just overwhelming. Aside from Chemistry and Physics, I enjoyed English, French and later Latin. During later years I began to like especially art, followed by geography, old German, history and music appreciation. Mathematics with algebra and trigonometry gave me most trouble and often brought me very close to failing grades. Nobody liked our mandatory school subjects, but later in life I was to appreciate everything I was required to learn.

Living in the Western sector in comparison with the East had many great advantages. Students generally had the same subjects we had been given before the end of the war. The teachers were usually the same, if they had survived and we were all at liberty to speak freely. Germans residing in the Soviet Sector in turn had to learn Russian instead of English in school and were subjected to a continuous barrage of pro-communist propaganda and the benefits of socialism. The instructors of the 'socialist camp' would not dare to criticize the new regime. Membership in the communist youth movement was expected, short of being mandatory, if one wanted to receive special privileges.

Following the first free elections in the city, it became clear that the overwhelming majority of the population, unless you were a Communist, rejected the communist ideology. From one day to the other, the Berliners could feel the increasing pressure put on by the Soviets. Traveling through Berlin and especially the Western Sectors, the East Berliners unmistakably noticed the great differences between the democracy in the West and their own life under communism. Many of them were putting out feelers to relatives in the West for a possibility of leaving the East and relocating. Although living space was extremely limited in West Berlin, with two and three families often living in one apartment, relatives nevertheless left the East for the freedom in the Western sector.

With the economy rapidly improving under the Western Allies, the Soviets realized that they were losing a lot of people. The newly found capitalism evolving outside the Soviet block seriously threatened their political and economical status in their occupied territories. It became clear to them that drastic steps had to be taken to improve their situation.

It did not take them long to react. We suddenly noted that traffic between Berlin and Western Germany through the Soviet Zone was being seriously hampered. Many Berliners now began to worry that they might become stranded on an island inside a Soviet satellite state. A possible isolation had never been felt to be possible. To underscore their power, the Soviet Army raised their communist hammer and sickle flag on top of Berlin's symbol, the Brandenburg Gate with its victory chariot, the '*Quadriga*'. This did not sit well with the West Berliners as it sat right on the sector border drawing a line between the East and the West, with the chariot pointing toward the West. We all got the impression the Soviets wanted to tell us that they intend to 'liberate' us again.

On a Sunday afternoon, following the placement of the flag, a couple of friends, I believe there were four of us, took the subway and we went to the Brandenburg Gate. Taking a chance of being caught, we entered the stairwell leading to the top and were surprised that everything was open for us to get to the top. After cautiously looking around to find a gap in the almost non-existent traffic, we slowly lowered the flag and then hurriedly ripped the flag off its pole rope. Running downstairs the narrow steps, we almost fell over each other dragging the flag downstairs.

One of our guys had stayed downstairs at the door on the street level to warn us of either police or soldiers approaching. None of the authorities had arrived but some Berliners nearby evidently watched our escapade and gathered next to the door. I was afraid some of them were communists, but it turned out they were politically on our side. They would not however let us leave with the flag intact and without at least getting a piece of it as a souvenir. Ripping off a larger piece we handed it to them and expecting someone would soon come, we ran off into the nearby *'Tiergarten-Park'*. There we paused and tore the flag in several pieces for each us. To this day I have no idea what happened to my piece of the flag. It did not take the Soviets long to hoist another 'red banner'. This event was to be the last time I had the chance to enter East Berlin until a little more than a decade later and under quite different circumstances.

Berlin Blockade in the Making – Saved by the Berlin Airlift

A week later the East German People's Police, the *'Volkspolizei'* continued restricting traffic of Berliners from either side of the sectors. Throughout Berlin rolls of barbed wire were suddenly placed along the border under the supervision of armed East German border police and Soviet troops. The 'creeping' blockade had started. The West Berliners now became seriously concerned. Far from being self-sufficient we largely depended on our German fellow citizens, especially farmers around Berlin to support us with essential goods, mostly fresh vegetables and flour. Any limitations in that area could cause severe hardships regarding food availability. But that was not to be the only threat.

Suddenly we experienced another very unpleasant shock, when the communists turned off our lights. Although we had one Berlin Government, the one and only functional electric power company was located in East Berlin under the Soviet control. By cutting the power off, all of West Berlin, civilians and allied forces were in the dark. Although, after stern allied protests, they finally turned it back on, it showed us in the West that they did have a significant control over critical facilities. Regrettably this also included water supply and removal of garbage, which was always shipped to an area outside of Berlin.

We had been without power before during the combat in the city, but this was a 'déjà vu' nobody expected. All main access roads to and from Berlin were blocked by the Soviets in an obvious effort to force the Allies either to succumb to their demands or to get out of Berlin. But they erred. The Western powers demanded compliance with international law and the Four Power Agreement. Signed by all Allies, including the Russians at the end of the war, the free access to the capital was guaranteed. This was granted in an exchange for other territories previously taken and occupied by the Western Allies.

Following another meeting of all four Allies, the Soviet imposed new restrictions in travel to and from the city through the Soviet Zone and Sector. Several main land routes and three air corridors were established for transport from the West to Berlin and return. To insure this new free travel agreement is valid the American, British and French forces began utilizing these routes to ferry troops and equipment from their zones into Berlin.

The Soviets did not make any attempt to restrict those, but when American military vehicles attempted to drive into East Berlin, they suddenly stopped them along the sector line. To underline their intent of limiting Allied traffic into the East, they moved tanks up to the newly erected barbed wire perimeter. This, of course, was countered by American Army tanks moving up from the West.

It was the 24th of June 1948. For several days the tanks and troops faced each other without either side ready to move against each other or open fire. All civilian traffic into and out of the city was totally blocked. However, the Allies, without any wavering, decided to stand the ground and defend their principles of democracy against Russia's totalitarianism. They were determined to do whatever it takes to keep Berlin free, even if it meant feeding all of West Berlin through an airlift of monumental proportions.

The only three airports in West Berlin were immediately improved and expanded. The American Military Command used Tempelhof Airport in the American Sector. The British and French in turn used a new rapidly constructed Tegel Airport, with the British also utilizing waterborne aircrafts on the Tegel Lake.

On the 26th June the largest airlift in the history was started, with the US bringing in food and coal with their first 100 of C46 cargo aircraft, followed by the British and their air transports. Thus was born the well-known *'Berliner Luftbrücke'* or "air bridge" of Berlin. Aside from the food and coal, they also brought in parts for a power plant, which the Russians had partially dismantled before the Allies came to Berlin. It was not an easy task to feed only their own troops and their dependents but also the entire civilian population of West Berlin numbering nearly 2.2 million people. Thanks to the determination of the Americans and the will to survive in freedom by the Berliners the planes came in no matter what the weather was.

When the first planes arrived at Tempelhof, my entire class (our school was only a few blocks away) assembled on several rubble hills surrounding the airfield. Thoroughly excited, everyone waved and cheered the incoming planes, with the pilots returning our hand waves and saluting as they came in only a few feet above our heads. To our pleasant surprise during the days following, miniature parachutes were dropped from the planes. Rushing to pick them up, we found bars of American chocolate attached to strings and suspended from handkerchiefs. As time went on, the word spread and more and more Berliners gathered on the surrounding mounds to welcome the planes and 'our' American heroes. From that day on the C-46 aircrafts were dubbed with an endearing name: "*Schokoladen Bomber*", Chocolate bombers.

The Berlin airlift strangely enough had another benefit, too. The US Military realized that there were too many half-starved and undernourished children in Berlin. Someone had the brilliant idea to reduce the younger population to be fed in Berlin by flying young children on the near empty returning aircrafts back to West-Germany. With an abundance of food in the West, they could more easily be taken care of by relatives or temporary foster families. The idea was accepted by the command and the mercy flights began under project '*Operation Kinderlift*'. Our family was very lucky as both my sister and little brother were considered malnourished qualifying them for participation in the operation.

They both left with one of the first aircrafts to stay near Heidelberg with a foster family of farmers for an indefinite period of recuperation. My mother was elated, as was I, since we now had more sleeping space, less noise and no argumentations. Aside from the daily, prescheduled disruptions of electrical power, we got along pretty well. Always looking for some type of entertainment, these blackout periods of course created a new fun game for us juveniles. Not so for the adults who considered our form of fun an aggravating nuisance. Armed with a box of toothpicks, we would sneak around the neighborhood following the start of the blackout. Stopping at each apartment building door we inserted our toothpicks between the pushbuttons of the bells and the panel, wedging them into a ringing position. After the two hours of regular blackout, when the power came back on again, the entire block with all the apartments had their door bells ringing. To stop it, it took someone to come down the stairs and remove the toothpicks. This was the only 'criminal activity' I remember ever committing. Not exactly an exemplary conduct for a Pfadfinder and Scout.

E&E – 'Escape and Evasion' from Communist Agents

It was the day following our four weeks of school vacation in late summer of 1948 when my best school buddy gave me some worrisome news. He had apparently talked to his father about his school friends and about me. Mentioning my surname, it seemed to sound very familiar to his father. He did not suspect anything bad when his father asked him more questions about me until later, when he overheard his father talking to another one of his 'comrades' discussing certain "steps to be taken". Having learned to be very suspicious when dealing with the communists, I had the feeling that those comrades were members of the communist party possibly attempting to find my father.

Even we did not know where he was, except that he was once listed as missing in combat. He could have been killed, taken prisoner, was missing in action or he could have been living covertly somewhere in hiding as many combatants did. We knew that a lot of military servicemen even went to South America or had joined the French Foreign Legion to escape certain reprisals from the victors. Worried about my friend's conversation I told my mother immediately after I got home. Oddly enough, she told me that she contacted the Red Cross weeks before and had finally been informed by the German Red Cross that morning that my father was being held in an Internment Camp outside the city of Darmstadt.

There were hundreds of high ranking political and military prisoners being held there. In a brief note he relayed to us that he was well and was there with his best friend AUWI, Prince August Wilhelm von Preussen, the son of Kaiser Wilhelm II. My father later also informed us through the Red Cross that he did not know when he was to be released. However, it was suggested to him by the Americans, that he should not return into Soviet controlled territory.

Prince AUWI, Kaiser Wilhelm II's son had been approached earlier by the Queen of England and offered an early release, but the Prince, being a remote relative, turned down the British Crown's help to get him released to Great Britain. As an old party member, he wanted to remain with his comrade-in-arms. He also convinced my father not to return to Berlin because of the possibility of a persecution by the Reds should he return. After my father's eventual release to Heidelberg, the Prince stayed behind but still sent him letters and hand drawn pencil sketches of his castle on the letterhead from the internment camp. I treasure those personal letters I later inherited.

Feeling safe from the Russians and the communists, while living in the American Sector, I continued to attend school, but did not dare tell my friend about finding my father and his new location. It was only a few days later that my teacher, walking along the row of windows during class, uttered "What are they doing here?" My friend, curious and sitting close to the window, looked down from our third floor, turned to me yelling that his father and his comrades were there with a black sedan. Apparently he must have remembered his father's conversation from weeks before, and visibly shaken urged me to leave and leave fast. I did not hesitate but grabbed my coat, leaving my school supplies behind, and ran out of the classroom to everybody's surprise and some with stymied expressions on their faces. When I heard men coming up the main stairway, I left through the rear emergency stairway sliding down the handrails of three flights to the bottom floor. Scared stiff, I quickly got off the school property climbing over the schoolyard wall. That was my last school day at Dürer H/S in 1948.

As terrified as I was, I moved fast and it did not take me long to get to the subway. I could not get home fast enough. On the way home I stopped by my mother's work place and related the strange incident at school to her. Mother was naturally worried that my friend's father would also find our place of residence. I just hoped the NKVD men, I was sure that's who they were, did not know where we lived. Mother probably expected something like this to happen some day. Although living in the American Sector, we didn't know who to turn to or trust in the local government. She told me to immediately pack only the important valuables while she returned to her office to make some important phone calls. It was clear to me then, that we had to leave again, but unclear as to where we could be going.

We were lucky that the full power had been restored only a few days before and was able to use a friend's telephone. She finally returned after several hours, checked the essentials and told the family we were living with that we had to leave for an emergency for a while. Mother assured them that we would keep them posted as to our time of return, although knowing full and well that we would probably not return at all. Again we had to give up most of our newly collected belongings.

After we had left the apartment, my mother finally told me that she had made several important contacts through her friend and gotten some money and several packs of American cigarettes, a valuable bartering item. Although feeling left out of important developments, I did not ask her how she got the money or the cigarettes. Although I guessed it beforehand, she now told me that we were fleeing from Berlin, which so far had provided security for us. My suggestions, that maybe we should inform the local police or the Allies, were rejected. The police could still not be trusted and the allies could not be bothered with internal matters, she stated. I was glad that my brother and sister were safe and sound in the West already and did not have to go through this escapade with us again. Finally mother told me why she had made this decision, after she had talked to some of her trusted friends.

Our plans were to leave the American Sector of Berlin, travel by train through Soviet occupied territory of the so-called Peoples Republic of East Germany and during the trip be guided by certain contact people living in East Germany. Once we reached the British Zone in West Germany, we would then continue to travel to the American Zone, from where we could contact my father in Heidelberg and later my siblings still living with their temporary foster family near Heidelberg. I had to admit, that mother had guts.

My mother had apparently made the right connections because she felt very confident that we would have no problems making it to the West. We left our sector via subway to the last station near the border between Berlin and the Soviet Zone. There we met a man at a farm at a prearranged time, who guided us through the border into East Germany. He gave us detailed information as to which train to take to the next rendezvous point with another agent, who would provide us with East German identity cards, just in case we get stopped. As we went along on our journey, mother paid each contact either with West Mark or cigarettes. She seemed very competent dealing with the contact persons and I was genuinely amazed at her handling these unusual matters. Staying and sleeping in barns during day and traveling during darkness, after three days we finally made it to our last contact near the Soviet/British Zone border.

The guide took us to about 100 yards from a trail, which was running parallel to the zone border. There we stopped at a somewhat camouflaged spot, waiting for the sun to set. From this vantage point we spotted and observed two Russian soldiers walking toward each other on the trail. Briefly talking to each other once they met, they then separated again walking into opposite directions. We were advised that, after the soldiers had separated again and passed out of our sight the next time, we would have to walk quickly across the trail without making any noise. It was imperative that we hurry, since we had only about three minutes to four minutes to make it across the trail into West Germany. Before leaving us on our own, the guide also cautioned us about the British patrols on the other side. He warned us that they would not hesitate to turn us back over to the Russians, should they catch us.

·"Believe me", he said, "the *Iwans* don't treat people who leave their 'workers paradise' mercifully at all". We said our thanks and *'Auf Wiedersehen'*, even though we never intended to see him again.

At the proper time we dashed across the trail as fast as we could without losing anything out of bags, watching the nearest Russian taking a smoke break in the distant. My heart was throbbing in excitement as we made it across safely. Following our previously given instructions, we reached the railroad station, exhausted but elated.

So far we had not seen any sign of a patrol by British soldiers. A train finally arrived and we climbed aboard but to our surprise and shock a patrol appeared and climbed aboard the wagon next to ours. It was one of their routine patrols, which we had been warned about. We immediately jumped off the wagon on the opposite side of the station and were surprised to find many others doing the same thing. Lying low in the dark along the embankment and close to the tracks, we peered underneath the wagon until we finally saw the soldiers with their white boot leggings leave the last wagon to return to the station.

We re-boarded the wagon with the help of some riders in just about time before it started leaving the station again. As the conductor came through we bought our tickets and to our surprise received new advice when to expect the next identity card check. Luckily we had only one more control to pass before we entered the American Zone and we navigated through that one without any problem.

After several hours we reached Heidelberg. Our first stop was the main police station, where we asked about my father's address. Since Germany requires all citizens to register and list their residence and moves, they had no trouble locating him. Registering as 'visitors' from Berlin, we were counseled that in order to become residents in Heidelberg like my father was, that we had to report to the nearest Refugee Camp in Karlsruhe, about 30 miles from Heidelberg. It was a requirement that we had to undergo a refugee screening process to obtain permission to legally establish residence in Heidelberg. The fact that my father already lived in Heidelberg did not seem to matter. Lacking a telephone and our abrupt departure from Berlin, he had absolutely no idea of our arrival and was taken by surprise but happy to see us after all these years. Communications in those days still were not exactly the best and as a result he did not even know that his daughter and youngest son lived with foster parents about 30 miles from Heidelberg, thanks to the US Air Force.

It was the first time in my life I saw my father, the old soldier, cry.

We stayed with my father that night and traveled to Karlsruhe the following day, expecting a quick release and return but it was to take a lot longer than expected.

Refugee Camp Experience

The refugee camp was located near downtown in Karlsruhe. It was a former German Army barracks and was crammed with refugees from many Eastern European countries, including of course families from the Soviet Zone seeking "asylum" in Western Germany. The atmosphere in the camp was very depressing. Everybody waiting for processing was hoping and praying that they would be permitted to stay in Western Germany. Looking out of the windows of the barracks, we could see a beautiful residential area with its occupants busily going about their business and children going to school. In contrast, each of the barrack's rooms had about 10 cots and housed females and males alike, regardless of age, just waiting. From early in the morning until late at night, the room was never quiet enough to let an individual take a good nap or read. But we also had one great benefit, something which we had been missing for a long time and which we had only available on rare occasions in Berlin. There were plenty of separate showers available for men and women and regular meals were served at no cost to the refugees.

One definitely got the feeling of being in a homeless shelter, which of course it was. The food served was unique and quite interesting, since volunteer refugees, supervised by some state agency, did the cooking for the roughly 1000 people. The dishes ranged from Baltic German and Polish, to Hungarian, Russian, Czech and various other German tastes. The daily menus constantly changed, depending on who was preparing the meals, which in most cases were dishes and tastes I had never experienced before. Naturally, good and healthy food was extremely important to the camp inhabitants to prevent sicknesses and diseases in such a closed compound. When we had an outbreak of a fever in our dormitory, the doctors first isolated our dormitory and suspecting diphtheria quarantined us on a castle near the town of Rieneck. Short of adequate medicines, we were placed on urine therapy, a treatment quite common in the old world and in India, but new to us. Although rejected by many people, it had proved to be a lifesaver many times, being understood as 'nature's medicine' by many medical authorities. Surprisingly, we all recovered after about several days and went back to our "normal" life in the refugee camp.

Residing in this type of close environment one has no choice but to adapt and learn not only other customs but also different languages since any proper communication is based upon the understanding of another language. Interestingly enough, after several weeks of cohabitation I could understand some of the basics of several languages. Since many refugees spoke some German words it made it easier to learn another language productively passing time.

Still, not knowing how long our stay in the camp would last, boredom was slowly setting in. Restless, I was looking for something worthwhile to do. Looking at the bare walls of our large dormitory room, I tried to imagine what the room could look like, if it had some pictures to brighten it up. Walking around the barracks compound I found myself in a community hall. The Red Cross maintained a little library there and tried to provide some entertainment making limited amounts of material available for self-help projects within the compound.

Explaining to the Red Cross personnel what I liked to do, they thought it to be a great idea to liven up the bare surroundings. The idea was not a new one, since POW's often painted murals of their home country to make them feel better in those unfamiliar surroundings. One of the workers took me to a storeroom, where I found an assortment of chalks and coloring pens, suitable for my project. It took me several days to sketch and color a wall-sized mural, depicting imaginary scenes from Bavaria and the Alps, although I had never been there. I just remembered some scenes from books and films. My artwork must have been pretty good since a lot of people came into our room just to admire it. Apparently stimulated by my mural, other people found it a nice way of visualizing their hopes, dreams and memories. Before we left the refugee camp about a week later, some Hungarians and Poles had painted landscapes of their homeland and pictures of their traditional dresses on the walls of their rooms.

While I was occupying myself with art, government agents, including representatives from the States, were questioning my mother. Based on their findings, we were finally released to my father's care.

Germany in 1945, divided into four occupation Zones. A Federal
Republic was created in the West, while the Soviet Zone became a
separate state as the socalled German Democratic Republic.

The divided City of Berlin with its three guaranteed air corridors
over the Soviet Occupied Zone. West-Berlin was being supplied
by the American and British Air Forces via these access routes.

Unit Shoulder insignia of the
German Labor Service Unit of
the US Army Europe.

On guard duty as Labor Service Engineer
with GI's in Karlsruhe, Germany 1951.

Working as a Medical Administration
Clerk as LS Sergeant

Attending the US Army Quartermaster
School at Lenggries, Vavaria in 1954.

Leaving Germany and smiling to family and well wishers
from aboard the USS General Langfitt on 5 June 1956.

With a heavy heart I said my farewell to many newfound friends, who were afraid that they might be there for a long time. When we packed our bags to leave for Heidelberg, I looked around our temporary home, sure that I would never return to Karlsruhe. As we left the old Army barracks, my thoughts were with those refugees remaining behind. I could not help but feel sorry for them, as many had no connections or relatives in Germany that they knew of. Unless they had a certain desirable profession, namely one needed in a postwar Germany, it would make their acceptance and a future in West Germany rather uncertain. Our family at least knew we had a home in form of an apartment in Heidelberg, prepared for us by my father. The thought of being a family again with a mother and father at home was going to be something new for me.

Never imaginable for me, life intended for me to be a guest of the city of Karlsruhe again. This city was to play a major role in different events and experiences during some later phases of my life; occurrences I could not have imagined in my wildest dreams. For the time being though, I was just looking forward to return to a normal life again, something I have not had for over five years.

Chapter III

Reaching Adulthood – Yearning for Independence

Starting a New Life– Working to Support the Family

Arriving in back in Heidelberg in mid-December 1948, we moved into a three-room apartment, about a block from the Neckar River, a contributory to the Rhein River. The first thing we did, was to retrieve our other two kids from their temporary foster family and hosts to bring them also to Heidelberg and the new home. Needless to say the kids had a great time having a fantastic vacation away from Berlin.

Although crammed with five people into a small apartment, we did manage quite well, especially since we had gone through worse times before. I immediately enrolled in the Robert Bunsen *'Real Gymnasium'* a High School in downtown Heidelberg, to pick up where I had left off in Berlin. It was not easy to try catch up with the material, since I had lost a lot of time during the war in Berlin, while the youth in Heidelberg had hardly been touched by the war.

The Allies had never even considered Heidelberg as a worthwhile target since it was absent of any important industry. Based on its historical stature, the US Army considered the city ideal for their future headquarters following the surrender. They had wisely selected a beautiful large barracks complex on the outskirts of Heidelberg in the suburb of Rohrbach, which was eventually established as the US Army Headquarters, Europe. In close proximity the Army had selected a former German hospital to serve as their major military medical facility. The rather significant number of military personnel at Heidelberg provided lucrative jobs for most Germans in the area. All large hotels in the city were "requisitioned" for visiting officer's quarters, while abandoned residences of some former Nazis were used by the military government to house some of their families. Lacking any large industry or employer, the American Army had soon become the largest employer in Heidelberg and nobody complained about the benefits the occupiers provided.

Our family, however, had a major problem. My parents, as former members of the Party were prohibited from holding any job, even though my father was well qualified for any job in the area of finance. My father only received a very small unemployment check as head of the household. Since my mother had been a housewife and mother after her marriage and birth of her three children, it disqualified her from receiving any unemployment pay. Seeing my parents struggle to feed us all, I decided to find me a small job, where I could contribute at least something to the family and earn some money toward my school tuition. Being a student and sixteen years old I could take part-time jobs if available.

Part time work was not really new to me, recalling a period at the beginning of 1946 before I resumed school. Somehow my mother located an old uncle, who used to own a small bakery in our district in Berlin, not too far from where we had lived. Fortunately, he still had the little bakery and after repairing some war damage was open for business again. He agreed to let me do '*Schwarzarbeit*', a term used for 'working under the table' in the "Grey Market". It was part-time help with some pay and goods in the form of bread and rolls. Before school resumed in Berlin, I used to get up at 4 o'clock in the morning, rode an old bike of his to the bakery to help him with making the dough and rolls until about 10 o'clock in the morning. I worked there for about two or three months, mostly for the bread. It did help the family out quite a bit while we were still in Berlin.

My new temporary part-time job would naturally bring in more than just a few tokens and some bread. With the help of a school friend I found employment close by in a carton manufacturing company, where I worked the night shift making boxes of various sizes. Of course this work and the lack of sleep caused my grades to gradually go downhill after several months. This was disappointing to me and my parents, as I had just begun to improve my grades and was catching up from being behind.

My parents decided that it was not worth it having me work while also going to school and made me quit. The following weeks were pretty austere again but fate meant well when my father received a very promising letter from the Government. He was informed that the Americans and the new German government had investigated his background and found him now officially classified *'Entnazifiziert'* (de-nazified) under "paragraph *131*". This in turn permitted the government to rehire the old 131'ers, especially professionals so badly needed. This was a certification declaring a person free of any involvement with political war crimes and that there were no charges against him. Regardless, the Russians of course were still looking for him and many other anti-communists. Well aware of this, he decided not to return to Berlin, where the East German communists arbitrarily "nationalized" some of our property we owned outside the city. It was a loss we were willing to assume.

It was indeed a great day in Germany's history when on 12 May 1949 the Soviets finally gave up on their blockade of West Berlin. The airlift had ended and with the three access roads to the city open again, a somewhat normal life returned, even though the Germans had to pay a stiff fee every time they traveled on the access roads. An appreciative citizenry of West Berlin would never forget the heroic efforts made by the Allies, especially the Americans. During the blockade over 200,000 flights moving 1.7 millions tons of supplies were made. Right outside the Frankfurt Rhein-Main Airbase next to the Autobahn, a very contemporary memorial in the shape of bridge section reaching skyward was erected, symbolizing the historic *'Luftbrücke'*. In front of the US Airbase in Berlin-Tempelhof, an identical memorial was erected, pointing towards West Germany's Frankfurt Airbase. Those memorials were to be a reminder of the past struggle for freedom to the people and the world and to honor those American pilots who gave their lives to save the Berliners from starvation and from communist domination.

While life under the Western Allies was good, the people of the Soviet Sector seeing the economic miracle in the West finally got fed up and staged a massive uprising against the East German regime and their Soviet occupiers on 17 June 1953. The desperate and helpless communists appealed to the Soviet Commandant of East Berlin, who declared a state of emergency and moved in his troops and tanks to restore order. The revolt unfortunately failed. Thousands of "agitators" were arrested and nineteen of them were subsequently sentenced to death. This action in the East promptly caused the Allies to place their troops on a high alert status. They wanted to make sure that the Soviets remained within their own territory on their side in East Berlin.

As an old Berliner, father watched the developments in the East with mixed feelings and desperation. He still loved the city remembering the glorious days, but based on the worsening situation and instability in East Berlin he decided not to return there even for a short visit. My father's decision to turn his back on Berlin was made easy by the fact that the city of Heidelberg offered him a state job as a federal officer and fiscal secretary working in the finance department. This opportunity greatly improved our living conditions, but not enough to find a better and larger apartment.

Even though we had a three-room apartment, we did not have a toilet or restroom within the apartment, but had to go half a flight up the stairwell to share it with a next-door neighbor. Of course this was not unusual at all in the older cities of Germany. Tradition had it that the family went to the swimming hall and bath house each Saturday to get our ritualistic bath or shower and, while there, naturally do some swimming. We did remember our house well in Berlin, where we enjoyed frequent baths until we had to make room for the rabbits in the bath tub during the periods of water shortages, as a result of bombardments, to supplement our meals.

Having left my Berlin and settled in Heidelberg I missed the excitement I had with the Pfadfinder in Berlin. I felt a great need for comradeship and started looking for a group again to continue my scouting. Luckily, I found one of them on the outskirts of Heidelberg and soon started going on trips throughout Germany. My greatest trip came in the summer of 1949, when I finally bought my first bicycle and with a group of four guys we left Heidelberg for a 600 km bike tour to Denmark. Camping along the Rhine River going north and hitch-hiking for about 100 km on a truck trailer, loaded with long pure rubber logs, was hilarious. We crossed the border into Denmark and traveled another few kilometers, just to be able to say that we visited that country. On the return trip we visited the famous Island of Sylt, actually our main destination. We camped on the island for several days, thoroughly enjoying the nudist beaches and the pure white sand searching for mother of pearl, amber and other "exotic" items.

Leaving College to Find Work

I continued my high school until I completed the *'Obersekunda'*, the equivalent of two years of college or junior college at the ripe old age of eighteen. Ute, my sister, had reached the age to go to high school, but my parents could not afford both of us to attend high school. My grades were average, but I lacked any enthusiasm for French and Latin, Mathematics and Physics, to name my worst subjects. This gave me a good excuse and the incentive to quit school and find a challenging job, with the idea to continue later. Ute now had the chance to get a better education.

I knew that I was definitely going to miss my art classes, which were often held in the open along the Neckar River. The panorama was enchanting. Sitting along the river bank we had a beautiful view of the charming old city of Heidelberg, its old stone bridge and the ancient castle nestled in the mountain side. From the castle itself, I could overlook the river and observe its boats cruising up and down.

Always favoring art, I decided to find myself a job where I could undergo an apprenticeship in graphic arts. The local newspaper in Heidelberg, the *'Rhein-Neckar Zeitung'*, had openings for draftsmen, graphic artists and apprentices and I immediately applied. A family friend, already working for the newspaper told my parents that my sketches I had submitted with a job application were some of the best. Unfortunately, I would probably not be accepted, because they had an unwritten policy, which disqualified non-Catholics for employment.

Since Germans were required to pay church taxes if they were either Protestants or Catholics, you had to list the religion on the application. Other unsanctioned religions were not obligated to pay taxes to the state. Among my many friends, religion never played a role and I cannot recall any friend ever mentioning the denomination they belonged to. Most Berliners were Protestants and we were really unaware of the fact that we were now living in a predominantly Catholic area. The first Chancellor of the new Federal Republic of Germany was Konrad Adenauer, a devout Catholic and a mentor and supporter of the Heidelberg newspaper. Well, my friend was correct in the feeling that I might not be accepted for employment. I was turned down as being "unqualified", not for my talent it seems, but for my religious orientation.

Disappointed but not discouraged I continued my search for another appropriate job. Since the federal government only recognized two religions for taxing purposes and employment; Catholics or Protestants. I decided to chose *'Gottgläubig'*, a term used for non-specific believers, including many Christian sects. Strangely enough many people also terminated their official affiliation avoiding taxation. Hating to be classified by any specific religion, I made it a point from then on to keep my religious preference strictly a personal matter, which later prevented many difficult situations in my life.

Joining the Labor Service – Para-military Training with the US Army

The American Army in Gemany had instituted a youth program, called the "German Youth Activity". The GYA (also called American Youth Activity, or AYA) regularly held dances and other cultural activities every weekend in one of their large villas along the Neckar River. It was there that I met my first girl friend from Heidelberg, Irmtraud, whom I seriously fell in love with. While attending one of their dances, we met a friend, who wore a black uniform, which looked like an American Army uniform except for its black color. When questioned he explained to me that the patch on his shoulder, which resembled a shield of an American flag with the inscription "Civilian Labor Service", is worn by members of a newly formed Para-military unit. This unit, he explained, was established during the airlift in Berlin to get additional personnel for specific work. They were an augmentation to the US Army and consisted of guard units, engineers and signal units with members from Germany and other displaced persons from Eastern Europe. I was intrigued and impressed when he told me about the pay, the training, free meals, housing, uniforms and cigarettes. In those days the latter were luxury items. This sounded like a great opportunity and Irmtraud agreed. After my parents gave me their approval and I had reached the qualifying age of eighteen, I took a train to Frankfurt-Eschborn, a small US Army Post and airfield, where the recruiting station was located.

One unit stationed there was the 6970th Engineer Battalion, made up mostly of Germans. There were also other units, among them Latvian, Estonian and even a Ukrainian IP company, an industrial police outfit. Most of the Baltic's and Ukrainians had been members of the former German SS units, fighting the Soviets during the war. A few weeks later, the Ukrainian unit was suddenly shipped out to the US for what we heard was "special" training. Considering the political situation of the cold war, the US military and government was seriously interested in former members of any of the Warsaw pact countries.

The promise of a US citizenship for service in the military or other intelligence organizations was, of course, a great incentive for those DPs, a term for Displaced Persons, which were refugees from the East. Clearly, Germany was a refuge for those, who had previously served against the Russians, now looking for a new home. They all had a great desire to start a new life in a country where personal freedom was guaranteed. Although being a German citizen, I was classified as a Class-A refugee from the East, a so-called *'Ostflüchtling'*. We qualified for this status since we had been evacuated from Berlin to the area along the German/Polish border, which after the war became a territory under Polish administration. Having lost all of our possessions at Meseritz during the flight from the advancing Red Army, the German government awarded us a $2,000 per person settlement for resettling in Western Germany.

Non-German refugees, classified as "DP", had priority in obtaining quotas for emigration to the United States and Canada. Many DP's served with the Labor Services (LS) prior to the relocation to the US, thereby familiarizing themselves with the English language and showing their willingness to work for the Americans. It was surprising to find a lot of them enlisting in the US Army even before going to the States.

Following a thorough interview and test, I was accepted for the Labor Service and assigned quarters, issued my uniform and other essential clothing. Undergoing some weapons training with the US carbine, familiarization of the US Army, its customs and structure, which was required before being permanently assigned to a labor service unit. Having completed this type of training I was informed that the battalion was soon going to be relocated to Karlsruhe-Ettlingen. Attached to the 555th Engineer Group of the US Army with its quarters at the Rheinland Kaserne meant a return to Karlsruhe for me. It was, however, only two years later from my last visit there under somewhat different circumstances.

Before our relocation I had a long weekend off and decided to visit my parents in Heidelberg about 50 miles south of Frankfurt. A friend gave me a ride but unfortunately could not take me back, which forced me to hitchhike back as my funds were rather low. That type of travel was quite popular in those days. Departing Heidelberg rather late, only about two hours before darkness, I found myself in a very difficult situation, which I had not anticipated. Catching a ride within the city was quite difficult and consequently I reached the interstate, the *'Autobahn'* during the onset of darkness. It became apparent to me that wearing a black uniform on a dark highway was not a smart decision I had made.

Rather than turning back and going by train, I decided to keep on hitchhiking in the hope and expectation that someone would give me a lift. No such luck. I realized that nobody would stop especially toward midnight but with no other choice I continued to hike along the roadside determined to make it to Frankfurt by sunrise and on time for reveille. It was around five o'clock in the morning when I finally reached the outskirts of the city and took the first streetcar back to the barracks. It was a forced march, to say the least. Totally wiped out, with blisters on both feet, I arrived at my unit on time with the resolution never to hitchhike again.

Our battalion's main purpose was to provide support in construction engineering from transporting equipment to pulling guard duty and providing security. Frequently we were also required to check bridges to determine their load bearing capabilities in case of another war. Quite often we also assisted another Labor Service unit, a Rhine River bridge battalion, which was responsible for operating so-called tactical swinging bridges across the Rhine River. Members of that battalion were mostly Latvians, who were experts in operating so-called DUKW, waterborne trucks that, after being connected became a floating bridge across the Rhine.

Being part of the US Army, having an essential mission and wearing a uniform gave us all the sense of importance. My knowledge of the English language gave me the advantage to vie for an administrative position as a clerk. Following attendance at an US Army Europe, USAREUR administrative course in Stuttgart near the Black Forest and successfully graduating from it, I was given a job as an administrative clerk in the supply field. Pulling guard duty with a carbine about every two weeks became a routine and I didn't mind it at all. As a matter of fact it filled me with pride to be a member of the Labor Service and as such a contributing member of the United States Army.

There were of course certain inherent privileges by being in the Labor Service, such as free rides on the busses and the streetcar, as long as we were wearing the military uniform. Needless to say, many tax-free "comfort" items such as cigarettes were considered a nice extra bonus.

Karlsruhe was a nice town but still, I badly wanted to get an assignment to the Heidelberg area. One of my comrades in the dispensary told me that the Army had formed a new medical ambulance company in the Heidelberg area. I understood that they were working for the US Army Hospital there but, when checking, I found they did not have any opening at that time. I opted instead for a unit in Mannheim, which was only 10 miles to Heidelberg, rather than 25 miles to Karlsruhe. At least it brought me closer to home.

After receiving some more drivers training there, I was lucky to get an assignment in another medical unit under the 5th Mobile Army Surgical Hospital (MASH), stationed at the 130th Station Hospital in Heidelberg.

This finally brought me home to my parents and naturally to my girl friend Irmtraud. Our primary mission as a mobile unit required us to conduct a lot of maneuvers and participate in training exercises throughout the southern part of Germany. Needless to say, I enjoyed field exercises because they always provided me a chance to meet new friends and gain valuable life experiences.

When Holland (The Netherlands) met with disastrous flooding in the early fifties, the Dutch asked the US Army for help and the Army immediately sent the DUKW battalion and our unit to give then urgently needed support. Arriving in the coastal disaster area, the Dutch were initially enthused and happy seeing Americans and their life saving equipment. To our surprise though, they suddenly became almost hostile when they heard German spoken by those men in American uniforms. It apparently reminded them of some bad experiences they had under German occupation before the end of the war. It took quite a bit of diplomacy on the part of American military personnel to convince them that those Germans and the Baltic personnel were part of the US Army and certainly good guys. After seeing the good work and dedication displayed by the Labor Service men, they were finally convinced of our good intentions. We made it a point to speak more English from then on. Regardless, we worked as a team and were proud finally getting the appropriate recognition as auxiliary members of the US Army.

It was a lot more fun participating in maneuvers in Germany, where we had many opportunities to "fraternize" with the local populace in the company of our GI's, who were just tickled pink to have their own interpreters. Wearing the same identical fatigue uniform as the American GIs, except for our identifying patch and red rank insignias, we were often mistaken for Americans. Sometimes questioned about our dialect by English speaking Germans, we usually tried to convince them that we were from Pennsylvania. Having found new friends among the Germans, we frequently jumped into our jeeps after the exercises to frequent the local 'Gasthaus' for the necessary 'stress relief'. It was always rewarding to be able to introduce our GIs to the various German customs, which they would probably rarely become acquainted with on their own. Showing their gratitude, they would seldom let a Labor Service "buddy" pay for the excursion.

Without a doubt, we had many unusual heartwarming incidents on and off-duty, especially with the girls, who all seemed to love men in uniform, especially Americans. My assignment to this unit also gave me the opportunity to travel to my old home town, Berlin, where another Labor Service Center was located, which had to be inspected frequently in the areas of medical supplies and support. Being part of the military, we were given special travel orders for military flights into Berlin or order with Russian translations for train travel through the Soviet Zone into Berlin. My first flight back to Berlin reminded me of the past when my mother and I escaped from Berlin, on foot, through unfriendly territory. I vividly recalled being fearful that we might get caught for illegally crossing the borders and deserting from "The Republic". Those days were finally behind me. I was grateful to be free and naturally excited to visit some of my old friends and relatives following the completion of my assigned tasks in Berlin, hoping that these trips would not be a rare occasion.

Developing Fondness for Americans

While stationed at the hospital I also met some other Labor Service personnel, who were members of a very Special unit, the 3331st US Army Labor Services Liaison Detachment. After talking with some of them, I realized that this would be an ideal unit for me. 'Lady luck' smiled upon me again when I found that this outfit had an opening for a draftsman in the grade of a Labor Service Sergeant. Naturally and most important for me as a young man, was the opportunity that I could spend more time with my girl friend. Being in a general staff unit, you have regular eight to five work hours, unusual for most military personnel, unless you were in a peacetime environment.

With quarters at the hospital compound, a job in the Headquarters of the US Army in Europe nearby and only minutes from my parents, it was an ideal assignment. My detachment had special housing units in the back of the hospital to include a separate mess hall and a LS Club House, which was quite similar to a military club. An added advantage was that we had quite a few nurses as customers. They liked to acquaint themselves with foreigners in an area free of harassment from GIs, yet still inside the US compound and very close to their personal quarters. I found out that it was a place where many serious friendships were made, which later led to sponsorships for emigration.

The personnel working at the headquarters were quite unique. I found several officers, who had previously served with the SS of countries like Lithuania, Latvia, Estonia, Czechoslovakia, the Ukraine and Poland. They had retreated from the advancing Soviet Army just as I did in 1945. All classified as "DP's", most of them were working for the Army while waiting to emigrate to the United States, Canada or Australia, under special immigration quotas. Since we were all working with American soldiers, including females, it was not unusual to either be invited to their homes, if they were married, to movies or even out on dates.

Having our housing right next to the quarters of WAC (Women's Army Corps) members presented even more chances to fraternize. Having worked with the US Army for over four years, I had formed many friendships with officers and NCOs. It was not unusual that I was frequently offered sponsorships for the immigration to the States, but somehow I did not feel ready yet to leave Germany for destinations unfamiliar to me. It would have been a very serious step and I just needed a little more time. Still feeling that I needed to support my family, I dutifully surrendered nearly my entire income to my mother each month. In addition, I realized that my English needed a lot more polishing if I intended to build a life in another country like America.

It was just then that I met an attractive, young WAC working at the hospital. Her name was Rymanta and she frequently visited our LS Club to meet one of the many LS men, who were from her former country, Lithuania.

We found ourselves attracted to each other, although she was twelve years older. She was a former refugee and DP from Riga, Lithuania. Rymanta had fled from the Russians in 1945 passed Berlin to finally end up in West Germany. From there subsequently immigrated to the United States in 1946. Joining the military, she returned to Germany as a member of the occupation troops because of her knowledge of the German language. I liked her very much and my parents immediately "adopted" Rymanta, especially since she never came empty-handed during her visits. The cigarettes as well as the excellent Bourbon definitely left a great impression with my parents. In return, Rymanta enjoyed some home-cooked meals whenever we visited, but occasionally visited my parents on her own. It became apparent to everybody very soon, that she was more than just fond of me. This became very clear one day, when she asked me to escort her to Frankfurt for some errand. Of course I agreed and after a short train ride we arrived at an American car dealership, which serviced military personnel. Walking past a variety of great looking cars, she asked me which one I would like best. A sleek looking two-colored blue Studebaker Commander

V8, a true jewel, looking like an oversized Porsche, caught my eyes. When she told the salesman that she would take that one, I asked her what she is going to do with a car, especially since she did neither like to drive, nor did she have a drivers license. How was she going to drive it back to Heidelberg? With a faint smile she answered me, that since I had a German and US military driver's license, it would be mine to drive. I was speechless. I knew that she had absolutely no desire to learn how to drive. What was I going to do with that big car?

Rymanta, evidently, had it all figured out. Since German civilians were not permitted to drive cars with US license plates, she had obtained a special permit for me to drive her car. Often, when she was on duty and I needed to go somewhere, she encouraged me to take the Studebaker and have fun. While all my comrades and friends envied me, I personally did not feel comfortable with that situation, because I looked like a kept man. When Rymanta one day told me that she longed to take a vacation in Italy, Austria and Switzerland, I was both embarrassed, yet eager to drive and be her dedicated driver. It was not only because I felt obligated to do so, but also because I enjoyed traveling. Her being a good Catholic, making such a proposal actually threw me. She must have noted my embarrassment and promised me to maintain a strictly platonic relationship throughout the trip.

Contrary to my personal expectations, we had a beautiful vacation, especially when being snowed in at the *Brenner Pass* in the Alps. She spoke perfect English and German with a cute Baltic accent, but we concentrated on speaking English or rather American to give me more experience. At work, as well as off duty, I continuously practiced my American language either through reading comic books, watching movies or common conversations. Following five years of close contact with Americans, I was able to pick up a lot of their habits and culture from those around me.

During my tour of duty at USAREUR headquarters I was again required to fly to Berlin in May 1954. I had to conduct required personnel records checks, which also gave me the opportunity to spend a short vacation there renewing old friendships. In December that same year my boss felt that I needed additional training in logistics and of course English.

When classes at an Army school became available and I was made an offer to go, I immediately accepted to attend. The course was given at the USAREUR Quarter-master School in Lenggries, Bavaria, near Garmisch-Partenkirchen. School attendance there also fulfilled a lifelong dream of mine to see and visit the Alps, which were only about twelve kilometers or eight miles from the Austrian border. Even though most Berliners would never admit that they loved Bavaria, they all take a certain liking to the laid-back life style of the Bavarians. They usually spend many of their vacations in that part of the country and its neighbors in Austria and Switzerland. The Quartermaster course proved to be quite a challenge.

Considering that I was the only German among the thirty to thirty-five American GI's, I not only had to study and increase my English vocabulary, but also get acquainted to the rather unfamiliar supply procedures of the Army. That certainly did not leave much time for me to enjoy either the people or countryside. But the award, graduating at least still in the top 33% was very satisfying, especially since I was just hoping not to fail the course. It gave me a good reason though to make plans to spend my next vacation in Bavaria to make up for lost 'fun' time. Since we had Labor Service units throughout the American Zone in Southern Germany and also in Garmisch-Partenkirchen supporting the Army Recreational Facilities there, we were occasionally given the privilege of staying in their barracks while on vacation in the area.

It was like a R&R Center, and when I was given a chance to spend a vacation there, I gladly accepted. It was unquestionably a new experience. While fraternizing with some Bavarians I was introduced to and given a chance to undergo one of the old Bavarian customs of *'fensterln'* or "window climbing". I always thought of it as being more like a joke.

Well, I was to find out more about it personally, when I met a pretty young local Bavarian girl at a local pub. Having enjoyed a few beers, she unfortunately had to leave, but she asked me to visit her at her home after I leave the pub and before going back to the barracks. Before departing she gave me her address and told me that her room was located on the second floor, where a ladder could be found and that she would leave the lights on.

Happy about the prospect of meeting this girl in private surroundings, I was getting few more hints from my Bavarian friends, who seemed to be very experienced in this sort of operation. Thoroughly briefed, I made a hasty exit and went on my way to the rendezvous. My heart beating for joy and excitement, I found the address, the house with two dimly lit windows on the second floor and the ladder, which took a while to locate because of the total darkness. After I had carefully raised the 18-foot ladder to the window, I quietly climbed up to the sill and knocked on the glass. With the windows usually opening to the outside I was staying below the window sill. I waited about a minute, but without getting a response, I knocked again. The window finally opened, but to my surprise it was a bearded old German in the window frame shouting apparent obscenities at me in a Bavarian dialect, which I did not all comprehend. He obviously did not appreciate being awakened in the middle of the night. I felt like I had been set up and found myself desperately hanging on to the ladder, which my "friendly" Bavarian had pushed away from the window. With the ladder slowly but surely falling away from the house, I was peering down and to the rear in darkness, where I could make out a big pile of hay or straw. Well, it was neither hay nor straw but newly "harvested" manure, which, in my excitement I had neither smelled nor noticed before. Fortunately, I made a soft landing, but my appearance after I emerged from the smelly pile must have been a comical sight. Glancing back up towards the house while quickly retreating from the property, I got a glimpse of the young girl behind the adjacent window, which I had knocked on. She was holding her head between her hands, shaking it in disbelief.

I realized then that I must have picked the wrong window, which she confirmed the next day when I saw her again. The girl apologized to me and explained that her parents usually go to bed early, but unfortunately for both of us they did not that evening. She promised that she would make up for my misfortune, which she did. It certainly helped lessen the pain and embarrassment I felt when my comrades in the barracks laughed about my appearance and the accompanying stench I carried after my return to the quarters.

The following day, having been thoroughly cleansed of all objectionable fumes, she showed me some of truly beautiful sights of Garmisch rarely visited by tourists. We took a five-hour hike to the top of the '*Alpspitze*', a mountain next the to the '*Zugspitze*', the highest mountaintop in Germany. This hike and sightseeing tour made up for any humiliation I may still have felt.

Rejection by the New German Army

When the Western Allies dissolved their Zones in 1949 and gave sovereignty back to West Germany, the Federal Republic of Germany became a new political entity. It was early 1955, when they were also granted to establish their own defense force, the '*Bundeswehr*'. Trained and equipped initially with the help of the US military, the new German Army was to be an allied partner within NATO, against any possible aggression by the communist Warsaw-Pact countries.

One of my very close friends in my LS unit, Berndt von der Decken, asked me one day out of the blue, if I would be interested in joining the new German Army with him. Questioning that I would probably not meet their qualifications, considering my parent's background, he assured me that his uncle the deputy Secretary of Defense, Dr. von Merkatz, would make sure that we could join as officer candidates. Berndt, being a blue-blooded German aristocrat's son, apparent by the "*von*" in his name, convinced me that his connections to another 'von', especially his uncle, should help us get in without any problems. I was really surprised, when he told me later, that we were invited to have tea with the Secretary of Defense. It all made it sound very positive. Accepting the invitation, Bernd and I went to Köln to visit Dr. Von Merkatz and spent an interesting afternoon in his office. After we took our entrance examination later that day, we were advised to expect to be informed of our outcome about 2 weeks later.

I was going to be in for a big shock. While Berndt was accepted, my application was rejected because of what they termed a lack of education and 'insufficient intelligence'. At least this is what the official records showed, which I later surreptitiously obtained from another friend working for the German Army. My honesty during the psychological interview, when I revealed a pro-American attitude, may have been true reason for the rejection. My admiration for the American way of life was so apparent, that it could not have been appreciated by the psychological testing official. I loved the American life style, its history, culture and its people, a feeling, which my father did not share at all understandably so, as a result of his negative experiences in the American Internment Camp as a POW.

My father was a proud German and, fearing that I might leave for the United States, he tried to talk me into applying for service in the Federal Border Defense Force, the '*Bundesgrenzschutz*' (BGS). Not to disappoint him and to please him, I subsequently did. Personally, I did not have any great hope, as most government agencies had the same established rules. Unexpectedly though I passed every category, but this time I was rejected for physical reasons. When questioned if I had ever had any unusual problems, I unintentionally mentioned that I had some minor stomach bleeding some time ago and with that, another disqualification for the service hit me square in the face.

Longing for Emigration

I was finally totally disillusioned with the German system and more than ever enthused and excited about the possibility of leaving Germany. Some of my comrades were playing with the idea of going to Australia or Canada, primarily because they had immediate openings in immigration quotas. The United States, however, had more of an appeal to me.

When I saw my friend Berndt again, he apologized that his uncle was not able to get me into the German Army. He would have liked nothing more than to have me next to him attending the German Officers Academy and, like him, become an Air Force pilot. I had the strange feeling that he was gloating about his personal prospects but I countered that since the German Army felt I was not good enough to serve in their ranks, I might as well emigrate and go to the United States. Berndt questioned my intentions, trying to assure me that, if I joined the military in the United States, they would also consider my parent's background. I would certainly never be able to even make corporal.

Coming from a good friend, I was very disappointed in his comments. Difficult as it may have been, I suppressed my anger about his statement, but still wished him good luck in his career. Berndt a few weeks thereafter departed to begin his officers academy schooling. Spurred by his attitude, I was then more than ever determined to show and prove, that I could "be all that I can be" in America and in the US military. I was to enlist the help of another unusual uncle, 'Uncle Sam'!

After a few more dates with Rymanta, she casually made the suggestion that, should I ever be interested in leaving Germany and immigrating to the United States, she would be more than willing to sponsor me. Somehow I had the feeling, however, that she would probably also be interested in a more serious relationship. Unsure of my personal future, I was not willing to make any promises or commitments and could not go any further than a close friendship. I was very anxious to get out of my stalemate situation before I turned too old and told her that I would definitely be interested and would gladly accept her offer. She told me that she understood.

Rymanta immediately made contact with some friends stateside, since she personally did not have the required $10,000 to sponsor me and could not provide me with a job being in the military in Europe. One of her friends, a pastor, turned out to be a chaplain and Colonel in the Army Reserve, who headed the Hope Lutheran Church in Cleveland, Ohio. He agreed to handle all the necessary paperwork. It still took a few months as I had expected, before I received permission and a visa to immigrate into the US.

While my sister and brother were excited for me, my parents were not quite as exuberant, considering the prospect of losing a family member. I tried to explain to them that I could not continue to live in barracks all my life. At the ripe old age of twenty-four I felt that it was high time to have a promising career; to start my very own family and have my own apartment or home. That prospect in Germany, only 10 years after the war, was very bleak. I had no desire to continue living with my parents, in a crammed apartment with five grown-ups in a two-bedroom apartment.

Every family living at my parents' apartment house had a very small attic room in the same building. Generally for storage only it was without electricity or running water. Looking for some occasional privacy, I had considered that attic room my private space. After I had dropped an extension cord off the roof outside and down two floors, I then even had electricity. For several years I used to take my sweetheart and we sneaked up into the attic for some privacy. We always enjoyed our little nest, until the day my mother noticed the extension cord downstairs leading up onto the roof. Knowing me too well and figuring out where it was going, she got the picture and pulled the plug while we were in the attic, putting us into total darkness. I neglected to tell her about my private space and the well-camouflaged cord, which made her mad. For a long time we had just used candles at night but during the day we also enjoyed the radio and music. I finally convinced her of my need to have some privacy and she plugged in the cord whenever I told her that I would be in the attic.

After I had received word about my immigration I knew that I had to tell Irmtraud, but was worried how she would feel about it. I wanted to tell her in private and took her to our "nest" where I told her that I am ready and willing to go to the 'Land of Opportunities' and what the GIs called the "Land of the great PX". We had previously talked about America and a life there, but she never really believed it could become a reality. She was very hesitant about the prospect of ever leaving her parents, who were old farmers near Heidelberg and expected her to run the farm once they retired. When I asked her if she would be willing to emigrate too or join me once I was established, she slowly shook her head and asked me to give her some time to think it over.

Getting
Married to
the Army…

and Christine

A suspicious team.
Five German Im-
migrants in Basic
Training.

Honor Guard at the
Phillips Barracks
Chapel.

The Sky is the limit.
Becoming a Parachutist.

Ranger Training in the
Georgia Mountains.

After talking about all the great opportunities available to us there, I had the distinct feeling that she might be willing to go too in the end. After a couple days and a long silence, and to my total disappointment, she told me that she would rather I go over first and then, if I get settled somewhere in the US, she would reconsider it. I really hated the thought of leaving her and had the feeling deep down, that it hurt her very deeply to disappoint me. I was the first man in her life and we had always considered building a life together. The love for her parents was obviously strong. I could not, however, reconsider my decision and was hopeful and determined that I would do well and then get her to join me later.

I sorted out my few belongings during the following weeks and made my mother promise to keep some of my personal mementos. Not wanting to be burdened with unnecessary things when starting my new life in the States, I planned to recover those things later, once I was settled. I was ready to go and nothing or nobody was going to stop me.

Chapter IV

A Dream Fulfilled - America

Leaving Germany for the United States

I received my release from Labor Service as a LS-5 Sergeant and travel orders from Heidelberg to the Bremerhaven Port of Embarkation for the purpose of immigration to the United States. It was the 5th June 1956 when my family escorted me to Bremerhaven POE. There, after a tearful good-bye, I boarded a large US Navy ship, the USNS General Langfitt with the destination of New York City. It took us about nine days to cross the Atlantic.

Travel on Navy vessels is not exactly like being on a cruise ship and bored stiff after an uneventful day, I was looking for something to do. I have not been one that could just sit around doing nothing. Coming across a Public Information member, I asked him if there was anything one could do to make the trip more exciting. I asked the right person apparently, because after a brief conversation with him I had found myself volunteering to be part of the ship's newspaper staff. They just happened to be in need of a graphic artist to create illustrations for their paper. It was a fun experience and helped me pass the time even faster, especially since the weather did not give us the smoothest ride across.

Being occupied also distracted me from any feeling of uncertainty. It had not really sunk in yet that I was strictly alone without anybody to lean on or get support from while starting a new life from scratch. A look at my meager belongings, packed in one small suitcase made me wonder how I am going to fare once I get to my final destination in Cleveland, Ohio. I only knew that my sponsor, whom I had never met before, will be there to pick me up, but I had no idea what these people were like. Rymanta only told me that someone nice from her church, by the name of Edith Brumbergs, would be there to steer me in the right direction. I was confident that everything had to be on the up and up because someone accepted the responsibility of sponsorship, paid for my trip and was providing me with a job, once I got there.

We arrived on a rather dreary day in New York and the dock was filled with people, probably friends and relatives picking up their people. Of course there was nobody there to personally greet me, where it not for this one beautiful lady I had heard so much about, the Statue of Liberty. She was truly a magnificent sight to see and, gazing at the skyscrapers all around me, I knew that I was ready to face whatever America had to throw at me.

Following the directions I had received from several people aboard the Langfitt, I felt that I should not have any problems. All I had to do was get to the train station. But once I arrived there I could not believe I was at the right place from what I saw. Certainly, this was not Germany, but the rundown place, which I faced and the impression that I got, was not at all what I expected to find in the States. For a moment, I thought to be at the wrong location. But when I read the sign Erie Station, I knew it had to be the right place. I was so shocked that this "eerie" sight, that my first instinct told me to turn around and go back home to Germany.

There was hardly anybody at the station except a conductor. Pulling myself together I asked him if this was the train station for passenger trains to Cleveland, Ohio. With a big disarming smile he assured me, that it was, but that I was early and just had to be patient and wait. Not having a ticket, I asked him how and where to get the ticket, which of course was quite different from Europe. After finally understanding the proper procedure, I pulled myself together, bought my ticket and returned to the platform to wait for the train. What really hit me was the neglect of the station buildings and the trash I saw everywhere. This was in great contrast to what I was used to in Germany or anywhere in Europe.

I finally spotted another rider, a GI in uniform, coming on to the platform. Somehow I could identify with him and felt the need to talk to someone familiar, which, wearing the uniform he was. After a brief introduction, he was happy and willing to share any information and answer the many questions I had as an immigrant. To my surprise, he himself felt uncomfortable with the trashy surroundings and quickly stated that I should not judge America by what I see at this station. The station was quite old and was about to be torn to be rebuilt. The few people who were forced to ride the train from here were used to it and put up with its appearance. He told me also that he never needed to take the train either because, like most Americans, he has his own car at home or typically takes the bus when without a vehicle. He knew many people that never rode a train in their life. His explanations made sense and I was resolved to overlook and forget this experience.

I was anxiously looking forward to get to Cleveland, Ohio, the city that Rymanta had bragged about so much. I was relieved when the train finally arrived and, in the company of the soldier, we departed, leaving Erie Station and New York City behind. My new acquaintance and fellow traveler was an eager talker and we found ourselves sharing experiences until we finally arrived in Cleveland.

I was to meet a young woman by the name of Edith, but, since neither one of us knew what the other looked like, I decided to wait until everybody is off the platform. In retrospect, I could not understand why we never exchanged pictures. The time had probably been too short for us to come up with some piece of identification for an easy recognition.

Well, I did not have to wait or worry about that too long, because, to my surprise, an attractive young lady steered right to me, before the area was even half cleared. Approaching me, she asked me if was Dieter. Caught by surprise, I countered with the question 'how did she know'. Her answer should not have surprised me, when she stated, that I just look too much like a German not to be the one she expected. Hearing her German dialect I almost felt like being home, because her Mannheim dialect was one I was quite familiar with. Her husband, Karlis, standing in the back, was accompanying her and greeted me with a big grin and I immediately recognized his accent as that of Estonia, one of the former German Baltic states. He had also been a member of the Labor Service at one time, who chose to immigrate to the US after he had married Edith, his wife. Offered a good job in Cleveland they decided to settle there, where he worked as a chemist. Like Rymanta felt about the area, Cleveland struck me also as a beautiful city and I was truly impressed, to say the least. What a difference from what I had seen in the New York harbor area.

Starting a New Life – Facing the Draft

The Brumbergs with their one teenage son, Peter, spared no effort to make me feel at home in their suburban home. Edith was a dedicated housewife and member of the church, while Karlis worked for a large chemical corporation. She usually did janitorial work at the church and it was there, where I finally met the Colonel, Rymanta's connection, who actually made it all possible. The real sponsor, I found out later, was Gertrud, a lady and a fellow member of the congregation Since she was too old to provide me with the required job, the Brumbergs had volunteered to assume her responsibilities. I never realized that there were so many people involved and I could never find out who actually paid for the trip on the navy ship and arranged for the job. Truly grateful for their support, I was determined to make up for it and work it off in time, starting with helping Edith with her daily janitorial job.

Pastor Grotefend, an Army Reserve Colonel (Chaplain), made it a point to greet and welcome me to the United States. Naturally, he also made it a point that the law requires I register with the Selective Service System and, at the same time, to apply for permanent residency by obtaining an "Alien Registration Card". This was essential to permit me to work in the United States.

The Brumbergs insisted that I first get acclimatized and get a better feel of the States for a couple weeks. This included a familiarization with the area, which included visiting downtown Cleveland. We drove around for a couple days, visiting a couple of their friends after which I decided to go it alone.

I still don't know why I did what I did, but since it was rather hot I got dressed in my Bavarian '*Lederhosen*' , my favorite leather shorts, and set out to check out Cleveland on foot. With a city map in my pockets, I strolled around in neighborhoods to get to know it better. By accident, I found myself in a colored neighborhood with many people staring and grinning at me. I finally realized that I must have stood out as a tourist and did not really fit in this area, especially in that traditional German garb. For traveling, I found leather shorts to be quite practical, at least in Germany, because you never have to wash them. I was told once that you wear them until they are black and stiff, able to stand up on their own. After a two or three hours hike, studying the unique architecture, I decided to turn around and go back to where I came from and, getting tired, finally made it back to the Brumbergs. It was an interesting experience and I still wonder what those Clevelanders must have thought about this strange tourist. My hosts and their friends were laughing for quite awhile when I related my excursion to them.

After about two weeks of lounging around I began feeling guilty. Accompanying Edith during her shopping and primarily watching American television programs until very late each night, I felt like I had to get going without wasting another day. The next item on my agenda was to get my job lined up, which I must say, was not as easy as I had imagined. Karlis took me downtown to the office of the General Electric Company, which had offered my sponsor a job for me in the graphic arts field.

During the interview they also went over my sketches I brought, which they liked, but when they asked me, if I had already served in the military, I had some trouble explaining my previous service. They had apparently never heard of the Labor Service, which I had served in with the US Army in Germany for over five years. The interviewer finally stated, that in my case and my age, in addition to official military discharge papers, I also needed a social security number to be eligible to work. As a new immigrant, I naturally had neither one. Finally, they recommended that I talk to the Selective Service Office first and if they recognized my five years Labor Service, they would be happy to have me as an employee. They feared that they might lose me to the draft once I started working, because I had reached that point where they would be prompted to draft me before I got any older.

Not being acquainted with this draft system Karlis explained to me after the interview, that there was a military draft in the United States. Most men my age would have already served by the time they reached my ripe age of twenty-four. Checking in with the Selective Service that same day, I found that the United States had an even greater and improved bureaucracy than the Germans ever had. I was not even close to being a legal immigrant. We had totally overlooked the fact, that although I was an immigrant according to my passport, I was not registered as an alien. This required an alien registration card, which then certified that I had the intention of becoming an American citizen.

Finally, armed with my immigration visa and German passport, we visited the INS, the Immigration and Naturalization Service office and obtained the alien registration card, which then allowed me to get a social security card and thereby permission to take and hold a job. Of course, there was still another visit to the Selective Service Office, which checked all my papers and documents, including my service in Germany. After carefully perusing them, they accepted all of them, except my paramilitary service. They strongly recommended I see the local recruiter. Because of my age, I would be subject to military service within six months, which definitely would not make me a likely candidate for a job with General Electric. Nevertheless, I called them to apprise them of my dilemma and they assured me that they would keep a job open for me, as promised, for two years, should I be required to serve. They recommended that I volunteer for the draft to get it over with faster, which would only be two years. During my military service I could even acquire special training, which I could later use in a civilian capacity.

This time, taking a bus downtown on my own again, I visited the Recruiting Office to talk to the Air Force representative. Service in the Air Force had always been my dream. Unfortunately, Air Force representative was out to lunch, but an Army sergeant readily offered to help. He explained the different opportunities in the various services and branches, while I kept studying pictures of aircraft hanging along the walls. I mentioned to him that my father had once been in the German Air Force and was a parachutist, whereupon he proudly pointed at his wings, stating that I could get those too in the airborne. Instead of even taking time to think it over, I told him that his offer sounded acceptable to me. I was so impressed when he showed me the different aircrafts he jumped from, that I did not realize that I was not talking to an Air Force but an Army Recruiter. Telling him that I did not want to wait to be drafted, that I wanted to volunteer, he assured me that it was no problem and after some more small talk he finished his paperwork. After a firm handshake he handed me a paper with additional instructions regarding my physical, swearing in and the reporting date. I was happy.

I left the recruiting station proud of myself and satisfied that I had made the right decision until I got home to Karlis, whom I showed my papers to with a big smile. He looked them over and shook his head asking me why I changed my mind and volunteered, but not only that, why I did not try to join the Air Force, but the Airborne. I was flabbergasted, when he explained to me that there is a fine distinction between just volunteering and volunteering for the draft and that the difference is three years versus two years. Besides, in the US military the Airborne is part of the Army and not the Force, like in Germany. At first I was disappointed, feeling that I had been tricked. Looking over the papers the recruiters had gone over with me, they clearly stated a volunteer status and Airborne assignment, thereby putting the blame squarely on me for not clearly knowing the fine differences.

After a few beers with Karlis, we both agreed both services had their advantages and no matter which one I had chosen, it was meant to be and I will undoubtedly make the best of it.

After another week of relaxation, during which I talked to Pastor Grotefend extensively, since he was an Army officer, he assured me, that I had made the right choice. After explaining the various opportunities available to me in the Army, I knew that I was going to happy with myself and my choice.

Basic and Advanced Training. My First Permanent Assignment

Following my physical examination, passing with flying colors, and my oath of enlistment, swearing allegiance to the United States of America, even as a German citizen, I was on my way to processing for basic training to Camp Chaffee, Arkansas.

The processing routine as a new recruit for the training in the Infantry were so overwhelming that I don't really remember much of it. Trying to learn the different and many alien terminologies in English kept me up late every night while the rest of my comrades were deep in sleep. My previous school attendance at the US Army Quartermaster School while serving with the Labor Service in Germany, undergoing training and schooling there, helped somewhat.

I am glad to admit, that being a German in the US Army, I never encountered any type of hostility or animosity towards me. Considering the fact that most of my fellow recruits had fathers or relatives, who had served in the US military during World War II, fought against Germany or even had died for their country, I could have expected resentment. Yet, I was fully accepted as an equal. All of my instructors and superiors were seriously interested in my well-being and training and only occasionally referred to me as *'Kraut'*. I never considered this an insult, but a term of endearment just as our term for Americans, like Yankee, was ever considered offensive to my knowledge. Besides, the Army instructors in general seemed to love to use various nick-names for individuals, when they did not exactly meet the desired standards.

Following our initial in-processing at Camp Chaffee for about a week, we were shipped out for basic and advanced training to Fort Hood, Texas, a training center for Armored Infantry, near Killeen, Texas. Training in those days was extremely time consuming and for the first eight weeks we could not even think about getting off post for some extracurricular activities. That was to come after my Basic Combat Training and during advanced training. I could never understand or rationalize, as to how and why I could end up in Armored Infantry training, when I was supposed to receive Airborne training and its appropriate assignment. Questioning my company commander, he told me that the Army is sometimes working in mysterious ways and assured me that this is probably still coming. He advised me, that I probably would have to volunteer for this assignment once again after my advanced training. One thing I was always warned about by my buddies during my training, which was never to volunteer for anything. I guess it was in my genes to be a determined volunteer, as it turned out later.

My advanced training was quite interesting and not as strenuous as basic training. To my surprise, I found four more trainees in my company, who had either emigrated from Germany alone or whose parents had recently come from the old country with them. Being from the same national origin, we naturally seemed to have mutual interests and likes.

Given off-post pass privileges over some weekends, we usually traveled together to places like Mexico and those counties, where it was legal to drink beer. This was not the case in the nearby town of Killeen, a "dry" county. We just could not understand this strange situation as Europeans, raised in a country, where alcohol is not a taboo. Most of us had tried beer and wine at a very early age and did not have to wait until reaching the magic age of eighteen or twenty one, before we could have a drink for the first time. We were properly conditioned. Eager to have a beer off and on, we had to resort to visiting the enlisted club on Post.

For us immigrants, however, the military low alcohol brew just did not cut it. We finally found a Club, where you could become a member, and as such, bring your own bottle and drink in private. Surprisingly, the sheriff was often 'sitting' next to you at the bar. It was strange to us, that a sheriff was insuring the law was being upheld and enforced in a "dry" county by sitting in a bar. Still being foreigners, we were eager to learn and to understand the customs of our new country, only to often getting thoroughly confused.

When traveling as a larger group, we found that our "colored" comrades had to use a different restroom in public places while on an Army post there was never any distinction made between the white and the colored soldiers. One exception however could be found on our written orders, such as travel orders and assignments, which always showed "Cau" or "Neg" behind the names, which we later understood to mean Caucasian or Negroid.

Occasionally, not having a home or parents in the States I was invited by several colored comrades to visit with their families, which I gladly accepted without any reservation. There were some fellow soldiers, who advised me against it, saying that visiting colored areas as a white may not be too well received by the other colored people living nearby. As a hard-headed German I refused to accept this unless I experienced it myself.

I must honestly admit that I never had any problems being in the company of people of a different culture. Regardless of different races I always considered people living in the United States as just Americans. Taking a shower in the military one will quickly find, when a large group soldiers are frolicking in the soap and being all wet, rank, race and nationality becomes nonexistent.

My basic training completed, I received my new assignment orders to the 78th Combat Engineer Battalion of the 2d Infantry Division stationed at Fort Benning, Georgia. This was a rather large military base that was to be my temporary home as it would frequently be later in my career.

I arrived there with several of my German buddies, who were also assigned to the same Division, but to different Battalions. Upon my arrival I was informed that my battalion was a so-called 'GYROSCOPE' Battalion, scheduled to move in its entirety to Germany. I did not know whether to laugh or cry. Here I was, glad to be in America, and the Army decides to send me be right back to where I just came from; and that in only about three months. The battalion was already in its final stages of preparation for the move and since they were not replacing just unit personnel already in Germany, all of the equipment had to be readied for shipment.

As a young Private, assigned to HQ&HQ Company of the Battalion, I was surprised to be summoned by the Battalion Commander, accompanied by the company commander. I expected something bad had happened, as you rarely get called to talk the Battalion Commander accompanied by your Company Commander for any good reason. After a lengthy conversation and question-and-answer session with several other staff officers present, my past history and experiences were discussed. I was finally asked if I would be willing to instruct members of the battalion in the customs, rules and regulations of Germany, primarily the common laws and traffic regulations with the expected "do's and don'ts".

Not having been previously exposed to such tasks as instructing or even talking to a larger group of people, the idea sounded scary to me at first. Obviously it must have shown, because the Battalion Commander quickly assured me, that even though this may be a new experience to me, he would do anything to make it as easy as possible. The Battalion was to provide me with any equipment and any other help that I may need to do a good job. Responding to my statement that I am only a Private and as such not quite comfortable in telling higher ranking soldiers what or how to do things, he stated that with my new responsibility would also come a promotion. Honored by their request for assistance and a possible promotion, I hesitatingly accepted with a promise to do my very best.

Following the briefing, my company commander handed me a promotion order, advancing me to PFC (Private First Class). With it also came a temporary promotion to 'Acting Sergeant', something I had never heard of before. My first Sergeant hunted me down later on and handed me a strange-looking wide black arm band, which almost looked like a band usually worn by mourners at a funeral, After he put it own my left arm I noticed Sergeant stripes sewn onto them. It took some getting used to it.

I realized that I had taken on a great responsibility, which came with the unusual promotion and I set out to prepare myself for the task ahead.

Setting up various classes for drivers explaining European traffic regulations and general classes for the troops about their expected behavior while stationed in Germany, also included a limited but essential basic German language familiarization and their customs. Creating my own graphic visual aids made my job a lot easier. Having witnessed the behavior of GIs in Germany over several years, I made sure that 'our' GIs did not commit the same blunders, which those that came before us had made.

To my surprise, the classes went smoothly and I began to enjoy every minute of it. Unexpectedly, at the beginning of January 1957, I was contacted by a senior warrant officer of our Battalion. He told me, that he had talked to the Battalion Commander, who suggested that I should accompany him to Germany as member of the Advance Party, preceding the main body, which would follow us by the end of January. When I asked him 'why me' and how many people are making up the Advance Party, he calmly told me that he and I are it. It is going to be a 'piece of cake', he stated, since I already knew Karlsruhe so well. I was almost speechless about this prospect of returning to Karlsruhe again, the second time, but quickly regained my composure.

It was mid-January, when Chief Warrant Officer Powell, accompanied by his wife and children, and I proceeded in his car to Ft Hamilton, New York to embark on a journey by naval transport back to the familiar Bremerhaven Port. It was a strange feeling going through the port again, only this time in uniform and with a definite mission as a member of the United States Army Corps of Engineers. CWO Powell's family car was loaded below deck so as to give us transportation once we arrived in Bremerhaven. I could hardly wait to see and surprise my family, friends and especially my girl friend. The thoughts crossed my mind at the same time, how I could tell them anything important about America having been there only about five months. Especially since most of that time was spent on military installations receiving training and instructing troops in conversational German and customs. My entire stay in the US was actually nothing more than a limited vacation.

Welcome Back to Bremerhaven POE

After we picked up the car at Bremerhaven, we slowly made our way south through Bremerhaven and onto the autobahn, Germany's interstate. Since the Powell family had never been to Germany before, I had my hands full just pointing out different sights and sounds and explaining them. The 400-mile trip from Bremerhaven to Karlsruhe took us only five hours after the family convinced me to drive, which I, of course, enjoyed immensely. Without any speed limits, except traveling through towns, I was back in my element with my fellow travelers getting very quiet, when the speedometer reached 100 mph. Traffic in those years was very light because of the small number of vehicles on the roads. I had to explain that in Germany, unlike in the US, most cars had been destroyed only 11 years ago. The German automobile industry was still being rebuilt and therefore a lot of vehicles on the road were American.

After an enjoyable ride, luckily without any snowfall, we finally arrived at the Karlsruhe Post Headquarters and made our first coordinations to locate and inspect the future quarters of our Battalion. After we dropped off the Chief's family at the guest quarters, we went to check out our new home. Phillips Barracks, was an old German Army barracks with beautiful buildings, located in a wooded area visibly untouched by the war. All

buildings were still empty but well maintained by a group of German civilian janitors. The ranking engineer proudly showed us the area and was
happy to hear, that our unit was a combat engineer unit, as he had been a
member of the German Army Engineers previously stationed there.

Over a welcoming drink, a local German beer, he was very proud to
show us an album of pictures from his last years with his unit in those
barracks. Under his advisement and my interpretations, whenever the
German's English was lacking, we spent a couple days assigning buildings
to the various companies and the headquarters. Once satisfied, we notified
our battalion at Fort Benning, that the barracks had been signed for and we
were ready to receive them.

The official tasks behind us, I was given a couple days off to visit my
family in Heidelberg, only about 30 miles from my new station. Since I
had not told my family about my arrival in Germany, it was a total surprise. I always liked to surprise people, which incidentally quite often
backfired. This surprise visit however worked, seeing by the tears in my
parent's eyes. I hugged my mother, brother and sister but not my father,
who for a strange reason did not want to see or talk to me. He had locked
himself in his room and no coaching would convince him to come out to
embrace me.

My mother finally explained. He had never liked the idea of my emigration to the US and even less the fact that I was now an American soldier. To him, according to my mother, it seemed I had betrayed Germany,
even though he understood my disgust with the German system, which
had prompted me to emigrate. Strangely enough, he admired and liked
Rymanta. He never took me seriously, it appeared, and never imagined
that I might really leave and even consider joining the US Army. Being a
member of the Labor Service did not seem to bother him that much, probably because I was given a chance to make a fairly good salary to support
the family. I personally could not see the difference.

I didn't push the issue however, and decided to wait it out, because I
thought I knew my father well enough. I hoped he would eventually see
the situation differently. But in the meantime, I chose to stay with a friend
until the Battalion arrived in order not to aggravate the situation. As far as
the rest of the family was concerned, they were happy that I was back in
Germany, that the Korean War was over and not flaring up again. In my
mother's eyes I was going to be safe for at least three years for the duration
of my enlistment.

My friend Irmtraud was ecstatic and happy to see me again. We made it a point to see each other more often, whenever my duties permitted me to do so. Remembering my friend Rymanta and grateful for all her help, I desperately wanted to see Rymanta to thank her for all the help she had given me. I felt the need to brief her on my experiences in the States so far and my future plans, but found out that, unfortunately, she had left Germany and rotated back to the States in the meantime. My sister Ute, who saw her quite often after I had left, told me that she had been filling in for me and driving her around, whenever she needed a drive. Rymanta was still unsure of her own driving, which she had finally learned. Her dislike of driving and her inexperience even resulted in an accident requiring some minor repairs to the car. Nonetheless, she loved still the car so much, probably for the all the memories she had experienced with it, that she had decided to take it back to the US. I found out later, from another close friend of hers, that she took it back to Cleveland to her sister, where she had it placed on blocks to conserve it for reasons unknown.

Our Battalion arrived in Germany and the troops began settling in their new home. Only a Private First Class, I was still an acting Sergeant and was given a squad to lead in B Company. I loved my new role and enjoyed my assignment and responsibilities tremendously. Since those acting stripes alone did not provide the respective pay, I had to be rather frugal. Limiting my occasional visits home I figured I could save enough money to eventually be able to buy a used car. During my visits to Heidelberg, I was surprised to find both my sister and my brother also showing a keen interest in immigrating to the States themselves, an effort that I certainly strongly supported. After some research I found a way for me to sponsor my sister and we started preparing for her emigration.

Having been in Germany for a few months already, I found most of the personnel of my Battalion enjoyed their duty station and for those difficulties with their German friends, I tried my best to be an intermediary and help them if possible. Not surprising, in most cases it involved relationships with their girls. One of the most difficult things was naturally the knowledge of the basics in German. It was amazing how many GIs had a great and sincere desire to learn German. In an attempt to learn a few phrases, they frequently picked up some words from Germans, which they believed to be proper language. Quite often though, some words and sayings were insulting rather than complimentary. There were always some jokers around, who disliked the GIs and considered it great fun to get them into trouble.

Feeling guilty sometimes, I occasionally invited a few of my fellow soldiers to my home to introduce them to a different kind of Germans. My sister was always delighted and enjoyed meeting some Americans first-hand. I made sure that those guys were all right. It would only cost them a train ride, but they always enjoyed guided tours of Heidelberg, escorted by my sister. Being invited to a German family and a home cooked meal prepared by my mother was always appreciated. After a couple months of visiting the family, my father, an avid smoker, finally came out of his self-imposed "exile". Our mother had anticipated his change of heart for quite a while. Attracted by the smell of American cigarette smoke, he finally mellowed and decided to join my friends and me toasting to our friendship with some good Kentucky Bourbon.

It must have been a truly awkward situation to finally come out of his isolation. After a few drinks, my father could not help but tell me the reason for his past withdrawal. He revealed to all of us his bad experiences he had while a POW at the hands of the Americans in Darmstadt. While visiting, we all tried hard to dispel his misconception about the wild American cowboys and the gun-toting gangsters in Chicago, who in his eyes, seemed to be running the states. More than ever, I was determined to correct his false image and invited him to see the country himself, once the opportunity presented itself.

After a few months of seriously limiting any extraordinary expenses I was able to buy my first car ever. It was an old 1950 '*Opel Kapitän*', which after some hard work of polishing looked impressive enough to show off to my friends. Regretfully, this hard-earned new pride did not last very long. Only a few weeks after I showed it off to my family, I was returning to Karlsruhe on the autobahn, when suddenly the road seemed blocked by some wooden structure. Before I can come to a stop my wheels seemed to collapse as I dropped into an approximately two to three feet deep hole in the right lane. The highway department had dug this hole for who knows what reason.

Climbing out of the hole in a daze, I noticed several pieces of a barricade buried underneath my car with extinguished Kerosene lamps still attached. I suspected another car, previously passing this spot, must have hit the barricade before, pushing it into the cavity. Another car approaching from my rear must have spotted me and my car stuck in the hole. He

stopped and inquired about the mishap. Noting no injuries, he recommended that I wait for the police. Before departing he promised to notify the
nearest highway authority. In the meantime I dug out the Kerosene lamps
and tried to light them but found that they were completely drained.

Sitting next to my wreck, smoking about three cigarettes, the *'Weisse
Mäuse'*, or "white mice", the nickname for the German highway police
and their green and white VW patrol cars, arrived. They could not believe
that I did not see a warning sign ahead of the construction site. Checking,
they were dumbfounded to find the lamps out of Kerosene, which obviously caused me to run into the pit with the barricade. They made out a report,
apologized and assured me that it clearly was not my fault, but neglect on
the part of the highway department. After I secured my personal items and
tags, they offered me a ride back to the barracks, which I gladly accepted.
On the way I wondered 'why me'? But sometimes things happened for a
good reason in my life, I surmised. This accident was probably in my cards
to change it for something better. I was soon to find out.

Kismet – Fate and Luck Bring Soul Mate

While waiting for the insurance company to settle my claim, I was back
to riding the train again to visit my family and invited Gene, one of my
best friends to visit with me. It happened in May of 1957, after a nice
weekend in Heidelberg, where I took out Irmtraud, accompanied by Gene,
who dated my sister Ute. Both Gene and I were returning to Karlsruhe on
a none-stop train ride from Heidelberg.

Standing on one end of the wagon I noticed, and was mesmerized, by
a strikingly attractive young girl on the other end. Turning to Gene I jokingly told him that my wife was standing on the end of the wagon. He only
looked at me in disbelief, smiling, and said that I must be kidding since I
was not even married. But I repeated myself staring at this lady. When he
shook his head, I told him straight to his face, that she was not yet my wife
but will be in the very near future. Taking me up on this, he made a bet that
she would never be my wife.

He wagered $50, which was more than a month's pay in the Army in
those days. Very sure of myself, for reasons unknown to me at that time, I
eagerly accepted his bet, without thinking about the possibility of losing.
For a moment I totally forgot about Irmtraut. Approaching our destination,
Karlsuhe, my heart was beating considerably faster as I was hoping that
she would get off the train with us. Still staring at her, I noticed her bend-

ing down to pick up her bag. I suddenly had the gut feeling that she would be getting off with us, which was exactly what she did. Departing the train, we followed her at a safe distance with Gene grinning all over his face and continuously shaking his head. He thought it was a crazy idea to follow her to an unknown destination. In his opinion it would have been much easier, if I had just introduced myself to see what would happen after that. Being somewhat shy concerning persons of the female persuasion, he figured that I would not come right out and introduce myself to a complete stranger. Besides, my method would definitely increase his chances for winning the bet. I thought it was my call and so we continued trailing behind her toward a nearby streetcar stop, which we fortunately had to go to also. While we were waiting near her for the streetcar, I kept my fingers crossed and hoped that she would also take the same one we needed to take.

Disregarding the first two lines she picked the following, the same numbered streetcar we had to take. Even if she had selected a different line, I would still have followed her to whatever the destination would have been. As we got onto the streetcar I was inching closer to her among the group of people standing up. As we climbed aboard, I sensed that she obviously noticed we were following her. I thought I detected a faint smile on her face as she was looking past us. I had my fingers crossed inside my pants pocket, hoping that she would also get off at the next transfer point. My luck seemed to be holding up.

Having reached that station, she did exit, with us still following her like puppies. I could have jumped for joy. We now needed to wait for another tram to transfer to which would take us to the barracks, but my mysterious dream girl must have reached her destination. Rather than changing the line with us again, she left the stop and crossed the main street, walking toward a row of residential apartment buildings.

It was pretty dark by now, but I was not about to leave her now and suggested to Gene to stay with me if he wanted to. I was going to follow her wherever she was going. Gene must have started worrying about losing his bet and followed with me, slowly walking at a fair distance from her toward a building not too far from the stop. She walked toward a large four-story apartment building and, reaching the entrance, fumbled for a key. Having stopped also, we tried to hide out of site in a dark recess of an adjacent building. After she had disappeared inside her building, I patiently waited hoping that she lived in one of the apartments facing our street.

Suddenly lights were turned on in a room facing us, with a person pulling the drapes shut while looking down onto the street where we were standing in the dark. Looking at the silhouette I had no doubt that it was her, since that room was the only one where the lights were turned on shortly after she entered the house. Now it was my turn to face Gene with a big grin on my face. I already felt like a newlywed, but had absolutely no concrete idea as to what my next step would be, especially considering all the unknowns about her. It depended on many things, such as how old she was, whether she was single, unattached to another German, working in Karlsruhe or maybe just visiting relatives. Most importantly, would she also be interested in me personally.

Leaving our position, all these thoughts went through my mind while we were walking back to the streetcar stop, where we caught the last scheduled streetcar taking us back to the barracks. Gene was also strangely quiet and deep in thought making me wonder if it was my sister, my future wife or the hasty bet he made that got him so quiet. Anyway, I had made definite plans to actively pick up on my pursuit the next day. I became very curious, when our First Sergeant called me. He asked me if I could find a replacement for Gene, who was scheduled for special duty, but claimed he needed the evening off for personal reasons. Since Gene never asked me, his squad leader, I had a growing suspicion and was curious to find out what he was up to.

I found a replacement for him and followed him when he left the barracks that evening. I was not really surprised when he departed the barracks heading towards our previous night's common location. Following in a great distance, he steered straight for the building into which "my" girl had disappeared in. He waited for about two hours, unaware of my presence in hiding. Probably discouraged, he finally gave up and left for an unknown destination. I was determined continue the wait, hoping that she would still show up from wherever she was, hopefully her place of work. I relocated myself to a bench next to the main road with a good view of her apartment and the streetcar stop. I remained there for about another hour when a car from out of town pulled up and the driver asked me for directions to a Bavarian Restaurant on the other end of Karlsruhe. My directions were pretty precise I thought, but he was still not quite clear. He then asked me if I would be willing to show him and as his guest, join him for a meal and a beer. Realizing that I could still continue my surveillance later,

I accepted. I enjoyed a good Bavarian dinner and a few beers listening to a Bavarian dance band.

I had just finished my meal when my eyes caught a glimpse of a familiar figure, the one person that I would never have expected to see at that place. It was her !!

I could not believe my eyes, but there she stood, at the door with another young lady, both skimming the crowd while apparently deciding whether to stay or leave. About to get up to greet her, she and her friend walked over to a table near the dance floor where they sat down. Noticing a few empty chairs at their table, I decided to join the two ladies after I thanked my hosts for their gracious invitation. I should have been quicker. Proceeding to join the two ladies, I was surprised to see several young men, some looking like GIs with their short haircuts, had taken the empty seats at their table.

That was disappointing but determined not to lose sight of my main subject, I selected a seat at the closest table to them. I had to have a seat with a good view, so that I could easily ask her for the next dance. Quite obviously, those guys on her table had the same idea, because as soon as the band started playing, two of them asked her for a dance, which she accepted. I was sure that she had neither seen nor recognized me in the restaurant. Recognizing that I had to be faster, I waited for the next dance just about to start, when I began moving toward her seat, this time though getting to her just at the right moment. Looking up at me, her eyes seemed to get bigger and her face flushed when she undoubtedly recognized me as the person who tailed her the night before.

Finally I had the chance to introduce myself, to get her name, which was Christine, and to exchange some other important information. I needed to know what she was doing and where she was from originally, since her accent gave her away as being from Eastern Germany. It was a dialect I was well familiar with. It was a cute Saxon slang, which Berliners always imitated and joked about. One dance was definitely not enough for me and I asked her for the next dance, primarily to keep her from going back to the imitation GI's. Christine accepted and instead of returning to the table to her friend, we stayed on the dance floor for the next few dances. Appearing totally occupied with each other, the other guys at the table were obviously getting discouraged. Not interested in her friend from work that much, they finally decided to leave.

I was quite relieved, as she appeared to be, and with a disarming smile on her face we returned to her girlfriend. As it was getting late and they both had to work the following morning they decided to call it a day. When her friend, who had invited her out straight from work, could not find her purse to settle their bill, I saw my chance to be the perfect gentleman and take care of the charges. After I escorted them outside, Christine's friend probably did not want to be the third wheel, said her thanks and good by. Finally alone we took a long walk along the main street, bypassing the next streetcar stops to catch a later streetcar. Talking about our lives, she told me that she was a refugee of East Germany living in Karlsruhe by herself. Her mother was still living under the Russians, while her father was already in the West in Heidelberg, living near my parents. She had found a well paying job through her aunt, who lived in Karlsruhe and she usually visited her father over the weekend traveling by train to Heidelberg.

My feelings toward her could not be described as anything other than love at first sight. Having told her about my past, she seemed impressed and I casually asked her if she would ever be interested to go to America too. My heart almost stopped when she unexpectedly answered with a "yes", which to me, sounded almost like an affirmative answer to a wedding proposal. I would never have dared to imply that we get married. I just wanted to find out if she would be inclined to visit the States, but her answer definitely uplifted my spirits and gave me unimagined hope. I finally got her home and saying our good byes, we agreed to see each other again the next weekend. For the first and "accidental date" I did not want to push it or dare to go beyond the traditional hand kiss.

Tying the Knot and Expecting

Excited as I was, I could not wait until I told Gene. My friend was obviously very surprised when I told him about my unexpected rendezvous with Christine the night before. However I was not about to tell him that I had watched him waiting for Christine for several hours. He felt a little better after I promised him another date with my sister, whom he definitely wanted to go out with again.

The insurance company finally settled the claim and I set out to get me another used car, which was not too difficult as many soldiers leave their old cars in Germany when returning to the States. It was another Opel of the same year and I was eager to fix it up nicely again, so I could take Christine and also Gene to Heidelberg to visit our parents. Usually just polishing it, but otherwise neglecting the regular maintenance, soon led to embarrassing situations and blisters on Christine's hands and feet. My neglect led to the battery frequently failing, which 'invited' Christine to help me push-start the car, when I had to return to the barracks from her apartment. Embarrassed I finally solved the problems by replacing the battery, fearing that I might otherwise lose my newly found soul mate.

Worried about losing my soul mate, I suddenly realized that I still had another girl friend. To be fair, I had to clear up a few loose ends. The following weekend visiting my parents, I met with Irmtraud again. Our talks touched on her feeling about going to the States with me, after my tour of duty was over. She finally admitted that she was seriously studying agriculture in college and that her parents would prefer that she stayed in Germany. Partially feeling rejected, I yet assured her that I understood. I was also realizing that I was free to pursue Christine. I was truly relieved.

Prepared to go on another serious date with Christine, I was informed that I had been selected to attend the Non-Commissioned Officers Academy of the 7th Army at Warner Barracks in Munich, which was a four-week course. Attendance and graduation from this academy was essential for any permanent promotion to Sergeant. I knew I had to attend it and of course graduate successfully. Besides, just wearing the Acting Sergeant stripes while getting paid only as a PFC did not sit too well with me.

Most people in my unit realized that it was merely a temporary position with limited prestige. The fact that I could not get paid for the responsibility unless the rank is permanent, made me strive harder to earn the real thing and the proper reward that came with the grade. Making sure that I was ready, I searched out some of the NCOs who had recently graduated from the academy to get briefed on the finer points. This was my first real attendance of any leadership institution and my preparations appeared to have paid off, when I received my diploma and certificate showing my standing in the upper fourth in my class.

Proud of my success, I was happy to return to my unit and subsequently receive a promotion to Corporal, while still wearing the stripes of the Acting Sergeant. At least fully qualified, it was only a matter of time to reach my goal and remove the black armband. Things were going well and I had high hopes that I would receive my real rank pretty soon because I had big plans for Christine and myself. We went to Heidelberg together to see our parents a few times. Gene and Ute were quite happy, as was Christine.

Naturally, I met Christine's father, who was now married to another woman, after a divorce from Christine's mother, who still lived in Plauen, in the Soviet occupation zone. She also became remarried to another East German. After about eight weeks since meeting Christine for the first time, I was getting serious and very anxious. I did not want to wait any longer and had built up enough courage to ask her if she would like to get married. It was a weak 'yes' it seemed, but I heard it loud and clear. Had she known then what she was getting into, I wonder if she would have made such a hasty decision. But she did agree to marry me, nevertheless. After she had accepted my proposal, I was anxious to see her father and stepmother to officially ask for her hand by bringing a dozen of roses to her father's wife. I could not believe it, however, when her stepmother bluntly turned me down, stating that she had already found a suitable future mate for Christine. He was apparently the son of a big factory owner. Christine was totally surprised to hear that. Her future and this subject had never come up before when she was visiting her father. She was visibly upset, because she should have been the one person to know about this man, whoever he was. Christine and I, we both looked at each other, and grinning as I remember, immediately turned around and left with our comment that she had no say in the matter anyway. Any decision and approval was actually up to her natural mother as her official guardian, since Christine was just about to turn eighteen and still needed parental approval.

Since Christine's mother was the guardian, we decided to invite her to come to the West for a visit, so that I could ask her personally for her permission and subsequently celebrate our engagement. The mother, being married in the Soviet zone was given an exceptional permission, provided her husband stayed behind. She arrived shortly afterwards and we received her blessing and the permission to get married. I was glad that German customs require only one ring. Worn during the engagement on the left hand, the plain gold ring is switched to the right ring finger when married.

The Army, however, was not so quick to grant its permission, because Christine came from the Soviet Zone and as such had to be cleared first. Being a member of the US Armed Forces, regulations covering marriages to a 'foreigner' required a thorough background investigation. Finally, after another eight months, we received permission and proceeded with our wedding plans.

I was very fortunate that my bride did neither expect nor demand a big wedding or an elaborate affair. I was very glad, since neither one of us could really afford it. Besides neither Christine nor I cared for anything extravagant. My mother was actually the one who desired a church wedding, even though she never went to church. Christine and I on the other hand, were more in favor of just a civil ceremony without much fanfare.

We had at beautiful ceremony at City Hall in Karlsruhe on 28th of February 1958, performed by the Mayor, as required by German law. To make my mother happy, we then followed up with a small ceremony the same day, held by Captain Cole, our Battalion Chaplain, at the Post Chapel. We were quite astonished when he conducted the short military wedding in German with only our immediate family members attending. About to leave the chapel we got another surprise. We found ourselves walking through an arch of troops, lined up with crossed rifles and fixed bayonets. The Chaplain had arranged for my squad to act as an honor guard in the old Army tradition. As expected for a military wedding, I was wearing my uniform, while Christine was wearing a beautiful gray suit in lieu of a white dress. The wedding could not have been any more dignified, regardless. Besides, none of us were virgins.

We were both happy especially considering the prospect of my moving out of the barracks to reside Off- Post in private quarters like all married troops with dependents in Germany were authorized to do. I was in seventh heaven, as was Christine. Being more familiar with Karlsruhe, she soon located a nice little furnished apartment not too far from the Barracks. After a few weeks of adjustment, we managed to get up early enough so that I could make it to the barracks before the troops even had their reveille.

My wife Christine did not want to waste any time to have a family. After only being married for a few days I agreed, even though my duties kept me thoroughly occupied. I had the feeling that my extended absences at exercises might be a hardship on her. Being nine months pregnant in December, we remember our well-meaning American friends reminding us of certain tax laws effecting the birth of a child. If we had the baby before New Year's eve we could claim the baby for the entire year.

Well, being young and just a little crazy, we didn't want to miss out on that chance and Christine and I took advantage of all dances at numerous Christmas parties to help along with the birth. But no matter how hard we tried, the last very lively dance on New Years eve still did not bring us the success we had hoped for. Our daughter Ines, Cora, Bianka was finally born on the 2nd of January. I had rushed the expectant mother to the 130th US Army Hospital in Heidelberg, my old LS home station from the days prior to my emigration to the United States. Christine, I and our families were all happy, except maybe her stepmother.

Receiving the birth certificate, we were both surprised to find the heading of this document not saying Certificate of Birth, but in typical military jargon 'Report of Child Born Abroad to American Parents'. Regardless, and unfortunately, being German citizens ourselves, we could not claim US citizenship for our daughter based upon that official document. Born in Germany as a German, she would later have to fight for her own US citizenship after she had received her German Birth Certificate.

That same year I received another surprise, a somewhat belated Christmas present in the form of a real set of Sergeant stripes, a promotion to Sergeant after a little over three years. Another hurdle in my newly selected career had been overcome and I was confident that I could master all future challenges with confidence.

Of course my parents, as well as Christine's father, were all excited about the baby, including her mother who stayed for about six weeks and not only taught her daughter, the young mother all the tricks and responsibilities of motherhood. She also introduced her to good cooking, which my mother did later-on as well. Her mother, unfortunately, had to return to her home in the Soviet Zone initially, but decided shortly thereafter to illegally leave the *'Deutsche Demokratische Republik'* after her husband died. She left the Soviet Zone and relocated to West Germany with Christine's younger brother Ulli to stay permanently in Karlsruhe. As a refugee from the East, her mother also had to visit another former temporary home of mine, the refugee camp in Karlsruhe. But, because I was a member of the US Army and married to her daughter, she was considered a dependant and we were able to get her out of the camp with only a few formalities.

Only about a month later, I had to return to my old hospital grounds again. WWII had caught up with me. I had a painful cyst in my neck, which had developed over several months. I had not paid much attention to this sore until the pain became such, that my Battalion surgeon recommended its surgical removal. While under local anesthesia, the operation took only about one hour after which the doctor asked me when and where I was wounded. He had apparently removed an old grenade fragment from my neck and for the record needed to know. Baffled, I suddenly realized that I never had my wound properly treated after I got injured behind my ear in 1945 in Berlin. He shook his head after I explained and he theorized that the approximately ¼" sized fragment had apparently wandered from my original area of injury to the center of my neck prompted by the continuous movement of the head. We both had to laugh over his suggestion to submit a request for the Purple Heart through channels to the German Army, as it was a combat wound, to receive their 'combat wounded' award. It was a good joke and the family decided to toast to this unusual experience with a good glass of German cognac.

Assigned to my Engineer Battalion I was constantly exposed to new experiences and became quite fond of my Company Commander, Captain Cox, a typical West Pointer, who always liked to test my various abilities. Christine and I were always welcomed in their home although I was an NCO. He, for some reason, had assumed the role of being my mentor. I was occasionally invited to attend Officers Club functions in civilian clothing, during which I frequently felt out of place. Both he and his wife repeatedly persuaded me to feel free, that he is the host and that there is a purpose for my being there. Several weeks before Christmas the military community started the annual contest of decorating homes and facilities to celebrate the holidays. The best themes and displays were always being awarded various prizes.

After he had recognized my artistic talents, I was selected to represent our Battalion and was charged with designing and painting certain Christmas themes at the club and, of course, at his quarters. I naturally liked the attention and accepted the challenges and started creating murals with winter and Christmas scenes painted onto windows. To my surprise I helped the Battalion and my Commander to receive several awards, which always filled me with great pride.

But I was not willing to stop there. A command-wide contest to award units for best mess halls challenged me again. During a two weekend period I painted over a dozen murals on the walls between the windows of our Battalion mess hall depicting famous vacation spots of Europe. Our unit won first place; not only for my art work but also for the culinary art and quality of food prepared by our mess personnel. It was good team work.

The military services always challenged their members. After several try-outs, I was fortunate enough to be selected and become a member of the respected USAREUR/7th US Army Rifle Team. Through continued training I was able to help our Battalion team to win numerous awards and citations.

Our battalion was frequently involved in improving sites and the construction of firing ranges maintained by the US forces in the Grafenwöhr, Hohenfels and Vilseck Training Areas. Asked how we can leave a visible reminder of our Battalion's presence in Germany, I proposed that, after the completion of a new rifle range in Grafenwöhr, we pour two large cement slabs about 6'x6' downrange on a slope facing the firers. With the help of three mess kit knives, which were eventually totally worn down, I carved out of the half-cured cement, by hand, our 78th Distinctive Unit Insignia and the 7th Army patch. Later, painted in color, it was plainly visible for approximately three miles from the air. I was sure they would still be there after several decades

Returning to the US. Preparing for OCS

My remaining months in Germany passed rather quickly, and nearing the end of my nearly three-year tour overseas and nearing the end of my term of enlistment, we were preparing to leave for a new home again. Having received my redeployment orders, including my new family, we were contemplating returning to the States to start a new life as civilians. The Army, always in need of qualified and well trained personnel, was always attempting to sway the soldiers to reenlist. I listened to the REUP talk, but the family decided to wait until we returned to the United States. I was scheduled to be discharged at Fort Hamilton, N.Y. for a further return to Cleveland, Ohio.

While clearing the Battalion I was helped by a young lieutenant, Lt Sumner, a close friend of my Company Commander, Captain Cox, who was also scheduled to return on the same ship, the USNS Buttner. I was certain that he was directed by Captain Cox not only to keep an eye on me but to give me a very good reenlistment talk while aboard the ship crossing the Atlantic; which he certainly did. He painted such a good picture of my possible future in the Army, that by the time we arrived in Fort Hamilton, NY, I was ready to raise my right hand and repeat after him what I had done only three years ago before. According to Lt Sumner, I would be assigned to his unit of assignment, another Engineer Battalion at Fort Belvoir, Virginia. He assured me that I would, after careful preparation, be able to attend OCS, the Army's Officer Candidate School, to become a commissioned Army officer.

Initially I was overwhelmed and was not quite sure if I should take this unusual step. Considering the faith some people had in me, there must have been something that convinced them that I would, beyond any doubt, succeed. Someone must have also indoctrinated Christine somehow at the same time. For reasons unknown to me, she had absolutely no qualms about staying in and in any plan of pursuing a career in the military 'for better or for worse'. Certainly, I needed her assurance too, since it had to be for the good of the whole family. Not having a permanent home, parents, relatives or other tangible assets in the States, this step would provide us with a good start, a satisfying career and security to work on finding a future permanent home. It was not going to be easy for the family, yet I was willing and able. With Christine and Ines standing nearby, the Lieutenant was swearing me in as I took the oath of allegiance for service to the United States again.

Prior to our departure from Germany we had purchased a used Mercedes Benz 180, which was shipped aboard our ship, the USNS Buttner. Taking about two days to unload the ship we stayed at a New York City Hotel, which provided rooms for in-processing military personnel. The thought of revisiting and retracing the day of my first arrival in the US and a visit to Erie Station crossed my mind but was subsequently dismissed as a bad idea.

After picking up our car, we arrived at Fort Belvoir, Virginia and I reported in to my new unit, A Company, 91st Combat Engineer Battalion. Since I had over sixty days of leave accrued I was advised to take at least thirty days of vacation until government quarters could be made available. Remembering my friends and sponsors in Cleveland, Ohio, we called them to inform them of our decision to remain in the Army and make it a career. They immediately invited us to stay and spend our vacation with them and we happily accepted their invitation. They were very kind and, of course, anxious to meet my wife and child for the first time. They all hit it off well and we thoroughly enjoyed our time with them. We had to promise that we would not be strangers whenever we are in the States. Unexpectedly, Christine would soon have another chance to revisit. Following our vacation, we all returned to Fort Belvoir so that I could assume my new duties.

Finding out that quarters had not yet become available, we were forced to choose temporary lodging in a nearby motel. It was a small efficiency apartment but we still found it comfortable enough to stay there for a short duration. Since we did not have many belongings, which were being held in storage pending assignment to more permanent housing, we knew that we could do with the minimum of comfort. At least I received a special shipment of uniforms and equipment so that I could still perform my regular duties, which I considered unexpected and unique. Lieutenant Sumner, now Company Commander, kept his word when he promised to prepare me for OCS, but it was not quite what I had expected.

My Platoon Sergeant, MSGT Pietrowsky, made it quite clear that he is of Polish descent and does not have any love for Germans. He remembered that they invaded his country, mistreated his family and relatives but that he is happy to finally be able to get even with a 'Kraut'. From the first day on he made sure I got the worst assignments and most difficult details, which I often felt bordering on pure harassment. Without any let-up he seemed bent on making my life as unpleasant as possible. Fellow NCOs even suggested to me that I report this unfair conduct to the Company Commander. Naturally, I could not do so, being afraid to disappoint the Lieutenant who had so much faith in me and was expecting to get me into OCS. I figured that somehow the Commander would find out anyway and then take appropriate action without me complaining about this treatment.

Several mornings in a row I noticed the Platoon Leader, a 2d Lieutenant, absent from the morning formations. The Platoon Sergeant, taking over the platoon for the Lieutenant, one day called me out to take over the platoon because he had to report to the Battalion. Suddenly it dawned on me, that I was being singled out for a purpose. None of the other ranking NCOs were that often chosen to take over or picked for special assignments or greater responsibilities. Finally I realized that all these assignments and unusual harassment and name-calling were obviously part of the preparation for OCS. Assuming this being the case, it gave me even greater strength and willpower to prevail in spite of all the obstacles and difficulties thrown in my path.

After about three months, my Company Commander called me in to his office, sat me down and informed me that I have performed my duties to his satisfaction. He noted also that I have stood fast in my beliefs against sometimes almost insurmountable odds and thus have shown that I have the fortitude and stamina to qualify for the attendance at OCS. Handing me my orders assigning me to the Student Brigade of the Infantry School at Fort Benning, Georgia he stated that he knew I was going to represent our Battalion well and make him proud. Coming from a West Point Officer, I considered that a great compliment.

On my way out, I saw the grinning *'Polak'* walking up to me and shaking my hand with the words that he would like to be the first one to render his salute and receive a dollar as is customary once I get my commission as an officer. During the remaining months I was not given any slack either but now I knew that it was definitely for my benefit. I deeply felt that, in return, my superiors and comrades deserved even more than expected from me.

Prior to my reassignment to the "Benning School for Boys", as the school was referred to, I was given one last task. To assist in building an auxiliary flight ramp at the Ft Belvoir Miller Army Airfield. I hoped the ramp would last for decades, but in retrospect I had developed some serious doubts. After felling nearly a hundred trees, which I could not get rid of or even sell, I decided to dig a couple deep trenches as it was usual and bury them alongside the concrete ramp. To this day I still wonder if the ground adjacent to the ramp is still solid and firm or maybe started to cave in.

During my assignment at Ft Belvoir I fortunately did not have much of any chance to form any serious friendships, as the time was just too short and I was too busy with assignments, This made saying the usual goodbyes so much easier. Still, I found throughout my tours of duty that it is always hard to say farewell to people you have so closely worked with. Preparing to leave Virginia, I remembered a very good friend of mine from Germany, Toni Lahnig. I had served with him for several years in my last Labor Service unit in Heidelberg and knew that he had emigrated to the US at about the same time I did. I never had the chance to say farewell then. He supposedly settled in Hagerstown, MD, only a stone throw away from Ft Belvoir. Checking the area telephone book, I eventually located him and called to tell him that I would like to visit him as soon as my time would permit to make up for the missed goodbye.

The U S Army Infantry School – A New Challenge through OCS

Having received my new reassignment orders to Fort Benning, Georgia, I considered it important that I immediately take care of my family before I left. First and foremost I needed to find them another temporary home, so

I can dedicate myself solely to my next important challenge at hand, the Officers Candidate School.

During the upcoming six months any contact with relatives and dependents were clearly out of the question I was told. Academic requirements and other duties were such that while there all personal time was virtually non-existent. I was also informed, that in order to assure myself of any chance to successfully graduate, the candidates would have to be free of any and all outside interferences and responsibilities.

Christine fully understood the separation and, after a long discussion with the Brumbergs, was prepared to stay with my sponsor, our friends in Cleveland again. They were happy to have both Christine and Ines. Therefore, before I reported in to the Infantry School, I made a quick trip to Cleveland to drop Christine and the baby off at the Brumbergs. After a brief and hearty farewell party with my friends and well-wishers, I said my goodbyes and left alone for my trip to Fort Benning. My arrival there was something I could not have imagined in my wildest dreams, as this was no ordinary in-processing for Class 3-60 of the 51st Company, 5th Student Battalion. The 5th Platoon was going to be my "home" for the next six months with Max, short for 'Maximillian', a colored roommate from Athens, Ohio. Besides a candidate from Agana, Guam, I was the only "foreign" student in the 5th Platoon, listing a residence of Heidelberg, Germany, since that was the only permanent residence I had. Strange as it may appear, not having a permanent home in the US, the Army listed my passport residence.

There is no way to specifically and properly describe that "first day". It was a unique mixture of timidity, confusion, ignorance and disorganization, all rolled up into a twenty-four hour period, crammed with orientations, administration procedures, rules and regulations that would govern our daily routines from then on. OCS attendance is divided into three phases, the plebe, an intermediate and a senior phase, of which the first one is naturally the hardest and most stressful.

Hanging up the regular uniform and replacing it with the candidate's fatigues, one loses not only the familiar freedoms but also part of your dignities it seemed. As a plebe, you were exposed to constant harassment by the blue-helmeted seniors. During class breaks, they seem to have it in for the new candidates whether inside and outside the buildings, except in the classroom. From the first waking moment to lights out after study time, we were yelled at, downgraded, forced to perform ridiculous tasks and exercises. It was an apparent attempt to make you feel sorry you ever entered the course and give you the option to quit, should you not have the stamina to prevail. There were moments when I asked myself if anything would really be worth this treatment, but then again I thought of the family and their expectations of me. Considering my past and what I had gone through before in Germany, I knew I would be able to handle this treatment hands down. Other men had gone through this before and managed to endure and so could I.

There were a few seniors that seemed to have it in particularly for me and I gradually devised ways to avoid them as much as I could. I vividly remember one, obviously a Russian immigrant, who enjoyed pushing me around and calling me names like 'little NAZI bastard', 'reject', 'imbecile' and others. Not that they were vulgar, but insulting nevertheless. Aside from basic military academics, emphasis at OCS was primarily placed on military leadership and discipline. It was clearly not for awarding degrees, after all, the Infantry needed leaders more than pure academicians.

Almost weekly, except for the position of the tactical officer supervising the student body, the leadership within the student companies changed. Most of the candidates were thereby exposed to various leadership and staff positions, such as Company Commander, Platoon Leader, Operations Officer and others. Physical exercises and double-time running was interwoven in the curriculum, which covered a tremendous number of subjects. The school program was designed to give the future officer such a wealth of military knowledge, that he could master the many situations he may be faced with during his career.

As a future Infantry officer, one had to be very familiar with many associated combat branches. Airborne and air mobility tactics as well as Ranger operations were stressed. But since the Infantry could never accomplish their objectives without proper combat support, the students were thoroughly familiarized with the capabilities of the other combat branches such as Armor, Artillery, Army Aviation and the other important combat arm, the Engineers.

Most significant for an Infantry man was that he was well trained on the latest equipment in weaponry and communications to be able to "shoot and communicate". This fact was underscored by weeks of training spent on the various ranges to familiarize the students with tank firing, guided missiles, machine guns, mortars and anti-tank weapons. It was essential of course that each future officer also be qualified in handling the basic weapons such as the carbine, the rifle, .45 caliber pistol, rocket launchers, hand grenades and mines. Another part of physical training included hand-to-hand combat with the bayonet, the confidence course, escape and evasion, and foot marches in conjunction with the important map reading techniques. Some of the other important subjects covered were chemical, biological and radiological warfare, the psychological and unconventional warfare, as well as intelligence and counterintelligence operations.

To eliminate the boring standing in line for chow, it was customary that before entering the dining hall, an ever-increasing number of pull-ups at the entrance was mandatory. While inside the mess, most movements were robot-like, rigid and timed, and certainly not very conducive to enjoying a leisure type meal. Candidates were not permitted to speak unless spoken to by either an officer or senior candidate.

Speaking of meals, I remember making a mistake just once taking more ice cream than I could comfortably eat under those circumstances. The Army did not believe in unnecessary waste. Served in small paper cartons, I should have realized that it was more than I could eat. When a senior candidate noticed some ice cream still left in the box when I turned in the tray, I was ordered to eat the rest including the paper box. Rest assured it was not very tasty and I learned quickly never to take more than I could eat. Raised in a society, where food never was in an abundance, this was one lesson that stayed with me all my life.

Constantly being under pressure from a 06:00 hours reveille formation in the morning to the end of study hour at 23:00 hours each day, the first eight weeks passed rather fast. The ninth week started our intermediate phase, ending the plebe phase after the Eighth Week Party held at the Gold Bar Club with entertainment put on by classmates. Since this new phase put us more into the field we hardly saw much of the seniors.

The 17th and 18th week were clearly significant ones. They included tactics in the culmination of all our training with a special JCOC luncheon and Operation MAN (Modern Army Needs). During the luncheon we met guests from industry, research and development and special VIPs including the Commander-in-Chief, then President Dwight D. Eisenhower.

The highlight of course was that significant day to which every candidate was looking forward to next to graduation, the 'Blue Day' and 'Blue Day Parade'. The last four days before turning 'blue' now saw all of us candidates drilling, spit shining shoes, adjusting and straightening out. We had finally reached a very important milestone at OCS and it quite clearly showed it in our bearing, as we donned our blue helmets as new seniors. Proudly parading past the reviewing stand, we reaffirmed to the public and the senior officers on the stand that we have what it takes to become Infantry Officers.

Having changed our helmets from black to infantry blue, we were not only permitted, but also encouraged to instill discipline into the plebes, candidates of a new class, by applying to them what we had been subjected to and endured ourselves previously. By 'getting into another candidate's face', we practiced our command voices until often hoarse. As a test in demonstrating our command voice we had to shout orders across the football field in such a way, that it could be clearly understood by someone on the other side.

With reaching senior status, one other benefit was derived from it. A limited pass policy came into effect, which permitted us to have visits by spouses and relatives. I found that several wives, who lived nearby, had joined the Candidate's Wives Club which was established to prepare them for a future as an officer's wife. The Club's purpose was to teach them customs, etiquette and traditions of the military. Having been without a wife for a rather long time, I immediately thought it a great idea to get Christine and the little Ines to move into Fort Benning's neighborhood to be nearby and gain a new experience.

Confident that I would now successfully graduate from OCS, I had also applied for Ranger training and subsequent Airborne training. Tentatively approved, it would keep me in the area for an additional nine weeks plus four weeks respectively. I had found a small and affordable apartment right outside the gates of Ft. Benning, which I planned to share with another candidate and friend. Christine agreed, left Cleveland and joined me in Columbus, Georgia. Our personal time together was often rather brief and limited to weekends, but it gave Christine the opportunity to learn more about the military and undoubtedly the southern hospitality.

The last weeks were filled with more tactics, bivouac, and introduction to survival techniques, Ranger operations and a general test of our tactical and technical proficiency we had acquired through our months of military training. After three more grueling months of tactical and technical education we finally reached the ultimate day, our graduation day.

It was amazing to see how a military school like OCS would not only reshape an individual in such a short period of time, but additionally form genuine friendships and mutual respect for each other. The unusual pressures and difficulties we were confronted with challenged us all tremendously and taught the candidates the importance of teamwork, mutual support, reliability and physical endurance, not to forget honesty and integrity.

Still rather new to my adopted country I never had the opportunity to really get to know the feeling and thinking of the individual American. In order to get a better understanding, it was of significant importance to me to learn a lot more about the psyche of the American fighting man. What I learned and experienced at the school made me more aware of what it takes to build true friendships and comradeships. Men with pride in the military, are apt to form strong brotherhoods, which are so essential when in combat situations.

Looking back I realized that I had met some of the finest individuals from all walks of life at OCS, all of whom had prior military experience as enlisted men. They had proven that they had the ability, the capability and the desire to become an important member and leader of men within the United States Army. Admittedly, our student body did shrink during the six months period, as some candidates failed academically and physically. A few others had a different problem. For various reasons they could not obtain their secret clearance following the required thorough background investigation. Fortunately, I received mine, though I was still a German citizen. One of the previous class members, an Eastern European, then a senior candidate, was held over pending his clearance. He finally obtained it to graduate as a commissioned officer. He was to become well-known eventually and achieve general rank after a long career.

Prior to graduation our class held a last social gathering. It was a reception held prior to graduation, where wives, relatives and dependents were to get their first taste of a formal military social function. The "Big Day" was the 17th of June 1960. This date had always been a highlight in my past life. It was the day when the people in Berlin rose up against the communist regime. It was later declared a national holiday in Germany.

Now this date had another special meaning. It became another even more significant milestone in my life. It is the day I proudly received not only my graduation diploma from OCS but concurrently my commission as a Second Lieutenant in the Infantry of the United States Army Reserve. The Congress had recognized each of us graduates as officers and gentlemen in the United States Army and along with it bestowed upon us not only the prestige and privileges, but also the responsibilities of a future combat leader.

Discharged from enlisted service, having received a commission, I was simultaneously called to Active Duty and watching Christine, I noted that she was without a doubt happy and proud to pin the gold bars of a 2nd Lt. on my uniform. Although I had applied for a Regular Army commission, I was not able to obtain it, because I was still a German citizen. I was encouraged to reapply once I received my US citizenship. Until then I would serve as a Reserve Officer for an indefinite term.

No doubt about it, my next priority was to inquire about the requirements for getting the citizenship. An INS check revealed that I had to be a resident in a State for at least six months before I could even apply for a US citizenship. This meant that I had to wait until my next assignment, which turned out to be Fort Knox, Kentucky, following my Ranger and Airborne training. Over the years I had learned to be patient and was grateful for the trust that the Army and Congress has had in me so far. I had the unshaken belief in the Army slogan that promises each individual that one can "Be all you can be".

Before I would leave Ft Benning though, I remembered the promise I made to that one Platoon Sergeant, my 'favorite Polak', who tried to make my life miserable preparing me for OCS and who helped me in receiving a commission. As tradition required, I went out of my way to visit my old unit, the 91st Combat Engineer Battalion to get the first salute from my old "Sarge" in exchange for a dollar. The fact that he was not quite the first one did not make a difference. I was proud indeed to see him again, as he was to see me.

More Training to Endure – Becoming an Army Ranger

I only had a few days to settle a few things, change all my fatigue uniforms to reflect the new rank before proceeding on Temporary Duty to the 1st Ranger Company at Eglin Air Force Base in Florida. There I was to undergo training for the next nine weeks to include a period in Dahlonega, Georgia with the 2nd Ranger Co. for jungle and mountain training. While the OCS attendance was constant spit and polish, this training was exactly the opposite. Ranger training I found was enormously challenging and one could tell by the mix of personnel volunteering for this adventure, they were all looking forward to being one of the elite within the military. Any rank of the individual during the training, regardless of grade, was abolished. Although we had not earned the title yet, everyone was being addressed as "Ranger". Just a plain old grunt.

Surprising to me was the fact that many of the officers attending the course were Allied officers from Asia and the Americas as well as the Middle East and Egypt. I noticed through close observation, that their home countries were extremely selective in sending only the country's best-qualified soldiers. One of the hardest parts of the training was the initial endurance march, designed to separate, early on, the best from the mediocre and unqualified. Students were broken down into two man buddy teams and if, during the endurance march, someone breaks down, the other had to carry him on. It frequently resulted in both of them finally quitting, if the burden became too much even for the stronger one. Witnessing guts and exemplary determination, I have seen one Egyptian student carry his team mate, an American all the way to the finish line within the allotted time frame after the team mate injured a tendon. They both qualified, receiving applause from the other teams.

Another basic qualifying requirement for Ranger training was the ability to swim well. Several students, who were either unable to swim well or were weak swimmers had previously drowned during the swamp training. To prove their abilities, all prospective Rangers were subjected to a jump from a 10-meter diving board with full combat gear including helmet and a rifle. Diving to the bottom of the swimming pool's deep end, we had to shed our gear and return to the surface for air, after which we then had to return to retrieve our rifle and personal gear. Watching some of my fellow students undergo their swim tests, I was a little leery about my ability to stay underwater for about 2 minutes. After doing some deep breathing exercises, I completed the test even with a couple seconds to spare. I often wondered about the limits of my own capabilities, but with my mind made up and focused I usually succeeded in most of my crucial efforts.

To test the future Ranger's confidence, training included the 'Slide for Life', where students in fatigues and boots had to slide down on a long cable, stretched across a lake with its deepest level about 30 feet above the water. Reaching the low point, the student had to release himself from the pully, hit the water and then return to shore swimming.

· During a different part of the Ranger training, and for the first time in my life, I was confronted with totally different operational areas. From high rock formations to deep water area operations and from dessert to swamp negotiating, I was constantly changing from one adversity to another. Having watched mountain climbers in Bavaria during my visits there, I had never actually climbed rocks myself. Other than hiking on trails, I never even had the desire to rope climb or rappel from high over-hangs and rocky cliffs. All this was about to change.

To my surprise, after my exposure to mountain climbing training along the mountain ranges of the Tennessee Valley Divide for a couple days, I even began to enjoy it. The initial apprehension was quickly over-come. As always, teamwork was constantly stressed throughout the train-ing, reminding me of the Ranger assaults on the beaches of Normandy in WWII and the necessity for this training. Rangers had to be prepared for all eventualities, especially since we could face different terrain through-out the world where our troops could be deployed.

Next after the mountain training phase, the Eglin phase introduced us to waterborne operations, where we were put aboard Navy submarines off the coast near Pensacola Naval Air Station in Florida. Under the cover of darkness the submarine approached the coast line submerged. Exiting through the torpedo tubes in telescope depth, we swam towards the beach to conduct a night assault, using night vision devices, against a power facility to destroy it.

And there was no letting up during training. Without much of a rest we were transported to the Okefenokee Swamps in Southern Georgia, bordering Florida along the Suwanee River. Here we got wet again. This time we were being introduced to patrolling in marshes and snake infested swamps. A thorough educational program then taught us the art of survival by identifying unknown but edible animals, fruits and other plants, some of which would have turned the stomach of most people. To convince us of the importance of food and its safety, we were 'invited' to ingest some of these exotic meals like turtles soup, snake meat and several other unmen-tionable edibles, such as bugs and raw monkey brain. The Darby Ranger Camp, our base during the training had one prominent mascot, which was admired by all students. It was a huge turtle, estimated to have been older than any of us, which could easily carry three of us skinny types for sev-eral yards, if it only could be persuaded to crawl.

Walking on a reconnaissance patrol all day and night without any sleep immediately reminded me of the great trek from the Polish border to Berlin in Germany, except for the jungle type terrain with intermittent swamps. It was déjà vu again, with one important difference. I was not under any live fire keeping me awake. I could definitely handle this; at least I thought.

Not permitted to use any lights at night, all Ranger students had two small luminous white tapes fastened on the back of their patrol caps. They were usually visible from a distance of about 10 feet to easily permit a soldier to follow the man in front of him to preclude getting lost or separated. Yet several students did nevertheless. It was the quiet and a lack of sleep, which will eventually overcome you.

The heat and quietness together with exhaustion, staring at the two small stripes on a cap in front of you in total darkness will almost put you into a state of hypnosis. Believing you are clearly seeing the strips you suddenly get slapped in your face. You suddenly realize that the luminous stripes, which were in front of you all the time, were gone. I had actually fallen asleep while walking until I hit an obstacle. Turning around I spotted the guy behind me, who was locked in on my cap and following me, but my front man was gone. I was embarrassed to no end, to say the least. It usually takes quite a while before the front of the patrol realizes that the rear was lost somewhere in the dark and then tries to find and reconnect to the rear end.

Despite the seriousness of the training, we encountered a lot of humorous incidents. There was not one day where we did not return to base camp dirty, hungry, tired and totally exhausted. All we were yearning for was just one hour or so of solid sleep. We all knew though that we had to go to the extremes and that the price to pay was well worth the effort in the end. After completion of the nine-week Ranger Training Course about 60% of the class graduated. I was excited and proud to receive the coveted Ranger Tab. For most Infantry soldiers earning this tab and becoming a Ranger was considered just one step below earning the Combat Infantry Badge, the award received only after having been engaged with an enemy in combat.

The Sky Has no Limits – Joining the Airborne Family

As if I had not suffered enough, it seems I was asking for more punishment. My last strenuous training before my actual troop assignment was staring me in the face. Returning to Fort Benning and my family for a brief three days of rest and recuperation, I enjoyed an hour long soaking bath, which I had to do without for several weeks. Fort Benning is the 'Home of the Infantry' and is also the Home of the Airborne School.

During our entire OCS course we could clearly see the huge jump towers in the distance, where future parachutists would be pulled up hanging on an open parachute. Reaching the top of the tower, the student would then be released and floating down to ground, practice the maneuvering of the chute and the 'PLF', the Principle Landing Fall. This was to be my next extraordinary experience.

I vividly remember the first time I was stationed at Benning with the 78th Engineer Battalion before going to Germany, when I stood next to the big sign proclaiming the site as the "Home of the Airborne". There I was with three other German buddies standing by my side and all of us were bragging, that one of these days we would be airborne too. I didn't know whether the other guys ever made it, but I personally was enthusiastic then, as it had been my dream before. I had finally made it at least to the school. Getting my silver airborne wings still lay in the future.

Reporting in for training was done running, in double-time and I continued double-time style for the duration of the four-week course. Having gone through Ranger training made jump training a lot easier than I expected. Whether it was the physical training or some minor punishments dished out by the cadre in form of push-ups, this training was easy to take. In retrospect, there was really not much classroom work involved and I cannot even remember what took us so long to qualify for the impressive looking silver wings. Obtaining a good physical condition though was top priority.

Following daily exercises practicing exiting an aircraft, we did feel worn out at the end of the duty day and were glad that we could go home to the family each evening for those living outside the base. Being a one-car family with the husband gone all day and unavailable in cases of an emergency, it was tough on the wife and the daughter. Christine though was lucky to have found good neighbors and a friend in Inge Nelson, who was also from Germany. Her husband, like many other students attending classes at Benning, and our family decided to rent and share the same house, while her husband and I attended Ranger and Airborne School. Living in Columbus, Georgia, Christine met many neighbors, especially one older couple working for the Morton Salt Company who were quite supportive. They were willing to take the time and introduced Christine to the many customs and traditions of America. Meeting the various families, I know Christine could hardly wait to have a home of her own. We were all looking forward to that day when we could be all together as a family and have our well deserved privacy.

Naturally, we all knew that military life would be quite different from that of a civilian and that we never knew for sure where we were going to be living. The Army alone always determined where I was needed and subsequently where we were going to be living, accompanied by the family or unaccompanied. Life in the military promised to be challenging, exciting and rewarding.

Jump school, I found, was actually quite short and after the first three weeks of continuous PT, the Physical Training was reduced and the technical and tactical aspects of airborne operations was increased. We could hardly wait to finally put our training into practice and get our five qualifying jumps in. Final qualification consisted of daylight drops and night time parachuting with combat gear. It was the 10th of October 1960 when we assembled for our first live jump on the Drop Zone (DZ) at Lee Field. We parachuted out of a C-123 Air Force Aircraft, our standard aircraft for airborne drops at that time. Even after all our training to build confidence in oneself, I felt quite uneasy and apprehensive, trying to reason as to why a man would want to jump out of a perfectly operating aircraft.

While climbing aboard the plane in numerical order, based on the large numbers painted on our helmets, I was trying to convince myself that nothing could seriously go wrong. We all had been carefully checked, from the main chute to the reserve chute by the riggers and jumpmasters and we also rechecked each other's parachutes. I was ready.

After we had entered the aircraft, we gave each other more words of encouragement while filing into the aircraft. It was rather tight after we all had squeezed in on the netted seats alongside the fuselage. We listened attentively to the last words and warnings of the jumpmaster, who was trying hard to be heard over the drowning sound of the engines.

The time had finally arrived for the aircraft to take off. We gradually lifted off the runway for a steep climb and a relatively short flight. After about five minutes, the engines appeared to be trimming down and the jumpmasters walked over to the rear of the aircraft. Opening the doors on each side, they gave us the hand signal to stand up and hook up. This was the moment when you realized that there was no other way out except through the open doors. Once the red light on the exit door turned green you would be shoved out of the door by at least 30 troopers behind you. Checking the parachute of the man in front of you again and insuring that the parachute cord was properly hooked up to the static line inside the air-craft, your eyes stayed focused on the light. Suddenly the red light turned green and after the jumpmaster looked outside the plane verifying the DZ was clear and in sight, the first man was tapped out and left the aircraft with the remaining paratroopers shuffling toward the exit.

Everything went by so fast and suddenly I found myself standing in the doorway, assumed the proper jump position and with one leap left the aircraft falling toward the ground, carefully counting a required 'one thou-sand, two thousand', hoping that by reaching 'four thousand' you would feel the shock of the chute opening. I don't remember ever reaching the count of four thousand, but I did feel the shock.

Looking up I saw the most beautiful sight ever, a huge parachute above me and the C-123 passing overhead, gradually fading in the dis-tance, while in total silence nearly a hundred paratroopers were slowly drifting toward the ground. The beautiful silence was suddenly disrupted by the orders shouted by drop zone personnel with megaphones. Slip right, slip left, and prepare to land… The ground came up so fast that one has hardly had any time to think about what to do next. Instinctively I assumed the proper landing position, as drilled in to you during weeks of rigorous training. Landing, I was told that I had expertly performed my first PLF, hitting the ground, rolling along and properly getting up from the roll. To me it seemed more like being dragged. I got up with a genuine sigh of relief, slowly unhooking my chute, rolling it up to be packed. My first live parachute jump was now a matter of record, with only four more to go to qualify for the wings.

The remaining four jumps were conducted during the following days with the second one strangely enough being the worst. For some unexplainable reason the realization set in, that because everything went smooth the first time, something could go wrong the second time. But it was quite the opposite and the remaining jumps on a different DZ, during good weather again with only frequent gusts of winds, were performed without any serious mishaps or injuries. You always find some troopers trying to show off by landing on the edge of the DZ attempting some tree landing. Those are by no means ideal landings and often cause injuries but they are often encountered in actual combat situations.

With all the required jumps successfully completed on the 14th October 1960, our Class # 10 of the 4th Student Battalion, all dressed in khakis lined up in formation, we proudly accepted the first airborne wings. Everyone naturally hoped that sometime, during our military careers, we may have the fortune to be assigned to an airborne unit being able to further qualify for the senior and later master wings. Being a young second lieutenant, the extra $110 a month bonus while assigned to an airborne unit or being on jump status made a big difference, as it almost doubled your pay. However, for the time being, I was just longing to be assigned to any regular Army unit, to be a leader and instructor and return to a halfway normal life. This was a wish that would not be fulfilled until far in the future.

With my major career obstacles successfully overcome and behind me, I was ready and willing to accept the challenges that awaited me at Fort Knox, Kentucky, my next assignment. Orders in hand, we said good by to all our friends and comrades-in-arms, to include the outstanding cadre of the Infantry School. Gathering our few family belongings, consisting of only a few suitcases we departed with a loaded Mercedes-Benz en route to Fort Knox, Kentucky, our next duty station.

My First Troop Command

Our first stop was the Headquarters of USATCA, the United States Army Training Center, Armor, at Fort Knox to sign in. With several other fellow graduates assigned to Ft Knox, it was somewhat disappointing that family quarters were not immediately available on the Post and we had to settle with temporary quarters on the economy again.

We found an old house close to the Post, which was more like a shack and scheduled for demolition, but this building was the only one we could find close by on the spur of the moment. It could be used for about two months for a very small rent, we were told, before it had to be torn down. Nothing else being affordable within our salary range, we looked it over and found it actually cute and worth the effort of fixing it up for the time being. Getting Kerosene on a daily basis to provide for heat and cooking was an inconvenience but no hardship.

Spotting a furniture store nearby, we determined that this was a good time to select what we needed to start a new home. I incidentally mentioned to the owner that we had a hard time locating him initially and almost missed his place because of a lack of signage and advertising. He admitted the shortcoming and stated he had been looking for someone with graphics talent to make signs and advertise on his large windows, but to no avail. Hardly anybody in that area was either willing or qualified to do that kind of work. Mentioning to him that I was in the Army and also had been doing graphic work, he was willing to barter with me for some appropriate layout and design work. I promptly accepted.

For the next few weeks, during my time off, I would find myself on a tall ladder lettering his windows and helping with his displays. We stayed in that house for just about two months, collecting a few new pieces of furniture in the meantime. When the Army finally offered us an available temporary efficiency apartment in a hotel complex, owned by the military and located right outside the gate, we gladly accepted and moved in.

Residing in better quarters for the family, I could now concentrate more on my required duties and was happy with my assignment to Company A, 9th Battalion, 3rd Training Regiment. My first day at "A" Company presented an unusual surprise when the Regimental Commander, Col Frankel, escorted me to the Company area to introduce me to the staff and troops. The entire company was standing tall in formation and over the loudspeaker I suddenly heard some very familiar music being played. It was the very old and traditional German march of *"Alte Kameraden"* or 'Old Comrades'. I was baffled. In the absence of the Executive Officer, First Sergeant Thomas Monteleone, an old Infantry man, wearing his second award of the CIB, the Combat Infantryman Badge, reported the Company as "All present and accounted for".

Noting my astonishment, COL. Frankel just smiled at me and handing me the Company guidon, he turned the command over to me. It was a great a feeling and I expressed my emotion to my new company of young trainees, promising to make them some of the best-trained soldiers on the Post. That, I found, was not as difficult as I had expected. The company cadre with the First Sergeant at its head, was one of the better units I had seen so far in my career. Curious about my reception I questioned the 1/SGT about his reason for playing this German march. Grinning from ear to ear, he admitted that he had been stationed in Germany for many years. His wife from Germany suggested that he play it, as it would make the new Company Commander feel more welcome to the Post and his new company. She was right.

It seemed rather unusual but every morning after reveille and until we departed the company area, we played old marching music from various eras of our history, not only from old Prussia. Actually expecting some opposition, we did not receive any complaints. We noticed though that playing some German marches it was creating some havoc among other companies marching through our area. The reason being that the normal marching step of the American soldier is slightly faster than the German or British Army step. The Prussian General Baron von Steuben during the revolutionary war, had written the so-called "Blue Book". It became the US Army Manual, covering everything from military training, close order drill and marching to military customs. Lacking appropriate march music, most of our military marches were then composed and written by an Austrian, John Phillip Sousa, who, for some reason increased the speed of our marching step.

Since part of our basic training is close order drill and marching, we had to teach the soldiers to get into and stay in step. Believing in setting the example, I requisitioned a drum from the Army band and pending training of a drummer, I did not hesitate positioning myself next to the guidon bearer in front of the company to drum and lead the company marching to and from the different training areas. Undoubtedly the drum made a difference and we were not surprised when our company won honors for "best marching unit" in the parade at the end of basic training. But maybe I was carrying it a bit too far when on a Sunday morning I marched the entire company to church for services. Not a traditional church attendee myself, being a free spirit, I instead tended to my administrative duties at the company. After the Battalion Commander had received a complaint from some non-believers and several of another religious belief, I was made to realize that not everybody is a Christian, and neither was he. Following a friendly discussion with the Battalion Commander about the individual's rights and freedoms in the States, I stood corrected and actually felt relieved. The Chaplain though was on my side, as he had a good attendance of his service for a change.

Training troops, I found was not as easy as many believe it to be, because as cadre you have to be constantly there for the troops. Aside from the training aspect, you are their "mother", looking out for their personal welfare and often solving some of their problems until they have matured.

Getting up at 04:00 hours in the morning to get to the company area in time for reveille and take care of administrative duties prior to leaving for the field can take a toll on the individual and his family, especially if he is married. Spending many hours in the company area during the weekends was not unusual, but I was fortunate that we had a hobby shop within the same block. I often stayed there for hours at a time between company tasks, doing ceramics for therapy. It was a hobby I had picked up, because it would give me chance to create works of art, which I could easily use in my own home.

By the time I had two companies of trainees successfully graduate, I had created a table of inlaid ceramics, depicting the coat of arms of major German cities, all hand-painted. Impressed by my work, some friends encouraged me to display it in public. It was hard to believe, but during a Fort Knox Arts Festival competition, I managed to win a prize for it. But my creativity did not stop there. Christine surprised me with another award I had achieved. I had created something, which would not be handed to me until about nine months later. Our doctor revealed we were going to be parents to our second child during the latter part of 1961.

Subsequent to my command time in Basic Training, I had a chance to be an instructor for several months, which permitted me to spend more time with the family, which suited me just fine.

Getting General Staff Experience and Jungle Warfare Training in Panama

It was obvious that the Army had too many Lieutenants graduating from its military academies. Having had the opportunity to command troops for several months, one had to move on to give others the chance to exercise and experience leadership. The opportunity to get a different experience presented itself, when USATCA, G2, the Intelligence Branch, had an opening for an Executive Officer or Deputy to the Assistant Chief of Staff, G2. This assistant's responsibilities included briefing foreign dignitaries and officers from Germany and Austria in German. His major function was to be a liaison officer to several Allied soldiers from their country's tank units training at Fort Knox with our Armor troops. After attending a course in intelligence, I also became responsible for initiating requests for security clearances and in addition I was giving weekly briefings, as necessary, to German speaking officers. It was a rewarding experience.

Receiving word that the housing shortage was finally overcome we were able to move into our 'permanent' quarters on Post. It was a two story duplex with plenty of space for the family, which we soon found we were going to need. Christine was determined to have a boy that year, probably in September with my parents expected to come during the summer before the baby would arrive. One notable shortcoming for us was the fact that the Army did not provide any significant pieces of furniture except for the bare necessities, such as beds. That meant, we had to bite into the sour apple and invest in additional items of furniture, in order to have sufficient comfort items enabling us finally to start entertaining guests.

Believing in preparedness for all eventualities, I submitted my request for a four-week training in jungle warfare. To my surprise the Chief of Staff approved my request. He could not believe that I was that crazy, but also realized I had the potential and could better serve the Army through additional training. Besides, this was only a temporary duty deal during a slow activity period after which I would return to continue with my obligations. Continued education, especially in military subjects, is always a plus in the eyes of the Army and since I was clearly doing a job well enough to warrant a promotion, I was pleased to receive my silver bars as a First Lieutenant prior to my departure for the Jungle Warfare Training Center at Fort Sherman, Panama Canal Zone.

As expected, Christine was not too thrilled about my leaving again for another adventure, while she had to stay home with the girl, expecting another child. As always, she seemed to understand that a man has to do what a man has to do. When my parents received word about the promotion and my plans to go to Panama, they made the decision to visit us in the United States, something I had hoped but would have never expected from my father. They had planned to visit us after my return from Panama in May 1961.

I left from Charleston Air Force Base to fly to Panama for a period of about thirty days. Arriving there in a tropical environment, following a long flight, it took me three days merely to adjust to the climate while going through in-processing and briefings. After the acclimatization to the extreme heat, I felt that I would be ready for whatever was to be thrown at me. I was naturally wondering how a city boy from Berlin would be able to adjust to this new environment and endure hardship training on top. After all, this Central American country seemed to be on the far end of civilization. As I was soon to find out, earning the patch of a Jungle Expert was not as easy as I imagined and the training course was full of surprises.

The main purpose of jungle warfare training clearly was to prepare us for a jungle war and the survival in a tropical environment for which Viet-Nam certainly qualified. Quartered at Fort Sherman during the periods not spent on patrol or in the jungle, we enjoyed our open-air buildings, which had large windows without glass. Huge ceiling fans were providing a constant cooling breeze in lieu of the customary air conditioning at home.

To get acclimatized, we had enough liberty during the first three days to get a good feel for the heat and try out the cooler water on the beaches of the Pacific Ocean near Panama City or the waters at Colon, on the Caribbean side of the Canal. The beaches looked inviting but they often hid some unpleasant inhabitants in the form of big jellyfish. Unexpected contacts with them quickly convinced me to avoid deeper waters unless it was absolutely necessary to cool off. The period of adjustment was unfortunately too short.

Our training included several extended patrols through jungle terrain. Prior to, and in preparation for these exercises we were exposed to a multitude of animals and vegetation, edible, non-edible, especially poisonous specimen. The instructors repeatedly stressed various diseases and viruses we would be exposed to in this type of environment. We were also reminded of the effects mosquito bites can have, as most of us could still feel the huge needle and the after effects of the shot we received. It was Gamma Globulin, given us to prevent yellow fever and other infectious diseases common in central and South America.

I always had a great respect even for little snakes, but when I saw some of those huge snakes weighing over a hundred pounds, like the boa and bushmaster, my respect increased a hundred-fold. Some of those snakes reached a reputable length of over 25 feet. The Vipers, even though smaller in size, were the most venomous types and repeatedly mentioned by the cadre. Having been advised of all the associated perils inherent in living in the jungle, all of us students became keenly aware of the threats we were going to be facing while in Panama.

We were about to find out soon after we started out on our first patrol. Given a rather scroungy looking dead chicken, which did not seem to have any meat on it at all, and a small bag of rice to survive, I started wondering what I was going to eat after that. The survival training assured us all that survival in the jungle was easy and food plentiful. Now, faced with reality, it started to worry most of us. After a few hours moving through the hot Jungle, the chicken started to smell so bad, that we had to bury them because nobody in his right mind would have wanted to eat anything like that. Having been taught about all the various types of food in the wilderness, we knew that the dead chickens were only meant as a joke to stimulate the students to look for more appealing nourishment. Without a doubt, this adventure was guaranteed to trim us down to a more acceptable weight even below the Army standards.

There was indeed plenty of food in the form of plantains (bananas) and various berries around, that could satisfy one's hunger. One of our best sources of meat came in the form of crabs, which seem to be running all over the place. Catching them though was a different matter. We plain forgot to ask one of the Panamanians we met on a bus during the first weekend of acclimatization, how they caught them. While riding on the bus, we noticed several burlap bags creeping along the floor, all by themselves. None of us imagined what the contents were, until we spotted this amazing crab escape out of the bag and run between the seats. One of the instructors, after prompting, finally told us later, that using a flashlight at night is the ideal way of catching them in the jungle. Most of those we found near a water source or in moist areas. Weirdly enough, one possibly good meal visited me during the first days on patrol while sleeping in the tent, when I felt something cool sliding up my leg inside the trousers. Slightly raising my head, I saw what appeared to be the end of a snake disappearing inside one of my pant legs. Knowing that disturbing a snake is the worst thing one could do, I tried hard to remain completely still, hoping the snake would just turn around or take the other trouser leg to leave, since I had my waist belt tight. Sensing the snake sliding across my lower abdomen, I felt paralyzed from fear not knowing what kind it was and relaxing all my muscles actually made me fall asleep.

Waking up in the morning, I suddenly remembered the visit of the snake. Carefully moving some of my muscles, I tried to feel for anything strange still being in my pants. When I felt no resistance or movement, I very slowly slid my hand alongside my pants. Not feeling any obstruction I was sure that the snake had left me again sometimes during the night. Looking around my immediate area, it seemed clear of my uninvited guest. Although not advisable, I made sure that I bloused my trousers and stuck them inside my boots from now on before going to sleep.

Blousing the trousers is generally not recommended in the jungle and I found the reason for that the next day, when I bumped against a small palmetto tree. All of a sudden I experienced a crucifying burning sensation all over my upper body. My teammates broke out in laughter, when they noticed fire ants which had fallen out of the tree crawling all over my hat and fatigue shirt, causing me to do a wild Indian dance. Ants had also fallen down inside my loose, un-bloused shirt with a lot of them slipping into my lose pants. Since my pants were tucked inside my boots, many of them could not fall out. Even though I immediately pulled my pants out of my boots, the damage had already been done.

Since we were moving along the shoreline I made a mad dash toward the water and was able to submerse myself in the water. Had I had open trousers, most of them would have fallen out and the pain would have been less. The primary reason for wearing your trousers open was to permit air circulation to keep the body cooler. I kept learning a lot of things the hard way. Either way, being a profusely perspiring type, my fatigues were always so wet, that they helped me stay cool anyway.

Ranger training had truly taught me a lot in survival and confidence, but the jungle in Panama was a different environment in comparison with the Florida swamps. Getting disoriented, which is a better way than saying getting lost, was not difficult at all. To this day most of us will swear that the maps we had were either incorrect or not up-to-date. At least that was the reason some teams gave when, after operating in the jungle, they returned back late to base camp. Returning on time guaranteed you to get a weekend pass fraternize with the indigenous people. Several teams had difficulties returning and thus missed out on some good times in Panama City, an unusual city.

The Main Street was divided by an imaginary line, separating jurisdictions. One side of the street was the Canal Zone under US jurisdiction, controlled by Canal Police in New York City style uniforms. More interesting however, was the other side belonging to Panama. It was heavily patrolled by the Guardia National, the Panamanian National Guard, their Police Force. Those chaps were usually not so friendly in contrast to the natives, who were extremely nice.

With tourism not exactly flourishing, our soldiers spent quite a bit of their payroll downtown. The fact that Panama used the US Dollar as their currency made it a lot easier for us to do comparison-shopping. Curiously enough, I found most stores being run by either Chinese or merchants from India. Looking for souvenirs and gifts, I was glad to find quite a selection of Chinese dresses to bring back home.

Although their bills and coins were US currency I found it unique that the Republic of Panama also had their own coins in addition to US coins. The equivalent to a Dollar coin was the Balboa and was minted from pure silver, even showing the silver content on its face.

Due to the rather low costs of entertainment and drinks, our troops occasionally got into trouble in the many bars on the Panamanian side. When in trouble, and before the Panamanian Police would get too close, they usually dashed across the street to the US side for protection, avoiding possible apprehension. It was quite easy to lose control of one's gentleman-like behavior as a result of an over-consumption of the really inexpensive rum and coke drinks, Panamanian style. It was a very potent drink, which we were not quite used to.

·Returning to the Fort from downtown with the gang one day, we noticed something truly unique. Crossing the Gatun Lock we were wondering why we had several small M-41 tanks sitting on concrete slabs along the canal near the lock. The cadre told us that they were protecting the canal operations, but to our surprise we found later that they were frequently pulled back from plain view anytime a Russian ship came through. Pulling them back occasionally did not make any sense to any of us. They knew we always had tanks there.

Completing the training course was an intriguing challenge but it was not that difficult considering the tougher Ranger training, which merited the Ranger tab. I actually classified the course as more of a Gentleman's tour.

Graduates of the Jungle Warfare School did not return home to their unit empty handed however. They received a neat looking patch with a classic white sailing vessel on a blue background, worn on fatigue uniforms only, identifying the wearer as a Jungle Expert.

With the relinquishing of US control over the Canal and our presence there at Fort Sherman, this special patch, a symbol of US Forces, Panama is now a relic, a collectible and part of history. We all knew then that the future of the Training School was very uncertain, I certainly appreciated the opportunity to prepare myself for future commitment into a jungle environment such as Indochina. Panama will be well remembered by me. My body's exposure to whatever natural plant caused the curing of my athlete's feet. I still wonder what the unknown remedy had been.

Before leaving Panama to return home to Fort Knox, I took another short trip to Panama City just to take in a few more sights and came to the conclusion, that Panama was rather interesting but certainly not a place, where I would take the family for a vacation.

I arrived back at Fort Knox, courtesy of the US Air Force, and was glad to be back home again, surrounded by the usual items of civilization, such as showers, clean clothes and a decent home-cooked meal.

Of course it was also great to be back in a clean office, regardless of the a huge amount of work that had piled up during my brief absence. Appreciating the opportunity offered to me to attend the course, I felt compelled to work late many nights to catch up with special projects. Once up-to-date, I was ready to get involved into my new hobby, searching for traces of American history. I noted that several areas where new ranges were being built revealed large amounts of Indian arrowheads. This thoroughly intrigued me, definitely more so than collecting bomb fragments during my youth. Following heavy rains I could usually be found scouring the countryside looking for these unusual artifacts.

Hardly settled in, and really loving it at Fort Knox, I got word from the Pentagon informing me of my upcoming assignment to Germany. I did not know how to break it to Christine and wondered how she would feel about the news. Would she even want to go back to Germany? I was looking for a way to gently break it to her. Hoping for her understanding, I told her that in the military you really don't have much of a choice of assignments and once you choose that career you must be prepared to face inconvenient moves and assignments.

Only this time it involved more than just packing up again and leave. Special instructions stated that my dependents had to be US citizens before they could return back to their home country. Never had the Department of Defense ever been mentioning anything about me becoming a US citizen. Shouldn't I become a citizen first too? Something seemed to be drastically wrong. I had been waiting for my US citizenship for over five years now. I definitely needed to clear this up.

Without telling Christine about her requirement and to make preliminary arrangements for Christine's citizenship, I went to Louisville, KY on 26th May 1961 to see a judge. I wanted to personally inquire not only about her status, but first and foremost about my very own citizenship.

Wearing my proper uniform, I saw a judge and asked him about receiving the US citizenship. The judge in turn asked me, who I was inquiring for. Stating that I was seeking citizenship for myself, he seemed baffled. Looking at my uniform, he was shaking his head assuming I misunderstood his question. When I repeated my questions, he answered that he did not quite understand why, as an American, I would want to be sworn in as a US citizen.

It should have been obvious to him listening to me and noticing my accent, that I was not what I appeared to be. After I explained my circumstances, he took down my personal data and asked me to wait outside his chambers for a couple minutes. Standing very close to the door, I could not help overhearing his telephone call to Washington inquiring about me and my status. After a few minutes he called me back in to tell me that he now understands my background. However, he was still a little confused about my past. He had a hard time understanding how my unique status was even possible.

When I explained my wife's position, he agreed with me, that it is imperative I become a citizen immediately. In my case he was willing to make an exception to the normal rules of waiting periods, since I had military orders pending to go overseas. Christine would have to go through normal procedures, but also as soon as possible.

Before becoming a US citizen during that time, one had to pass a citizenship test and, as the law requires, prove that the applicant could read, write and speak English. With a broad smile the judge asked me if I could speak, read and write English, even though he heard me speak. After my affirmative response, he stated that he believes me, but he still needed to ask me to write something in English. I will never forget it when I wrote: "Now is the time for all good citizens to come to the aid of their country".

The judge accepted the proof and asked me if I was willing to take the oath of allegiance. When I answered in the affirmative, he started by saying "repeat after me", when he suddenly stopped. He said that he was curious and asked me if I had ever taken the oath before, because I simply got ahead of him reciting the oath. I could not help but tell him that I had. Not only had I taken the oath several times before, especially when I received my commission, but I had also sworn in other GIs previously without any hesitation, and even though I had still been a German citizen. Both of us again raising our hands, I was finally sworn in as a new citizen of the United States of America.

The judge, again shaking his head in disbelief, shook my hand and wished me good luck in all my future endeavors as an American citizen. It was a great moment in my life giving me a hard to explain feeling of suddenly being a full-fledged member of this great nation.

Now that I had finally received my citizenship, even though I had always felt like an American with or without the paper, I was proud to finally be a legitimate and proud member of a great nation.

It was the end of May 1961, when my parents arrived in Fort Knox and I had my hands full explaining to my father what life in the States was all about. It soon became clear to him that we did not have any gangsters running around lose in Chicago and that the wild cowboys were also rather tame.

After I showed him the Armor Museum at Fort Knox, he was ready to jump into the German Tiger Tank sitting out front and he could not believe the huge amount of 'Third Reich' memorabilia displayed there. Having been a former parachutist and Armor Infantry officer in Africa, I found him spending a lot of time at this place of history; his history. He loved the Post, unusually large in comparison to German barracks, and to my surprise I heard that he had walked around the entire Fort several times. Appropriate for the season, he was dressed in his old khaki 'Afrika Korps' outfit, minus insignias, of course. He was excited and proud to tell me all about the various sites, including the Fort Knox Gold Depository.

My father's English language proficiency was not really that good, but to our surprise he brought home a friend one day, whom he met in the Officers Club. His friend was a big colored Major with a towering figure, who looked like a quarterback and, to our surprise, spoke fairly good German. He was proud to tell us that he had learned the language while he was stationed in Germany. Not used to fraternizing with higher ranking officers as a young Lieutenant, especially with a field grade officer, I could not believe my eyes how well these two were getting along. I was certainly happy that my father had found someone else to talk to.

A Son Enters into Our Life

The women naturally had their own special interests, especially after the arrival of our son Dieter on 14th of September 1961 at the Ireland Army Hospital in Fort Knox. My mother was a great help during the first weeks after Dieter's arrival and my dad was far from being content with just sitting around and made it his personal responsibility to frequently make breakfast and fry the special 'Kartoffelpuffer' his German potato pancakes. He had a knack for this dish and we are still wondering what he used, as I often tried to copy him without really mastering it.

It was the end of October, when both my parents departed from Fort Knox to visit my sister in Cleveland for a couple weeks before they were to return to Germany. Knowing my pending reassignment, I promised them that I would see them again soon. Thanks to the Army I was able to keep that promise later.

Having received my own citizenship, Christine was to be next. To get ready, I had previously received some material from the judge, who swore me in. It was a study booklet from the Daughters of the American Revolution published to prepare immigrants for naturalization. It was essential that she became a US citizen soon, before I received my final orders for Germany.

I was amazed to find that not all military wives are necessarily pleased when the husband accepts additional obligations, like by inviting a group of four Austrian Officers and several NCOs to their home. When Christmas approached, the Commanding General of the Post hosting those foreign troops, I felt compelled to participate in some type of celebration. Looking for some ideas from his staff, my Chief of Staff suggested that maybe I could, if able and willing, host them at my home and have a German style celebration. Not daring to turn the recommendation down I accepted, unfortunately without first asking the wife.

Among the guests was the Military Attaché to the US from Vienna, a General Paul von Klein accompanied by two Colonels and several Austrian NCOs. Christine was first a bit shocked, but still agreed to prepare a home-cooked Christmas dinner of '*Wiener Schnitzel*'. Served with the appropriate dessert and toasts with '*Cognac*' we were sure to make the guests feel at home while in the States.

Having that many guests though, we could only get pork meat, since that many veal steaks were not available. Most Germans use the less expensive pork anyway instead of veal for the Schnitzel, yet we first felt somewhat uncomfortable to serve pork.

After the guests arrived, they were all very happy to spend an evening with us instead at an official function. To our surprise, we were also glad and gratified to learn that the original Viennese dish of Wienerschnitzel was actually made from pork, because it was a traditional dish of the middle income people of Austria.

Needless to say, the evening was a success, resulting in several invitations from them to visit them in Austria and to attend the upcoming Olympic Games at Innsbruck, Austria. Traditionally, the Austrian Army had the responsibility for the overall organization and security of the games. We gladly accepted and expected to attend but the Army had other plans for my family and me. Members of the military understand the Army's priorities. We now had a war going on in Viet-Nam and we all realized that pretty soon it would be my turn to do my part.

With our orders in hand to go back to Germany, Christine and I went back to Louisville, KY where she was sworn in and received her US Citizenship on the 23rd of July 1962 at the same Court House, where I had received mine a year before. We are glad, that we would never have to worry about our son's citizenship. He was the only born US Citizen. Not so our daughter, Ines. She would have to apply for her citizenship some day in the future.

Chapter V

Back to the Old Country

An Airborne Tour in the "Fatherland"

Getting ready for shipment and packing all of our possessions was something we were gradually getting accustomed to. Moving was to become a routine procedure just about every two to three years. I had intended to take the Mercedes back to Germany, when we unexpectedly experienced engine trouble with the car. Owning an expensive German car in the US carried with it higher costs in repairs and maintenance. The engine showed a crack in the engine block. Finding that having it fixed would have cost us more than we had originally spent for the whole car in Germany, we decided that it was time for us to get a new car.

As new citizens we also felt, that as Americans we should drive an American car. After a few days of searching and comparing, we finally found one that everyone in the family truly liked. Sleek and white with black leather interior, this brand new Ford Galaxy 500 convertible was just perfect for us. Gas prices in those days were really low, so the size of the car did not matter much.

Departing from Fort Knox, we looked back to the great time we had. From searching for Indian arrow- heads on the firing ranges, attending the horse races at Louisville's Churchill Downs to touring the Kentucky country side and working with our hobbies, we all had rewarding experiences. My assigned duties were all fulfilling and I hoped that some day we might return to Fort Knox and Kentucky.

After we arrived back at our now familiar departure site, Fort Hamilton, New York, we turned in our car at the port for shipment to Europe.

We hoped that we would get it back soon after our arrival in Germany. The family, this time with two children, proceeded to John F. Kennedy International Airport from where we departed by commercial air this time with the destination of Frankfurt, Germany. This was fairly close to our new duty station in Gonsenheim, Germany, along the Rhine River and only forty miles from Heidelberg.

An assignment to an Airborne unit had obviously been my preference since graduating from the school. Being a paratrooper I definitely felt the need to put into practice what I had been trained for. To my surprise, I was privileged to be a platoon leader of Co E, 504th Infantry, now under the 1st Airborne Battle Group of the 8th Infantry Division, which was part of the 82nd Airborne Division. The unit had a long, outstanding history, including parachuting into France during WWII. It was hard to determine, but those troops had probably faced my father's German paratrooper unit at some time in France.

Before I reported for duty I had thirty days accumulated annual leave, which certainly came in very handy to help the family to settle down. It also gave me a chance to pick up the car from the port about a week later. Pending the receipt of government quarters, delayed by the common temporary non-availability, Christine and our two children were granted temporary residence with my parents in Heidelberg.

They did not mind that at all for the time being while I stayed at the Bachelor Officers Quarters for a couple of weeks. The dormitory provided me with all the basics yet I would have to do without the customary niceties one expected at home. Being alone, without a wife doing things for you, one also seems to be careless. And carelessness can lead to very embarrassing situations.

It happened to me when I had lied down under a sunlamp one evening to get a little tan for the parade the following day. The soothing light naturally had its effect on me, putting me soundly to sleep. Several hours later, luck had it, that a young lady, who walked by my apartment, noticed the unusual bright light through the curtains and nosily peeped through a small gap. When she spotted me, obviously sound asleep on my bed with an already noticeable sunburn, she knocked on the window to wake me up. Without a response from me, she came inside the building, and entered my unlocked room and carefully woke me up. Opening my eyes and seeing a young lady standing next to my couch, I momentarily felt embarrassed. Attempting to get up and cover myself I felt a burning sensation and noticed my red skin. Disregarding the pain, I finally raised up and covered my body, as much as I could. I was in excruciating pain.

My guardian angel had turned off the sun lamp and apologized for entering my quarters. She casually told me, that she was a German nurse in the dispensary and felt the need to help me as much as she could. Considering, that there was not that much one can do with a sunburn like that, she briefly left to pick up some medication. She returned with a powder, which she carefully sprinkled over my entire body. She advised me to lay low for a couple days, if I can, because the blisters will break open and, after soaking my clothes, start sticking to my skin causing even more pain.

I was fortunate only having been burned on the front of my body. Her advice, never to take a sunbath by myself, unfortunately came too late. As she predicted, the burn and the resulting blisters were extremely painful. I was very grateful for her help and could not thank her enough before she left.

My biggest problem however emerged when I realized that I had to report for duty the next morning and was wondering how I could hide my burns and overcome the pain. Getting a severe sunburn like I had, which might prevent the individual to perform normal duties, is considered self-mutilation. As ridiculous as it may sound, it was actually considered a court-martial offense.

After a painful night I woke up early the next morning and, covering up all the blisters, I carefully put on my uniform and proceeded to the parade grounds. My starched fatigue uniform did hide my problem for quite awhile, since I limited my walking as much as I could. However, once I got in front of the unit, I felt the sap running down my skin and the uniform started showing some wet spots. Fortunately nobody noticed it from the distance, except for my troops and I had a rather difficult time explaining to them what had happened. At the same time I cautioned them never to make the same mistake.

Aside from a few grins here and there I received at lot of expressions of empathy. They realized how painful it must have been for me just to grit my teeth and march with them. I was sure glad that it happened on a Saturday, giving me chance to return to the quarters and lick my wounds over the weekend. I still kept the lamp as a constant reminder of my stupidity. We were finally assigned permanent quarters in the housing area, next to the Officers Club. It was time for me to gather up the family from my parents and move into the new apartment.

It was a custom that a new member of the Airborne unit undergo the annual ritual of an initiation. This traditional event, the famous "Prop Blast" is administered to every soldier before he can become a full-fledged paratrooper and participate in unit Airborne operations. This special event was something I had never expected, because one rarely talks about it. Even while at the Airborne school this ritual had never been mentioned.

The Prop Blast was usually conducted by the unit to welcome the new team members to instill in the individual a sense of belonging, as well as pride in his unit. As I was to find out, it also tests one's stamina of being an Airborne trooper.

When a section of the fuselage of a C-123 aircraft showed up in the back of the Officers Club one afternoon, it did not raise any curiosity. We had Airborne and paratrooper mementos all around the area Since we were getting ready for the annual German-American Open House festival that week this was a natural piece of decoration. Being called to attend a special meeting on a Sunday afternoon at the Headquarters was nothing really unusual either. It struck me as somewhat strange though when I was told to show up in combat fatigues.

Dutifully, I reported in to find a group of about thirty newly assigned officers standing around, wondering what this meeting was all about. Finally the Battle Group Commander showed up with his entire staff. With big grins on their faces, they put us into a formation and marched us from the Headquarters building to the Officers Club, only about three blocks away. Upon our arrival we spotted two big thirty-men tents, which were erected in the back of the Club. A big banner with the inscription "Welcome to the Prop Blast" was hung between two trees, suddenly clarifying what this uncommon meeting was really about.

After a brief greeting by a welcoming "baptism committee", we were ordered to don reserve parachutes and steel pots in the first tent. Lined up, we were moved to the second tent, which held another surprise for us. On a long table I spotted several dishes of unrecognizable origin and several large bowls of strange looking brews for toasting. I noticed one of them even having some dead fish and worms floating in it. Several senior Sergeants were seen busy adding mustard, Tabasco sauce and other condiments to the mixture. This stuff could really make someone throw up right then and there just looking at it. Never mind being invited to drink a full glass of that mixture.

Prior to drinking this concoction, we were all given a black pill by the regimental surgeon to preclude any possibility of high altitude exposure, as we were told. Luckily, aside from this aforementioned brew of non-alcoholic contents, Prop Blast participants were given another choice of a drink. That one was quite less repulsive looking except for the odd purple color. The label of a '151' Rum bottle alongside other potent beverages did not bother any of us. It was not surprising, that the alcoholic brew appealed to the majority and obviously became the preferred choice.

Following the downing of a large sized goblet everyone was ordered to participate in our typical 'daily dozen' exercise, after which we were invited to have another drink of a different unidentifiable taste. After about twenty to thirty minutes, nobody felt any pain except for those poor fellows, who chose the non-alcoholic mixture. Quickly reconsidering, they now decided to kill the rotten taste of their first choice with the drink of an alcoholic medicine.

The initial somber mood of the group rapidly changed to one of elevated spirits. The increasing roaring laughter nearly drowned out the playing of military march music and our traditional Airborne songs. Having reached the expected climax of intoxication, our ever-present leadership finally lined us up for the parachute jump out of the 'aircraft'. I recognized it as the section of the fuselage I had spotted the day earlier in the back of the Club.

Led into the aircraft to hook up, we began lining up, staggering toward the exit door where we were slowly shoved out of the exit. As I approached the door, I assumed the proper jump position inside the door, firmly holding on to the outside of the fuselage. Waiting for the green light to turn on, I suddenly felt the shock of my life when 220 Volts were sent through my body. Jumping forward to disconnect from the current I ended up in a large tub of ice-cold water, face down. I felt absolutely no pain, when a couple of guys lifted me out of the water to stand me up next to my other fellow prop blasted paratroopers to be marched out of the "drop zone" in a rather unmilitary formation.

Following a short congratulatory speech by the Battle Group Commander, we were released to our pre-selected "St. Michaels". St. Michael is the internationally recognized guarding saint of the paratroopers. The job of those "Saints" was to deliver us safely to our families and quarters for a well-deserved nap. An unexpected aftermath became visible during the night and the next morning, when the blackened mattress clearly showed the embarrassing evidence of the previous day's blast. Christine was quite embarrassed, when she had to call the Quartermaster to have the mattress picked for cleaning. I must admit, I was embarrassed , even though I was not the only one.

The first months in the unit kept me very busy participating in exercises and parachuting into a beautiful countryside under the watchful eyes not only of the German civilian population, but also my parents.

What really surprised me, however, was the day when my father invited me to attend one of his *Afrika Korps* Association meeting in Heidelberg, where I was given the opportunity to be a guest speaker at their get-together. Besides it being an honor, this was a truly invigorating experience. I felt no hesitation talking about my previous difficulties and experiences in Germany. Having been rejected as a prospective German Army officer candidate, it prompted me to emigrate and choose a career in the US Army. It showed the Afrika-Korps members the great chances to succeed most immigrants have in the States. It was a very interesting, enlightening meeting and a very beneficial exchanging of ideas. I felt a keen sense of satisfaction receiving congratulations from those German old-timers and warhorses from WWII. It undoubtedly was a proud moment in my young career.

Knowing the language of the host country, of course, can have its advantages, but it may also be a disadvantage as it was in my case. When my Battle Group Commander needed a new Club officer, the ideal solution seemed to get someone, who spoke the language and could thus better control the German employees. The Officers Club was in financial trouble and it was believed the difficulties could be remedied. A better management was needed to get out of the red. Some of the losses were attributed to suspected theft and misappropriations.

As the only native German in the Battalion, it seemed logical to him to assign me to the job. I explained that I was not too eager to accept that job, because I had no experience in this field. More importantly I did not like the idea of possibly loosing a leadership position and maybe even my jump status. After he assured me, that I would still remain assigned to the unit and on jump status, receiving parachute pay, I reluctantly accepted. My "better half" did not like the idea at all and neither did I.

Primarily Infantry Officers, as I learned earlier, had to be prepared to assume many varied types of assignments during their career. This job, I found out soon, was definitely far removed from troop duty. It was absolutely frustrating, especially for a man who believed in being "gung-ho" and preferred serving with soldiers. Instead, I was tasked to deal with civilian personnel and their related problems.

Managing the entire operation of the Mainz Officers Club that served around a thousand military and some DA civilian government employees of a large area, insuring adequate daily food preparation, proper maintenance of the facility and providing entertainment until midnight each day, was not a pleasant task.

Considering everything this job entailed, it also had a few bright spots, I must admit. In order to serve the military community properly, I was given with the more pleasant task of providing a good selection of local wines. It required me to reconnoiter the entire wine areas nearby to taste and select the best harvests. This of course meant spending time in the immediate Rhine and Mosel River territories attending some outstanding wine-tasting events.

Naturally, I was always happy to see my fellow officers come into the club after duty, but dreaded the meetings the Wives Club held. They always expected special treatment and occasional freebees, which I was not privileged to provide and would not. The Club's top priority was the serving the officers, our members.

I remember one special occasion, however, when the Wives Club asked me, if I could serve them a special drink during their session. It was the so-called *'Berliner Weisse'* or Berlin White (Wheat) Beer. It was a unique mixture of regular Pils beer with a shot of raspberry syrup, traditional in Berlin but scarcely known in our area. Agreeing to prepare it and having it served turned the entire Club into a party of extremely happy ladies. The mixture hardly tasted like beer or alcohol but its result was just as effective. For weeks to come I could not do anything wrong in their eyes, even though they did not receive their usual extras.

Still, some time later, I was called to meet the Battalion Commander. His wife had complained that her club did not get the usual free coffee and German cookies, as they used to. I had to remind him that he had previously stated the reason I was placed into this position, was to properly run the operation to reduce losses. Some people liked to blame the losses on the workforce but I soon found that to be incorrect. The previous managers failed to be cost conscious and had the habit to please the wives more than the actual members. In addition, I detected several military managers were regularly helping themselves to the easily obtainable change of the slot machines.

It was not easy to explain to a young wife sitting at home most of the time with the kids, why I had to spend so much time in the Club, while my fellow officers did not. Since their duties didn't leave much time for them to relax, it was clear that they would rather spend it with the family, as I would prefer.

The German Army Experience

A desired break from the overwhelming Club chores came when the Seventh Army needed to send an exchange student to the German Army College, the *'Bundeswehrschule für Innere Führung'* to attend the new Army's Political Education and Moral Leadership Course. This school was created to instill in the officers of the German armed forces the new morals versus those of the old "Wehrmacht". It seemed apparent that they needed to show to the Americans and other Western Allies that the German Army had indeed changed politically and morally into a democratic defense force.

Not so surprising to me, I was selected to attend as an American officer, probably because the Commander felt I had the best chance to make the grade, considering the course was conducted in German, with only occasional interpretations. Desperately in need of a break and a chance of getting back to soldiering again I looked forward to participating in something unusual with members of a different military.

The college was located at Koblenz, a medium sized city with a great historical background, right on the border of France in one of the better wine areas of Germany. It was only about eighty kilometer (50 miles) away from home and was only three weeks in duration. Christine, not needing the car during the week, agreed that I should take our convertible. It was a beautiful ride on a sunny June day, cruising westward alongside the romantic Mosel River. Along the route many old castles and ruins were looking down on me, while large ships carrying goods moved up and down the waterways.

Signing in to the college was very new to me, since I had never had any direct dealing with the new German Army, its customs and procedures. Deep in my mind, I was truly glad I never pursued joining the new German Army any further and joined the US Army instead.

During the first introduction of the instructors and the curriculum, the ranking instructor also introduced and welcomed me, as the one and only American student, in English. He added that he will be happy to frequently interpret the instructional material for me, should I have any questions or trouble understanding German. Speaking German, I expressed my appreciation for the invitation to the course and told him that I am grateful for his offer, but that I was quite proficient in German, so that he would not have to interpret. Surprised, he asked me where I had learned to speak such a good German, even with a Berliner accent. I replied honestly, that I was born in Berlin and as a matter of fact had briefly fought against the Russians in 1945, being finally overrun.

I could sense that he was taken aback and somewhat confused, but with a smile he added, that he was proud to have an American paratrooper and Ranger in their midst. I accepted his compliment and did not have the heart to tell him that, until recently I had been a German citizen. I was also tempted to tell him, that only a few years ago, I had applied for service in the new German Army, but was rejected prompting me to emigrate.

To my surprise, after the first hour of class, I was called into the office of the Commandant of the college, General Hinkelbein. He wanted to personally welcome me to the college, he said, but was surprised and somehow disappointed that the US Army did not send a real American Officer, but sent a German native exchange student instead. Although not a born US citizen, I replied that I was indeed an American officer and that the US Army felt it would be more appropriate to send a German speaking American officer to attend. This would make it easier on the instructors and a lot easier for me to relate my experience to my fellow officers.

After exchanging a few compliments, I returned to the class. While at the college I had some very pleasant exchanges of ideas with my German fellow officers. Again I was instilled with pride to be an American serviceman.

As you would expect in such an environment, it included so-called 'Kameradschaftsabende', evenings of comradeship, identical to our "Happy Hour". These gatherings were held in various local restaurants and pubs. I only regretted that I had not had any new combat experiences to talk about, since Viet-Nam had not fully been developed yet and my knowledge about that war was only from hearsay. Certainly, I had no desire to speak about my bad experiences in Berlin during WWII. I still had plenty of experiences to relate though, pertaining to our officers schooling at OCS, as well as Ranger and Airborne training. Answering some of their questions when it came to sophisticated equipment, new developments and techniques, I sometimes felt uncomfortable considering the degrees of classifications of the subject matter. Even though I realized that they were NATO allies and probably had access to some classified information. Knowing that the German Government, including the military arm, had many spies and moles from East Germany collecting intelligence, I found it easier to just tell them that I either had no knowledge of that particular subject or item.

Returning from this rather unusual temporary duty I was immediately subjected to another challenging interlude with the German Army. The entire 8th Infantry Division was conducting training exercises each year and in 1963, named "Operation Big Lift". It was an exercise involving airlifting units from the United States to Germany for combined tactical maneuvers. That year the maneuvers also included a German unit of the *42nd Panzer Grenadier Battalion,* an Armored Infantry unit from northern Germany.

Together, with two other German speaking soldiers, a Captain Lueders, and Sgt Bruno Seewald, both immigrants, we found ourselves joining the 42nd Grenadiers as liaison officers and interpreters on temporary duty.

Our mission was to make sure the communication between US units and the Germans were such that the coordination of operations was flawless. It was only for ten days of TDY but our work seemed a lot longer and more difficult than we had expected. The German commander, one heck of a guy and driving force from the WWII vintage, just would not want to stop for administrative purposes, as advised, but took his M-41 tanks (he called them tank hunters) and ran them all over the simulated Eastern front lines.

When an administrative halt had been called to allow a non-tactical ambulance movement his actions of course confused the other units, which had been told to stand by. Without doubt, he just did not like what we were advising him to do. We were all convinced that he probably believed he was back in WWII and this time he was going to beat the Russians. I was glad Captain Lueders was the ranking interpreter and had to answer and explain to our Commander, who did not understand how hard it was being only a Captain trying to stop a German Colonel from what he believes to be the best tactical move.

Still, we all had a good experience, a lot of laughs and fun, especially trying to keep Russian military observers from the Soviet Military Mission out of the maneuver area. In order to collect intelligence, they constantly tried to sneak in and monitor our operations and tactics. I am sure they were utterly confused by the German's actions and tactical moves, as we were. Once stopped trying to pass as Germans, I was called to interpret, immediately realizing that they were Russians. The German Press representatives nearby noticed our handling of the trespassers. When they interviewed us, they found it very amusing that an American Officer, formerly a German from Berlin, had arrested Russian Officers spying on NATO maneuvers. In retrospect, we all thought it quite humerous.

It was not to be the only incident. During a different exercise, code-named REFORGER during one of my later assignments to Germany, the German Press had another field day, covering a similar incident, where I was involved in combined operations with German military units. Reading those newspaper articles from my historical files always make me laugh about those rather hilarious incidents.

A Déjà Vu with My Birthplace Berlin with a Classified Assignment

Once our exercise was terminated, the German battalion held their customary maneuver ball and we were invited to live a new experience of working hard and playing even harder. We constantly enjoyed our comradeships, after which it was very hard to say goodbye, but there was always hope for another field experience.

I did not have to wait too long for that to happen, when I received new temporary duty orders to participate in another exercise with the Germany Army's III Corps operation of *'Spätlese'*, the German for 'Late Harvest', lasting one week. I must admit I enjoyed the work relationship with the new German military tremendously, which I believed to be mutual. The best part of it was being an American Liaison Officer giving me a feeling of gratification and pride in my own achievements in the US Army.

Germany, referring to the bureaucrats, who had previously considered me unqualified for service in their forces now had to accept me as an equal. Every time, when asked by my counterparts about my background, I made no secret of my past efforts to join the German Army prior to my emigration. To my astonishment, several German officers relayed to me that the head of the Army's selective service system during my application period had been fired for falsifying his professional qualifications as a psychologist. This development subsequently resulted in an investigation and reinstatement of most applicants who had previously been turned down for psychological reasons, as it was in my case. Deep inside I was glad that fate had prevailed, giving me a chance to succeed in the United States in my chosen career.

Life was indeed full of surprises. Returning to my Battle Group, I was presented with another surprise, which I felt topped it all. I knew then and there that my social job as a Club Officer was passé. I was handed new assignment orders from the Department of the Army, the Pentagon. It was a special assignment to a Detachment A, Berlin Brigade in West-Berlin, Germany.

Nobody could or wanted to tell me anything about this unknown unit, but suddenly I recalled someone in the Intelligence Division at Fort Knox, who once mentioned this unit, as being the perfect assignment for me, whereupon I later had sent a letter to the commander of that unit, inquiring if they had any openings and providing him with some of my qualifications and background. I finally received an answer and his statement that I had all the required qualifications for such an assignment. He was however wondering from whom I received the information about his unit. Since I could not remember the NCO's name, I could not tell him. No other reply was ever received.

It was hard to believe that, after all these months, I was to be transferred to this unit in my old home town and birthplace. I was still wondering what kind of unit I was getting in to, because I was not being told for security reasons. Christine was probably upset, but didn't tell me. We had only been with my Airborne unit for about a year now, when we had to pack and move again. On top of it, we were moving behind the Iron Curtain, right in the middle of the Soviet Occupied Zone, as we still called it, although they called it the German Democratic Republic or DDR.

If Christine was a little disturbed I could have understood her feeling, because we were both going right back to where we once fled from, onto a political 'island', surrounded by hostile forces, where your travel is restricted to within the city limits and travel outside was made very difficult. Facing the very same communist troops, who we both hated, on a daily basis was not exactly a pleasure.

Leaving my club job was the easiest departure ever. The direct assignment by Washington to a unit veiled in secrecy, with yet unknown responsibilities and challenges waiting for me, filled me with anxiety and excitement.

It was October 1963 and about three months after President John F. Kennedy had visited Berlin where, in his speech in front of Berlin-

Schöneberg's City Hall, he proclaimed *'Ich bin ein Berliner'*, translated from the German "I am a Berliner". Reporting in to Berlin's Detachment A unfortunately presented us with the same dilemma we were so accustomed to. Family quarters were not going to be available until a month later. I decided then that the family should remain in Mainz until I had reported in to my new station and had everything prepared for them to move to Berlin.

Traveling by car alone across the Soviet occupied territory was not exactly what I had in mind or enjoyed. Trips through East Germany were quite unpleasant and tightly controlled and you had to be briefed before you did. I had no other choice but to travel by myself.

Arriving at Helmstedt, the border crossing point on the Autobahn in West Germany, leading to Berlin, I received a thorough briefing by the US Army Military Police, as to the do's and don'ts for the security of the travelers. All American personnel were required to fill up their fuel tanks and strictly adhere to the posted speed limit in order to make it through the checkpoints exactly on time. Missing the projected arrival time at Berlin's check point would immediately cause MP patrols to be sent out to search for the missing overdue vehicle and its occupants.

The route through the Zone was approximately two hundred kilometer long (120 miles). Having traveled nearly three hundred miles already just to get to the border crossing, I soon became tired. Travelers had been strictly warned against driving when tired, but the circumstances required that I do. It was to be the typical late fall weather, until it unexpectedly started snowing after I crossed the border. The snow was only in form of light flurries, rare for this area and season, but nevertheless a nuisance.

Driving with the convertible top down I knew that I would be able to stay awake and maintain the required speed. Pulling into a rest area I noticed several East German Army soldiers checking some West-German travelers. Noticing me pulling in, they signaled to me to pull over. Remembering our strict orders never to follow any order other than that of a Russian officer, I continued driving slowly at almost a crawl. While automatically lowering my top, I passed them without stopping. They were shaking their heads in disbelief, when I pulled out again into the Autobahn, taking off while it was snowing into my car. My only concern was to stay awake and reach Berlin safely. I finally reached the Berlin checkpoint on time and after processing through the US Checkpoint, I continued. Only this time my convertible top was back up again, noting the smiles on the MP's faces, after I explained my strange behavior.

My Elite Assignment with the "Quiet Professionals". Earning the "Green Beret"

Not having been to Berlin for quite a few years, I was surprised about the many visual changes that had taken place while I was gone. It took me awhile to find my way to the Headquarters of the US Army Berlin Command. After I had signed in there, I was given guest quarters next to the Headquarters pending the arrival of the family and furniture from West Germany after we would move into new quarters in the family housing area.

Having reported in, I made my way to Andrews Barracks, the former SS Barracks, to sign in at Detachment "A" Berlin Brigade, my new unit. I was eager to find out more about its mission and classified existence.

Arriving at the building complex, I found all the doors locked. Trying unsuccessfully some other doors went back to the first entrance, where I spotted several outside mirrors covering the entire adjacent area. The door was finally opened after several minutes had passed and I entered a large dimly lit foyer with a man armed with a Russian Kalashnikov sitting next to a large drum. After producing my orders and my ID card I was escorted upstairs to the second floor where we entered one open office, where I was greeted by the Detachment Commander, a colonel, who welcomed me in German displaying a big smile.

I still had no clear idea of what kind of an outfit I had landed in, but felt a lot more at ease noticing that he wore the Combat Infantryman's Badge, senior Airborne wings and a Ranger tab. Looking for a special unit patch, the only patch his uniform showed was the normal Berlin patch, not revealing any other patch. After he offered me a cup of freshly brewed coffee, he called his staff into his office and introduced the unit's staff officers. Most of them seemed senior captains with the exception of the Operations officer, who was a major. Colonel Piernick, the Detachment Commander, stated that had been trying to get me assigned for a long time.

He welcomed me to the most unique military unit in the United States, Army, the Detachment "A", Berlin Brigade, a unit of the 1st Special Forces, who are more commonly called the "Green Berets". The troops properly referred to themselves as the "quiet professionals", while others also called them "snake eaters".

He immediately stressed and emphasized that the unit, because of its sensitive mission and operations, does not have a numerical Special Forces designation. Its present unit ID was used to give the impression that it was merely an administrative unit of the Berlin Command. Co-located with an Army Security (ASA) unit, for cover, it made it appear normal for the SF to wear civilian clothes, since they generally wore only civilian clothing. Normally a Special Forces "A" Detachment has 12 members, but this special detachment had several small groups with several individual cells. In general, a Special Forces Group has SFOBs, Special Forces Operational Bases with C, B and A Detachments.

The cold war and the fact that the city of Berlin was located behind the "iron curtain", surrounded by the Soviet Army with its subordinate East Germany Army, the Volks Armee. Its primary purpose was that of a stay-behind unit in case Berlin was overrun by an enemy. Other operational techniques were, infiltration by air, land, or sea.

Being a German native, especially a born Berliner, undoubtedly gave me a significant advantage qualifying for such an assignment. After being given the command of one of its groups, I soon found that I was not the only one with an edge and special qualifications. The majority of assigned SF personnel were of Eastern European origin, some even former immigrants from Poland, Czechoslovakia, Russia, Latvia, Estonia, Lithuania, Hungary and several other countries.

Not to my surprise they all spoke German, although with various accents but they could well pass as Germans. Operational personnel showed no signs, which might reveal an American, such as tattoos or even the customary circumcision, not usually found in Europe, especially in Germany. The other group commanders were from Latvia, Poland and Czechoslovakia. We were all assigned different operational areas of responsibility of West Berlin to work in.

To provide a so-called compartmentalization, neither one of us knew about any particular methods of operation in the area of another group. To minimize any possibility of compromise, my AO (Area of Operation) did not coincide with the area in which I previously resided and attended school during my younger years. Any possible risk of running into one of my old school buddies from the '40s, was avoided. After I had been familiarized with the operations, I was given a couple of weeks to get the family into quarters, which were going to be available shortly. Eager to get to work, I returned to West Germany and Mainz to pack and move to Berlin. Returning to the family was uneventful as I was now familiar with the route, but still cautious. Security and my new classification stipulated, that after I moved my family to Berlin, I was no longer able to travel through the Soviet Occupied Zone by car.

We spent a few days with my family in Heidelberg and with quarters already waiting for me in Berlin, we started packing while the movers did their part to ship it to the big city. This time we all traveled by car and looked forward to our new home, about four hundred twenty miles away. We traveled through West Germany without any incidents until we arrived at the Helmstedt border crossing check point.

Checking in at the US military check point in West Germany first we then proceeded through the Soviet military check point in East Germany, where all our papers were carefully checked, especially the Soviet Travel Authorization printed in four languages. My family stayed inside the vehicle with the car doors locked and the windows nearly closed to prevent an easy entry by outsiders.

By myself, I proceeded to the building, where a Russian officer checked my ID card and our travel documents, only leaving the room briefly for a few minutes. After his return I received my stamped papers and ID and returned to my car, where I noted a Russian soldier, who had been at the car door, slowly leaving the vehicle. Getting inside the car, Christine told me that the "Russian" had asked her in her own dialect of a Saxony-German why she had left the Republic and why she had married me. Of course, she did not answer him, but it really irritated her and me because her new American passport listed her native country as Germany. A check by the Russians of their records apparently revealed that she was born and had lived in the Soviet Zone before she fled to the West. It became clear to me that their intelligence collection efforts were not to be underestimated and that the US made it quite easy for them to gather whatever vital information they needed.

While the civilian German nationals and commercial trucks had to wait in long lines for processing, we were processed by the military through a separate lane designated only for Allied personnel with Soviet travel documents. Unfamiliar with the strange regulations governing the occupation of East Germany, I explained to the family that, once through the checkpoints and on the Autobahn on the other side, we had exactly two hours, traveling at sixty mph to make it to the next checkpoint entering the US sector at Berlin.

Carefully checking our official route map and the attached pictures of road signs, we had to make sure we do not get off the interstate by mistake, as it would be considered a severe violation of the Allied agreement. For harassment, the East Germans often moved or changed directional signs to harass Americans and mislead them into taking wrong routes and exits, whereupon they would be stopped and interrogated.

The issued route map explicitly showed kilometer markers and pictures of the appropriate signs they would have to be reached along the trip. Any unusual delay at the arrival check point prompted surveillance vehicles to be dispatched to check the route for the delayed or missing vehicle. Everybody dreaded the thought of breaking down while in the Soviet Zone, and we therefore did everything possible to have our car thoroughly checked. It was also essential to carry emergency gas and tools to be able to help yourself and other travelers, in case of a breakdown or the need for towing.

Staying within our assigned limits we safely reached our destination at the crossing into the US Sector of Berlin without any mishaps and with a great feeling of relief. Having completed our debriefing for our travel, we took in our first deep breaths of fresh Berlin air, which was to surround us for the next two years.

Our initial happiness after arriving in Berlin was to be severely shattered though the following day when we visited an old family friend on 23 November 1963. This was the day when we heard a German TV commentator announce that the US President, John Fitzgerald Kennedy had been assassinated in Dallas, Texas.

A quick check with the AFN, the Armed Forces Network and RIAS, the Radio in the American Sector of Berlin, verified our worst fears. His death immediately prompted all Western stations to cease their regular programs and to play appropriate solemn music. All Berliners were showing their respect and openly mourned an American President, whom they loved and admired and who had just visited them only a few months before.

On all government buildings the flags of the United States, Germany and Berlin were lowered to half-mast. Not only Berlin, but also the remaining Germany mourned the loss together with our military forces, who had not only lost a President but also their Commander-in-Chief. Special Forces in particular had lost its idol, the founder and "father" of this unique elite unit of the United States Army. It was JFK who had awarded them the Green Beret, their distinctive headgear, proudly worn by those who earned it.

It was astonishing to see Berliners showing tears after they heard the news, even lining up at American installations to sign lists of condolence. For several weeks I was handing out freshly minted special issues of silver dollars of John F. Kennedy to close friends and acquaintances. Members of our detachment were all visibly shaken. But it was also a period of heightened alertness. Getting down to business, I was reminded that I still had to undergo some highly specialized training to be able to assume the extensive responsibilities as a Special Forces trooper. Not yet authorized to wear a Green Beret, I needed to fully qualify in my new MOS, my Military Occupational Specialty to earn it.

Familiar with some of the operational concepts from my Ranger and unconventional warfare training, I knew that to qualify for Special Forces it takes a lot more, aside from the foreign language requirements, three of which I was fluent in. Excluding the administrative staff, all operational detachment personnel were quite well trained in Special Forces operational techniques. My lack of such specialized training was to be quickly remedied by the Detachment. I was scheduled for this additional Special Forces training with the 10th Special Forces Group at Bad Tölz, in Southern Bavaria, my favorite vacation area.

The school attendance was anything but a vacation however, especially the one subject near the end of the period of instruction, when students are subjected to a period of a Prisoner of War environment.

It began quite harmless. With students loaded on trucks, we were driven along desolate country roads for a while and into a wooded area, when we were ambushed and taken prisoner by a group of Russian soldiers. At least it was so realistic, that many of us actually were uncertain whether this was real or training. After being blindfolded the students were taken to a prison type facility. With the blindfolds removed inside the structure, we were segregated. I was stripped naked by prison guards and my buttocks were painted with big swastikas, after which I was locked up in a totally dark cell with a black painted window and only one dimly lit bulb in the ceiling.

The cell was bare of any furniture without even a bunk and absent of any heat source whatsoever. Dirty walls showed all kinds of graffiti with mostly Russian, but also some German writing. Outside the cell, the tier corridor was resounding with Russian military music and songs, while Russian speaking guards constantly beat against, what sounded like, a fifty-five gallon drum. Occasionally they hit on the solid cell door with the intent of keeping you awake and prepared for an interrogation, which evidently had to come at any time.

I cannot recall how long I stayed huddled in the bad smelling cold corner hoping for something to happen soon, as time slipped by without any indication of how long I had been there. It was impossible to reach the window near the ceiling to scrape some of the paint off and to see what time it was. Any attempt by me to take a nap encouraged a guard to stick a water hose through a small peep hole in the door and spray me with ice cold water. Asking for water or food prompted the same reaction by the guard, but at least you could catch some water to drink, regardless of the source of the water. At least it helped flush away any urine and other excretions left in the corner, which had to serve as toilet.

Any attempt to communicate with someone next door failed miserably with all the noise created by the guards and the frequent yelling from other prisoners. Having lost any sense of time, it seemed as if I had been there for several days, particularly my increasing noticeable hunger. Finally my cell door was opened and I was taken out of the cell to be confronted by a uniformed Russian officer in a separate room. He offered me a cigarette and asked me in broken English to sit down. Handed an old blanket, I wrapped myself in it and gladly accepted the cigarette, which was of typically Russian manufacture. Briefly studying him, he definitely looked like a genuine Soviet NKVD officer. When I asked him where I was and why I was being held, complaining about this inhuman treatment, he uttered a few words in Russian and began talking to me again in pigeon English. When I tried to tell him that I did not understand English well enough, he did not question my statement and instead switched to German.

He asked me the typical questions usually asked from POWs such as your unit, its strength, its mission and other military information, followed by questions of a more private nature pertaining to family. Playing the Geneva Convention card, I stuck to the 'Code of Conduct', giving him only my name, rank and serial number and lied about the last item. Reminding me that, unless I cooperate, I will be stuck here for a long time until being shipped out to Siberia. There I could join some other American POWs from Korea. Mad and cold, I was pushed back to my cell and locked up again.

They let me keep the blanket but I was still hungry without any hope of food and still doubtful whether this situation was for real or just a game being played. The whole situation appeared so real. At least I found out that it was getting dark outside and estimated my time spent in that hell-hole to be about two days, maybe. I figured that they have to feed me one of these days and could tolerate it as long as I had some water off and on. I knew how to get, even if it meant getting wet again. Doing exercises I realized would dry me off and warm me up.

Shifting my position into the corner next to the door, I was finally able to get some naptime even through all the noise. All of a sudden I was abruptly shaken awake and led out of the cell again, this time facing a different interrogator in Russian fatigues, who got up to shake my hand, congratulating me for passing the test and handing me my uniform. In passing he inquired if I would like something to eat. Asking him how many days I had been in the cell, he replied just a day and a half, which I could hardly believe, as it seemed to me more like three to four days.

He then casually asked me how long I had lived in Germany and where, before I went to the US. I told him and he then asked me more about my new assignment, when I suddenly got suspicious and instinctively clammed up. To my surprise, he slammed down his hand on the desk and stated in beautiful southern accent, that I almost flunked the test.

My assumption that he was an instructor was wrong, and had this been a real situation I could have revealed more information than permitted by the code. I learned another important lesson; that in a similar situation like this you trust no one!

I must give credit to the school (CIA?) for running a very realistic situation, as they had fooled just about everyone, except the few very suspicious doubters who you find in many situations. I then realized why nobody had clued us in about the special facets of this SF training.

Following the graduation from the course I returned to Berlin quite a bit wiser and more confident about my assignment, the risks involved and a much better awareness for whatever might face us in the event the Russians decided to take Berlin by force.

The course was challenging, highly educational, while also stressful and physically demanding. Back at home in the big city I got more involved in the critical areas of operations. I was ready to get my feet wet and to get to know my men and their capabilities better. One of my men, Henryk Zbieransky, of Polish background asked me out of the blue, if I happened to know a young Berliner a redheaded lady named Regine.

For a moment I was stunned about his question, but when I told him that I did, he told me that Regine was his wife. Flabbergasted is not the right expression for how I felt to find my cousin again in Berlin after all these years and especially married to a member of my unit. After fleeing from Berlin in 1948 I had never even tried to locate her. Certainly, it was embarrassing for Henryk to finding out that his commander was related to his wife. But given the special circumstances, I assured him that I would never hold it against him, but that he could also not expect any special treatment because of this relationship. Had he not mentioned my name to his wife, Regine would probably never have found out about me since I had broken all contact with most of my relatives in Germany after my emigration.

While serving in this unit we rarely had any social affairs for security reasons. After several weeks we finally had a chance to meet. It was a rather emotional reunion when we finally faced each other again. We had both matured and such changed significantly.

My life seemed to be full of unexpected events. Another emotional occurrence was not far behind, when my mother called me from Heidelberg. She told me that my brother, who had also emigrated to the United States on his own in the meantime, had joined the Army and returned to Germany. However, he disliked the service so much that he just deserted his unit following some problems he had with his superior officers. Military Police officers attempting to arrest him at the home of my parents could not gain entrance, because it was private German property, while the German police, summoned to assist, would not enter the area either, because my brother had not broken any German law.

It was apparently a standoff. Obligated to assist I took the next flight from Berlin to Heidelberg and met with the MP's to be briefed. Being a relative, I was authorized to enter the apartment alone to arrest my brother. He had, of course, gotten wind of my arrival and fled the apartment via the rear exit with the help of one of my old friends. My friend did not realize what my brother Reiner had done and that I was there to arrest him. My father was naturally embarrassed and mad about his youngest son's actions, but calmed down after I talked to him. Assisting the MP's we finally caught up with him and following his later arrest, he was his subsequently court-martialed and discharged from the Army.

I never expected him to become our family's black sheep nor could I understand what made him act like he did. Strongly believing in such character traits like honesty and loyalty as well as duty, honor and country,

I could no longer respect him and broke off all ties with him, as did my sister Ute.

It made my previous decision to sever ties even easier, when he unexpectedly changed his name and "acquired" the new name of 'Von Ziethen' added to our family name. Taking this well-respected name of the late Cavalry General and Field Marshal under King Frederick the Great was, I felt, a terrible insult to this hero. My brother apparently believed that this would gain him prestige, which comes being a so-called 'blue-blood' aristocratic relative.

Still in possession of his alien registration card, the "green card", he had returned to the states after his dishonorable discharge. Somehow he had entered college and a university in California, where he earned a doctor's degree in anthropology. Without a proper education from Germany, except high school, I will never understand how he did it. I learned later on that he was back in Germany as a professor at the Goethe University in Frankfurt, where he supposedly lives with his family and wife, a former Canadian and Baroness from Hungary.

Operating Incognito

Being relatively new to the city of Berlin and its recent economical developments, I spent many days and nights reconnoitering my area of responsibility within the limits of West Berlin and the adjacent area in East Germany. West-Berlin had been so well rebuilt that I could hardly find any traces of the war, giving the impression it had never been destroyed. The Marshall Plan had definitely been a blessing to the capitol.

Conducting covert operations, incognito, it was common practice for us to dress in German clothing to check out the sites next to the Berlin wall and the barb wired sections, the '*Eiserner Vorhang*', known to the allies as the "Iron Curtain", separating the Zones. Collecting intelligence, we surreptitiously took pictures of some of the vital areas and weak points.

Naturally, our enemies observed and watched us too and for a while we looked at each other through binoculars. We knew quite well that they were taking pictures of us at the same time, probably to determine who we were. Making their job more difficult was often a pain in the neck for us. We frequently changed our facial appearances and dresses. By adding beards, mustaches, wigs and other gimmicks, we attempted to fool them. Quite often we were not able to recognize each other.

The first time I bought my make-up kit at a German theatrical supply shop, I felt compelled to tell the sales person that I was a new member of a theatre group and needed to replace my entire worn out set. I hated to wear a mustache because my perspiration often caused the make up to slip. This required me to frequently check in a mirror, if it was still in place. Not realizing it was out of place could be quite embarrassing, when other people looked at you frowning or outright telling you that your mustache is out of place. I was glad that we did not have to abide by Army regulations concerning our haircuts. Wearing wigs was also very uncomfortable. To most of the military community we were thought to be civilians or belonged to the Army Security Agency or CID, which was the whole purpose behind the camouflage.

Equipped with the necessary ID's identifying me as a member of the Berlin police, I was free to gain information vital to our operations without raising suspicion. Living in an environment such as Berlin, surrounded by a hostile power, made most of the population very distrustful.

My car was a little German Ford Taunus with German government license plates, which I used for all covert operations. Because some ridiculous Army regulation required us to carry fire extinguishers between the front seats, we always made sure to cover them up, so as not to reveal it was US government owned. Germans never carried extinguishers in their cars, especially not extinguisher made in the USA.

Playing another role, once every two weeks I was putting on my regular green uniform of an officer of the US Army, minus Ranger tab, airborne wings and the SF patch. Our job was to take a special US Army staff car and conduct a G-2 patrol in East Berlin. Departing from West Berlin and proceeding through Checkpoint Charlie our main purpose was to drive through the Soviet occupied territory and check out their military facilities, their transport systems and observe their troop movements. To update information on vital installations we collected information through observation and personal contact, if possible, just like the Soviet Military Mission personnel did in West Germany.

These patrols were conducted mutually, based on a reciprocal agreement among the Allies following the establishment of the Allied Zones of occupation. While the Soviets had the chance to freely roam without problems, we did not have the same freedom entering the East Sector. Instantly, a plain car with several occupants, quite often some in civilian clothes, tailed us. Apparently they wanted to make sure we did not get the opportunity to see something we were not supposed to and, if necessary, to block our access by any means.

All our drivers were specially selected and the sedans were equipped with a special high powered antenna centered on the car roof, which permitted us to be in constant contact with the Headquarters to relay any unusual occurrences. Protecting the antenna was an open can shaped contraption to prevent the border guards from touching and possibly breaking off the antenna, while leaning against the car. As soon as the driver noticed any such attempt, the driver keyed his mike sending a burst of electricity thru the canned antenna shocking him. Once tried, they would never repeat it.

Once in East German territory and being followed by a "tail", it was the driver's job to loose the tail, to permit us to venture out into areas of military importance. Not limited to gaining information about railroad crossings, bridges, power stations and communications facilities, we also looked for individuals we deemed pro-American, who would provide us with worthwhile information. Loaded with goodies, such as nylons, cigarettes, good whisky and chocolate we often made contact with people revealing such an attitude or pronounced anticommunist feeling.

Frequently, when not followed by tailing vehicle, people would give us a friendly hand wave or smile and, while stopped along the road, even well meant words of support when they knew to be free of observation. Following several trips we had found several sympathizers, who willingly provided us with information about troop and equipment movements. All information we received was classified into different categories of reliability following verification, to eliminate invalid statements and rumors.

Always considering the possibility of an outbreak of open hostilities, we needed to collect all such intelligence, which could some day be vital to the survival of our unit, its personnel and primarily the accomplishment of our mission. This effort also required personnel assets, reliable individuals, who could be helpful in case of a war.

I remember an older lady working for the railroad at one particular railroad crossing signal tower, who always waved at us when sure that we were not being followed. Once she considered it safe to talk, she even came down from her tower to talk to us briefly and to give us written information regarding trains carrying military equipment and personnel. In turn, we always showed our appreciation for her courage and gladly shared some of our valuables with her, usual nylons and sometimes bananas, and other items unavailable to normal citizens in the East. We never considered our action bribery or hers treason.

But just as we were usually tailed in the Soviet Sector, we sometimes found ourselves occasionally being followed in West Berlin, whether we were in the French, British or American Sector. Frequently I spotted someone following or watching me for an extended period of time. It was no secret that West Berlin was full of Eastern agents. Movements of American personnel throughout the city could easily be monitored.

Personnel leaving the military barracks in civilian clothes especially were suspect of being members of some type of intelligence unit, particularly when operating an unmarked civilian vehicle. Using various ways and means to shake off anybody tailing us became part of a routine after a while. In order to pursue covert operations I usually chose the guise of being a student of the Free Berlin University, visiting there often, and as such tried to appear to be a German in every respect. This obviously meant that I had to avoid most military facilities, except our barracks, where we could be considered members of the Security Agency or civilian help working there.

Without a doubt, subversive groups from the East were constantly monitoring our military operations and functions. It was therefore strongly recommended that we do not use the PX and commissary or the officers and NCO club. It was Christine and the other wives who did all the purchasing. I preferred shopping in German stores during my reconnaissance of the city. Regarding the clubs, we suspected some of the bartenders to be East Block agents, who probably functioned as double agents for some other intelligence outfit. Valuable information was often gained by frequenting bars in areas near the wall and border, as people in those places were more apt to talk under the influence of alcohol.

As some of our personnel in the unit left, changes were necessary to be made in our assets in the East. Essentially, this required our members to initiate new contacts with trustworthy and reliable people while also maintaining the old sources. We constantly needed data, which could help us in the assessment of the enemy's capabilities and intentions. Such an ideal asset presented itself, when my father revealed to me that I had a sister living in East Berlin under the Soviets.

I was stunned by this revelation because I had never heard of such a sister before, who actually was a half-sister. She was born to my father's secretary during his only indiscretion, while he was working in the Air

Ministry. Although my mother knew about this girl, she preferred never to talk about this event to any of us children while we were younger.

Out of sheer curiosity, my father was wondering, if I could possibly find her since I had easier access to police records as a member of the Allied forces in Berlin. Recalling an old friend of mine, Dieter Kohlsch, from my Labor Service days when I visited Berlin, I searched him out and found him working as a *'Kriminal Kommissar'* a detective superintendent of the Berlin police. Our reunion was a total surprise for him, especially when I brought him up-to-date with my more recent past to include my emigration to the States and joining the Army.

We renewed our friendship and had several get-togethers at his home, during which we talked about his job and naturally mine, where I had to draw the line of course, as to the real purpose of my being in Berlin. Every once in awhile in one's life, you have to tell half-truths or even a lie. I consequently told him that I was working for the Army Security Agency as a lieutenant, which employed many civilians working on security classifications for employees to the US Army. This job logically required me to wear civilian clothing most of the time.

We made it a point not to discuss our jobs in the future, since his assignments were also fairly critical, but he offered to help me out in anyway he could, since the Allied occupation forces had jurisdiction over the police departments in Berlin. In his position he had access to many areas and establishments and taking me around to meet numerous people, he usually presented me as an old friend and student of the university using my two middle names as an alias, rather than my true identity to play it safe.

Meeting Another Sister the First Time. Adjusting to Covert Operations

When I mentioned a half-sister to Dieter, he assured me that he could find out details about her through some contact in East Berlin. After a week, he gave me her address, place of employment and other personal information. Without knowing her political orientation and for her own safety, I decided not to visit her at her home but to meet her casually in her place of employment. Heidi worked in a boutique close to the Brandenburg Gate, but on the eastern side.

During my next G-2 patrol, I had the driver stop near the shop, rather than in front to make sure we do not attract unnecessary attention with an American military sedan. I instructed him to wait for my return while I go inside the store. After I entered the boutique, several women in a lively conversation suddenly fell silent, just staring at me as if they had never seen an American soldier before. When one saleslady came over to ask me in English if she could help me, I answered her in German if a Heidi was in and if I could speak to her.

After I had mentioned her name, I noticed a pretty young lady walking towards us. Briefly looking over my uniform she noticed my nametag and suddenly burst out loud in German with "no, that can't be"! Unsure, she hesitatingly stretched out her hand to greet me. Personally, of course, I was also excited to meet my thirty year old sister for the first time in my life.

I was certainly tempted to give her a big hug but common sense told me to refrain from that emotional gesture, as we had several people watching us curiously. Such a contact could be very detrimental to her safety. I only told her that I was indeed her older brother, with another younger one and a sister living in the West. I also relayed to her that "our" father sends his greetings in the hope that they could, maybe meet some day soon, which she gladly agreed to.

It was not long after our introduction, when she noticed an East German police car from the *'Volkspolizei'* slowly drive by. She quickly pointed it out to me, asking me to say a hasty goodbye with a brief kiss on the cheek and my promise to return. I left the store hoping that my visit would not implicate her by talking to a 'western agent', a rather serious offense in the *DDR* and that her coworkers and customers would not turn her in.

Having visited the East a few times by then, I found that no matter where you went, there was always somebody watching your every move. A lot of people had the habit of sitting nearby their windows or even leaning out to observe suspicious activities in their neighborhood and immediately report those to the police.

Nevertheless, I had to see her again and the following week I made another trip to her shop. To my surprise, I was hardly out of the sedan, this time parking in front, when she walked out of the store to greet me, as if she had been expecting me. After a friendly 'hello', she told me that she was surprised to see me again It was a coincidence, as she was just about to meet her boyfriend. He had not shown up yet and this. gave us the chance to talk some more. At least we hoped, when a police car drove up and a policeman got out and came over to us. Disregarding me, he immediately asked for her identity card and when she stated that she did not have one with her, he told her to get into the patrol car.

This infuriated me and prompted me to step between them while asking him what right he had to arrest her for no apparent reason. As an Allied military officer I had every right to talk to anybody in this "democratic" state I wanted to, telling him to immediately call a Russian Officer. Before he could answer me however, a man came up behind him, tapping him on the shoulder demanding what was going on between him and his fiancée. He identified himself as a leader and head of the youth league, a member of the party, who cannot and will not tolerate his behavior.

Suddenly, two more policemen emerged from the patrol car, as did two of my fellow officers, who were with me on patrol. We seemed to be getting close to an apparent serious conflict. Realizing that we were facing armed reinforcements from the German police patrol car, I was asked by a Captain on my patrol not to cause an incident and instead to leave the area. It was quite clear that they had the upper hand and we were unable to forcefully intervene. I regretted to have exposed my sister to unnecessary trouble and had to witness both my sister and her fiancée, still protesting loudly, being arrested and taken away. Any future attempts of contacting her were futile and I realized that any further pursuit could have only made things worse for my sister.

Berlin was well known by everybody as a meeting place for foreign agents and conspirators. This became very apparent to me one evening when I was stopping by one of my cozy little pubs not too far from the Soviet Zone border and the iron curtain. The pub owner, well known to me from frequent visits, asked me if I had any connections with Americans. About to deny it, I reconsidered. It was obvious I knew some GIs, having made a mistake of smoking an American cigarette. I told him, that I am only sometimes invited to one of their parties. He told me that there was a guest at one table, who was trying to make contact with an American for some help he needed. I replied that I doubted I could help, but curious and intrigued, I joined the man looking like a Mediterranean, possibly a Turk. I introduced myself with my alias, after which he gave me his name, after which he identified himself as a Turk. Turks were a rather well represented population in Berlin working as foreign laborers, as many younger Germans had left the area for better work and higher living standards in the West.

He came right to the point and plainly stated in his heavy accent that he is looking to buy weapons, anti-tank weapons in particular, to fight foreign invaders in his home country. He was not very specific regarding the enemy but made mention of Iraq's involvement. I had to admit that I did not have any idea about any fighting going on in Turkey. He explained that he could only get those weapons from Americans, because the Germans he knew could not own or obtain any type of weapons, let alone get bazookas.

After I got his name and address, I promised him that he would hear from me again if I find some American friends who might be able to help. To show me that he is serious, he invited me to one of their "freedom fighter" meetings and encouraged me to bring my American friend, too.

He bought me a drink after which he departed. Checking with my friend Dieter first and telling him about my encounter with that strange individual, he did some checking and assured me that the guy was genuine. However, he was not quite sure whose side he was on since they had a lot of Kurds living in Berlin who fought against the Turkish government while others were waging war against the Iraqis.

I reported this strange encounter to my Commander, who thought another non-committal meeting with the group might be worthwhile intelligence. Making contact with the Turk again, it was arranged for me to attend a meeting a few days later in Kreuzberg, a district heavily saturated by Turks. I met my acquaintance again and saw his friends, who definitely looked like guerilla fighters from that Mediterranean area. I did not stay long for the meeting since it was all held in Turkish, I presumed, and only frequently translated into German for my benefit. I had no idea whether the translation was correct or not. Before I left, I assured them that I will try to find an American contact, who usually transports ammunition and bazookas to Berlin to meet with him at the same pub a week later. I told them, I can have nothing to do with weapons as it was illegal, and they will be on their own. Intrigued with some of the flyers and the unfamiliar writing, I took the liberty to take some with me.

After I submitted my report, with the flyers attached, to my Detachment, it was deemed advisable to turn this information over to the CIA., This type of operation was clearly outside our operational area of responsibility, but quite certainly possibly of interest to German and American intelligence.

The following week, I stopped by the pub again and was not surprised to find the Turk sitting at a table in the corner talking to a colored individual, who had trouble conversing with the Turk in German. Spotting me, he waved me over to the table. Somewhat obligated to help I joined them briefly to show them that my English is not that good to properly translate or interpret. I advised the Turk to get someone from his group who could speak better English or for the American to get a hold of someone, who could either speak German or Turkish. I was sure that this guy was sent by the CIA, but could not believe that the agency did not have a better language qualified agent to take the place of a soldier. As directed by my command I had removed myself from this strange dealing.

At least that's what I thought. The next time I stopped by the watering hole the proprietor told me that the German police had arrested the Turk. They showed the Turk a piece of paper, a report from an American officer with a German name, who had reported him. This report supposedly proved that he was suspected of attempting to deal in weapons smuggling. I had the feeling that this was my report, forwarded from the CIA to the German police. The bar keeper only knew me as a German student, who was friends with Americans. He did not even know my name. I convinced him, that the Turk probably made so many contacts that he slipped with one of them. I realized it was time for me to change my favorite place for another to preclude another run-in with the Kurd.

Shortly after the encounter with the Kurds, I received a directive from some security agency to report to a 'safe house', which was not one of our Detachment's property. Very suspicious, I questioned this directive and checked with my Commander. My suspicions were erased when he told me that this interview with the other agency is routine for all people assigned to the Detachment.

What was generally known as the "ice box", the interview consisted of a routine polygraph examination. Unknown to me, this interview was designed to make sure members did not have any unusual contact with hostile agents, which might present a breach of security.

Naturally, looking at the past military conduct in the execution of my duties, I knew that I did not have anything to hide but resented revealing my personal life to complete strangers. During the interview I found some of the questions were rather intrusive into my intimate life. A polygraph was something totally new to me.

After I answered some of the questions in a somewhat evasive manner, my answers were probably being read as not being the entire truth. I was assured by the agent, that I can be totally open and truthful as the information gained would not be accessible by anyone outside that room.

I still found the procedure quite objectionable, feeling that my loyalty was being questioned.

On the other hand, I realized that there are security breaches here and there and it was for my own good if everybody is being checked. After a few repeats and clearer answers, I passed, according to the examiner, Deep in my mind, I wondered, who certifies the tester's loyalty? I was sure that we were dealing with a lot of double agents every day in Berlin. 'Trust no one', was a slogan, which I constantly recalled when dealing with people outside my "inner Circle".   .

To become very familiar with the remaining districts along the center of Berlin and the Berlin Wall, I took frequent rides and walks along the heavily guarded wall and the greatly fortified and mined border of the iron curtain separating West Berlin from the Soviet Zone. Aside from a few not publicly known but existing underground tunnels between the East and the West there were of course also the waterways, such as the Teltow Canal, which many Berliners used trying to flee from the East to the West.

The biggest problem was the unavailability of appropriate diving gear, because swimming across would clearly be noticeable by the East German border guards, who would immediately open fire on them. They repeatedly shot people trying to cross over the wall, should they be lucky enough to negotiate the mine fields, the dogs and finally reach the wall. Climbing it always exposes escapees long enough to easily get shot.

My district included the Havel River running through Berlin along the Western border, which connected several lakes, one of which was the Wannsee. This beautiful lake, a recreational area, had an island, the *'Pfauen Insel'*. For the public restricted, this island, considered an environmentally protected area, was located along the border, but still inside the American sector. West Berliners used the River and the lakes for their recreational purposes such as enjoying a nude beach, camping, swimming and sail boating. They were cautioned however to avoid the island since it was very close to the border, which ran down the middle of the River, between the Island and the East German beach. It was naturally heavily patrolled by river boat border patrols from the East German Army.

There were no private boats or ships on the beaches of the communist side. To get a better look at their facilities and their security on the other side of the river without getting the US MP River Patrol involved, I talked to my friend Dieter. He was able to provide me and some of my team members with a private boat. After we were dropped off on the island, we selected a perfect area under camouflage from where we were able to observe several military patrol boats berthed in an area, which appeared to be part of a troop compound.

One of the boats was flying the special flag of a Regimental Commander at the rear end. It almost beckoned to be liberated and brought to the West. Of course, we were not merely interested in the flag.

After we had sufficiently surveyed the ongoing activities watching several boats come and go, we determined it was the right time to do something unusual. With the sun beginning to set and the light condition almost perfect for reduced visibility. Two of us donned our swimsuits and cautiously started swimming across the nearly two hundred meters to the target along the shore line. Coming up every so often to remain oriented we steered towards the one boat with the East German flag. Without any visible obstacles or being detected, we reached it and, with our hearts beating rapidly, we quickly cut the rope holding the flag.

Immediately submerging again to prevent being spotted either from the beach or by patrol boats in the vicinity, we dragged the flag under water swimming towards our little island only briefly surfacing to get air for a minute or two until we returned to the island again.

When we reached the undergrowth it was already pretty dark. Walking to the opposite side of the nearly three-acre island, we spotted our boat, which was already anxiously waiting for us. Hiding the trophy, we returned to our starting point thanking our friends, who had no idea of our doings, for the boat ride.

We could not reveal the reason for our visit to the island, but we knew they were eager to find out. They respected our silence without any question. We knew that Dieter's friend had been helping a few people flee from the East, but I did not want to question him at that time, since trust had to be earned over a longer period of time. Dieter had never been involved in either inserting or extracting agents. There was a time though, when he was approached by some agent from the other side, who had promised him preferential treatment of distant relatives living in the East, if he would work for them. Knowing that they had been devout communists, he declined.

Not One Boring Day in Berlin – Unforgettable Experiences

I had too many strange experiences in Berlin to write about them all, but there were quite a few that I could write about but not without embarrassing myself. While working in the city, most communication with assets in the East was done through dead letter drops. Messages were usually dropped or picked up at previously selected locations. Spotting a special sign or mark, which indicated the drop had been serviced, I carefully removed the message.

Dead letter drops could be behind mirrors and toilet tanks in bars or restaurants, behind advertisement posters in subways, under benches in parks and just about anywhere, where one feels they cannot be easily detected. Mostly encoded, some agents without access to a valid code, may just list a rendezvous point, where a face to face meeting was feasible.

Quite often a message was transported via public transportation from the East to the West and vice versa, such as the Berlin S-Bahn, a metro rail system, that did run into and through the West in some areas, but without East Berliners. East Berlin police cleared the train of personnel before it entered the West. Sending written messages to the East and to the West through the train system was no problem.

After servicing one drop I received a message requesting a face-to-face meeting for an exchange of information. I was prepared to comply, but unexpectedly ran into a situation, where I had to involve someone I had never dreamed of involving. I had no other choice. It was actually hilarious, come to think of it.

Proceeding to my rendezvous point, a "Club 10" in West Berlin, I found myself at a locked door. Ringing at the prominently marked door, I noticed a small window being opened. After I had been found to be alone, I was advised that I could not be admitted without a female escort. Even though I insisted, that I was being expected I was again told that I was required to be escorted. This was indeed strange.

Looking for a telephone booth I finally found one and called Christine at the quarters. I asked her to come to my location where I urgently needed her and emphasized that it was not for pleasure but strictly Army business. She first hesitated but finally agreed to come. She met me at the nearby station from where we proceeded to the Night Club where I was finally admitted after she declared that she was my escort. Neither Christine nor I had any idea what we were getting into. To our surprise, we had entered a night club filled with mostly women, who were not so much looking at me, but at Christine. I asked her to sit at the bar while I look for a "friend", who had to be somewhere in the club. I finally found and recognized my contact after my eyes got adjusted to the dark interior.

We had a brief talk and exchanged our information, which took a couple minutes. About to depart she asked me how I managed to get into the club because she had not yet advised the door manager to expect me. When I told her that I brought my wife, her eyes widened apologizing immediately and asking me, where I had left her. After I told her that I left her at the bar, she quickly walked toward the bar with me, where I found Christine quite embarrassed. Apparently a young girl was trying to get intimate with her and started caressing her. Having rescued her, I said a quick good-bye to my contact and we hurriedly left the bar. Christine was still in disbelief about this unexpected experience. I had to promise her never again to put her into such an extremely uncomfortable position, even if it was for the good of the country. I never did anything like that again.

Considering my work exhilarating is putting it mildly. It looked like the assignment was a twenty-four-hour job, since our daily operations in the city could not be limited to a certain time frame. I found that we could often not differentiate between on duty and off duty work. Each of us, alone or as a team, worked whenever a project or incident required it. This meant an individual had to be totally available.

Military families of Special Forces members knew what they had to put up with and gradually adjusted to it. It was not unusual that a soldier called home, telling the family something had come up and that he would not able to make it home that day, but will contact them as soon as possible. The assurance that they are fine and not to worry was generally all they could give the dependents. Subsequent absences of weeks and even months with only brief contacts were not unusual. Working in Berlin was quite different, as we were restricted to our operational area, which could easily be monitored by a hostile force.

This situation created some close calls. Using the S-Bahn train in West Berlin in plain clothes one day, I accidentally missed getting off at the last stop before the train entered the Soviet sector and stopped at the next station. Looking at the people and noticing an East German border policeman, who had just finished clearing the Westbound train of East Germans, I knew I was in the East.

While my train was picking up East Berliners for the continuing ride I had to get off fast and get on the train on the opposite side. It was about to leave the East and continue to the West. As the doors were about to close I dashed across, dodging some people, and barely squeezed through the automatically closing door of the West bound metro train when it started moving. I was fortunate that the police had not noticed me jumping on, otherwise they could have stopped it. It was a close call and it could have been an embarrassing situation getting caught with papers that would have undoubtedly raised some serious questions about my true identity.

Only a few weeks before this near disaster, we had been alerted to be on the lookout for an American deserter, a young Captain. I believe his name was Swenson, who was stationed in West Berlin and had gone over to the East and stayed there, apparently because of his romantic involvement to an East Berliner girl. After the propaganda machine of the communists had praised his anti-capitalist actions and sufficiently benefited from his desertion, he must have become disgruntled with his communist hosts. Through the underground he had finally made contact with the West again expressing his desire to return.

Clearly, the Soviets were not about to let him leave again and made every effort to prevent him from doing so voluntarily. Our G-2 patrols were advised to be on the lookout for him while in the East and to bring him back, if possible. We were not really enthused about bringing a traitor back should we have the chance to do so. Also, previous bad experiences with attempts to smuggle people out of the Soviet Sector, made us very cautious.

There had been cases, where some East Berliners approached our patrols and pleaded, citing knowledge of classified information, to take them to West Berlin in the trunk of our sedans. As soon as a sedan was between the East and the West barrier at Checkpoint "Charlie" they reportedly had screamed and knocked on the trunk lid, yelling that they are being kidnapped and demanded to be set free. While our patrols were not subject to searches by anyone, with the road barriers in place, submachine guns pointing at you and the media's cameras miraculously on hand recording the incident, you don't have much of a choice but to release the fake escapee.

Certain staged incidents were trying to make the Allies look bad and look like gangsters. These were frequently staged accidents involving our patrols. Unexpectedly, a "stunt" motorcyclist would come from a side street and purposely collide with the American sedan on patrol. Not so surprisingly, the 'VoPo' , the ever-present "Volks-Polizei" (People's Police) usually tailing us, would show up to record this 'imperialist' crime. These accidents were always made to appear bad for us.

Such staged accidents had often incited an outraged mob to attack the military sedan. At one time they even turned the sedan over when the occupants refused to get out. Incidents like this in return prompted the Western Allies to retaliate against the "Soviet Military Mission" patrols in the West. Usually, within hours after Berlin Command had been notified by radio of such incident, they had located one of their vehicles to stop and detain them for some reason.

There rarely seemed to be any dull days in this occupied city. No wonder that even after almost 40 years, troops stationed in Berlin received the World War II Occupation Medal. Berlin was still considered "Occupied Territory" until, I believe 1989 when the wall came down.

Playing Games with the 'Other Side'

Stationed in an area of a very limited size, surrounded by a hostile force and barbed wire, heightens one's desire to get out every once in a while. To enjoy travel without restrictions, such vacation required thorough planning. Having a sensitive security clearance prohibited me now from driving my own car through the Soviet Zone. Instead, provisions had been made for such personnel to have a military policeman drive the car through the zone, while the family took a military duty train from West Berlin to West Germany through the zone.

Once arriving at the checkpoint in the West, we would then pick up the vehicle at the border crossing point, pay the MP a small gratuity and start the vacation. The American and the British Forces had their own trains, which were escorted by armed military police to preclude any Russian or East Germany soldier from entering or harassing the travelers. In a way they were still irritating us by pulling our trains off to the side to let other second-rate local trains pass.

While parked on the side-line we had to sit and wait with windows drawn shut, not permitted to take pictures of their outside, while being served a meal. We could never understand why we were caving in to the Soviets and German Communists' demands.

The Brits unquestionably had class. Their trains were never held up or stopped, because they kept their windows open, refused to close the shades, and permitted travelers to take pictures, regardless. To top it all, the British served their riders on the train mouthwatering meals during the two to three hour train ride. Evidently, the Soviets did not want to let their own people watch while a train was stopped. As a result, the train was hurriedly moved out of the area. Whenever I had a chance or choice, I preferred to ride with the British even though I had always had a bad taste in my mouth from previous personal experience with the British Army. I still recall the days, when I fled from Berlin to West Germany and we had to avoid them so that I would not be turned over to the Soviets.

Following one of my very rare official military functions in the British Sector, I stopped by their Officers Club. Somehow getting involved in a lively conversation concerning the Germans from both the East and West, I could not help but mention the fact that, had I not been vigilant at one time in my life and succeeded in hiding from the British, I would probably not be there. Instead, I would probably have ended up in a slave labor camp or worse.

When I told them that I was once a refugee, afraid to be caught by their Army, they could hardly believe my story, especially being an American officer. They quickly apologized for their parents and I accepted, under the group's laughter, realizing that most of them were still in Kindergarten during that period. After a few toasts we parted, still as friends and Allies.

Broadening one's horizon and getting to know the enemy better, was of course a constant effort. The Soviets having undoubtedly been our most dangerous enemy, I was very much interested in learning more about the Russian Army and their language. The fact that we had several team members, who came from the Eastern block, the so-called Warsaw Pact countries, those men naturally provided the detachment with an ability to understand the various languages, including Russian.

For my own benefit, I decided to learn Russian, fast and furious and through any means available. While picking up a few words and sentences here and there from the members of the detachment, I definitely wanted to know more. I envied Christine, who had learned Russian in school while she was growing up in East Germany, the *'Deutsche Demokratische Republic'* or DDR. The allies referred to the East Germany as the German Democratic Republic, although they were neither democratic nor a republic.

In my role as a university student I found myself comfortably blending in at cultural gatherings and social functions of an ethnic nature. One rather stimulating event occurred when servicing one of my dead letter drops in a park. I was surprised to retrieve a message written in Russian, obviously not legible to me. Doubting that some Russian agent used the same unusual spot by coincidence for information exchange, I suspected that maybe one of our detachment members used the drop to contact some asset from the other side.

Getting a translation from one team member familiar with Russian, we found that most of the text was coded and abbreviated but it revealed a location in Berlin. Finding the word Masurka, we assumed it to be the "Masurka" Restaurant in the French Sector, named after a polish dance. Intrigued by the message, we decided to visit this place soon to find out who would be frequenting this spot, if that was what the text referred to.

Assured that none of our detachment members wrote this message and since the message had no value to us, I returned it to its original location, minus fingerprints. Under surveillance for two days, out of sheer curiosity if anyone would pick it up, we were disappointed when nobody showed up. For security reasons, we decided not to use the drop any longer, considering it compromised.

Along with two team members I visited the "Masurka" restaurant early in the evening and found it quite interesting. Judging from the décor, the food, the drinks served and the type of customers, we found the majority of them to be Poles and Russians. The atmosphere, with the Balalaika music and Polka dancers, seemed very traditional Russian and Polish. The language commonly spoken there appeared to be Russian.

Berlin had always been an international mixing bowl and as such it was not unusual to find many people of Eastern origin in our city. At the same time one would suspect restaurants like this one to be a possible meeting place for sympathizers of the communist system, especially since the communist party was not illegal in West Berlin. Thanks to my Slavic team members we had some interesting conversations over a period of several hours. It was mix of German, Polish, Russian and Czech, but no English.

Having indulged in some good Russian Vodka, traditionally served from an open carafe and some excellent *'Borscht'* soup, we could not find anything unusual and left the restaurant cutting through a heavy layer of cigarette smoke. The absence of any American tobacco aroma made the long exposure to the strong Turkish and other foreign tobacco smells almost unbearable. For security reasons we did not use our assigned vehicles but rather relied on public transportation.

It was not too far to walk to the next U-Bahn station, the Berlin Subway near the Kurfürstendamm, Berlin's "5th Avenue". Having walked for about two blocks, only exchanging a few words in German, we had the feeling that we were being followed. It was difficult to make out the person or persons tailing us because of the darkness. As we got closer to the main avenue, lights became more prevailing, and stopping to look at store layouts, we noticed one individual trying to fade into a doorway, reemerging again when we continued our walk. It was clear to us that someone was shadowing us. We decided to find a larger department store, where we could possibly shake him in a crowd.

This was the usual technique used during daytime, but we had trouble finding anything appropriate this time at night, because German stores usually closed around six o'clock. We could have easily confronted him by playing cops, but decided against it and try to shake him at the subway station. Since we all had free passes for the train while he, hopefully, would have had to purchase a ticket, we quickly went down the steps to race to the other end, where we left again through the exit. He must have lost track of us, as we could no longer spot him anywhere.

We were wondering why he tailed us and what made him suspicious of us. I could not remember speaking anything other than German with my team members, who frequently conversed in their native tongues. The only cigarettes we smoked were the common German brands. Whatever the reason, it made us aware of the fact that this place could well be a meeting place for hostile elements. Otherwise no one would have showed any interest in us, unless it was someone from the German or Allied counterintelligence.

I must admit though, that even acting like a German and carrying proper genuine German IDs, some Germans have still recognized me as an American in the past. Habits I had picked up, like a 'military' walk, the way I held a cigarette or how I used my fork and knife, which is totally different from the Europeans, may have tended to give me away. I was repeatedly reminded that not only the language and clothing, but also the behavior could be a dead giveaway. To blend in appropriately, team members were instructed to purchase new fashionable German clothing and utilize a local barber shop for the customary haircut. Some members who preferred facial hair had no restrictions, as long as it looked European. Our looks did frequently raise some questions about our unit, when we had to parachute in Bavaria. We did look so unlike typical Airborne personnel.

Maintaining Proficiency

Aside from the vital role of our special assignment, we still had to maintain the basic requirements of an Airborne soldier. This required that we conduct a monthly parachute jump not only for efficiency but also for hazardous duty pay purposes. That, of course, could not be accomplished within the confines of the city. After my qualification as a commercial bus driver, I was usually taking a group of team members, dressed in plain fatigues without any special identification on their fatigues to Tempelhof Airfield, the site used for the Berlin Airlift.

Taking a military flight to Frankfurt Rhein-Main Airbase, we changed aircraft and donned our parachutes. Our final destination was a drop zone outside Bad Tölz, the home base of the 10th Special Forces Group in Bavaria, where we parachuted in either during daylight hours or sometimes also during nighttime. Because of security considerations only select SF personnel from the Group were aware of our mission and assignment.

Germans were always inquisitive and curious. Most people figured that we were some kind of "spooks" or intelligence people using their field for a practice jump. Generally, my jumps were not too exiting except for one night drop. I clearly remember one time jumping during a light drizzle. After exiting the C-46 aircraft, and nearing the ground, I spotted several cone-shaped piles of hay on the field. Although there was the temptation to pick one of those haystacks to land softly, I knew there were tent-like poles inside, which could make it a rather unpleasant landing. I made every effort to avoid them.

What I did not see though, was a barely visible wire fence surrounding the field. Landing on top and straddling it I was getting an unforgettable pulsating jolt from the 220-Volt electrical current running through lines, designed to keep the cows outside the field. Even though I struggled hard to get off the wire with my parachute draped over me, I still had to endure several minutes of very unpleasant electrification. Embarrassed, but still proud, I chose not to reveal my unusual experience to my fellow teammates. At least I now had a better understanding and justification of "hazardous duty" pay.

With members of the SF Group handling the collection of parachutes, we quietly vacated the area by trucking to Fürstenfeldbruck Airfield near Munich. Departing from there, we flew to Wiesbaden changing aircraft again for our final destination in Berlin. Returning home to our Detachment, I was greeted with a rather pleasant surprise, which made me forget my unusual principal landing procedure in Bavaria. The Detachment Commander handed me my special order, promoting me from First Lieutenant to the rank of Captain, a grade my position had called for. Together with my fellow Group Commanders and our staff officers we had a not so quiet promotion party at a little restaurant outside my district.

I still wonder what the other guests may have thought about our group and their wives speaking at least four different languages, including German with many different accents. But then again, Berlin was an international city, which could suggest that we were all from some international corporation, celebrating.

Even being locked in and somewhat isolated in Berlin, our schooling requirements demanded that we participate in concurrent training not available in Berlin. Several members of our unit and I still needed to upgrade our Winter training. Placed in charge of a group of twelve Master Sergeants and several other Sergeants, we received travel orders to proceed to Berchtesgaden, Bavaria, not too far from Innsbruck, Austria, to undergo Ski Training.

Aside from some occasional skiing in my earlier youth I had never seriously skied. Special Forces training required that we were more than just familiar with various types of mobility, which included skiing. Berchtesgaden, the site of previous winter Olympics, offered great ski slopes and outstanding facilities in a Winter wonderland.

Authorized to wear civilian clothing of duty, we intended to make the most of it for this ten-day temporary duty. Under the tutelage of German ski instructors, we worked those alpine slopes of the "Jenner" ski area for the entire time, with a brief weekend break and visit to Salzburg, Austria for R&R. Without a doubt, this strenuous exercise was unusual for us and our R&R therefore was richly deserved since we all suffered from severe muscle aches. Skiing on our own and without instructors during the last days, we decided to get up to the top of one of those mountain peaks with the ski lift and to execute some cross country for a while before skiing downhill.

Everything seemed to go fine, until our point man for reasons unknown, but probably having become disoriented, took a wrong turn and instead of going North, he moved south, which was quite easy to do. Unaware of our exact location, we heard some distant shots and were subsequently stopped by an Austrian Border Patrol asking for our purpose of being in Austria. Lacking appropriate civilian skiing jackets, we were all wearing US Army winter overalls, which naturally caused them to be suspicious especially seeing half a platoon of soldiers coming down the slopes from Germany towards Austria.

Since we did not carry any weapons and after explaining to them that we were just in training and learning how to ski, they clearly saw and agreed that we were not poachers. This area evidently was often used by illegal hunters going after mountain goats. After a few laughs they directed us to the nearest downhill slope back to the Jenner area.

Stopping at a little ski hut to warm up, we enjoyed the company and conversation with a group of Germans taking a break with *'Glühwein'*, a glass of hot red wine with cinnamon. During the cold season, this is a typical German and Austrian Winter drink taken to warm up cold bodies.

Skiing downhill on a well used slope turned out to be more difficult than I had anticipated. For overuse of the slope, the tracks were packed and in some areas iced over to the extent that slowing down was almost impossible. In many cases we had to actually squat down, dragging on our buttocks to slow down a little bit. It was definitely not the professional way of slowing down on skies. I remember being catapulted from one elevated bump to another for what seemed to be hours, until finally reaching the bottom almost crashing into the area, where skiers stacked up their skies. Never again did I experience such a case of tired, involuntarily jerking muscles. This downhill skiing was undoubtedly extreme.

Collecting Pieces of German History

Scrutinizing the Iron Curtain around Berlin and the Wall, which was constantly being improved by East German work crews through-out Berlin, we made concerted efforts to survey and identify possible weak points in their fortified fencing, the mine fields and the wall, the "Berliner Mauer". It all started on 13 August 1961, when the Russians and Communist East Germany began dividing their Sector from the Western Allied sectors by initially just placing rolls of barbed wire throughout the entire city of Berlin, prohibiting any free traffic.

Obviously this wire presented a serious obstacle for the Berliner families and friends. Suddenly separated by a guarded wire obstacle, even Berliners living just across the street were blocked access and forbidden the usual visits. Several East German soldiers of their *'Nationale Volks-Armee'* standing guard right at the wire, in despair dared to jump the concertina wire and flee to freedom in the Western sector. When the East German regime recognized they could not even trust their own troops, the government decided to go one step further. The wire obviously being inadequate took steps to remedy this problem.

Several weeks later, brigades of workers and bricklayers under supervision of armed guards from the "Volkspolizei" began erecting a wall. Large concrete blocks and bricks, which were previously designated for building houses, were brought in to build a wall about ten to twelve feet high. Both Army and Police units supervised the work on foot and from hastily constructed guard towers with machine guns covering the entire area. A few openings in the new barrier were tightly controlled and required special permits to pass through. Even though the wall was extremely high and topped with barbed wire, several people still managed to scale them and make it across to the West. Even several members of the East German border police, who had been drafted into service, still managed to flee across.

The communists, realizing they could not stop determined freedom-seeking citizens, gradually widened the control strips along and adjacent to the wall. They were eventually deploying minefields, specially trained dogs and walking patrols between the tall watchtowers. At first they left houses located along the wall facing the west standing. When people started to jump from second and third floors into large nets held by West Berliners to brake their fall, they blocked all windows by mortaring them in.

Some desperate people still continued escaping, sometimes using even old, still undiscovered cellar tunnels. Never-ending escape attempts finally prompted the regime to tear down and bulldoze all houses along the sector line. To clear the area for increased vision and additional mine fields they created a flattened strip nearly a city block wide.

Despite the improvements to their obstacles, thousands of East Berliners had still tried to escape. Many have paid with their lives, while thousands others have been sentenced to long terms of imprisonment for their attempts to flee their 'democratic republic'.

In the first eighteen months after erecting the wall, forty-seven people were killed trying to seek freedom. Little memorials on the Western side, erected along the wall on the spots were they were shot reminded Berliners and visitors of the sacrifices made by desperate people. Many refugees, who tried to swim across the dividing Teltow Canal were shot and killed by patrolling river patrols. Watched by West Berliners, they retrieved the bodies dragging them toward their shoreline. The names of most victims were never released. Some names however and pictures of them bleeding to death were published in West Berlin and will never be forgotten, like the one casualty, Peter Fechter.

He was an eighteen-year-old youth and construction worker from East Berlin who was shot by Communist border guards while trying to escape over the wall into West Berlin. Although seriously wounded and bleeding, lying next to the wall on the East German side. He was neither helped by the Communists, nor could he receive any aid from the West sector. After he had died, he was finally removed by those who had shot him. This murder, observed by Berliners from the West, resulted in numerous West Berlin protest demonstrations at the place where he was killed.

Because the people's desperation for attaining freedom was clearly stronger than the communist regime anticipated and sometimes still successful, the government decided to reinforce the border by removing the old wall and its blocks and replace it with a brand new wall.

This new structure consisted of large sections of solid concrete slabs with a smooth and rounded top in lieu of barbed wire, which prevented potential escapees from getting a firm hold, even with grappling hooks. It took heavy equipment and cranes this time to assemble the huge sections in place.

One evening, with the help of my friend Dieter, we proceeded in my private car to a street where one of my uncles lived on Bernauer Street. Out of sight from the East, we climbed up the wall on the West side and managed to remove a large forty-pound concrete block during relative darkness. As an old Berliner I wanted to make sure that I own a piece of the original wall in memory of those Berliners who had given their life to reach freedom.

Saving on cement building the initial wall, the communists had mixed concrete with crushed red bricks left over from the ruins of houses destroyed during the war to make cinder blocks. I now owned one of those blocks. Some creative person had the great idea to recover several blocks during the re-building process to use these blocks again. Cutting them up into small hand-sized slices and mounted on a piece of wood those marbleized pieces of the block and a piece of barbed wire made unique and memorable souvenirs for American personnel departing from Berlin for a reassignment.

West Berlin was a metropolitan area with a tremendous vitality and an ever-growing economy as seen in the expanding housing construction.

The expansion was only limited by the border. This area limitation forced the government to building taller structures and skyscrapers and improving road systems.

One day, visiting and driving through the district where I was born, I noticed the old street signs, which were originally made of steel with baked white enamel showing the name and the numbers of the houses in the block. Hearing that the old street signs were to be replaced with newer signs, I had the feeling that part of my past was going to be destroyed.

As an old Berliner, I couldn't let this happen. Removing a concrete block from the infamous wall for historical preservation was quite all right, but taking a street sign of the lamppost, even on an isolated path, could probably not be considered legitimate. But in my mind, those signs pending destruction by the city needed to be saved for posterity.

Imposing on my friend again, he contacted the proper department, which gave him the go ahead for a particular date, when they had planned to replace it. Just to be sure, with that approval and Dieter in his police uniform, he assisted me in removing the heavy street sign. It was going to have a prominent and proud place in the United States somewhere in my back yard. It was to be a constant reminder of the years of pain and suffering by a freedom loving people, my people in Berlin. The sign read '*Am Kleinen Wannsee*' (On the little Lake Wannsee) and showed my house number.

Reassuring to the West Berliners that their freedom was guaranteed by the Allies, was the daily rumble of American tanks driving down the streets early in the morning. There were fourteen M-41 tanks, each one displaying the name of one of the West Berlin districts. Sitting in our living room during breakfast and watching the tanks go by also made us, the military community, repeatedly aware of our mission. We all were proud to protect not only the civilian German population, but also our democracy and freedom against a cruel and totalitarian system.

We knew that we were the bulwark against the Soviets, firmly standing in their way and insuring that they could not take over West Berlin to make it part of their 'socialist camp'. Operating under often less than desirable conditions, for practically 24 hours a day, I accepted all challenges with pride, knowing that my job was one of the more important ones in the United States Army. Gratification for our accomplishments was always felt in our dealings with the Berliners, especially on the annual German-

American Day, held near the Command Headquarters in the American Housing Area.

During this open house day, Americans and Berliners celebrated their common friendship. My son Dieter will also remember this day well, when, at age four, during heavy traffic and a slick road, a car rear-ended our convertible. Pushed into a car in front of us, it threw him forward against the dashboard slightly opening the skin over his eyebrows, requiring minor surgery in the Army Hospital. As he has grown, so has his scar, reminding him of his time in Berlin each morning looking in the mirror. My own lower lip cut near the top of the chin also brings back memories of Berlin.

Nearing the End of My Tour in My Home Town to Return to the States

Looking back to my tour of duty in Berlin, I must admit that I have enjoyed serving at my place of birth during times when our presence in Germany's capital was more important than in any other part of the world. The fact that several of our presidents visited Berlin voicing their personal and our government's support, as well as the backing of the free world to the survival of the free bastion of democracy, lent credibility to our mission.

After three years in Germany, most of which I spent in Berlin in sensitive operations, our family was making plans again to return to the "Land of the Big PX". Not knowing if and when we would ever return to my hometown, I collected all the souvenirs which I felt important and said goodbye to some of my closest friends. Many friends presented me with some old German artifacts as farewell gifts, as they felt these were safer in the United States than in Berlin.

Among the many presents I received several books, one printed in 1859 and others printed during a time when photography was still barely known. All pictures were pen and ink drawings. One book in particular, a hall of pictures of the German history, was printed in 1890. With its size of 12x15 inches, the book weighs 12 pounds containing over 500 pictures and probably is worthy of display in the Library of Congress or the Smithsonian.

Considering the tremendous destruction of Berlin during World War II, it is a wonder that some of these valuable articles survived. Even an old WWI flag of an Imperial German Battleship, battered but still in excellent shape considering the age, is one of my treasures. It was not difficult at all for me to promise my friends that I would respect and protect the artifacts. Saying farewell is never easy, particularly knowing you may never see them again.

Having learned from my experiences of past moves, I made sure that certain valuable articles were separately wrapped and packaged to insure that the movers did not pilfer them, as some of my weapons had been before. Strangely enough, while most people were looking forward to leaving the old capital and returning to an area where you are free to move and travel, I felt like leaving home for good, never to return.

As expected, my orders came with an assignment to the John F. Kennedy Center for Special Warfare, Airborne, at Fort Bragg, NC, the Home of Special Forces. Prior to assuming my new job I had the pleasure of attending the Advanced Officers Career Course at Fort Benning, GA for about 19 weeks. The moving company was scheduled to pick up our household goods again for shipment to the good old USA.

Military life, I had found, has only one drawback. Unavoidable separations and the loss of comrades and friends made during short assignments. Berlin was not an exception, especially when you work with individuals your life may depend on should a serious conflict arise, requiring absolute trust and loyalty to your fellow soldiers and the unit.

After the furniture had been picked up for shipment to the US, we turned our car over to the MPs, to be driven through the Soviet Zone. This left the family to take the military duty train from Berlin to the West. After we picked up our car again in the West, we went to Heidelberg to visit my parents one last time before departing for the States by air from Frankfurt's Rhein-Main Airbase. Again it was my job to take the family car to Bremerhaven for shipment to Charlestown, SC. Both of our kids were also anxiously looking forward to going back to the US after their 'Germanization' period. Speaking fluent German having spent most of their life so far in Germany, they could hardly wait to return to the States and a home still unknown to all of us and another language they both would still have to learn.

Viet-Nam is on My Mind. Getting the Reserve Components Trained for SF Commitment

The commercial airline flight made our return much more comfortable, but it did present me with a snafu prior to leaving Germany. Customs officials refused to let me take a freshly smoked German salami style sausage, because regulations prohibited shipment of certain agricultural foodstuffs. I was not about to leave the sausage behind and argued with him, promising him that the salami will go to the States, regardless of his regulation.

He just smiled shaking his head insisting that he will prevail, while I was determined to take the prize with me, no matter what it takes. After a brief discussion with my wife and kids I made it clear that no one will deny me my delicacy. I was going to have it my way, no matter what.

I decided to sit down and, removing the sausage from my carry-on under the watchful eyes of the customs officials, sharing the sausage with my family I began to devour the over two pound weighing sausage. Finishing it in time to board the plane, I felt quite satisfied to have won the battle; admittedly, this unusual meal made me feel extremely full. So full indeed, that I was forced to loosen my belt and jacket before getting aboard the plane past the surprised customs people.

Needless to say, I did not eat another bite until after our arrival in New York, where my sister Ute and her husband, who lived near New York greeted and welcomed our family back home. We finally made it to Fort Bragg, NC. After I signed in to the United States Army John F. Kennedy Center for Special Warfare (USAJFKCENSPWAR), we were scheduled to eventually get government quarters on Post following my schooling at Fort Benning, GA. The arrival of our household goods had been postponed until then. I took two weeks of vacation to pick up my vehicle at Charleston, SC, and briefly visited our friends in Cleveland, Ohio. Not wanting to leave the family in limbo at Ft Bragg, we all decided to go to Ft Benning together for the duration of the nineteen-week course. Our family was fortunate to find a small furnished apartment near the main gate as temporary quarters during my schooling.

Attending the Infantry Officers Career Course was mandatory for all career-oriented officers. It introduced the individual to new developments in weapons and tactics in the military. Consideration was also given to new rules, regulations and certain responsibilities commensurate with attaining higher ranks and positions of increased importance. Those nineteen weeks of classroom work and field training passed relatively fast. Studies and homework did not leave much room for recreational activities except for those few occasional visits to the Officers Club. Christine was doing her best to care for the children. Ines was finally introduced to her first Kindergarten attendance.

During the Career Course we were also acquainted to the students from several other countries as I found going through the Ranger Course. This time we met several officers from Australia, Cambodia, Viet-Nam, the Philippines and Thailand. One young Thai officer, Nyom Sansana-koom, a Captain in the Royal Thai Kings Guard befriended me and we became pretty close friends.

During the course I acquainted him not only with the American culture but also with my country of birth, Germany, while he tried to familiarize me with some need-to-know facts about his proud country, his King and Queen. He seriously hoped that the end of the course would not terminate our friendship, but that it would somehow continue and hopefully we would get to know each other a lot better. Unknown to both of us, Kismet was to bring us back together again.

We all knew very well that the military career demands that their members often have to leave on assignments, which may take them away from the family for months and sometimes years. Aware of this, the GI makes sure that those days he does have available with his family are well spent at home.

Returning from the US Army Infantry Center and School, we all set-tled in our new quarters. Mandatory schooling behind me, I was ready to report for work at the Special Warfare Center. Actually I expected and had hoped for a troop assignment, but as usual, the need of the Army always comes first. This time it was my turn for a General Staff assignment again. Unlike my past experience in G-2, this time I was to assume the responsi-bilities of a Chief, Special Forces Reserve Components Branch under the Chief of Staff for Operations, G-3.

Training our four Army Reserve and the National Guard Special Forces Groups was the responsibility of the active duty units under the direction of the Reserve Components Branch. With only four senior NCOs assigned to my branch, I was responsible for conducting MOS testing of the Military Occupational Specialties (MOS) of all soldiers assigned to two Army Reserve Groups and two Army National Groups. Their A, B and C Detachments were dispersed over the entire United States including Alaska and Puerto Rico.

This was not exactly a desirable job for a happily married man with children, but I soon found out that any dedicated soldier would find it an extremely important and rewarding assignment. Requiring continuous travel over the weekends when the Reserves trained, meant more than just occasional absences from home and the kids. There were rarely going to be any weekends to spend with the family.

Generally leaving on Thursdays I visited the various Detachments from Friday through Sunday, returning on Monday. Leaving only two days a week, namely Tuesday and Wednesday at the home base, I was busy writing reports and preparing for training and testing of the next unit. Among the Reserve Groups were the 11th Special Forces Group with its headquarters on Staten Island, N.Y. and the 12th SF Group at Chicago. The Army National Guard Group headquarters of the 19th SF Group was located at Salt Lake City, Utah with the 20th SF Group in Birmingham, Alabama. Even though it appears that the groups have their separate districts, we found that Reserve Detachments from the 11th Group could be found throughout the United States. Similarly, we found several National Guard detachments throughout the States often with a National Guard and an Army Reserve SF Detachment co-located.

I personally found the overall organizational layout absurd, but apparently political considerations were overriding factors in their set-up. Common throughout all Special Forces Reserve Component Units (RC) at that time was the fact that the majority of their members were unqualified. They urgently needed the basic Special Forces Training that would qualify them for earning and the wearing of the green beret, the culmination of their training and a proud testimonial to the individual's accomplishment. It was the job of my branch to provide the appropriate training with the active duty units during their ANACDUTRA, the Annual Active Duty Training and subsequent Testing, which had to be conducted at their home station. Many commanders of RC units naturally did not like the idea of active duty troops testing them. They had good reason. During the first year we found that the units were not even close to being qualified for any possible call-up to active duty to operate in conjunction with Special Operations.

With the Viet-Nam deployment of SF Teams to our new war zone, it was extremely important that all RC units, our backbone, be competent enough to assume the roles of the active Army personnel. National Guard units did have some units, who were found better trained and equipped. Their States' governors made sure that their boys had what it takes, such as one Georgia Governor. He even used his SF personnel as body guards, giving them extra training in security and covert operations. But then there were those States, who were afraid that their boys might not meet the standards. They instead tried to make us Federal Troops feel quite unwelcome when we indicated that they did not meet the basic requirements. As a result they could not be considered qualified in their MOS unless additional training was provided.

I remember it well, when our testing team went to Camp Dawson in West Virginia and was welcomed West Virginia style, with open arms and all the amenities for the first days. After the first results of testing came in and I made the commanders aware of the status, they tried to blame poor testing methods on their failure. Furious, they actually banned my entire team with representatives from several active SF Groups from the State training camp.

We left temporarily, moving off the Base into a nearby motel. I contacted the Special Forces Warfare Center and subsequently the Chief, National Guard Bureau, a 3-star General, who advised me to immediately return to the Base, as the Commander of Camp Dawson had been federalized and as such was thereby under my jurisdiction. It turned out to be a great day, as we accepted the Commander's apology and I handed him a caricature sketch drawn by me while we were off the base. It depicted me sitting on a suitcase under the entrance to the Camp showing a sign stating "banned". It prompted all to laugh.

Of course, the test scores did not change, but the men of the unit were mature enough to appreciate our efforts and expressed their desire to be better trained. I promised them we would strive for an improvement of their training after our return to Ft. Bragg. Being not fully qualified, they could not wear their full "flash" of their unit on the beret. They could only wear the stripe, part of the flash, showing that they were in training to earn it.

For about two years, our teams crossed the US, training and testing Special Forces in practically all states. For that, we utilized either commercial or military air transport and occasionally, for short distances, our own vehicles. For foreign weapons training, unless they had their own supply, we usually brought those weapons if we traveled by military aircraft, or carried them in our private vehicles. In the latter case it sometimes became hazardous. Quite often we transported anywhere from ten to twenty different types of foreign weapons and the appropriate ammunition in our trunks from Ft. Bragg to New York or Chicago for example. Although our special orders permitted us under special instructions that we were "Authorized to carry bulk of foreign automatic weapons for military purposes", we had to be constantly alert to protect the weapons, whether off-loaded in the motel room or left in the car trunk.

One Chicago detachment however really surprised us. The team took us to the residence of one of their commanders, who owned a big piece of real estate with the fitting gated residential palace and total security. Impressed, our team was taken to a basement, where we found a complete firing range and a weapons arsenal that almost put ours to shame. They even bragged that their counterpart Reserve SF unit in Chicago did not have equipment like that, even though most of those members belonged to the vice squad of the Police Department. There always appeared to be some rivalry between the units, which I found rather healthy.

They also empathized and stressed that, regardless of their jobs, whether in law enforcement or as civilians, they were all getting along just fine. It was hard for me to believe this strange setup among the Reserve Components. Several of my NCOs assured me that I have not seen anything yet; and they were so right. I found a similar situation in Miami, Florida. I was wondering what some of these guys were doing in civilian life and if outside their military responsibilities, there could ever be a professional confrontation, such as mafia versus Cops. To their credit I must admit that some units were truly outstanding and their members so dedicated that I would have been proud to have them serve with me anywhere in the world.

Our travels and testing took us to many places, including the 38th Special Forces Detachment in Anchorage, Alaska. Alaskans, I found were a totally different breed. I honestly meant it, when I stated once that I would be proud to serve with any of them.

One Master Sergeant in Alaska, an Eskimo, was so enthused about our training and mission that later on he took me up on my statement. The Alaska trip was a lot more extensive, since we were training them for two whole weeks, following an invitation by the Governor, who also required that our training team took a special Winter driving test. Traveling to Alaska proved to be something quite challenging, because most of the Special Forces Teams consisted of Eskimos, who were practically working full time, deployed along the Bering Strait out of Nome, Alaska.

My special travel orders were also truly special. It was a one-of-a kind document as it specifically stated that the individual will travel by the shortest available route. Travel is authorized to be performed by rail, bus, ferry, skin boat, government auto, riverboat, dogsled, skidoo and foot, covering all eventualities.

Luckily for my team, we were able to at least fly from Pope Air Force Base, NC directly to Fort Richardson, Alaska, where we met with several National Guard advisors. Our mission was to provide special MOS training for the SF team for a two-week period. It seemed very strange initially that each evening before turning in, we had to park our staff car in a clearly marked parking lot. Unusual for us from the "lower 48", we were required to plug our car into a 110V power receptacle, otherwise we would not have been able to start the car the next morning. All vehicle engines had a heating blanket installed to keep the oil in a liquid state.

Completing the essential winter driving training for Alaska and getting into the habit of plugging in your vehicle to keep the engine warm was one thing. Actually driving on nearly unmarked roads after a heavy snowfall was something entirely different. One incident stands out in my mind. Several members of the local Detachment took me out to take a look at their training facility, when we met a huge moose standing in the middle of the road. Honking the horn did not seem to help, so I turned on the headlights and the flashing blue light on top of the patrol car I was driving. Still no reaction. Moving closer to the moose in the hopes that it would move out of the way, the animal must have gotten irritated and decided to just block the road and stare at us.

Figuring that we obviously were at a stalemate, I decided to just pass it after a lot of encouragement from my fellow passengers. The moose, convinced it was much bigger than the car, now slowly moved toward us instead of getting out of the way. To our amazement it even made contact with the vehicle and actually started pushing us sideways. Since we did not have that much traction, even with chains on our tires, we knew immediately, that we could not win this battle. The car's tires still spinning, trying to move forward, it nevertheless began moving sideways until it slid into a snow-covered ditch.

Stranded in snow, leaning sideways with the right side doors blocked, we finally succeeded in climbing out of the vehicle on the driver's side. Our moose still staring at us, watched us exit the car before it finally backed off. Turning around slowly, it trotted off without giving us another glance. It must have been a pathetic sight having a moose defeating five grown men and walking away without a scratch and not even leaving a dent in our car. Even though we had weapons in the trunk for range firing and the moose would have made a great meal for some needy people, I felt that this incident was meant to be, call it 'Kismet'.

After I had called for help from the dispatcher and explaining our mishap, we were finally pulled back on the road and continued our trip with our eyes scanning the road ahead looking for another moose. I had the feeling my Alaskan friends were grinning behind me.

Even though our stay in Alaska was brief but crammed with training, we all made a lot of friends during our breaks and regretted leaving so soon. Our training and experiences benefited all of us, instructors and trainees alike. There was so much more our team could have learned from the "natives". An older Master Sergeant, who assumed that I was going to be leaving for Viet-Nam pretty soon asked me straight out, would I consider giving him a job in a unit in Viet-Nam, no matter where it is. Having observed his expert handling of equipment, I was convinced that he would be a great asset in his field of communication and I stated that I would, without hesitation.

In the back of mind, I was sure that he just wanted to impress me and the others, but would never make it to Viet-Nam. I had never heard of an Eskimo, who would voluntarily choose to fight in the jungle and expose himself to extreme heat.

During our last weekend, after we had completed our instructions and testing, we all got together at one of the renowned high-rise restaurants in Anchorage, the 'Captain Cook' for a farewell dinner and drinks. The top floor eating place, gave us a fantastic view of Anchorage. This evening was going to be another unique happening. Having spent several hours of intense conversation, we all admired the beautiful sunset.

Waiting and expecting the sun to disappear overt the horizon, we noticed after hours, that the sun never really set and disappeared but just kept sliding from the left to the right window, after which seemed to be rising again. After several hours of watching it never really turned dark. Nothing unusual for the locals, but it was quite impressive for us North Carolinians.

Stopping by at another watering hole close to the base, the 'Idle-hour Supper Club' for a 'nite cap' the next evening, I met an Ex-German compatriot working behind the bar. She had made Alaska her home and after I was making compliments about the beautiful Huskies, who had just completed their annual races, she asked me if I would like to have one. Telling her that I certainly would, she promised me that I would have one to take home to North Carolina for my kids. After a brief absence she returned with a pocket radio, placing it next to me, advising me to listen to the radio announcer coming up shortly.

Indeed, after about 5 minutes and some music a broadcaster came on saying that a young captain from the Green Berets stationed in North Carolina was so impressed by the huskies that he was looking for a young husky to take back home. Anyone interested was asked to please call the Club if one is available for free. With the room full of people listening in, the telephone rang a couple times and finally someone was happy and willing to give me a puppy.

A tall Alaskan stopped by shortly thereafter and asked me to pick a dog out of a litter. I selected the cutest looking pup and armed with an old cage I was given, I made the necessary arrangements to fly him back to the lower 48's. I knew that my kids were going to be ecstatic.

Returning to Ft. Bragg, I was wondering what my family was going to say about the new family member, and if they were ready to accept him. And they did. Throwing around a few suggestions, we all agreed to call him "mukluk" named after the Eskimo footwear. I was hoping that he would get along with our "guard dog" 'Henry', a Road Island Rooster we bought as a tiny chicken for Easter. This rooster was the best guardian our back yard ever had. Henry would never let any stranger enter the yard without dropping his wings and attacking the individual, should the individual not heed his obvious posture of a fighter.

Henry had his own house, of course, which was big enough to take in a big shepherd dog. As a matter of fact, I even crawled inside at one time to put the final interior touches on when I built it. Mukluk on the other hand, we felt, deserved a structure reminding him of Alaska. I immediately set out to build him a white igloo out of concrete and placed it in the shade so that he could tolerate the upcoming hot climate better. Since he was still a small pup, I hoped that he would get acclimatized, something I had not even thought about when I brought him down from the cold North.

Well, it did not take him too long to adjust to his new surroundings and our other family pet. Both of them quickly became good friends and shared the food, except Henry would not share his occasional sip of rum. He loved it, just as he liked eating rubber bands, after he had his occasional ration of rum by then probably thinking they were worms. Even though a lot of people found Mukluk to look very much like a German Shepherd dog, except for his blue eyes, he displayed behavior which in my opinion clearly showed his husky genes.

Right after I had built him the igloo, he started digging a deep tunnel underneath the hut in an apparent attempt to find a cooler spot inside the ground. This really did not make much sense to me, because I figured in Alaska he would dig a hole to keep himself warmer underground rather than colder.

Our family always got a surprise look on people's faces visiting, when they saw my big husky walking around in our fenced-in yard. The warning sign on the gate, however, showed a hand painted picture warning not of a dog but of a vicious Rhode Island rooster. My son Dieter always enjoyed teasing his Henry, so that he would chase him. To Dieter's surprise he would often catch up with him running and frequently draw blood pecking on his leg. The rooster was neat, to say the least.

When my coordination and training duties took me to about twenty Reserve Detachments along the Atlantic coast locations, I often used an aircraft from the Special Warfare Center's special fleet of U-10 aircrafts. They were single engine helio-courier aircrafts with a short take-off and landing capability. They were of a special design with strange looking bat wings on the wingtips and a powerful engine with four large propeller blades. The absence of the normal large identification number except for a very small ID number and the small US Army stenciled on the rudder made it suspiciously covert looking.

Its special features even allowed it to land sideways and on several occasions we touched down on baseball fields without any problem. My pilot, a rather large-built, Special Forces warrant officer truly enjoyed those flights to small community airfields, which were located close to our Detachment's location we needed to visit.

Our plane never failed to create special interest and usually attracted a small crowd looking it over while we were refueling. Those flights also gave me the rare opportunity to fly this aircraft for hours at times. I was privileged to have a pilot who enjoyed teaching me the rudimental facets of the aircraft and of flight itself. Once familiar with its basic operation, I had the chance to fly the U-10 using either instruments or flying visual by following the interstate highways. Flights were mostly along the eastern Atlantic states, generally following I-95 between Miami and Westchester County, N.Y.

It was on one of these trips during winter, flying from Ft. Bragg to a

Detachment in Westchester County, when we developed a problem of icing up of the rudders making navigation difficult. My pilot however had some ideas of correcting this problem. He decided to get off our normal flight pattern by flying lower over the New York city skyline to take advantage of the warmer air over the city. It seemed to work as it eliminated the problem, after which we readjusted our flight route and proceeded to Westchester. County. Radioing in for landing clearance we found out that that airport was not in operation due to poor weather conditions.

I was disappointed to hear that, because I had previously called my sister Ute, who lived in Westchester County and told her to meet us at the airfield. At the same time we also informed the SF Detachment located there and advised them of our approximate time of arrival. My pilot got back on the radio and informed the tower that we have a problem and need to land, regardless of the runway condition. When the tower requested more information on the type of aircraft, its ID and other data, which we provided, they stated they could not accept it, because our aircraft was not registered anywhere.

The pilot got quite irritated and insisted that this was a military aircraft and that we are going to land at the airfield according to our flight plan and that we will also require refueling. There was no further discussion.

We found the airfield and noted that the runway was not cleared of snow, but my pilot stated that this had never been a problem before and that we will hopefully be able to get some fuel. Although the previous conversation with an air traffic controller before gave us the impression that the airfield was closed to all traffic, we were surprised to find several vehicles moving and driving near the runway and the small control tower.

We touched down without any problem and rolled towards the parking ramp and the tower, when we suddenly noticed several vehicles coming toward our aircraft with red and blue lights flashing. It became clear to us that our insistence on landing must have inadvertently attracted state, federal and local police departments. Before we could even deplane, we were surrounded as if we had landed in some foreign country and were about to be placed under arrest. When one law enforcement officer got next to the fuselage he spotted the automatic weapons inside the aircraft.

Apparently he was surprised and unsure of our intentions and made an attempt to unholster his revolver, making us wonder what we had run into. After I had gotten out of the aircraft, it took me a few minutes to explain to him and several other law enforcement officers who we were. Showing them our military orders, the young trooper who had first approached us was told by a senior member to holster his gun and relax. By that time two vehicles from the Special Forces drove up and the matter was quickly cleared up.

The civilian officials still had questions about the strange looking camouflaged aircraft without the regular FAA identification numbers. The pilot explained that the equipment was strictly military, designed for special operations and therefore not registered except with the Department of Defense and the military, which their tower failed to check out. They quickly apologized for the misunderstanding, with the SF Reserve guys standing nearby, grinning from ear to ear about the bumbling by some inefficient county official, who had believed to have stumbled upon some high-class illegal smuggling operation.

My sister and her husband were watching this whole thing from the distance. They were surprised of course and wondering what her dear brother had gotten into this time. While I stayed with them overnight, the rest my team stayed at the Reserve Center. It took quite some time to explain the entire story and my work to the family. Special Forces rarely talk about their work and accomplishments. Knowing to be a well-trained elite force, we prefer to be known as the "quiet Professionals".

During my assignment dealing with the Reserve Components, I experienced many such similar incidents. Those stories are usually conversation pieces and proper material for many get-togethers. They are often bragged about when fellow veterans remembering the "good old days" from the world wars to more recent conflicts.

Attending numerous SF conferences, participating in two week annual training exercises and MOS testing, it became quite clear that Special Forces personnel needed a lot more time to become fully qualified. Not only in their basic fields, but also be cross-trained in other specialties to include another language or two. The standard weekend per month and two week active duty training per year could never adequately qualify them to reach the same standard which you expect and find in active duty personnel.

Completing a study about the reserve components I submitted a recommendation to the Commander of the JFK Center for Special Warfare, which also suggested the call-up of all Reserve Component Special Forces personnel. These men could then be thoroughly trained by active duty personnel during a proposed six-month period.

Once implemented, however, it was determined that it was a hardship for many "weekend warriors". Many of them faced radical pay cuts for this period of active duty just to get qualified, become a full-fledged member of the Special Forces and subsequently be authorized to wear the Green Beret. Unaware of the sometimes significant differences between their civilian income and the military pay, I did get some negative feedback from some personnel. It was my conviction, that if you really wanted to be a member of the elite, you have to make considerable sacrifices. Men, truly feeling the calling to become a 'quiet professional' never hesitate to take that step.

Chapter VI

My First Taste of the Orient

A Wish Fulfilled

Although I had returned from Europe only about two years ago, I was often asked by Reserve Component SF grunts what Viet-Nam was like. I certainly wished that I had been there already to answer their questions, but all I could tell them was that my time to serve there had not come yet.

On many evenings, stopping by the SF Branch Officers Club, I enviously listened to those, who had already been in Viet-Nam, telling war stories and relating their unique experiences. Several of my friends had been in "Nam" for several years as advisors already, even before the US officially began committing regular troops. I could not understand why I had not already been picked for an Asian tour. I felt left out of a rewarding career opportunity.

Finally, not wanting to wait in limbo I called the Department of the Army to find out what their plans were concerning my future personal career. I was told that I was in for a three year tour stateside before I was slated for another overseas tour, unless I volunteered. Even then, considering all other SF personnel volunteering for Viet-Nam, it would take quite a while before I was given a command assignment overseas.

But the Personnel Assignment Officer strongly recommended that I take up Russian language training, since my records indicated the knowledge of Russian to be advisable for my next assignment. For an accompanied tour it was also recommended that my wife brush up on her Russian. This statement really baffled me and left me at a loss since he could not explain any further. Usually officers could submit their assignment "wish list" of five choices, with number five being the least desirable. Past experiences revealed that most of us received the least desirable and rarely the one tour we preferred most. I considered several options, but eventually decided not to make a choice and let DA make the assignment, no matter where it would take me.

I was intrigued by the Personnel Officer's suggestion. I also felt another language might be beneficial in the long run. Considering my Reserve Component responsibilities I figured that I could make some time available after duty hours. I immediately enrolled in a language course with the United States Armed Forces Institute, USAFI, helped by my wife, Christine, who had Russian in school before. I suddenly realized that I should have had that training before I was assigned to Berlin. Chances were obviously very good for another repeat assignment with Detachment "A" in the near future.

As usual, you had to be prepared and expect the unexpected. Out of the blue sky it came in the form of new orders from the Department of the Army. Probably as a result of my inquiry I received my orders, as a gift on my birthday, the 29th April 1967. The orders assigned me to the 5th Special Forces Group (Airborne), with the US Army Viet-Nam. Besides some specifics about immunization, it only stipulated that travel be conducted in Khaki uniform with shorts and that a dress uniform was definitely not required.

With an arrival date in Viet-Nam of 17 June 1967, I knew time was short to make the necessary preparation for the family to be on their own for about a year. Not being assigned and stationed in Fort Bragg for a whole year, we had to leave the Government Quarters and I had to find them a home off post as no family could live on post unaccompanied. Fortunately, we had made many friends from previous Airborne assignments, who now were also stationed at Bragg, the Home of the Airborne or lived off-Post nearby. Some of them had even been with us in Berlin. Christine did not have to worry about being completely left alone to fend for herself and the children.

We knew that the military would always support the military families.

Fayetteville, North Carolina was a small "military" town, adjacent to the post, which was practically an extension of Fort Bragg. A great number of military families, active duty and retired, lived in surrounding areas, where they always supported each other should a member leave for an

unaccompanied temporary tour of assignment. We were lucky to be able
to purchase a house from another military family the following month. We
still had enough time prior to my departure to make all necessary arrangements to move our furniture, as we had done so many times before. To our
surprise we had an unexpected surprise visit before our move off-Post,
which turned into quite a memorable farewell party.

One morning, upon entering the office, I noticed someone's unusual
back of a uniform, not too common in the States, but still somewhat familiar to me. When I got closer and the soldier turned to face me, I was
surprised to find my Thai friend Nyom standing in front of me, with a big
smile on his face. He was telling me that he is on temporary duty at Fort
Bragg to attend another class, only this time in Unconventional Warfare.
Talking to my office staff prior to my arrival, he had already been informed
by them, that I was scheduled to go to Viet-Nam the following month.

He insisted that we have a farewell party before I had to leave for
overseas. Of course he would also bring some other fellow officers from
Thailand, if I did not mind, to give me a proper sendoff. Christine knew
that I liked parties, but she was always worried that she would not be able
to do enough to please the guests. I tried to convince her, that friends of
mine never worry about the little stuff and having some foreign officers
over is no big deal. Captain Nyom Sansanakoom was a little party animal
himself and when he showed up the following weekend, he came with an
entourage of four other Asian officers, most of them from Thailand.

Prepared to show us some of their cuisine, they brought several bags
of oriental food, which they all decided they would prepare themselves,
with Christine only showing them where the pots and pans were. To be
an instrumental part of the affair, I produced the beverages, a unique mix
of American and European drinks. It was one outstanding and impressive
party and Nyom continuously expressed his admiration and gratitude to
us for being such great hosts. The longer the party lasted, the more often
our guests repeatedly toasted to the United States to a point where I almost
expected them to sing our National Anthem at any moment. Nyom told
me confidentially, that his officer friends had been in the States for several months already. However, this was the first time they could actually
let their hair down, without having to be afraid that they could ruin their
country's reputation in America.

It was quite late, more like in the early morning, when we decided to
call it quits. Besides, I had run out of film and a few of them, exhausted,

started to fall asleep. We did take a lot of snapshots, but I had to promise them that I would never show anybody those pictures as they might reflect badly upon their country. Feeling extremely well and being proud of their friendship, I decided to make Nyom an "honorary citizen of Berlin" by presenting him with a lapel flag from Berlin, after which he had to repeat President Kennedy's famous statement "Ich bin ein Berliner". Thailand, previously called Siam, means "Land of the Free" and Thai people could relate well to Berlin, as their freedom was also being protected and maintained by the United States.

In parting, rather then telling them goodbye or farewell, we settled on "*Auf Wiedersehen*" the German for "until we see each other again", which I sincerely hoped for and which actually was going to become true.

Departing for Viet-Nam

The family was very glad when we were finally settled in our new home. After I had done some essential work to make them feel safe and secure, I felt ready to leave. Being surrounded by good friends has always been my priority. With varying assignments, you could never tell when you had to leave abruptly without much preparation. It gave me a good feeling leaving the dependents in the hands of friends and good neighbors. We all knew that the assignment would only be of a short duration. Never-the-less it was a fact that no one ever knew whether you would survive or not. Even though the individual rarely thinks about the worst that could happen, we are often made aware of these unpleasant facts of life when you hear about another friend and neighbor having been killed in action or been severely wounded.

Kids are usually the ones, who will ask why the dad has to go, why not somebody else. They might also question you, whether you really loved them or not. If you really did, then why did you want to leave them. As small as they were, this was awfully hard to explain or even justify your decision. Saying goodbye was always the hardest thing to do. Hoping that they were going to be alright, one usually puts the family in the back of one's mind. Concentrating instead on the job at hand and making the right decisions is crucial in order to survive and return home sound and safe.

After a tearful farewell, I departed Fort Bragg and after a short refueling stop at Travis Air Force Base in California, our plane loaded with troops finally landed at Camp Long Binh near Saigon, Viet-Nam's Capitol for in-processing through the 90th Replacement Battalion. On top of the nearly unbearable heat, I found myself in a situation, where confusion seemed to be the motto of the day.

Hundreds of troops were milling around trying to figure out what to do next and where to go from here, while some processing personnel were attempting to bring order into the chaos. It was easy to identify those who had just arrived in country from those who were leaving Viet-Nam . They were the ones with the bad smell and happy grin on their face, in contrast to those just arriving for the first time, wearing clean uniforms and an expression on their face that seemed to say "what am I doing here and where am I going to now". The newly arrived officers were told to report to one specific desk for further processing and while lining up, I noticed that I was the only one wearing the Green Beret.

When a young Sergeant checked my orders, he compared my data with a list he had and informed me, that my orders had been changed and that I would be picked up by a representative of the 1st Infantry Division. I could not believe what I heard. This was not what I had expected and I pointed out to him that there must have been a mistake. My orders specifically showed my assignment to the 5th Special Forces Group located at Da Nang. This young trooper only apologized, shaking his head. As did I.

There was no way, I was going to be diverted if I could help it. It was my intention to see someone in authority, who could clear up this misunderstanding and get me out of this place and on my way. Grabbing my orders from the Sergeant, I picked up my duffel bag and made my way out of the stench filled room to the outside of the building for some fresher air and to find a Personnel Officer.

The sky was filled with aircraft continuously coming in while others were leaving at nearly the same intervals. Setting down my bag to rethink the situation, I spotted a HU-1A helicopter, which had just landed discharging a 1st Lieutenant with a Green Beret. He was approaching the building, accompanied by the co-pilot helping him to carry some of his gear. Calling over to the Lieutenant, who was clearly leaving the country, I asked him if he was from the 5th SF Group. He nodded and laughed, saying that I was lucky, because there was my ride, waiting.

Naturally he assumed that I was assigned to the 5th Group. But when I told him that some Personnel Sergeant informed me that my orders had been changed to another "straight leg" Infantry Division he became upset. He told me that he had been the Adjutant of the 5th and that they had frequently noted before that several SF troopers, Officers and NCOs had arbitrarily been diverted from Special Forces and assigned to regular units. This left the SF units seriously under strength and short of qualified of personnel. Someone at the US Army Headquarters in Viet-Nam, who disliked Special Forces apparently reassigned those highly qualified people, creating havoc among our SF units. Since I had my orders assigning me to the 5th Group, he advised me to get on his chopper and head straight to my new unit.

Both the co-pilot and he shook my hand, welcoming me to Viet Nam and the 5th Special Forces Group. Before anyone else could hold us up, the co-pilot dropped the Lieutenant's bag and picked up mine. Without looking back, we strutted fast pace towards the helicopter, which immediately lifted off, since the rotors had still been running. Expressing my appreciation for the ride, he just nodded his head and gave me the "thumb up" sign, while I heaved a big sigh of relief.

Departing the processing station and the airfield lifted a huge burden off my mind, because I could not have imagined being assigned to a regular unit. Especially not after having been trained and qualified for unconventional warfare. Not processing in properly did not bother me at all, because I had my orders to report to the Group and I was going to do just that. In my mind, I rationalized that somebody had made an error trying to change my assignment. It was my obligation, no, my duty to correct an obvious mistake.

With the chopper doors wide open and a door gunner scanning the ground and horizon, I took in the beautiful view of palm trees and clouds reflecting in the water of glistening rice paddies. It took over an hour before we touched down at the Headquarters in Nha Trang, I Corps, where I was properly processed in. The Group Commander welcomed me officially and thanked me for disregarding the blatant attempt by the Replacement Battalion personnel and the Commander, US Army Viet-Nam to defy the orders from Department of the Army and our Special Warfare Center. As I found out later, there were several staff officers at Saigon, who did not look favorably at the "Sneaky Petes". In most cases it was petty jealousy. Even though the Group had stressed to Fort Bragg repeatedly to send more SF qualified personnel, which they said they had complied with, some personnel still got diverted for the benefit of Regular Army units. I hinted to him, that maybe placing a representative of the Group at the Replacement Battalion to immediately pick up SF people, might help solve the problem.

After a thorough briefing and overnight stay, I was assigned to C Company at Da-Nang. Located in I Corps, it was generally controlled by the Marine Corps, except for those operational areas run by Special Forces, who had their own jurisdiction under the 5th Group.

The flight from Group HQ to Da-Nang took about two hours, across fascinating territory from breathtaking mountains to rice paddies and coastal areas with small islands with high mountain peaks jutting out of the water. Coming in to the C-Team Headquarters, a mountaintop nearby with a beautiful huge white Buddha greeted us. It was visible for miles around showing an approximately 20 feet high swastika, the symbol of Buddhism. This was my first time I found a swastika depicting Buddhism anywhere, but it was not to be the last time. We had learned a little bit about Buddhism, but no specific mention was ever made of its religious symbols. I remember Ute's husband was a member of the Jains, a Hindu sect, who uses the swastika in religious ceremonies.

Camp Commander with an A-Detachment

Amazed at the sight of the big gleaming white Buddha, who seemed to be smiling at me, I got off the helicopter and was greeted by Colonel Dan Schungel. Immediately taken to a briefing room for another more detailed briefing, I was presented with an up-date of present operations of the Company and specifically my Detachment A-105 at Kham Duc. He was very specific in his expectations of me as the Commander of the Detachment.

This Detachment was obviously critically under strength by having only half the normal 12-man team. The last commander who had been kept longer than required, had just left the day before my arrival. LTC Schungel immediately got on the single sideband radio and informed the Executive Officer, Lt Harrington of my pending arrival at the Camp. Personnel shortages in many Special Forces camps were undoubtedly the result of diversions, which I almost became a victim of, too, after my arrival in the country. The Commander assured me, that my very competent XO would brief me thoroughly as soon as I got to Kham Duc, to which he accompanied me for the short 45-minute flight.

As it was explained to me at the briefing, my camp was located in a very mountainous area, inaccessible by road, but easily accessible by air. Outside the camp and next to the village of Kham Duc, the camp had its own airstrip with a large runway, long enough to permit C-130s, the four engine turboprop aircrafts to land and take-off. Coming in for a landing, I noticed the long runway with several smaller planes lined up alongside. It almost looked like a regular county airport stateside. Adjacent to the runway was a large, heavily fortified camp, flying the Viet-Namese flag while across the strip on the other side I clearly saw the little village of Kham Duc. The village had approximately sixty little buildings and huts, for a population of about three hundred natives.

The mountain rising at the beginning of the landing strip, was cut low and leveled at one time to permit a clear approach from the North onto the camp's airstrip. All the other sides were lined with high peak mountains, providing natural walls, but militarily presenting a drawback. An occupation of those hill tops by an enemy would provide clear fire into the camp, the village below, and the approximately six thousand feet long concrete runway. Only about three hundred meters to the East of the camp was a gradual drop off, revealing a small river nearly six to ten meters (approx. 30') wide below the camp's plateau.

During our descent LTC Schungel pointed out a few weaknesses in the defense of the camp and offered some suggestions for the improvement. During the short stay and before returning to his HQ, he introduced me to three Air Force Majors in the camp, who were FACs (Forward Air Controllers), pilots of the O-1 Bird Dogs. These single engine aircrafts and several OV-10s were stationed at Kham Duc to support SF and Air Force operations along the border of Cambodia and nearby Laos. A few Air Force NCOs were part of their staff responsible for maintaining the aircrafts and the ammunition their planes required. Mostly rockets with either high explosives or white phosphorus contents were used either to intercept or mark targets during their recon flights.

With a laugh, joined in by the pilots, he reminded me never to be intimidated and that, no matter what their grade, the ranking Army Infantry Officer on the ground is traditionally always in command, referring to me. It goes without saying he further stated that, as such, I was also responsible to house and feed them and to look out for their welfare.

In the air, however, that would be a different story, but he felt sure, that we would provide him with a great Army-Air Force team. Before departing, he took me over to the hutch, where our Viet-Namese counterpart, the Viet-Namese Special Forces (LLDB) detachment was housed. Some of our guys, who had more experience with their counterparts also referred to them as "Lousy Little Dirty Bastards".

Colonel Schungel left me with a serious warning. All these guys were mostly politically selected for their assignments and as such, unlike our own SF personnel, could not be completely trusted. The LLDB was officially in charge of the Civilian Irregular Defense Group (CIDG) personnel, which were made up of Viet-Namese and Montagnard soldiers. In reality, the US Special Forces team was actually in command, providing operational support, equipment and pay. Having met all my team members, I was sure that I could handle any unusual situation. They were well trained and had many years of experience in Special Forces, the majority even more than I had. They could be expected to take on various responsibilities commensurate with those normally expected from officers.

While NCOs had the choice of making special operations their life-long career, officers had to be more versatile and were more often likely to be given other duty assignments to round off their capabilities. The Army's requirements mandated flexibility, achieved generally by exposing officers to different training and various assignments. Some Army brass, not familiar with the mission of Special Forces, felt that a Captain commanding twelve men would have no more responsibility than a Sergeant being a squad leader.

My Executive Officer, Lt. Harrington, proved to be an outstanding leader, quick to respond, a thinker and problem solver. He proved unusually inventive, when it came to makeshift improvements in our defensive capabilities. Serious increases in enemy activity in our area of operation and within I Corps, made it necessary for us to anticipate the worst scenario. Located in the most Northern Corps of South Vietnam, without any allied forces nearby, we realized that we were practically on our own without any nearby support or quick reaction force to assist our camp in case of a North Viet-Namese attack.

A surprise courtesy visit by a Marine Corps General made that quite clear, when he stated that, should we ever get attacked, his troops would be too vulnerable to fly in without adequate air support. We were aware of the fact that the Marines did not like our indigenous troops. He made it clear to me that the Marines would not sacrifice any of their men for a Viet-Namese, especially the Montagnards. We in turn learned that our indigenous people proved to be outstanding loyal soldiers, who were willing to give their lives for us. We now realized for certain, that we could not rely on any support from the General.

It gave us the initiative and drive to get prepared for any eventuality. I found myself quite overwhelmed with all the various projects. I was extremely confident that our team consisting of the Senior NCO and Operations Sergeant, a Weapons Sergeant, Communications Sergeant, Team Medic and Intelligence Sergeant, all of them cross trained, could be relied on to do their assigned job without constant supervision. This left Lt. Harrington and me to deal with all problems involving the Viet-Namese troops, their families and the population of the village of Kham Duc. "Winning the hearts and the minds of the people" required us to provide Civic Action support to improve their life and win their trust and confidence.

Primitive Life in the Jungle. Improving the Art of Scrounging

My "baptism" as the new "camp" commander was not too far off. My team mates warned me about my Viet-Namese counterpart, Dai Uy (Cpt) Lich right after my arrival. He was as sly as a fox and was known for pulling the wool over the eyes of his American equals. Looking forward to some moves by him and his staff I got some feedback from an unexpected source. It came from my interpreter, whose job it was to translate my conversations with the Viet-Namese Captain and his staff.

This poor chap, going by the name Phan-Thanh-Long, was in a bind. Because some of the Viet-Namese officers spoke English he could not dare to tell me anything negative concerning the VNSF in their presence. Any attempt on his part to tell me the truth or warn me, would be overheard by those guys and get him into trouble. Fortunately, he found out that I was from Germany after which he confided in me when we had a chance to be alone. To my total surprise he told me in German that he had learned my language working for the German Beneficial Organization *"Malteser Hilfsdienst"*.

Long was eager to talk to me about some of the problems which I might be confronted with in dealing with the Viet-Namese Commander. I promised him that I would sit down with him soon so we could exchange our ideas, which I could tell made him visibly happy. Considering a possible set-up I decided to talk to my Intelligence Sergeant and Lt Harrington first before getting into something I would later regret.

Caution was indispensable, especially since I didn't know my indigenous troops at all and remembering LTC Schungel's advice and warnings when dealing with my counterparts. Briefed by my XO about the village, their problems and needs, I figured Civic Action, being one of our missions, should be tackled sooner rather than later.

Our vehicles were in a less than good shape and in many cases haphazardly fixed and held together by wire and Duct tape. Without any trafficable roads and just a few trails around the village and camp, trucks were hardly used except for transporting supplies and equipment from the airfield, off-loading aircraft, to the camp covering only about 500 yards.

The next morning I decided to take a walk from the camp into the Kham Duc village "coffee shop', the village meeting place, which I could quickly reach crossing the runway and walking for about another three minutes. Assured by my team that the area is relatively safe and secure, I took my Intelligence Sergeant with me, making sure though, that our route was covered by weapons from the tower. Even though the area had been relatively quiet, except for some occasional sniper fire, one never knew when an enemy attack could happen. The few SF camps along the Laotian border to our North had already been either overrun or were being attacked.

The "café" was a rather primitive small shack with only three little tables, but the coffee not only looked like the typical French brew I had in Paris before, but it was also served in a large glass and tasted like the real thing. It surprised me since they did not seem to have any store in the village, which could provide them with big city food items.

I found out later on, that my Viet-Namese "mess" personnel were permitted to fly on our military aircraft to either Da Nang or Nha Trang. Both destinations were two large coastal cities, in which we had the Special Forces Company and Group Headquarters stationed. On their trip they were accompanied by one of the team members, when they needed to pick up certain supplies and purchase whatever food supplies the SF team needed. A Viet-Namese and the Chinese Nung cook in turn bought whatever was needed which also included items for the village. A flight to the city on such scrounging missions usually gave the Green Berets a chance to meet and stay with friends overnight, while the cook visited one of his several wives.

This was the first time in my Army life, where an Army mess hall was not available and the food consisted strictly of native dishes with our meals consumed in our "Team House". Hunger usually lets you forget what kind of food is offered, as long it tastes good. We had to admit that the meals were quite good. Rarely did anybody ever question what we were actually eating. The question of the food possibly being poisoned, a definite possibility, never entered our mind.

Our Air Force guests in contrast were not too fond of eating the native food on a daily basis. That proved to be of surprisingly great benefit for the team. Longing for a change in cuisine they offered to fly in some steaks and beer to improve our menu. We made it clear to them that the main reason for our limited choice was the fact that meat had to be refrigerated, but the camp lacked this convenience. Our location in a jungle area precluded any access to extra power to run a cooler or refrigerator.

The flyboys naturally had a remedy for this problem, but they would not elaborate. Two days later, a huge Air Force load-bearing helicopter approached our camp. We spotted a container, resembling a walk-in reefer, suspended on cables underneath the chopper. One of our pilots standing nearby the Team House kitchen was seen directing the chopper to lower the refrigerator. Unfortunately their aim was not very accurate and he dropped the load straight through the thatched roof of the kitchen. Looking at the big refrigerator and the hole in the roof, the cooks seemed worried. The Americans on the other hand saw no problem getting it fixed. But then came the second surprise. One can hardly run a refrigerator or reefer without power and I could hardly believe my eyes, when shortly thereafter another chopper came in to drop off a 30 KW generator. More accurate this time, they zeroed in better and dropped it off adjacent to the kitchen.

In expectation of good things to come, our team was eager to repair the roof. The newly acquired equipment, its future use explained to her by our interpreter, put a big smile back on the face of our Chinese "chef", exposing her awful looking teeth. The majority of the natives had black teeth, because of their bad habit chewing the beetle nut and smoking some terrible smelling tobacco. It was rolled up in a strange looking cone shaped cigar. As far as smoking was concerned, our team did not have to resort to that kind of tobacco use. The USO was gracious enough to supply us adequately with free cigarettes, so that we never had to scrounge for them.

Getting the appropriate steaks and some beer to fill the cooler was another challenge, but was easily met and overcome by our Air Force boys through bartering with Montagnard cross bows and arrows, as well as other souvenirs of war such as "captured" Viet Cong flags. Families living in the camp with talents and crafts galore, we were able to produce quite a few items for barter.

Another great source of food proved to be the river adjacent to the camp with its ample fish population. Absent of any kind of fishing gear, my indigenous troops had a simple solution to catch a great supply of fish, whenever needed. Being reminded of the last days of the war in Berlin, they did it just like we did. Dropping a hand grenade into the river upstream, several soldiers stood in the water downstream, quickly removing the shell-shocked fish from the water. This unknown type of fish often weighed close to twenty pounds. They had a great taste and the best part of it, there were plenty of them to harvest.

Speaking French was a rather rare occasion for me and hearing it from a Viet-Namese surprised me, when "Papa San", the café owner, greeted me in French. It took me awhile to refresh my school French I had for six years in my youthful school days. After some serious vocabulary recall and thought-provoking gesticulation, I understood that he had once served with the *Légion Étrangére*, the French Foreign Legion.

Frequent visits to the café permitted me to improve my language fluency. Among other things I found out that right outside the village, nestled in the slopes of the hill, the former President of Viet-Nam, Diem had maintained a small resort facility. It had several ceramic tiled bath houses, which had been destroyed after his fall, but traces were still visible. I spotted those leveled buildings, when I took a reconnaissance patrol through the area for familiarization.

Not too far from the camp, to the West, we found many remnants from the French colonial days. The leftovers consisted mostly of heavy construction equipment that had been abandoned at least over a decade ago before we established the camp. The bulldozers and tractors were sitting alongside the old highway 14 running North to South. The "highway" was still showing on the maps, but had totally disappeared. Long overgrown and reclaimed by the jungle, one could detect not only the machinery but also some of the road surface, which used to be asphalt.

A hill located next to the former highway was occupied by one of our outposts. It was constantly manned by our indigenous troops, while our camp's patrols frequently checked the slope facing our camp to make sure our fresh water supply coming off a mountain spring was safe.

One of the previous Camp Commanders had the bright idea to take advantage of a spring halfway up the hill. Tapping in to it, he ran a pipe down hill and underneath the runway into a large water tank on stilts, thereby providing the camp with running fresh spring water. While it was cleverly camouflaged, we still had to make sure it was not being tampered with.

Poisoning the water source would be disastrous to the entire camp population. The camp not only housed the troops but also the dependant families, which were mostly Viet-Namese and not from the indigenous area of Kham Duc. This precious water source gave us water for the kitchen, the shower for the SF and Air Force personnel, including the immediate medical staff; our three Viet-Namese nurses. Separate trailers provided extra water supply throughout the camp.

Close to my "hooch", situated next to the gate, the camp had a tall flagpole on a large concrete platform flying the South Viet-Namese flag since it was officially a Viet-Namese camp. Realizing that the 4th of July was coming up, I talked to my team members about flying the American colors on our holiday. They all thought it would be unusual but great, so I approached the Viet-Namese Camp Commander and told him about our most important holiday coming up. Asking him if it wouldn't be a good idea and nice gesture if we could fly the American flag on the American holiday, I almost expected him to turn down my request. Certainly, it was South Viet-Namese territory and his prerogative to deny my request.

I sincerely wanted to fly our flag and figured that by somewhat modifying my request and suggesting that we fly both flags we would make it easier for him to concur. The idea was also to show a mutual comradeship and to get all troops involved. Our troops would participate in a brief formation, each rendering and saluting their respective flag. Specially rigged, both flags were to fly at the same level, side by side. He agreed and on our Independence Day, the Viet-Namese leadership and our American troops stood in formation rendering a salute to old glory.

It was a proud day for the US troops, Army and Air Force alike. That evening, the Americans and South Viet-Namese alike lifted their glasses in the traditional toast to our Commander-in-Chief and the United States, not forgetting our Allies fighting for their freedom.

South of Kham Duc and only about 2 miles away was the old satellite Special Forces camp of Ngok Tavok, previously evacuated but later reoccupied by a SOG (Special Operations Group, aka Studies & Observations Group) unit. Commanded by an Australian Special Forces Captain John White and US Captain Miller, they were training Montagnards, indigenous people of the area, for special operations into nearby Laos and Cambodia.

This special unit was constantly being re-supplied and supported by their very own C-130 "Blackbirds", who used Kham Duc's airstrip since it was the closest airfield to their camp. Even though they had different missions from us, being part of our elite fighting force it formed a strong bond among fellow Green Berets. We were like a family from which you can unquestionably expect help as well as depend on for mutual support.

Even though we were located in I Corps and within the Marine Corps' Area of Responsibility, we were about 50 miles away from the nearest Marine unit. On the other hand, the nearest Special Forces Camp, besides Ngok Tavok, was at Dak Pek, which was located twenty miles South of us, only 5 minutes away by air. To get acquainted with the units on your flanks, I made it a point to visit them shortly after I took command, because personal contacts are a must to strengthen a bond.

Unexpectedly, it was not long after my first personal meeting with Captain Miller, when I had to rely on his and his troops' support.

Payday was always very important, not so much for the US personnel, because our need for cash in the camp was next to zero and was always automatically deposited. For the South Viet-Namese however, it was very important. I could never understand why the US was paying the Viet-Namese Special Forces Troops for their service. It should have been the other way around.

On payday I saw long lines of Viet-Namese soldiers lining up to get paid. Yet, I heard, when it came to send people out on patrol, the "actual" Camp Commander, Captain Lich seemed to have problems to muster enough men for the different missions. While the SF personnel were officially only advisors, we were actually making all tactical decisions, provide the appropriate training, their pay and supplies. Practically giving them the total support. My own personal suspicion that we were not really getting what we were paying for would soon manifest itself.

Mutiny by Viet-Namese Counterparts

My first impression of the unusual number of personnel on paydays made me wonder, if the Viet-Namese Captain did not provide us with an inflated number of their strength. Confronting him initially with my doubts, but no concrete proof, would have been an insult to him.

My translator was giving me a lot of hints about the Viet-Namese officers raking in a lot of extra money on paydays, without coming right out with facts. His hints though made me wonder. I decided to find a foolproof and accurate way to control and verify individual payments to them. As it was hard for me to identify the various Viet-Namese, I properly asked my interpreter to help me.

Immediately I noticed the Viet-Namese SF officers looking at him and quite obviously intimidating him. It was apparent to me then, that he could not say much, even in German. Following the payout, I took him to my hutch, offered him a beer and got him to openly admit that the Viet-Nam-ese Officers had been sending several of their soldiers through the pay line twice. Not being part of the VN SF troops, but a civilian, the poor guy was genuinely so afraid for his own safety, that he asked me for a pistol for his own protection and at the same time give him a little more prestige as my "right hand man". I agreed and gave him an old .38 revolver from our ex-tra weapons stash, which my Weapons Sergeant cautioned me may not be the most accurate or safest revolver any more, because of excessive wear. But my interpreter was happy just to have a weapon he can carry and use just in case.

Calling the team together, I asked for a better idea and way to con-trol payday operations. We came up with several suggestions and a most promising system which would insure a proper accountability.

When the next payday came around, my Operations & Intelligence Sergeant showed up with a stamp and a black light set-up for stamping each payee's hand when signing for, but only just before he received his pay. Without really explaining to them this new and unusual "inoculation", we were not really surprised when we suddenly found several soldiers showing up to sign for their pay with the stamp already on the hand. Wear-ing a different or mixed "Tiger" uniform and being cleverly mixed among troops in line, not yet paid, the soldier brazenly tried to get paid again. We pulled them out of the line and made them stay in a separate area, while we continued paying those without the stamp.

There were quite a few of them and my team and I were very dis-appointed in the honesty of those troops. My inner feeling and instinct, based on stories from other SF people, told me that it was probably not the individual's decision to cheat, but rather their Commander's in forcing them to go through twice.

Information that I received seemed to validate the suspicion that by collecting the additional pay they would, in exchange, be kept safe inside the camp, instead of being sent out on operations. When I had more Viet-Namese Dong, their currency, left over than I had paid the last time, I talk-ed to Dai Uy Lich. I told him, without laying blame on him, that we now have a new pay system, because some troops were suspected of cheating. To my surprise, I told him, we had money left over in comparison with last payday. Seeking his advice I asked him if he would he be aware of any VC infiltrators maybe collecting moneys from the troops?

Or perhaps we had some VC sympathizers, who had left our camp, because of a pending attack as that had happened before in other camps. He was obviously very embarrassed, shrugged his shoulders and turned to his fellow officers, who all shook their heads. Without any further comments they departed toward their head shed. My team members, including the interpreter, just grinned after we released those caught attempting to collect twice. I wondered if I had by any chance stirred up a hornet's nest.

I was quite content with our successful operation but did not expect the surprise our counterparts presented to us later. Long, my interpreter, came running into our Team House to deliver a message from Dai Uy Lich to the Americans. Apparently angered by our action, he refused to work with us any longer and ordered his troops to lay down their weapons.

This development seemed unreal and ridiculous. His action could put him up for a court martial Viet-Namese style. His command's response to his action had me wonder.

Well, I found myself alone with my handful of Americans defending the camp and decided to give him an alternative. Either he immediately reverses his orders or the US troops will leave the camp, leaving him and his troops at the mercy of the Viet Cong and the North Viet-Namese Army.

Sending Long back to him with my message, I immediately had the communications Sergeant call my Company Headquarters advising LTC Schungel of the mutiny in our camp. He promised me that he would get with his counterpart and call me back, but in the meantime to inform CPT Miller from SOG and clue him in, especially since I had an under-strength team in the camp. My team immediately went on high alert manning all critical defense positions to defend towards the outside as well as inside of the camp.

Not having heard from my VN SF camp commander for about five minutes, I contacted CPT Miller using my landline and apprised him of my situation. His response was brief and to the point, telling me to stand by and not to open fire when he approaches my camp entrance with his troops. I was delighted to hear that. When Long returned after he delivered my message, he told me that Lich was playing it cool and would take his time to respond.

It only took about half an hour of sweating it out, when I got word from my guys manning the guard towers that CPT Miller and his "Yards" were crossing the runway and approaching the camp. To my delight about 30-40 mean looking Montagnards in full battle gear were approaching in double time toward the camp, armed with their automatic CAR–15 at port arms. While all critical towers in the camp were manned by my team members on the machine guns for perimeter defense, the SOG men lead by their Green Beret Commander approached the gate.

The well-known dislike between the "Yards" (Montagnards) and the Viet-Namese suddenly became quite apparent, when we noticed some of our indigenous CIDG people disappear in their shacks to quickly reappear clutching their carbines. It was a rather tense moment when CPT Miller and I met at the flagpole, exchanging salutes with his troops standing by. CPT Miller shouted several commands and his Yards dispersed, calmly strolling through the entire camp, smiling, their automatics at the ready. Showing the Viet-Namese who was in charge, one could see the Yards' pride and personal satisfaction of being in control.

No one was more relieved and gratified than I, because this situation could have turned into something very ugly. Talking to CPT Miller, I expressed my team's appreciation for his help, but he only smiled and told me that he, as well as his troops, enjoyed this episode more than I could imagine. After about another hour a helicopter arrived with COL Schungel, accompanied by the Viet-Namese SF Commander, who immediately talked to Dai Uy Lich and took him and several other counterpart officers back to Da Nang, promising a full replacement next day. I never heard from those counterparts again.

CPT Miller and his troops departed again and leaving the obvious impression that they are prepared and willing to return when needed, locked and loaded.

Naturally it was a slap in the face of the remaining Viet-Namese leaders, but they tried to apologize, reassuring us, that it was all the mistake of the other officers, a political clique, and that they were ready to defend their flag, their country and their camp. What they did not tell me, but my interpreter confidentially related to me was the fact that one of the indigenous troops, after receiving his pay, had secretly left the camp for a destination unknown.

It was safe to assume that he probably was a VC, who needed to inform "Charlie", the Viet Cong, of our counterpart problem in the camp. A quick check with some villagers, who we believed we could trust, showed that he did not leave through the village. It was wise for us to increase our vigilance. Our team started to double check our positions, the extensive barbed wire and booby traps around the camp, including all wiring leading to concealed antipersonnel Claymore mines and buried *"Fugas"* drums. These improvised antipersonnel devices were old fifty-five gallon drums, filled with a mixture of oil and fuel. Once detonated, they caused an effect similar to Napalm, being blown out of the ground and spread over a wide area.

Aside from tightening our security within the compound, we increased our patrols into sensitive areas from which we could receive ground fire. As promised, replacements for the departed VN SF personnel arrived. They made a good initial impression, giving us hope that they would be better than the previous leadership. The Commander seemed to be an old warhorse and not a mere politician, looking to make a bundle of loot for himself.

One night, I took two Viet-Namese soldiers with me for a check of an area from which suspected some sniper fire came once before. Usually carrying either a Kalashnikov or Swedish K submachine gun, I decided to take my M-16 with my night vision Starlight scope. After a short walk toward the edge of the jungle, we heard a noise to our front. Immediately hitting the ground, I looked through my scope, mounted on top of the M-16 and started scanning the entire area in front of me attempting to pick up the cause of the noise. Out of the jungle background I picked up some movement and spotted the cause, but could not believe my eyes. I spotted a big tiger through my bluish illuminated scope and was tempted to shoot it, but for some unknown reason restrained myself.

Instead, I quietly handed the rifle to the soldier next to me. He seemed to have picked up the tiger in the sight, looked at it for a moment and then, handing the weapon back to me he seriously cautioned and seemingly pleaded with me in his broken English not to kill the tiger. It was a beautiful animal and I could already see it hanging in my living room at home. Appreciating the beauty of this animal, I would not have been able to justify killing it.

I later found it was a wise decision. Long later told me that I would have left a bad image in the eyes of the local people. Most of them consider tigers sacred. As they believe in reincarnation, the tiger could have the soul of a former relative. He furthermore told me that, if I really wanted to hunt an animal other than a Viet Cong, he could show me, where the elephants usually roam, which are often used by the VC as a means of transportation. Watching the beautiful tiger though was truly enjoyable. I wished I could have seen him in daylight.

Previous encounters with elephants by our troops had proven though, that our automatic rifles do not have the power to kill an elephant that easily. Hunting elephants was not exactly on the list of my priorities, considering, we were surrounded by a more serious enemy. I was reminded of this tiger every time I looked at the Viet-Namese SF badge I wore, depicting a parachute with a leaping tiger in front.

To learn more about the indigenous people I was working and living with, I not only listened to their plights, but also attempted to understand their way of life and their beliefs. Even though the village was very small, I found a small church and a temple, which served my indigenous troops and families. Although the people were undoubtedly very poor according to our standards, after entering the Buddhist temple I found a beautiful golden Buddha with a charming smile and large swastika on his chest sitting on a large elevated podium appearing to be looking down on me. I was so impressed, that I had to sit down for several minutes inhaling the delicate fumes of the burning incense.

A sudden calmness came over me. Suddenly I found myself in a kind of meditating state, almost forgetting where I was. It was not until one of my Viet-Namese soldiers tapped me on the shoulder when I was brought back to reality. He gave me a small piece of orange cloth with Chinese calligraphy and a drawing on it, which he told me, holds a lot of power. He assured me it would protect me from all evils and help me to stay healthy and alive.

While being a skeptic when it comes to religion, I gracefully accepted it. Not really placing much value in it and just considering a nice little token, I nevertheless carried it faithfully with me wherever I went, like a little rabbit's foot. Now, in retrospect I feel that since my first visit to this Buddhist temple and the acceptance of this ominous piece of material, I tended to believe in having been mysteriously protected during many serious events, disasters and close calls.

Fighting a Plague

Talking about disasters. Our medic reported to me one day that he found several villagers suddenly quite sick. We could be confronted with an outbreak of a disease similar to the plague. Quite a few people among the camp's families had contracted it. With the Command notified, a special medical team from the Air Force immediately came to Kham Duc and determined it was indeed the plague.

An initial investigation suggested that it was probably disseminated by rats. Indeed, we had thousands of them everywhere. During the first night at Kham Duc, while soundly asleep in my "VIP" quarters, a tin- roofed hut, two big rabbit-sized rats fell down from the rafters above me. Not forewarned about my houseguests, they scared the hell out of me. Wondering why I had a fine net stretched over my bunk, I finally got my answer. The net was obviously not strong enough or fragile from age, to carry any significant weight, allowing the rats to break through. The following nights I was often awakened from my now light sleep to see several rats running along the beams below the roof.

After the medical evacuation of the ill by air, the Air Force determined that the best way to fight this disease is the eradication of the lice carried by the rats by putting out rattraps. To carry the process one step further, the Air Force even sprayed the camp and village with a dust to kill the lice. To give a hand to the all-out effort we established a special program offering the people a few '*dongs*' (piasters) for each rat killed and turned in.

The rat hunt by the people went quite well. Certainly the monetary rewards did the trick as it encouraged them to kill close to 100 rats. I advised the Viet-Namese SF to put the rats inside a crater outside the camp and, using gasoline, to burn them. Heavy black smoke rising out of the pit assured me that they did. At least I believed they did. The same evening I was invited by my new counterpart to sit down with them for an exchange of ideas and a Viet-Namese meal. It was quite an appetizing and delicious feast with absolutely great tasting shaved meat. I had never tasted meat like this before, but it had a similar taste of wild hare. Tempted to inquire about the kind of dish, I reconsidered as I didn't want to appear too ignorant and didn't ask them about the delicacy I was enjoying. Neither did my team members.

My interpreter, who was at my side, eating off a big plate, grinned and slightly shook his head toward the Viet-Namese Commander, who could speak some English and was just about to tell me something, I guess about the food. He must have reconsidered as I was indulging in more, since there was plenty of food for a change.

. After we had departed, Long pulled my arm and when I stopped and looked at him, he asked me if I really had no idea what I had eaten. When I told him that I didn't, but that I really enjoyed it, he stated that I should have enjoyed the meal because I had in a sense paid for it, which I could not understand. "Well, Dai Uy" he said "if you promise me you will not get mad at me or want your gun back, I will tell you". I agreed, whereupon he told me, after a brief hesitation, that I had eaten some of the delicious rats·I had paid for.

They actually did correctly burn most of them in the pit, while other select field rats were turned into a great dinner. Unknown to me, it was a favorite meat among some of the population, which also ate dog meat, as I had found out before. At least we had successfully accomplished our task. We seemed to have succeeded in eliminating the plague, especially after the Air Force Medical Team immunized the entire Kham Duc populace and personnel at the base camp.

Looking over the camp, the overall view was less than enlightening. Most of the buildings surrounded by walls of corrugated steel and sandbags topped with barbed wire. The ground was reddish and completely bare lacking any grass, let alone some plants or flowers. The only plant I could find in the entire camp was a lonely banana tree next to my quarters, about five feet tall, but absent of any fruit.

I thought that just because we were in an isolated area at wartime did not mean that we had to be without beautiful surroundings. I was thinking what a nice sight some flowers would make and decided to write to Christine asking her to send a variety of flower seeds, which I would try to cultivate and plant hoping to get them to grow.

I finally received several packs of a variety of flowers and got together with my nurses, who were surprised that a warrior could even think about such a thing. Not to my surprise, they got truly excited and immediately went to work to plant them next to my quarters and the team house. Even though the nurses and I watered them regularly, for some reason the plants never developed too well and besides a few leaves, I never found a single flower. I could not understand why and started blaming it on the climate. Was that an omen maybe of what was to come?

The Enemy is Closing in. Preparing for Attacks

From time to time we received some incoming small arms fire from the jungle area to which we responded with mortar fire to discourage the snipers we could not spot. To get a better look of what may have been building up beyond our range of observation, I began taking one of the Forward Air Controllers (FAC) up in one of their aircrafts to check out the area. Occasionally we had heard distant rumbling at night time, a noise sounding like trucks moving. Frequent spraying of the jungle area in our immediate vicinity by the Air Force with "Agent Orange" defoliant significantly increased the sound. Pilots had reported earlier that they had seen convoys from the North traveling on a new Ho Chi Min Trail only about three to five miles inside Laos along the border with South Viet-Nam. We never noticed any border markers, but according to our map and judging by the sound of traffic inside Laos, that placed them pretty close to our outposts. Enemy activity had been picking up considering several attacks on most Special Forces Camps just North of us, such as Khe Sanh and Lang Vei. When one of our patrols met with some VCs several days out, we lost two indigenous soldiers in the firefight, before the remaining patrol withdrew to the base camp.

We immediately informed the C Team, which arranged for an "arc light", a saturation bombing by the Air Force along the disputed area. We could clearly hear the impacts and see the flashes in the distance standing on top of our bunkers.

Besides our own patrols from the camp, SOG constantly dispatched various special teams into Laos and Cambodia to engage the regular North Viet-Namese troops moving South along the Ho Chi Minh Trail. Our SF Detachment was responsible for advising troops who were members of the Civilian Irregular Defense Groups (CIDG). They in turn were responsible for the pacification and defense of their immediate area and settlements by conducting foot patrols. The SOG (Special Operations) units consisted of highly trained and motivated Montagnards, Nungs and members of various other tribes, who were well known for their loyalty to the Americans.

Equipped with the most advanced weapons in our arsenal, they were under the direct command of US Special Forces soldiers. Operating in known hostile areas, they searched out, ambushed and destroyed North Viet-Namese troops infiltrating the South through areas bordering South Vietnam. I always envied those friends of mine in SF, who were lucky enough to be assigned to these special units. Unfortunately, our greatest losses came from those units.

Camp Kham Duc was lucky to have FACs located at our base airstrip, who often offered to fly us over our immediate area once they returned from an interdiction mission. Through this support we could at least be forewarned should any larger VC or North Viet-Namese unit get close to our camp.

Being below authorized strength in our US personnel, our ability to advise each CIDG patrol going out was limited. We therefore had to rely more on our counterpart, the Viet-Namese Special Forces to conduct patrols. They usually did it without any qualms, but after several weeks of increased enemy activity in closer proximity and with the closest SF camp in the North under siege, we noticed the CIDG troops returning from patrol a lot earlier and still looking well and refreshed.

Our team suspected that those patrols, without US personnel escorting them, probably did not even try to reach their assigned destination. We had the feeling they stopped and stood down only about a mile from our base camp, waited and then returned after they had finished their rations. I did not like to be misled or considered to be ignorant. To confirm our suspicions we planned to test the accuracy of their patrol report.

After two days out on patrol, we flew over the target area where they should have been and contacted them by radio to insure they were at the proper destination about four miles from the base camp. They confirmed their location, but on the return flight with my FAC we spotted the patrol in the jungle only about one mile outside the camp. There was, of course, a possibility that we were wrong and it could have been an enemy unit, which, that close to our perimeter should have been taken under fire.

Assuming an enemy patrol that close, we fired, as usual in the past a few rounds of either our 60mm or 4.2 inch mortar into the suspected area. After the second round had been fired, we received a frantic call in Viet-Namese that they had made contact with an overwhelming number of the enemy, were under mortar and rocket fire and requested permission to break contact and withdraw. We advised the patrol to break contact and withdraw to where apparently an enemy patrol outside our perimeter was spotted. We will keep firing on them until they are eliminated.

Not one of our counterparts got into any argument with the patrol, only asked for the number of casualties and confirmed to withdraw. After we fired another round, they came back on the radio and told their own SF that they must have made a mistake on the map, because they seem to be getting fired upon by the camp.

Following their return, the VN Camp Commander briefed us and admitted that his troops were apparently afraid to get too far away from the camp and had never made it to the assigned target area. There were no casualties on part of the patrol and their weapons had not even been fired.

He promised us adequate punishment for the cowards, assuring us that the next patrols will be properly executed.

Leaving my XO in charge, I decided to take the next patrol out, even if only for a few days. Christine would just have to wait a couple days before I would write her and send some mail. I generally made some tapes, as it was quicker and at least she would hear my voice.

Loaded with an adequate amount of ammunition and food supplies we set out for a five-day patrol West of the camp to find proof of enemy activity. Except for some elephant dung and some tie-down devices, we found nothing substantial. I could tell though that the Viet-Namese showed some signs of restlessness and extreme caution in their movements, as if they could smell the close proximity of the Viet Cong, nicknamed "Charlie".

Their wariness could probably be attributed to some visible damage previous B-52 bombings had done and finding fresh traces of some visible trails. Once in the jungle it was difficult to orient yourself on the map unless you find an open area and some reference point like a body of water or hilltop to be able to pinpoint your exact location. After three days, we decided to turn around returning by cutting a new trail parallel to the path we used before.

To our surprise we stumbled on more evidence of the previous occupation of a rest area of North Viet-Namese troops. It was a good indication that a major road of the Ho Chi Minh trail within Laos was nearby. Running low of rations and especially water, we decided not to probe any further, called in our location and continued to return back to the base camp.

Arriving at the camp, I briefed the Air Force pilots and made another flight over the area our patrol had returned on to see if I could find the major trail or a road next to the area we had patrolled. The jungle canopy covered the area to such an extent, that we could hardly find any opening in the canopy. Occasionally we spotted some signs of possible tracks and recorded the coordinates which we then called in to the Air Force to request defoliation. The North Viet-Namese were experts in camouflage, but once the area was bare and without foliage, it would undoubtedly reveal any road system alongside the Laotian-Viet-Namese border.

Flying back to Kham Duc, the pilot made a swing around the base to show me an area where the river flowed around the plateau of our camp to the South. The river bed was fairly shallow with a sandy bank and the pilot, who had surveyed this area often before, noticed something new and unusual looking at one point and decided to take the aircraft down to follow the river only about 50 feet above the water level with mountain slopes rising above us on one side. A sudden crack heard over the engine noise and the intercom prompted the pilot to yell at me to take my flack jacket off and sit on it.

We had just been fired on, but being a curious type, he was turning around to make another pass to check out something he spotted. The Major did his best to impress me with the agility of the aircraft climbing and turning, but I did not exactly appreciate his sudden dive after advising me to hang on tight. Diving toward a now obvious river crossing site with some ropes still showing on the banks, he fired a HE, high explosive rocket. Not ever having experienced the firing of a rocket from such a small aircraft, it momentarily shook me up. He followed up with one marking round at the target, pulling up and leveling off.

Climbing to a higher altitude, he circled around the site and after he had scanned the area again he told me that he was running low on gas and needed to refuel. He was intent, however, to check the target area out again once he dropped me off. Feeling like getting off an extreme roller coaster I was glad to feel solid ground under my feet again.

After landing and parking the bird dog at the ramp, we checked out the fuselage of the plane and found two rifle bullet holes between his seat and mine coming through the bottom and leaving through the top indicating that there were some VC in the area. Since it was only about one mile from the camp perimeter and also close to the SOG Camp at Nhoc Tovak, the area needed to be better reconnoitered. The Aussie to the South of us appreciated the info we had passed on to him.

Coincidentally, the Detachment's Escape & Evasion (E&E) route from the camp, in case we ever are in danger of getting overrun, was leading right through that area along the riverbank. This escape route either needed to be reconsidered or cleared.

After refueling and reloading both rocket pods which held about a dozen high explosive (HE) or marking rounds to mark targets for Air Force fighter aircraft and bombers, he took off again to recheck the last target. It took only about ten minutes, when we received a distress call from him, that his aircraft was hit again and that he was going down in the same area we both had been fired on before he had fired rockets along the river. A follow up call advised us that he had destroyed sensitive equipment left on board and was moving toward the camp along the riverbank.

We immediately contacted our Headquarters in Da Nang and requested a helicopter for an extraction, but were advised that they were short of a required flight crew. Contacting the Marines for air support, they were turned down because of a lack of fighter escort or such, after which the C-Team dispatched a helicopter with a skeleton crew.

In the meantime I returned to the crash site with another FAC and making out the downed aircraft, we fired a couple rockets and a marking round at the bird dog blowing it up and destroying it. The pilot told me though that he did not score a direct hit, but the nearby impact had moved the plane apparently setting off a secondary explosion probably caused by the booby-trapped plane. Unless the downed pilot did it, that would have been another indication that "Charlie" was active in the area, booby trapping the plane in case Americans would return to retrieve the pilot.

Communication received from the pilot nearby revealed his approximate location and his hope that he could remain free. He suspects possibly being tailed by the enemy. We assured him that extraction is on the way and to be prepared.

Returning to the camp, we waited for the chopper and after his arrival quickly briefed the warrant officer pilot. Adding a door gunner from our camp, he left with an added crew, including the other Air Force pilot, who had flown with me to the target area. Waiting anxiously for what seemed hours, they all returned with the downed pilot, who had successfully evaded and escaped any tailing enemy.

Following a brief toast to the helicopter rescue crew those gutsy guys returned to Da Nang. I was advised by my commander, LTC Schungel not to rely on any Marine support. They seemed to have a bad attitude towards our indigenous troops. One of our allied SF trained Laotian units, I believe it was the 33rd Elephant Battalion, which had to withdraw back to Viet Nam after an operation, was stopped by Marines, who did not know how to handle them. Instead of informing the nearest Special Forces Detachment, they just disarmed them and sent them back to Laos. Unarmed, they were left to an unknown fate.

It was a disappointment of course and we truly regretted those occasional "mishaps", which were also expressed on several occasions by General Westmoreland, the US Forces Commander in South Viet-Nam in 1968-69.

August and September proved to be really depressing, as the regular monsoon season arrived blanketing our area with heavy daily rains and fog around the surrounding mountains and hills. The weather was practically grounding our FACs and stopping any incoming flights of C-130 transports we depended upon for material support such as food, ammunition and personnel.

Fortunately, it also restricted enemy movement from the North along our border inside Laos. Continuing our improvements of defenses, we also added a new homemade weapons system designed and built by Lt. Harrington. He mounted discarded Air Force rocket pods onto the rear of one of our jeeps. Utterly impressive looking, it was to be used as a defensive rocket launcher system against possible enemy sightings on the hilltops surrounding the camp.

The rocket pods, mounted on the aircraft's wings, contained multiple tubes. Once they showed excessive wear or cracks making them unfit for further use by the Air Force, they were removed and placed out of commission. By blocking all damaged tubes, we, however, could still use the remaining operational tubes. Without a question it made a nice, mobile rocket launcher, considering we had plenty of ammunition available, stockpiled next to the runway.

The "home-made" stand for the launch pod was anchored in half of a fifty-gallon drum filled with concrete and placed in the back of the jeep. The pod had an adjustable frame that permitted rotation and elevation of the launching tubes, directing the fire to various locations. A crude board with an electrical wiring diagram permitted the firer to select individual rockets to be launched at selected targets. Successfully tested, our team was proud to have the only unique small rocket firing system not only in I Corps but surely in South Viet-Nam. I wonder if it was ever patented.

Something was definitely developing West of our camp as we received repeated fire from across the runway from inside the jungle next to the village at nightfall. Spotting the muzzle flashes of the firing weapons during darkness, we returned the fire with our M-16s. Because of its distance we dispatched some of our troops hoping to encircle the snipers, but they must have observed our soldiers leaving the only gate of the camp and quickly disappeared in the jungle.

Although we had several safe passages we could have used to encircle them, like to the rear of the camp in case we ever had to escape and evade through the perimeter's minefields, we did not want to take the risk and reveal these routes to either our Viet-Namese troops or the VC.

There were many precautionary measures US personnel maintained to insure ourselves, that we could defend the camp even against a possible attack by covert VC operators from within the camp. It meant having certain critical positions booby-trapped in case they ever get taken over by the enemy.

The next morning a surveillance team checked out the area from which we had received the fire before and found several bullet holes in the front bucket of a tractor left by the French. Spent cartridges revealed the position the VC had occupied. It also showed the bullet holes we made returning the fire.

While half of our team was on increased alert following the frequent sniper fire, we considered it more of a nuisance. Thankful for everything the Air Force guys had done for us our Detachment personnel assisted the Air Force at the camp to build new quarters. The flyboys certainly made sure to bring in sufficient material before the monsoon set in.

It looked like the connections with their people in Clark Air Force Base in the Philippines allowed them to requisition just about anything they needed for their personal comfort. While the SF team only had a small generator for the communications bunker, the Air Force guys dreamed of air-conditioning their quarters especially since we now had the 30 kw generators. Our team was still content with the one ceiling fan in our team house. It provided a breeze and a chance to occasionally relax, listen to favorite music, eat and have a rare beer.

The wall's decorations were something else. Several state flags, representing each member of the team were proudly displayed next to each other. Not being from any particular home state it included my flag, the flag of Berlin, which had, at one time, been flying at city hall during President Kennedy's visit.

For some reason, our Viet-Namese SF officers liked the flag, which depicted an upright walking black bear on a white background, and flanked by bold red stripes, it was similar to the state flag of California. When the Viet-Namese flag had been torn to the extent it could no longer be flown and flying the American flag was not permissible, I was surprised when I jokingly mentioned to the Viet-Namese Commander that the Berlin flag would be a good temporary substitute, he agreed.

Maybe one of my team sergeants was on the right track when he thought our counterparts might feel that by not flying a South Viet-Namese flag and flying a different, unknown flag it could prevent the VC and North VN troops from bothering our camp. If nothing else, it would at least confuse them, I thought. So, the next morning, I hoisted the flag of

Berlin, depicting a bear, over our camp. It proudly flew over the camp for several days until it was replaced again by new national colors of South Viet Nam and my home-town flag took its customary place along the team house wall. Before taking the "Berliner Bär" down though, the South Viet-Namese SF personnel demanded and got a picture of the flag with them posing in front of it.

It tried to write letters home almost every day, as did most of our team members. While the Viet-Namese troops had their dependents living in the camp with them, the SF could only dream of their wives and kids at home, hoping they were alright back in the land of the big PX. Besides writing, I found myself debating and planning various projects, which I contemplated starting as soon as I returned to the States. During the night, while on duty, I found ample time, not only to write letters, but also record my daily impressions and feelings on small tapes.

Being located in this remote area was often frustrating. This was especially true during the monsoon season, because the weather prevented any re-supply for weeks and many projects had to be postponed. The fear of being cut off from civilization and being totally dependent on one another within the camp without any prospect of outside help pushed us even more to be prepared for all eventualities.

Stopping the bombing of North Viet-Nam ordered by Washington put our troops in more danger than ever before and was considered by all of our troops on the ground as a grave mistake. They were now being overwhelmed by the ever-increasing North Viet-Namese hordes of division-sized units. Our immediate Headquarters in Da Nang had always been considered a relatively safe and secure area but it soon became clear that no place in South Vietnam was any longer a safe haven.

When we received the message over our short wave radio that Da Nang was under mortar attack and the closest SF Camp north of us was being overrun by North Viet-Namese regular troops with Russian PT-76 tanks, we knew that our days might be numbered, too. The message also informed us that the APO, the Army Post Office, had received a direct hit and we should forget about getting any mail for the next few days.

The introduction of tanks by the North was the first sign that the enemy was mounting for an all-out attack. Returning patrols now reported increased enemy contacts closer to the camp suffering several wounded. We knew it was definitely getting very serious. Since the Air Force pilots could not fly during the monsoon season and were grounded, they suggested and we whole-heartily agreed with the idea, to train them on our 4.2 inch mortars. It was a sight to behold to watch our Weapons Sergeant teach Air Force Field Grade officers and their enlisted personnel in the use of heavy weapons of the Infantry. They all realized that our situation suggested every man be fully prepared to defend the camp, which included relocating rockets stored outside the camp perimeter to a safe area inside the camp.

Following the monsoon season, normal bombardment of the Ho Chi Minh trail finally resumed and our pilots again continued their mission. Looking forward to better weather we realized that the enemy is probably just as happy and eager to expand their attacks.

At least we could expect a return of our re-supply with food, ammunition as well as moral and welfare items, such as mail among other items. With the frequent carpet-bombing, which contributed to heavy destruction of enemy convoys, the probing actions by the North was visibly reduced, but nevertheless, we all knew that they would soon be ready to expand their activity.

The camouflaged black birds, our favorite and reliable C-130 aircraft, who usually supported Special Operations Units, became more frequent in their visits to Kham Duc as those units were resuming their interdiction operations into neighboring Laos with their indigenous troops and other Montagnard tribesmen. I must admit that I have never developed more respect for any other soldiers than for those loyal troops. They were not only fierce fighters but would willingly give their own lives to protect their American comrade-in-arms.

Assignment to a More "Peaceful" and Civilized Area

Checking the messages one morning in mid-December, I found a message from the C-Team in Da Nang reassigning me to Detachment B-55 at, of all places, the capitol of South Vietnam, Saigon. My new job was to be the Executive Officer of a B-Detachment. Such a choice assignment definitely beat the job of operating an isolated post in the jungle.

True, we lacked all kinds of comfort, but the camaraderie you experience often makes up for it. Soldiers in the field are a different breed. They have a lot of pride and fortitude to share the common miseries and still prevail under circumstances rarely found anywhere else. With a heavy heart I collected my few possessions, said my farewell to my team members and some of the close Viet-Namese friends and counterparts. For the last time,

I visited Papa San in his café and took my last pictures with several of my young friends and the kids of the village.

Carrying my Berlin flag, properly signed by our allied Viet-Namese and Chinese natives, I said my farewells to my team. After the helicopter touched down on the runway to pick me up and drop off the new camp and Detachment Commander, Captain Sylva, I briefed him quickly and introduced him to the team, especially my XO, Lt. Harrington. I could only wish him good luck and express my hope that he will enjoy his assignment as much as I did.

Regardless of the problems we had encountered, which were rather common and expected serving at outposts such as Kham Duc, it was a rewarding assignment. As a farewell present, the Montagnards presented me with their tribal bracelet, a memento to remind me of our mutual admiration and the many rice wine tasting events we had shared together.

Lifting off, I sat in the door, looking at my camp for the last time wondering how long this camp would be able to remain free before it was overrun. Our experience definitely showed that it certainly was in the cards. My report to the C-Team expressed my worries about a major offensive by the North based on my experiences, but unfortunately my assessment seemed to be ignored.

Before I could depart for Saigon, I was ordered to return to Da Nang for a debriefing, where LTC Schungel greeted me and congratulated me on my new assignment. He was surprised how I could have gotten such a good deal. He made arrangements to have me flown to Saigon the following day, which was to be quite a long flight, because the Capitol was located pretty much at the more southern tip of South Vietnam.

To my amazement I was invited to participate in a troop formation to be greeted by the local Viet-Namese I Corps Commander of the Army, General Lam. The General had informed the C-Team Commander, that he was honored to present several awards to US and Viet-Namese personnel. Standing in formation, the General went down the line shaking each officer's hand. I was still curious why I was in that formation. When he came to stand in front of me he congratulated me and pinned the Viet-Namese Cross of Gallantry with Palm on my uniform. In addition, I was also awarded honorary Viet-Namese jump wings.

To top it all, I had another surprise coming. LTC Schungel presented me with the much-coveted Combat Infantryman's Badge, the CIB, for service in a Combat Zone, while engaged with a hostile force and being under enemy fire. Following the ceremony I had time to take a breather and walked along the beach only a few hundred meters from my visiting quarters to take in the beautiful view of the water.

Taking in the breathtaking view of the junkets floating on the waters of the China Sea, I noticed a little mountain projecting out of the water only about a mile away. I could not believe the sign posted on the beach next to a roll of barbed wire. It was warning everybody in several languages that walking past the sign will endanger a person's safety, also stating that personnel passing this point was now within the range of snipers.

VCs were consistently occupying the hill in the waters of the coast line and even after each shelling and bombing they always returned. Considering it a joke, I proceeded for about another fifty yards, being whistled at and called to turn back. When the sand around me suddenly erupted from two or three bullet rounds impacting on the beach sand, I did get the message, loud and clear. Turning around, I didn't hesitate one second to quickly return to the safe area.

I wanted to remember Da Nang and before leaving the city and the C-Team I took another ride up the little mountain outside the city to visit the great white Buddha, with its mysterious smile I had carried in my mind since I first saw him. I had always visualized him while in Kham Duc. Besides the Montagnard bracelet I had received as a memento I also wore a small necklace with a little Jade Buddhist and a mother of pearl swastika. I had picked up the Jade Buddha and a bracelet earlier during one of my visits to Da Nang.

Not that I was superstitious, but for some unknown reason those ornaments had always given me a lot of comfort. Flying out of Da Nang I noticed the tremendous damage the last VC attack had caused to the area and wondered, when the next attack would occur. How many more casualties would we, and the population have to endure.

Gazing at the country below, flying at a rather high altitude sitting next to the door gunner, I tried to imagine what kind of a great life the people could have if there were no fighting and no destruction. Does our presence in Viet-Nam really contribute to an eventual peace and if so, how many years would it take to rebuild the country and the cities. Hue, the capital of Central Viet-Nam and the northern most city of South Viet-Nam on the coast of the South China Sea, was once one of the more beautiful cities with great cultural sites. The war saw to it that most sacred sites were destroyed.

After another refueling stop at the 5th Special Forces Group Headquarters in Nha Trang, we flew another two hours before we arrived at Tan Son Nhut Air Force Base in Saigon. Saigon was also the seat of the Headquarters of MACV, the Military Advisory Command, Viet-Nam.

Major Ranger, the Detachment Commander, picked me up welcoming me to Saigon and our Detachment B-55. A little black compact car, bearing what appeared to be Viet-Namese license plates and a tall Viet-Namese driver was waiting for us. I was told that he was a Nung, a Viet-Namese tribesman of Chinese origin. Dressed in a special camouflaged "Tiger" uniform, he saluted and hurriedly opened the doors for us.

Leaving the airport, we drove by the MACV (Military Advisory Command, Viet-Nam) Headquarters, where its commander, Gen. Westmoreland, was located. Actually, the name 'advisory' should have been eliminated a long time ago. With all our conventional troops in country we were no longer just advising but totally involved in operations of our own. Only a few Regular Army and Special Forces advisors were still working with some of the Viet-Namese troop units.

The drive toward the inner city also brought us past the Detachment's S-5 Logistical Camp, Camp Goodman. The remainder of the Detachment was located near the center of the city and not too far from the American Embassy. To my surprise, we entered one of the more prominent streets of Saigon, the Le Van Duet and finally arrived at 240 Duong Pasteur Street.

An impressive large villa complex was guarded by Nungs. Very thorough in security, one of them even looked underneath the car with large mirrors to insure the bottom of the vehicle had not been tampered with. The Viet Cong had made it a habit to attach bombs underneath the vehicles to later command-detonate them.

We all had to admit that they were a formidable enemy. They were repeatedly convincing us that there were no safe territories in southern Viet Nam. I was very impressed by the correctness of the personnel and the cleanliness of the entire complex. The conspicuous absence of any type of weapon was almost leading me to believe that we were not in any hostile territory at all. That impression was soon to change.

R&R in the Homeland of My Allied Friends

Deserving or not, following six months of a hardship tour and combat, all troops were entitled to seven days of R&R. This Rest and Recuperation period, could be taken in a number of choice locations in the Far East, including Thailand, Kuala Lumpur, The Philippines, Hong Kong and even Australia. Recalling the stories my friends told me about their homelands, I naturally picked Bangkok in Thailand, as my favorite.

The flight from Saigon to Bangkok was short and sweet and after arriving at the airport, military representatives from the MACTHAI R&R Office were at hand to greet and brief the visitors. They offered recommendations of facilities, sites and other information to make our stay more enjoyable. Their slogan "The Beauties of Thailand await you" was no exaggeration. Wherever I looked I could see nothing but exotic beauties and it was not because I had been exposed to jungle life for too long. For some strange reason the air seemed to be a lot cleaner and drier compared to the weather in Vietnam, which was a lot more humid.

"Tommie's Tourist Agency" appeared to be geared to serve our servicemen in all aspects of our R&R. Following their recommendation I selected the Chavalit Hotel and found myself in a splendid room with an excellent view over Bangkok. I proceeded to the lobby, where several tables were set up by the USO to give you even more choices of entertainment readily available to the tired troops. Considering the shortness of this type of vacation, I wanted to get the most out of the stay.

I found a Taxi driver, who was willing to drive me wherever I wanted to go, twenty-four hours a day for seven days for a total of only $75. His very attractive younger sister, who he introduced, spoke surprisingly good English and was willing and happy to help make my stay a memorable one. I must admit that I had never seen so many polite, pleasant and good-looking young ladies for quite a long time. After I briefly explained my background, likes and dislikes over a few cool drinks, she made several recommendations.

Of course I added my own suggestions, including a visit to my two friends I had previously met in Fort Benning and Fort Bragg. We soon had our program together. Knowing that my 'better half' back in the United States would understand, I left it up to my female companion to show me her country, introduce me to its customs and traditions and help me enjoy my brief stay to the fullest. Needless to say, both she and her brother were an excellent team and I could not find anything to complain about.

Unfortunately we were not able to meet with my friend Nyom, who was a member of the Royal Guard Battalion, responsible for the protection of Queen Sirikit and King Bumipol. At the palace gate, we were advised that my friend was still undergoing some training in the United States. My driver told me that Nyom was also a member of the Royal Thai Special Forces. He had frequently been working on a US Airbase north of Bangkok. As the time of my visit was short I had to be content with the effort of at least having tried to find him.

· Thailand is extremely beautiful and I felt somehow bad that Christine could not be there with me to enjoy my R&R with me. As a matter of fact, I felt so strongly about it, that I decided to take her to Thailand some day after my return to the States, even if it would take several years.

Remembering WWII and the death march of Bataan, I also recalled the events at the bridge across the River Kwai. Mentioning this historical fact to my beautiful tour guide, she was glad to show me not only that site and the adjacent POW graves, but also the natural treasures of overwhelming caves with stalactites and stalagmites.

Every day was filled with a new adventure from the fascinating floating market to the Grand Palace and the temple of the Emerald Buddha. Another unforgettable site was TIMLAND. It was a huge park, portraying 'Thailand In Miniature', revealing to the visitors a mixture of animal life, the people, their culture, old traditions and typical everyday life. Watching Thai classical dancing, one could observe the rhythmic grace and the enchanting exotic charm of its native dancers. It was also in that park where I had the chance to hold the undoubtedly biggest snake I have ever seen, not in my hands but on my shoulders. My guide and her brother had to help me pick it up, since it weighed over one hundred pounds and was impossible to hold by oneself because of its length. It was one huge Boa.

The unusual sights and sounds were just overwhelming. After a long night out on the city, the most rewarding and relaxing feature of R&R I found was a Turkish bath and a massage. Escorted by my two faithful guides, who I had already grown fond of after only two days, I ventured out on a shopping tour. Visiting several competing Jewelry Stores, I was amazed about the choice of rings and jewelry being offered.

Talking about good old days. Gold was only $34 an ounce and the selection was so great that it was customary that the customers sit down for a small snack and drink while deciding on a purchase. Immediately paying the advertised price was apparently an insult to the seller. Tutored by my guides, I quickly learned the oriental way to haggle until both parties were satisfied. Loaded down with trinkets, jewelry and an assortment of souvenirs I was happy and satisfied. At the end of my vacation I sincerely regretted not having purchased more pieces.

The sights of the Grand Palace and the most beautiful structures and temples with its statutes of giants, half human, half animal, and dominating statues of lions are still imbedded in my mind. Overwhelmingly glistening in gold, mixed with beautiful, brilliant colors, the buildings and paintings were the most impressive I had ever seen. Considering that Thailand was only about one hour flight from Vietnam, the difference in their people, their attitude, wealth and culture was amazing.

I dreaded the day when I had to leave this beautiful country behind to return to the war scene.

Impressed by this experience I was seriously determined to return very soon to share another visit to this fantastic paradise with my wife. Not wanting to waste any minute I was an early riser for the remaining days. Finally, I even had a chance to see His Majesty the King of Thailand floating by in his royal barge "Sri Suwannahongse". Manned by at least 40 rowers, all dressed in gold and red uniforms, this was a sight to behold.

On my seventh and last day of R&R, I finally had to bid farewell to my newly found acquaintances, and expressed my heartfelt thanks, assuring them that I would try to return some day soon. I was sure that we all enjoyed each other. Feeling a sense of sadness, I left Bangkok to return to Saigon.

The Quiet before the Storm. Seeing Bad Omens

I soon found that Detachment B-55 had a unique role within the 5th Special Forces Group. Previously an operational B-Team, the Detachment had a unique and specific role. Its role included communications, logistical support, briefing and debriefing as well as processing Special Forces personnel. The detachment Commander was also the SF Liaison Officer with the Military Advisory Command, Vietnam, MACV Commander, General Westmoreland.

Several months after my assignment to B-55, the 5th SF Group changed our detachment's designation from B-55 to the Command Liaison Detachment (CLD). Its mission basically remained unchanged, except the Detachment was now headed by a Captain. Major Ranger, the Detachment Commander had been reassigned to a more responsible position, after which I assumed Command of the Detachment. Sergeant Major Campbell, the Detachment's senior NCO, was an old hand in Special Forces and proved outstanding in running the compound and its Enlisted Personnel.

It was amusing to see him feed the Detachment's mascot, a caged, huge and nearly six foot long Bushmaster snake. Kept in a small front yard it lived there together with several domesticated deer. The snake usually consumed a duck a week, which the SGM Campbell fed the snake on a regular basis. With the increase of enemy activity around Saigon, this quiet little showcase of a yard changed after we decided to quarter a squad of Nungs in the front yard. The area was surrounded by a two meter high wall providing external security and limiting the view of the compound from the outside.

As one of our functions we conducted frequent checks with CICV, the Central Intelligence Center in Viet-Nam. Daily situation reports showing tactical changes were essential in our planning and assessments. The most recent information at that time indicated that North Vietnam and the Viet Cong had planned an extraordinary offensive, with Saigon as its main target. Assuring that our unit is sufficiently prepared for possible combat in this urban environment, it prompted me to build additional fortifications. To fend off any possible assault upon the compound we immediately built a concrete bunker-type structure with several firing ports outside but adjacent to the entrance of the compound.

Manned by our Detachment's Nungs, armed with a machine gun, it provided a field of fire of 180 degrees within Rue Pasteur. This bunker also gave relative protection to a Hotel next to our compound, which housed American personnel of USAID, our US Agency for International Development and others. Our foresight paid off, as this extra defensive position proved to be a great plus in the weeks to come.

Christmas 1967 went by pretty fast, mainly because unlike in the United States, we were not exposed to weeks of constant commercial reminders of the upcoming season. The tropical surroundings and the weather reminded us more of the 4th of July than the winter season. Besides, the pressing tasks and requirements helped us forget the niceties and comforts of life stateside.

Required to make frequent liaison flights to Special Forces Camps in all four Corps from the mountainous I Corps to the flatlands of IV Corps in the Delta in Viet-Nam I found myself flying more than 200 hours over hostile territory. While visiting one of the camps in the Delta I met with Sergeant First Class Dave Boyd, my neighbor and friend from Fayetteville, NC.

He had been patrolling his operational area, which consisted of huge rice paddies, using Florida style airboats whenever the area was flooded. Most of the SF Compounds were uniquely built on large floating platforms, constructed on top of numerous fifty-five gallon drums. As the water was rising in the Delta rice fields it helped to keep them always above the water and dry. It was a nice experience to find and meet with old friends in this otherwise hostile atmosphere.

Only about a week after my visit, SFC Boyd. having his bags already packed, was waiting for his return flight home. When one of his patrols got involved in a firefight with some VCs not too far from the camp, he volunteered to go on a final mission into an area he knew well. Unfortunately, on the way to the objective, his team ran into an ambush. Both he and his small crew on the airboat were killed. Sorry to say, he was not going to be the only friend I had known for many years, who was going to be killed in Vietnam.

Nothing is worse than to find out a friend or close comrade you had just recently or even the day before talked to, had been killed, captured or been declared missing in action. As a member of the military you soon learn to cope, adjust and accept all the adverse effects of life experiences as to be expected.

Saigon did not turn out to be what I envisioned, regarding the previously envisioned peaceful life in this capitol. Quite soon, I was to find the opposite to be true during a training program on the rifle range just outside the city limits. Our Detachment and its assigned Nungs were preparing to zero in their weapons in anticipation of certain pending hostilities. We had just dismounted from our trucks and jeeps and proceeded to our firing positions, when suddenly a volley of fire was hitting our positions.

Totally unprepared for such an ambush in an area generally void of an enemy, we immediately searched for cover. It was definitely a rude wake-up call. It took our troops a few moments to get a hold of enough ammunition to return fire. Personnel with available side arms, such as .45 pistols provided covering fire toward the ambushers. The Viet-Cong apparently hid near the actual firing targets, a location nobody would ever have figured anyone to pick as a position. Once the initial shock of the unexpected attack had subsided our troops were fully armed and we returned fire. A small group of our troops, at the same time, tried to make a flanking movement to assault the attacker from the side or the rear. After a few minutes, the fire subsided and the assault team returned having found the positions vacated by the VC.

Establishing special security around the range, we completed zeroing our weapons and returned to our compound. It did not take any more incidents such as this to convince us that nobody was totally secure in the city any more. It unquestionably reinforced our feeling that the enemy was planning to achieve some significant victory in Saigon itself, until then believed to be a safe haven and secure.

Returning from a briefing with Gen. Westmoreland one day, I was told by SGM Campbell that an old friend of mine has been assigned to the Detachment and he was eager to talk to me. When I walked into my office, I saw a towering figure standing there. I did not recognize him immediately, but after he uttered his first words, I finally placed him. Still in awe, I could not believe my eyes, that it was the old Master Sergeant I had last seen in Alaska. It was the same one, who once had asked me to be assigned and allowed to serve with me in Viet Nam. Incredible as it seemed, he had actually succeeded in locating me.

With an opening at our location in Camp Goodman, I assigned him there, where he quickly seemed to adjust to his job. My staff there soon reported, however, that he had a very difficult time adjusting to the extreme heat as an Eskimo and was found spending a lot of time in the few areas, which were air conditioned. The man probably never imagined how hot it could actually get in Viet-Nam. He would have been in shock serving at Kham Duc.

I must admit, I felt bad but also proud of him considering the fact that this man had the guts to volunteer for service in a theatre that would be so hot and hard to live in. I doubted very much, if he could have survived in any of our outposts in the jungle without a long period of adjustments. After a few weeks however he got adjusted to the heat continuously wearing soaking wet fatigues. He never openly complained.

Firefight with Viet Cong in Saigon

On my way to one of my briefings to the commander at MACV at the Tan Son Nhut Air Base in early January 1968, I was sitting in the back seat of my small black sedan approaching the Air Base. Scanning the area, I heard what sounded like intermittent weapons fire. Suddenly, I spotted several MPs crouched next to their vehicles in front of us, their .45 pistols pulled, aiming and firing at one of the buildings lining the street. After one round hit our sedan, my driver suddenly stepped on the brakes and started to pull over.

Asking me to lie low, he pulled out a strange looking carbine, I had never seen before. Slipping out of the vehicle he started well-aimed fire supporting the Military Police, who had neither carbines nor rifles. After a few more rounds, the firing ceased. I was glad the fire fight, apparently a small ambush directed at the MP's ceased abruptly. When the MP's returned to their vehicle, my driver also returned, broadly smiling, assuring me not to worry. We continued without any further delay.

My driver's carbine, I noticed had been modified by changing the big stock to form a small handle. The barrel was shortened and reminded me of the TV show, where the western hero carried a long holstered gun which he only needed to pull forward to fire. Following standing military orders, staff officers in Saigon did not carry a weapon openly at that time. It was supposedly to reassure the Viet-Namese and impress on all people that they had nothing to be afraid of.

Our Nungs knew better, of course. Increased assaults on outlying areas and even inside the city limits forced many military and even some civilians to start carrying concealed weapons. As a result of this incident and my very own sense of survival, I carried a small .25 cal. pistol under my belt in the back. I made it a point to carry a weapon that way, especially when wearing civilian clothes working outside the compound.

The presence of many foreign agents operating in South Vietnam made the city a Mecca for intelligence operatives. Many of them worked out of their Embassies to support one side or the other. Coincidentally, the opportunity presented itself, when I accidentally met the 'Number Two' man of the West German Embassy, the Baron Hasso Rued von Collenberg. After a few get-togethers, I befriended him, telling him that I was from Germany originally and worked for USAID. Naturally speaking German, he openly discussed problems of mutual interest and concern.

It was interesting to hear that he had often met with some wounded Viet Cong. The German Red Cross Hospital Ship *"Helgoland"*, docked off the coast of South Viet-Nam, was obligated to treat the wounded as an act of humanitarian service. I was hoping that eventually I might get some vital information and even find out if the German intelligence was collecting tactical information, which might be of some help to us. Most of his information though was not of much significance for us. I seriously was hoping he could enlighten me about the operations of the French and their Michelin Rubber Plantations.

Across from our compound we could see a rather large Villa with about three floors, owned by the French Michelin Rubber Company. Most windows facing our facility were closed with all of their roll-down shutters. Only occasionally did they open the shutters a few inches and I spotted what appeared to be large panels of communication equipment along a wall. Using starlight night scopes, our team occasionally saw what appeared to be several armed small sized figures moving about in their yard. Presumably they were security personnel, most likely VC, but we never spotted any of them during daylight hours.

Since the French obviously had a special status in Saigon, we were not able to investigate their peculiar behavior or do anything about it. Besides, we assumed they were our old friends. I sincerely hoped though, that the Baron could eventually provide me with some information about the French connections. One thing was very clear to us; just as we watched them, our compound and our operations were under constant scrutiny by the Viet Cong and their special agents as well.

Our guards frequently pointed out to us that a little old lady, carrying a baby, suspiciously kept walking up and down the Rue in front of the French building. Several times during the day she stopped briefly, handling the baby, but always keeping an eye on our gate. It was very plain that she was observing all vehicles leaving and entering past our guards at the front. When this woman was finally stopped by one of my irritated guards to be questioned, she reportedly uttered some insulting words and started hitting the guard.

Grabbed by the guard to be taken into the compound, she managed to free herself, starting to run down the street. Pursued, she dropped the little kid and to our guard's surprise, a hand grenade, which she must have carried underneath her dress. A Viet-Namese National Police patrol in the area noticed her running from the guard and promptly apprehended her, after our security people reported her suspicious activity to them. It had been common knowledge, that some female operatives were carrying explosive devices in their body cavities. Well-known to our indigenous soldiers, but hard to believe for most Americans, those innocent looking females often used different types of explosives on various targets of opportunity.

I must have had my Buddha or a guardian angel with me one evening, when I took a ride in a jeep with an American civilian friend of mine. We visited a Viet-Namese Bar near the German Embassy, leaving the vehicle parked across the street. After a brief visit, we were about to leave the establishment, when a young Viet-Namese girl, who had met my friend before, called us back inside, insisting that we have another glass of "Saigon Tea", a customary alcoholic concoction. Hesitating, and suspicious, we gave in and returned inside for another drink.

It was not more than about a minute thereafter when a detonation occurred across the street. It was our jeep, in flames, but nobody nearby. Had I been sitting in the vehicle during the explosion, it would undoubtedly have killed my friend and me. After the shock had worn off, the girl explained, that she had watched a younger man walk around the vehicle and, covering the gas tank with his body, drop something into the gas tank. We heard of such sabotage acts before, where an incendiary device of some sort would explode shortly after insertion into gasoline tank. When the man either saw us or was told by someone we were leaving the bar, he must have dropped it in the tank, giving him adequate time to leave before we climbed into the vehicle and have an unexpected blast.

Needless to say, I never left a vehicle unattended again, no matter how safe the area appeared to be, especially in Saigon, where incidents like this became more and more common.

Looking at the brighter side of combat service in 'Nam, one of the more exciting and pleasurable times were those when the entertainer June Collins showed up after she entertained the troops at various US troop facilities and bases. Our Detachment was privileged to provide her temporary safe quarters at our compound during her visit in Saigon. She was one of many Australian beauties who, like Bob Hope, were given special protection while visiting Viet Nam and whenever she came to Saigon. Strange as it may seem but it became my job to see to her needs, including escorting her to dinner whenever she stayed overnight.

It was a riot whenever she visited. Martha Raye, our very own US entertainer was also a frequent visitor. She was undoubtedly the darling of the Special Forces, who made no beans about the fact that she loved her SF NCOs. Known to be a registered nurse, she proudly wore a green beret with a Lieutenant Colonel rank insignia. She was known to be rather foulmouthed and famous for leaving the dirtiest jokes on the restroom walls, but her unique character added humor to the often-bizarre happenings around us.

A Happy Chinese New Year It Was Not - Têt Offensive Brings Combat to Saigon

It was a rather rude awakening on 30 January 1968, when I heard weapons firing outside my quarters facing the street. Jumping out of my bed I reached for my weapon nearby in anticipation of a possible attack on the compound. When no further rounds were fired and everything seemed quiet, I figured the firing to be just an accidental discharge of weapons by the jittery security personnel. It was beginning to get light outside and I immediately met with my staff and duty personnel to check into the weapons firing.

Incidentally, "Têt", the Chinese Lunar New Year, is considered a time to relax and was customarily celebrated with fireworks. Not that time. The fireworks we were going to experience were not what we expected. As the first messages came in rapid succession, they could not be misunderstood. Our communications section reported some unusual VC activity during the night in the Cholon district. This was the Chinese section of Saigon, where Russian-type trucks had been spotted nearby. Several of my security personnel living in Cholon had previously given us information about unusual movements of groups of people throughout their district. This type of activity violated established curfew hours and was very abnormal. Coming from reliable sources it became quite disturbing. Our suspicions were to be correct.

All of a sudden, all hell broke loose. Reports were received that several of our Chinese Nungs did not report for duty. Information trickled in that they apparently had been caught in the battle with regular North Viet-Namese troops. These Regulars had emerged from tunnels dug and built underneath the Phu To Race Track. Those troops were engaged in open battles with the South Viet-Namese Army units and the National Police throughout that part of the city.

While the battles raged on around the Race Track, a message came in from our CIA contacts that the US Embassy had just been attacked. Several MP guards had been killed or wounded and VCs were swarming all over the compound. Several scarcely armed Americans had isolated themselves on the upper floors. They were hoping for relief troops to free them and to regain control of the compound. But with several trouble spots suddenly developing in many areas in and around Saigon, priorities must have gotten lost.

One Military Police unit from the 716th MP Battalion attempting to rescue the embassy personnel was held up by engagements with other VC units along their relief route. It took nearly an hour before they could finally make it to the Embassy, to engage the VCs regain control of the grounds and the building again. It took nearly another two hours before a platoon of the 101st Airborne Division landed by helicopter to add to the security of the embassy. Through all this fighting and turmoil, Ambassador Ellsworth Bunker fortunately remained unhurt.

Next to our compound was a big four-story building, which housed several US Government agencies. Most of the personnel were civilians working for USAID, while others were providing support and assistance to several Viet-Namese Government Operations. Totally unexpected, we received some frantic calls from them, asking us, if we could provide some security for them. According to them, they had been receiving incoming rifle fire and felt extremely vulnerable. We had gotten reports, that the VC had selected and assaulted several government facilities throughout the city. After they had penetrated the buildings they had either executed the inhabitants or taken them hostage.

Our Detachment's mission was very specific which did not require us to provide protection for civilian complexes. Considering that American lives were at stake, we could at least make arrangements to provide them with a supply of hand grenades for their own personal protection. Our Nung security personnel at the gate were also advised that there was a possibility of VC suicide squads attacking our facility and the adjacent buildings. To protect our compound they were instructed to provide cover by fire to buildings next to ours should any suspicious activity become apparent. Any occupation of adjacent buildings by an enemy would seriously compromise our own security.

Although generally enjoyed by a mutually agreed upon and accepted cease-fire period throughout Viet-Nam, this Têt was to be nothing even close to a peaceful holiday season. We soon found that the US Embassy was not to be an isolated target of the communists. Various elements of the over two hundred fifty men strong VC Sapper unit assaulted other targets such as the Viet-Namese Presidential Palace, the Vietnam Navy Headquarters and the US Airbase at Tan Son Nhut.

General Westmoreland's MACV Headquarters and other main Headquarters critical to our military operations in South Viet-Nam were among prize objectives. Unable to give Gen. Westmoreland my regular briefing, I planned to take an armed jeep with a two-man team of Nungs and try to possibly retrieve some of my security people from Cholon. Passing the Race Track, we got under heavy fire. Realizing, that I did not have the proper firepower to respond and still had a Detachment to run, I decided to drop the effort. There was hope that those missing would make it out of the area somehow.

Returning past one of the Officer Billets for Majors and Colonels near the Track, we spotted an Army jeep, shot up, with several US officers lying nearby on the ground. It appeared they were shot execution style. Because of our "no weapon carrying" policy before Têt, they obviously did not have a chance to defend themselves against their attackers. Among them I found my old friend, another immigrant from Germany, Maximillian Simmeth, an Infantry Major, who I had served with in Germany with the Airborne Group. He had been working with General Westmoreland's staff.

His body was later retrieved and even though I tried hard to escort and return his body to his parents, my efforts were fruitless. Our situation in Vietnam at that that time just did not permit it. Returning to my compound, I was brought up to date of additional developments during the day. Some days seemed to be longer and busier than any others.

One message read that our Special Forces Headquarters and that of our counterparts in Nha Trang had been attacked repeatedly. They successfully repelled the VC and the North Viet-Namese, with most losses suffered by the VC. Aside from the Nha Trang, they also had significant losses from their assaults of provincial capitols and smaller cities, including our military facilities. Considered only harassing actions, Da Nang, with its airbase and my former C-Team Headquarters location and LTC Schungle, was also under a ground attack by several companies of VC infiltrators.

Obviously the VC and North Viet-Namese had disregarded the cease-fire throughout South Vietnam. MACV finally cancelled our cease-fire and directed resumption of normal operations in preparation of a pending all-out offensive by the enemy. We realized that the early morning assaults were only a prelude of what this Têt Offensive was really going to be like for the following days.

As in any war, the free world also lost a lot of civilians caught in the middle. Reading the newspaper the following day, I was deeply moved by the reported loss of the German Embassy official Baron von Collenberg, who was caught by the Viet Cong during street fighting also near the Phu To Race Track. He was found blindfolded, his hands tied behind him and shot in his back of his head. The Baron was left near his white Volkswagen only about three blocks from a site where four correspondents, from

Australia and Great Britain were brutally slain by the Viet Cong that same day.

The US Command decided to improve security around all sensitive and strategic facilities. After about a week of search and destroy operations, the enemy appeared to either withdraw or disappear after their unsuccessful attempts to gain overall control during Têt. All indications were that they were regrouping for future renewed major assaults on US military facilities.

Most of the Special Forces camps along the Laotian border and near larger cities, such as Hue and Da Nang came under heavy ground attacks by the regular North Viet-Namese Divisions and during the first week of February 1968. Our SF camp at Lang Vei was overrun by North Viet-Namese P-76 Russian-made tanks. I had the feeling that my old camp of Kham Duc would undoubtedly be next.

The troops at Lang Vei resisted the onslaught and fought bravely with their C-Team Commander, LTC Schungel flown in, fighting at their side. With thirteen Green Berets wounded and ten declared missing or dead out of a total of twenty-four, they finally had to be extracted. Three quarters of the CIDG Montagnards at Lang Vei were unaccounted for but, considered fierce and loyal troops, they were probably killed during the assault.

Constantly monitoring communications between 5th SF Group in Nha Trang and other units, there were clear signs that the North Viet-Namese were moving major units South within Laos past Kham Duc. While control had been reestablished within the capitol, it was an uneasy quiet that had returned to Saigon. It was apparent that the Viet Cong had not achieved any significant victory in the Capitol, but it clearly showed the vulnerabilities and weaknesses because of our false sense of security living in the capitol. It was quite obvious that, since our halting of the bombing of North Viet-Nam, the North Viet-Namese Army was fiercely building up their combat elements in Laos and Cambodia.

Shockingly bad news reached me on Mothers Day, 10 May 1968, when a message stated that our Kham Duc satellite Special Forces Camp of Ngok Tavak was being attacked by an estimated full battalion of North Viet-Namese troops. Following a report from a prisoner, captured around the beginning of the month of May, who revealed the pending attack on Kham Duc and Ngok Tavak, their fortifications had been significantly improved.

Aerial view of Camp Kham Duc,
Viet-Nam. Home of Det. A-105, 5th
Special Forces Group.

Insignia of Viet-
Nam Special Forces
(LLDB)

Some of my Camp's LLDB troops
posing under the Berlin Flag.

My Detachment Team members with the
Viet-Namese LLDB Team Commander.

"Bringing home the bacon"
Amazing what hand grenade
fishing can do.

Civic Action with the locals. Could not beat a good
french coffee in our only Kham Duc Village Cafe.

Additional US Artillery and CIDG mortar units, plus a one hundred twenty-two man Nung Mobile Strike Force of the US Special Forces were deployed to strengthen both areas. A later message revealed that despite all the efforts to hold the complexes, including close air and helicopter gunship fire support, both camps fell into the hands of the enemy after some successful escape and evasion operations by US troops.

Out of some forty-four Aussies and Americans at Ngok Tavak, fifteen were killed in action, two were declared missing and twenty three wounded. Casualties from Kham Duc amounted to nearly six Americans missing and thirty-two KIA. Losses among the Nungs and CIDG troops were about the same. The runways of both Ngok Tavak and Kham Duc were littered with shot-down helicopters and several burned out C-130 Air Force aircraft. Other C-130s, which were attempting to evacuate civilians, women and children from Kham Duc were shot down as they were barely clearing the hill surrounding the camp.

Surprisingly enough, the North Viet-Namese had reportedly ceased firing to permit three medical evacuation helicopters retrieve and fly out wounded. It did not stop them though from subsequently shooting down a larger CH-46 Helicopter attempting to land more indigenous troops. Although little known, the Battle of Kham Duc-Nogk Tavak, although short in duration, was the most devastating fight and showed the highest number of missing of any battle in Viet-Nam.

I must admit that I am proud of my service in Vietnam yet I still feel sorry for the loss of all those I knew and admired at Kham Duc, who lost their lives in this senseless conflict.

Goodbye Saigon, Farewell Friends

Although my combat tour in Viet-Nam was quite eventful and often extremely frustrating, I had mixed feelings, when I received my orders the following month to return to the US. After my exciting one year stint in South Vietnam, I felt that I had not quite completed my part of the assigned tasks. One year in Viet-Nam was just too short. Although happy to be returning to my family in the US, I felt that I was disappointing those, who I had made friends with while in country and that I was actually deserting them. I can now understand why so many Special Forces men elected to return to Viet-Nam a second or even a third time to finish what they did not have time to accomplish before.

On my last day in Saigon, my Chinese Nungs presented me with a beautifully old heavy solid brass incense burner and two matching candleholders. I promised myself that I will treasure those pieces forever. Receiving the air medal for participating in flights for over two hundred hours over hostile territory and surviving without a scratch on my body only strengthened my belief in Kismet. I strongly felt the power of my good luck charms, from my little Buddha, the Montagnard bracelet and the time-battered orange-colored Chinese good luck cloth.

After a brief farewell, with my personal belongings all packed and shipped, I left the CLD compound and made my way to Ton San Nhut Air Base. I kept my fingers crossed that "Charlie" would not try anything stupid to prevent me from leaving this war-torn country in one piece to see my family again. Watching several military ambulance evacuation aircraft departing for the US, I felt gratified and lucky to be still intact, while wishing those guys aboard the evacuation planes the best of luck in their future.

During the flight back to the States, everybody aboard the aircraft appeared deep in thought and hopeful that they find everything unchanged stateside with the families still unharmed and healthy. My new orders assigned me to Fort Bragg, NC and I expected to Special Forces again.

However, Department of the Army felt differently and assigned me instead to the 82nd Airborne Division. This, of course meant that I had to be without my green beret for the time being. At least I had another Airborne assignment for which I was grateful. Naturally, the first thing on my mind was a reunion with my family and a thirty-day vacation, which I looked forward to spending it with the kids. As it was June and they were out of school and on vacation, it gave us ample time to travel and visit friends.

Chapter VII

After a Brief Stay at Home, the Far East Beckons Again

Welcome Back to Fort Bragg

Recalling my previous experience as the Assistant G-2 at Fort Knox, I was actually looking forward to experience the challenges as the S-2 of the 1st Brigade, 82nd Airborne Division. This at least gave me more time to spend with the family. That was something I was not used to while being in Special Forces, considering the many varied projects and operations I was involved in.

Part of my responsibilities involved processing security clearances for all troops requiring one for their sensitive position and job. The primary task involved providing intelligence and counterintelligence information for exercises and special operations conducted by the Brigade.

Still thinking 'SF', I found the Brigade needed some special means to collect intelligence in the field. When I proposed to the Brigade Commander LTC Brooks that we create a unique small unit within the Brigade, assigned to and working for the Intelligence Section, he agreed. This special reconnaissance unit would be tasked to work like scouts with the specific mission to obtain essential intelligence information for the Brigade. After some serious planning, I was finally able to establish the first so-called LRRP or Long Range Reconnaissance Patrol. It was made up of a team of specially selected and highly qualified intelligence personnel. The LRRPs turned out to be an important asset and important resource for reliable information in our operations.

It was during the last week of January 1969, when I received a call from Germany informing me that my father, the old warrior was seriously ill in the Hospital in Heidelberg. My mother thought it important enough to call me and recommended that I come to visit him.

Granted emergency leave, I took a commercial flight via New York to Frankfurt and continued by rental car to Heidelberg. Apparently he had a relapse of his Malaria he had picked up while serving in Africa during World War II. Following my visit and a few good old soldier jokes, he seemed to become his old self again and expressed his embarrassment that mother had even sent for me. He was sure I had better things to do and urged me to take advantage of my time available until my return flight and visit friends in Germany.

I frequently visited him, since I had two weeks until my scheduled departure. Visiting numerous friends, I could not get out of talking about my tour and repeating my experiences in Viet Nam. After a while though it became quite tiring. I was longing to get back home to the States. On the day of my departure from Germany I said my goodbyes to my father and the family and left Heidelberg hoping for the best for my father's total recovery.

Showing up in the Frankfurt Airport for my regularly scheduled flight I was told that New York had such a bad snowstorm that all flights had been delayed for at least a full day. Unsure as to what to do, I remembered a good friend living near the airport. Calling him just to talk on the phone, he heard about my dilemma and insisted that I visit him and his family and even spend the night there. Frequent calls to the airline to check on outgoing flights could easily made from his home.

My friend Heinz was a German Army Officer, who was glad that I could visit him and his wife to spend some relaxing time exchanging ideas and talking about Viet Nam. Receiving confirmation for the next flight, I returned to the airport. Although some flights had resumed to the East Coast, most flights were diverted to Philadelphia because of continued snowing in New York. I was glad to finally make it back to Fort Bragg, where I found myself up to my neck in work, which had piled up during my absence.

Parachuting into Turkey

Our Brigade was frequently tasked by the Division to participate in a NATO Exercise dubbed Deep Furrow 69. It required the Brigade Commander and an Operations or Intelligence Officer with a high level NATO Security Clearance to attend a Final Planning and Coordination Conference at Izmir, Turkey. My wife and my children could hardly believe that I would have to leave again. Traveling to unusual places seemed to have become a pattern in my life. I seemed to be destined to spend an enormous amount of time away from home.

Although the conference itself only lasted four days, we had the opportunity to visit the surrounding area and actually check out the site, where our parachute drop would be executed. The Drop Zone was near the city of Izmir in Turkey and involved close coordination with the US Air Force and the Turkish Armed Forces. Since it was my first time in that part of Europe, it was quite interesting for me to observe the customs and traditions of the Turkish Army.

What a difference in discipline from our military when considering their conduct and apparent total obedience of their troops toward their officers. While at the conference, we also noted several Greek Army Officers present at the conference. Since we were going to use some of their air space it required special coordination between these two neighboring nations. It became quite obvious, the Greeks and the Turks did not like each other.

During a general conversation the Greeks mentioned that they were disappointed, because the US did not extend the airborne operation into their country, especially since our former first lady had married a Greek, which the Turks did not like. Because of that relationship, the Greeks almost expected that we give them a larger part in participation. We stated that the decision had been made by higher Headquarters and was strictly non-political, but this was hard to explain to them. It was not easy to diplomatically ease out of this rather sensitive issue, but we eventually did.

To please both sides, we told the Greeks that we will consider deploying our Naval forces during this exercise to provide some Naval support from the Greek side and the Aegean Sea. They thought this plan to be a grand idea and we left it at that.

While in Turkey, our Turkish hosts did their best to show us around Instanbul and Izmir, and gave us some valuable tips at a brief shopping trip. Being among men, they also showed us the red light district in Izmir, which was somewhat different from the one in Hamburg, Germany, where the "ladies" sit inside a display window like a model. There was nothing that extravagant in Izmir and I was told that most of those women were not professionals. Most of them were supposedly wives of men who were working off their husband's prison sentences or fines handed down by a court for crimes committed by men, who could not pay their fines.

Even though it sounded strange, I had no reason to doubt them. I even noticed a very old woman leaving the health check building, where regular medical check-ups were being given. Aside from the red light district, the overall tour somehow reminded me of Kreuzberg, one of the districts in Berlin, which was heavily populated by Turks. During a period of severe labor shortages in Berlin, the German government invited many migrant workers from Turkey to fill jobs in Germany. Settling down in Kreuzberg, they brought with them their culture, traditions and way of life. This district was commonly known as "Little Turkey".

Living in Berlin, with all its amenities and big salaries, I could understand why they would not desire to return to Turkey, but rather bring part of their culture and lifestyle to Germany including food specialty stores. Following our visit, we returned to the States to make final preparations for the Brigade's NATO Exercise. The operation found the entire Brigade flying non-stop from Ft Bragg, NC to Izmir, Turkey for one grand parachute landing just outside the city of Izmir. It was an impressive way to demonstrate our capability to rapidly deploy to Europe for the possible defense of this NATO ally.

Join the Army and See the World. Enjoying Another Far East Tour

Following the exercise, our Brigade returned to Fort Bragg and, of course, Fayetteville and the family, who had missed me, I was told. The unique souvenirs I always brought back from the various countries I visited were always appreciated. Christine was not so enthused however, as she was always thinking about our repeated moves and the ever-increasing added weight and work in future packing and unwrapping.

The collection of mementos, like street signs, cement blocks from the Berlin Wall, to mention just a few, became so voluminous that we ran out of room to display them. We were all looking forward to the day, when we could find a more permanent home to call our own, where we have adequate space to display all the souvenirs and trinkets. Having served only a little over half of my planned twenty year service career, this little house would have to suffice for the time being.

At least we could consider it home to which we were always able to return to when getting stationed at Ft Bragg following overseas assignments. Especially when faced with an unaccompanied tour, the family could stay behind at our home and the kids could have an uninterrupted school education. Fort Bragg was a post, where frequent troop rotations were a norm. Following a minimum of a one-year assignment there, one could usually expect to leave for a one-year assignment to either Viet Nam or Korea. Without doubt, there was still the possibility of another accompanied three-year commitment to Europe.

The Army was not exactly the best place to foster long lasting friendships, especially among fellow soldiers. And so the day came, when, after having been back at Fort Bragg for only about fifteen months, that I had to tell my wife and kids that I had received new orders for the Orient again. Only this time it was not Viet Nam as I had expected, but Korea. We had a Special Forces Unit in Korea and I was hopeful that I would find a home there. However, to my disappointment, I was assigned to a "leg" unit, the non-airborne 2nd Infantry Division of the 8th US Army.

The Pentagon's reason, when questioned, was that I needed to round out my career pattern. Our SF Detachment in Korea had no openings for a promotable Captain or a Major. Unknown to me, I had passed the promotion board for field grade officers and on 8 September 1969 I was summoned to the Brigade Commander's office where I found Christine visiting. After Colonel Brooks called me on the carpet, he read a promotion order to me whereupon both she and the Brigade Commander pinned the golden Major leaves on my uniform.

But that was not the only surprise that awaited me. He also congratulated me and pinned my Senior Parachute Wings on my uniform. I had not counted my Airborne jumps and therefore had lost track of the number of jumps I had made. It was a very gratifying day for this old refugee to have reached another unusual and rewarding moment in his career.

Strangely enough, tapped for another unaccompanied overseas tour again, I did not mind it too much leaving again, although I was sure the family did. Slated for a thirteen-month tour of duty this time, I realized once again that I had volunteered for this life style and was content to do the expected. Life had obviously at lot of challenges planned for me, but I was fortunate to have a very understanding wife and children, who, I am sure, knew that in the end I did it all for them.

But before leaving for Korea, I was granted thirty days of ordinary leave. It was almost becoming a routine that I take a vacation around the time I was scheduled for another assignment. Army regulations required that I take it because I had accumulated almost ninety days of vacation. Not using at least thirty days, I would lose all days over sixty. Needless to say, I had no qualms about taking a vacation. Who in his right mind would? I had a very extensive 'Honey-do-List' for planned projects around the house. Beautifying the grounds and modifying some parts of the house itself were always tasks I thoroughly enjoyed.

Building a new driveway entrance to the property by constructing a new stone gate was one undertaking, which challenged my talents as a stonemason, not used since my days I was a combat engineer. Adding a new nice split rail fence, it seemed to give the family the feeling of having a little more security. Accumulating an assortment of various tools over the years, there was also a definite need for a shed. Admittedly, tools were really not the only reason for a tool shed. I had that great offer, and I was sure it was a one-time opportunity, to acquire a genuine German BMW 660 motorcycle from an Air Force Captain. He had been newly assigned to Pope Air Force Base adjacent to Fort Bragg and must have either grown tired of it or found the weather quite different from Florida to warrant its future use. The bike was a dream machine.

I still don't know to this day whether Christine was really in favor of this purchase or not, but at least it gave her the total use of the car, while I drove the BMW to work. Having the only motorcycle on Post, it took me awhile to get the appropriate Post tags. Riding the BMW was not only fun for me but also the rest of the family, especially Ines and son Dieter who could hardly wait to be taken for rides. Throughout the year the weather was generally very favorable for motorcycle riding.

Owning a home, I found, was requiring me to learn a lot about maintenance. Fixing and repairing different items became increasingly challenging. Whether it was removing a kitchen window and enlarging the hole to install a sliding door for the planned patio or pouring concrete, it was always a rewarding experience finishing and later admiring the end product. Unaware of certain requirements I did all work without a building permit, thinking it was unnecessary. I always liked to make things appear more expensive than they actually were. Painting lines on a poured patio, I imitated slates making the new porch looking almost like real slates.

After a few weeks of actually enjoying the improvements, I got down to preparing for my departure to my next assignment, unsure of exactly what unit I would be assigned to. Saying farewell to the family always seemed to be rather brief, while the goodbyes from friends and fellow comrades usually turned out to be rather lengthy and drawn out affairs. Visiting various homes and subsequently the Officers Clubs to find out specifics about my future destination, usually took more than just a few hours. Old customs, traditions and the strong feeling of the old Esprit de Corps, were just so different in those days compared to later imposed rules and regulations. You never left your unit or comrades-in-arms without properly toasting to the past and the future, which undoubtedly can take considerable time. We were always wondering if we would ever see each other again.

Welcome to the "Land of Morning Calm", the Republic of South Korea

Surviving several headaches and a lot of farewell parties later, I finally said goodbye to the family and Fort Bragg. Departing in November 1969 from Fayetteville Airport by commercial air, I arrived at McCord Air Force Base, Tacoma, Washington for a continued flight by Military Air Transport to KIMPO Airbase. The airbase was located right outside of Seoul, the capitol of the Republic of South Korea.

My arrival in Korea was quite a bit different in comparison with my previous experiences in Viet-Nam. Both the wartime climate and the heat were totally absent. The weather was similar to the temperature in North Carolina, but I was reminded by some people, that it was unusually warm in Korea for that year's season.

Picked up by a sedan, we traveled only a few miles North to Camp Howze, Headquarters of the 2nd Division of the 8th United States Army. The 8th Army was first line of defense for the United Nations Command, responsible for the security of the Demilitarized Zone at the 38th Parallel. The drive was quite short and led us past numerous rice paddies, encountering hardly any traffic except military vehicles.

In-Processing, including a briefing explaining the mission of the division and the threat from Communist North Korea was short but thorough. After hours of anxious waiting I finally received my assignment, which was more than what I had expected, but then I had always been lucky and usually content with my duties. General Michaelis, the Division Commander greeted all of us new arrivals and welcomed us to the 2nd Infantry Division, where he reiterated the importance of our assignments within the UN Command.

He also stressed our excellent relationship with our counterparts, the KATUSA, or "Korean Augmentation To the US Army".

I received my orders assigning me as the Battalion Executive Officer to the 1st Battalion of the 9th Infantry (Manchu), a historical unit with a long and outstanding military record going back to the boxer rebellion in China. I was very impressed by his speech and knew that I was not going to be disappointed. Although I was not going to be parachuting during my assignment in Korea, the fact that I was going to be part of a unique unit with a mission to maintain peace and guard the frontier, made up for my initial disappointment.

Coincidentally, I was again facing a communist block country quite similar to my past assignment in Berlin. The mission of the unit convinced me of the importance of my assignment, especially when I realized the fact that my Battalion was operating in a hostile area. The Army realized the adversities troops had to face in a combat zone along the border with North Korea and consequently considered it a hardship tour of only thirteen months.

An assignment along the Demilitarized Zone was quite different from duties at 8th Army Headquarters in the Capitol itself, which was generally considered a cushy job. Some lucky soldiers assigned to Seoul, even had the privilege of serving in a general staff position enjoying a three year tour accompanied by the families, being housed in outstanding quarters with live-in maid service.

A young driver, SP4 Doug Perry, picked me up in a black jeep from Division Headquarters and after we loaded my gear he took me on a relaxing drive along a country road. Traveling through several quaint little villages and along large rice paddies and an occasionally straw-thatched hut, we eventually reached Munsan, a larger town just South of the Demilitarized Zone. Out of the blue, my driver suddenly asked me to watch the spare tire mounted on the back of the jeep.

Naturally, I was baffled, but he quickly explained. He had just lost his spare tire only a couple weeks ago driving thru town within the posted 10 mile speed limit. Going into more details, he told me that kids usually run alongside and following behind the jeep waving and yelling, drawing your attention. At that moment, someone in the crowd to your rear cleverly removed the spare tire taking off with it. Watching the excited, seemingly friendly kids, I had my doubts about the truth of his story. It was later confirmed and I felt like I had to apologize for doubting him.

My own personal impression of the Koreans was, that they were a very proud, graceful and courteous people. They also seem to have a keen sense of humor and were quick to laugh, as information brochures stated, but I decided to keep an open mind to reserve my judgment for later. My initial feeling was later to be confirmed, with only very few exceptions as you find them among any race and in any country. From all the information I had received and read, I knew that I had entered a country with an ancient culture and proud traditions both of which I was eager to observe, study and learn from.

In retrospect, I regretted only that I had not been given the opportunity to study the Korean Language, but I was seriously hoping that I might have the opportunity to learn it while serving in Korea.

After a forty-minute ride from Division Headquarters departure, we approached a military checkpoint at "Freedom Bridge", spanning the Imjin River. Entering a restricted area, the road crossing the bridge was guarded by a combined detail of US Military MPs and South Korean Soldiers, members of the KATUSA. After clearing the checkpoint, we arrived at the Battalion's Post, located right at the Demilitarized Zone, my new home, off and on, for the next thirteen months.

The Battalion actually had two camps. One 'forward', Camp Liberty Bell, was located just North of the Imjin River in a restricted area and the combat zone. The other one was just South of the river, which permitted troops to have more leisure time and freedom of movement following an occasional rotation from the North to the South Camp Dodge.

While at the northern camp, troops were on constant alert and twenty-four hours duty, monitoring the movements of the Communist troops from several outposts located in the center of the DMZ. Flying from the three flagpoles at the Battalion Headquarters, I noticed the center pole flying the blue flag of the United Nations, flanked by the American and the Korean flags. Lieutenant Colonel Hansen, the Battalion Commander welcomed me with a smile, a firm handshake and the question if I played chess, which I answered in the affirmative but adding that I am probably a lousy player not having played for many years. That was soon to change.

Settling in Along the DMZ

Following his introduction to my new staff, he took me on a tour of the camp, its defenses and quarters, as well as the support facilities, such as the dispensary, mess hall and dayrooms. When we walked up to a predominant hilltop and a high barbed wired hurricane fence, the southern border of the DMZ. He pointed out a large Quonset hut sitting right on top of the bald hill. The hut was overlooking the fence and the DMZ, which revealed a picturesque looking village nestled just beyond the border in the ·no-mans land. The commander smiled and told me that this was our home, while we were located north of the Imjin River.

The building, if one wants to call it that, sat there exposed, resembling a half buried large drum with tiny windows cut out. Not exactly appearing very inviting nor attractive, it was surrounded by sandbags and a water tank outside to provide water for the quarters inside. Korean guards were constantly walking their post on a trail alongside the fence and the building. The Quonset hut was divided into two sections, providing quarters for the Battalion Commander and myself, with my section facing the DMZ and the enemy. We both shared the shower and restroom in the center.

The idea of my quarters possibly being a reference point for the enemy artillery was not exactly a comforting feeling. LTC Hansen's residence pointed toward the lower laying battalion area with a view of all activities going on within the compound.

Generally, the rooms were fairly comfortable with potbellied stoves of WWII vintage sitting in the middle of the rooms. The one thing I did not like was the fact that my room was facing the enemy but had no window to view the no-mans land. When I asked the Commander if I could have a window put in to be able to watch across the DMZ, he told me that I could do whatever I liked to make the quarters more comfortable. I was determined to change it as soon as I had my feet on the ground and was acclimated to my new job.

Adjacent to our camp, located at Panmunjom inside the DMZ, was the United Nations Command Security Force (UNCSF-JSA) or Joint Security Area. US Army personnel stationed at the JSA were responsible for the security and operation of the frequent Military Armistice Commission's negotiation talks between the North Koreans and the United Nations Command. Representing the UNC were Officers of the United States Army and the Republic of Korea (ROK). At all times, both, the US Military Police with the KATUSA and the North Koreans were patrolling their respective side of the territory of the conference building.

A wide yellow line was running straight through the building and conference table, separating the North from the South at the 38th Parallel. To show their imaginary power and superiority, the communists constantly changed the appearance of several items of importance. By sometimes raising their chairs, their microphones or their often enlarged flags they attempted to irritate the UN representatives. It seemed rather childish to us, but our side nevertheless just played along with their games to show them we cannot be intimidated.

It was different with the uniformed neutral representatives of Sweden and Switzerland, as well as those from Poland and Czechoslovakia They were stationed separately in camps in the Southern and Northern part of the DMZ adjacent to the JSA. Although they had the responsibility of assuring neutrality of the talks as a result of the armistice talks following the signing in July 1953, they rarely intervened in clashes between the North and the South. Quite familiar with the communist system, I could well imagine the conditions these members had to live under and the hardships they had to endure.

We had information which revealed neither one of the neutral representatives had any freedom of movement to check or investigate anything within the North Korean territory as stipulated by the UN. A young Swedish Lieutenant was reportedly killed with a baseball bat wrapped with barbed wire by some members of the North Korean People's Army because he offended some communist soldier.

Later, in 1984 a young Captain Bonifas and a Lieutenant Barrett overseeing a work detail near the famous "Bridge of No Return" were viciously attacked by Communist Korean Troops and murdered with axes. It became known as the Panmunjom Axe Murder.

Initiation into the "Manchu" Battalion

Well, since nobody had ever related to me the history of the Battalion before joining the unit, this oversight was soon to be remedied at an upcoming weekend. My driver pulled up to the office with my jeep one evening to inform me that the Colonel wanted to see me at the JSA immediately. When I looked around to find one of my staff officers to man the office I could not find anybody. Perry stated that it was urgent and that the Commander needed to see me there immediately. The Sergeant Major was on his way to hold down the fort.

It was my first visit to the area and I was surprised to find the JSA to have all amenities the soldiers needed in an isolated area. I did not, however, expect them to have a nice little Officers Club, the "Monastery", where Perry had been instructed to drop me off. He left me with a mysterious grin on his face. Reminding him to stand by to pick me up, he stated that I would not have to worry about that, because the Commander assured him that he would bring me back after the meeting. And what a meeting it was.

Entering the club I found just about everybody I was familiar with from my staff standing around a large table with a very sizeable silver bowl in the center. The bowl was surrounded by about twenty or more smaller pint sized silver goblets. The Commander asked me to join the group and apologized for calling me away from my work, but that this was necessary, as a matter of fact essential. A serious mistake had been made, he stated, through an oversight.

The problem was, he went on to say that I was not really yet an official member of the unit. It was an error he intended to correct immediately. With those words he instructed the Adjutant, LT Perna, to fill the goblets in order to initiate a new member into the brother-hood of the Manchu. After a brief recitation of the proud history of the Battalion, LTC Hansen proposed a toast to the President, our Commander-in Chief, the Army Commander, Division Commander and the new XO. My pint-sized goblet, with my name engraved was filled to the rim, while the other members only had theirs maybe one third full. I was somewhat uneasy, but not unwilling, to execute the toasting. Lifting my full goblet, which was lit and burning, I joined in with the chorus calling out the Manchu motto "Keep up the Fire"!

Without hesitation and as ordered, I downed the entire drink without stopping. My Commander reached out to congratulate me and handed to me an official, historical belt buckle of the 1st Battalion, 9th Infantry, the only battalion in the history of the United States Army, whose personnel was authorized by Congress to wear this special buckle.

Naturally, with an empty stomach and '151' Puerto Rican Rum in my stomach, my war stories I was asked to tell, only lasted about ten minutes when I unexpectedly saw my driver enter the room. And I felt it was time, because I suddenly experienced a weakness in my knees and was about to excuse myself, when two fellow officers escorted my out of the club under the applause of those present. I was advised to wear this buckle proudly throughout my career with my authorization handy, should I ever be questioned. Perry slowly drove me back to my quarters.

Before I fell asleep, feeling somewhat embarrassed, I wondered what the rest of my fellow officers would think about me, an old Ranger and

SF guy, nearly passing out so quickly. The next day I met a lot of smiling faces but no other comments, which I assumed to be the equivalent to an official acceptance into the unit.

Aside from routine administrative duties, our unit had the responsibility to conduct daily patrols of the No-mans land by jeep and check with the outpost bunkers located within the DMZ. At random times I left my office, mounted a jeep clearly marked with a US Military Police sign in English and Korean below the windshield. Flying a large white flag and carrying a mounted M-60 machine gun we passed a gate in the fence and drove into the DMZ. Slowly driving through the area, we stopped at our Command Post bunkers situated on several hilltops overlooking the northern part of the zone to insure North Korean troops had not attempted to penetrate our sector.

It was only a few months prior to my arrival that one of our patrol vehicles had been ambushed and the three occupants killed. This serious violation required us from that time on to patrol with armed vehicles. My previous curiosity as to why the DMZ was considered a combat or hostile area was fully answered as a result of this incident. This incident was not the only reason, because there had been several sniper actions taken by the North Koreans. Even I had a personal taste of what hostile fire meant.

I was routinely visiting one of the bunkers one night to check our night vision devices and other alert systems. As I was peering through the opening of the bunker, I felt like smoking a cigarette. Lighting it and taking a first drag, I heard a loud crack followed by a feeling of something burning hot slipping down my neck. Taking off my helmet to check the cause, I found a deformed bullet lodged between my skin and the jacket. When I looked closer at my helmet, I noticed a small bullet hole on front near the top of the steel pot. Undoubtedly it was the entry point of a bullet. Without a doubt the round had penetrated the outer shell of the helmet and then, slowed down by the plastic insert, it traveled in a circle inside until it dropped. No other evidence was needed to convince me that this was a combat zone and receiving monthly combat pay while in the DMZ was certainly warranted.

On the return trip to the base I checked a few more individual posts to insure the guards were not tempted to smoke thereby exposing themselves, when lighting the cigarette. Since we had below freezing temperatures, the soldiers often huddled in some foxholes near the bunkers, trying to keep warm. Isolated guard duty could sometimes be very boring, prompting negligence in maintaining vigilance.

Luckily, I checked one position just in time, because as I approached the position, I saw some small flames and an individual trying to extinguish the flames. Boredom and the cold had apparently contributed to the GI's mishap. He had a miniature kerosene stove under his poncho to keep warm, when he apparently fell asleep, setting himself on fire. His reaction and behavior when I talked to him, made me very suspicious. Further observation of him, while calling for his relief, convinced me that he was on some type of drug.

An examination by the battalion surgeon confirmed that the individual had smoked pot and probably dozed, causing the accident. He suffered some severe burns. Never having witnessed drug use by the troops in any of my previous units, it finally made me aware of a not so rare problem in the military. To my knowledge, there had never been any drug usage among the more mature Special Forces soldiers. Questioning my staff and several of the platoon leaders of the companies, I was briefed on several previous incidents. Soliciting recommendations to reduce or eliminate future intolerable situations within a combat zone, I considered implementing frequent drug testing.

Unless better controlled, incidents and accidents such as this could be very detrimental to the welfare of the entire command. Frequent rotations of units from the front line area to the rear was being considered to be one of the ways to reduce stress and boredom from the routine duties. The battalion did offer some recreational activities in our day rooms, where movies were shown several evenings a week. Young soldiers, however, definitely looked for more pleasant distractions. One solution, which most soldiers believed could make their tour more pleasant while off duty, would be occasional dances.

Arrangements with the USO and subsequent bi-monthly visits North of the Imjin River by young Korean ladies definitely raised the morale of the troops in the following months. The leadership agreed that caring for the troops and improving the overall morale and welfare of the command is essential to the accomplishment of the mission. Seeing smiles on the faces of the troops during those dancing affairs was gratifying. Being chaperoned and monitored during the events did not bother the troops at all.

After several weeks on the DMZ, one gets used to the lack of many customary conveniences. Once I had been exposed to deprivations found in Viet-Nam, it was relatively easy for me to deal with those "minor" shortcomings.

As in Germany in the earlier years after the war, we were issued ration cards and military script, the "funny money" of Korea. Designed to prevent a black market, it flourished nevertheless. Assigned a houseboy to take care of the Officers Quarters, I did not have to worry about my laundry or care-taking of my "home". They tried to do their best to please you, considering the pay was more than generous in comparison with the local economy.

Korea in the 70's had definite shortcomings of many things, especially in the technical area. Korea could not quite compete with Japan, but they did their best to copy items. I had purchased a brand new Japanese fan in the Post Exchange for my quarters but it unexpectedly quit after only a few weeks. When I took it back for an exchange, as it was under warranty, I was told that the warranty covers only the original Japanese make, but does not apply to Korean-made fans. Protesting was useless I was advised. I had been had. I may have bought a fine product in the PX before, as shown on my cashier's slip, but the serial numbers did not match. The Korean saleslady recommended that I better have a serious talk with my houseboy and ask him what had happened to my original fan.

Water was always a critical item up North and I was trying to make sure that water was not being wasted. When I complained to Maintenance, that my showerhead was constantly dripping, they told me that the washers were replaced just recently and could not be bad already. Checking the washer, I noticed that it could not have been the original but was evidently a substitute. It seemed that the houseboys had a habit of replacing the good washer, made in the USA, with a "kimchee"-rigged plastic or old rubber substitute. My stern warning to him not to alter any of the equipment was only received with a humbling smile. I now seriously suspected him of not only replacing the washers but also switching my fan.

Christine could not believe my request for assorted washers to bring my shower and faucet back to speed. Of course it took several weeks and additional thorough explanations of my strange request. When I mentioned that one would really have to be there to better understand the problems we have, she obviously understood that comment to be an invitation for her to come to Korea. She promptly replied, that she would be happy to come to Korea for a visit to see for herself, if she had the money for the trip.

Well, after giving it some serious thought, I checked with the Brigade Commander South of the Imjin River about such possibility. I don't believe it had been done before. He must have liked me, because he believed this to be a splendid idea and even offered his personal quarters for her in Korea. We would just swap quarters for this brief period. I immediately got on my PRC 125 radio on the jeep, called our Division's base station and through the switchboard placed a call to the States, which totally surprised her of course. When I told her, that I was calling her from my jeep at the DMZ, she only believed me after the switchboard operator explaining the "over" after each response on the radio. After several tries we finally got to communicate to everybody's satisfaction.

R&R in Korea?

Obtaining the necessary money required a great sacrifice on my part. We had to sell my BMW 660 motorcycle. I was sure that I could always save up some coins later on to buy myself a new one upon my return stateside. Excited about this unusual adventure, Christine had no problem selling the BMW to another fellow soldier on post. She was intrigued and determined the see the orient. My wife figured this trip could be a once in a lifetime opportunity and parking the two kids temporarily with friends in Hagerstown, MD was also easy. The Lahnigs had always liked our kids and they did not mind playing substitute parents to them.

Evidently, I really wanted to show her a good time, so I made some special arrangements with some local Koreans, with whom I had formed friendships over the past months. A principal of the local high school, where I spent some of my leisure time teaching English, and the headmaster of the "Love Orphanage" which our battalion sponsored and supported, they all looked forward to meeting Christine. I had to rely on Kim, a young lady to help me with special preparations. Kim was my translator who I trusted to escort and guide me through the occasional good will ambassador meetings with the local mayor. She would be ideal to also give Christine an insight into a Korean woman's life.

The Battalion Commander was not too fond of entertaining Koreans and preferred to stay away from the required civic action affairs. In his opinion, that was the Executive's job. Kim was a very pleasant woman, a terrific translator and my tutor in Korean culture and traditions. Under her tutelage I was beginning to learn more about their civilization and appreciated the Oriental culture more and more. She lived in a typical Korean rice-thatched building nearby in the little town of Kyong-gi-Do and, while in the South Camp Dodge, I always looked forward to spending some of my off-duty time with her. At the same time, I tried to tell her about German customs and way of life.

When I told her, that I planned to have my wife visit me in Korea, she was thrilled to meet a German woman and show her what life was like in Korea. She was afraid though that Christine might be somewhat disappointed, when she sees the conditions many Koreans live under. I managed to ease her apprehensions, assuring her that, if I liked the Koreans and their life style, she would also. That certainly would include some of the very peculiar foods and drinks. I was confident that Christine would love to be introduced to some real oriental food, such as 'Kim-chi' and their customary potent drink of Makli.

It was going to be quite interesting for her to try the home-made rice wine, not to mention the unheard of variations of American Whiskey. Unusual as it may seem to Westerners, Koreans soaked some kind of black water bugs in the Whiskey to produce, what they believe, a 'healthy' vitamin-rich Bourbon. Assured that this drink will definitely provide the consumer with extra vitality and vitamins I did try a few of those concoctions and some of their freshly harvested ginseng, which actually kept me in an unbelievable shape.

Ginseng was being grown in a very fertile area just South of the DMZ. As explained to me, it was brought to Korea from West Virginia by missionaries.

Koreans favored the root and consumed it in many different forms such as in soups and in salads but also soaked in a variety of alcoholic beverages, including Bourbon and Vodka. On one occasion I had to drink the root after I had a plate full of fried grasshoppers. I definitely needed that. Christine was certainly going to be thrilled with this unique cuisine and I convinced Kim that my wife was very open-minded, because she had also lived through some very hard times when she was young and that she appreciated different cultures. I hoped that I was right. After I had received Christine's itinerary, I scheduled my leave of absence to coincide with her vacation.

Christine flew via Tokyo, Japan where she had to stay overnight because of South Korea's nightly curfew. After she arrived at Kimpo, Perry and I picked her up with the jeep and brought her to Camp Dodge, South of the DMZ, where the Brigade Commander welcomed her and officially offered her to stay in his quarters, while he moved into mine. As I had two weeks of furlough, I had made arrangements to show her as much of Korea as possible, to include a visit to Osaka, Japan and the 1970 World EXPO. Once Christine had gotten over her jetlag feeling, I took her by jeep into the Demilitarized Zone to Panmunjom.

During the tour I took her inside the guarded conference building under the watchful eyes of the North Korean soldiers. Without warning she unknowingly crossed the yellow demarcation line and actually sat down at the conference table on the northern side, within the territory of the Peoples Republic of Korea. When the communists peering through the windows started to gesticulate, with their arms waving, I advised her immediately to come back to our side, as we certainly did not want to start an incident between North and South Korea. I am sure she got a kick out of this Panmunjom visit.

Experiences, such as this, seem to last forever and the pictures we had taken are a constant reminder of the good times we had, even when under some less than ideal conditions. It was quite obvious that my driver, Perry, surely enjoyed driving my wife around, as we visited the children in the orphanage and the local high school. The principal went all out and had the entire school assemble in the courtyard in formation, military style, where they sang a Korean song for her. Invited inside the school, she was asked to address the students in English, which, to my surprise she did, although I knew she was not too comfortable to speak to a larger group in public.

When the principal's wife asked me if she could take her for a little shopping trip, I couldn't say no and had Perry drive them to wherever they needed to go, while I stayed with the school children. Returning, I hardly recognized Christine at first, because she was completely dressed in Korean attire. It was a gift from the school, she was told, which I was sure to be able to return in kind, when the next opportunity availed itself.

Korea can truly boast about the many outstanding, hardly known achievements and their influence on other cultures and countries, especially on the Chinese. One can notice the mixture of the Korean language characters with those of the Chinese. Unknown to me, I found out that the Korean language is considered one of the oldest in the world. Touring the countryside, we found the oldest astronomical observatory in the world in the town of Kyongju. We were impressed with those splendid oriental structures and magnificent Buddhist temples throughout the area. According to history, it was in 1232, when Korean printers began using moveable metal type. This was nearly two centuries before Gutenberg used this process.

Surprising, as it may seem, the Korean culture is said to be the oldest culture in the world. I was repeatedly impressed by the so-called "gentlemen scholars of the East" and their leadership in artistic creations of oriental art. You find it expressed in woodcarvings, paintings or brass, to name just a few applications. While visiting some friends at their homes during the winter, which could be like the Siberian cold, I was genuinely impressed with the warmth in their residences. There was, to my amazement, a total absence of any type of visible heating device, except for a kiln-type structure on one side outside the dwelling and a small chimney on the other side. Commenting to the host about their comforting heat, I was shown a simple but very effective system. It was surely worth copying. People not only sat, as is customary, but also slept on the wooden floors, covered only with a small mat or mattress.

Since my arrival in Korea I was being taught first hand, that just about everything we tended to throw away, the Koreans had found a way to recycle and reuse. Naturally, our society had recently changed too and was beginning to recycle still valuable materials. Revealing the "inners" of their heating system, I found hundreds of aluminum cans, carefully soldered together in a maze of piping underneath the floor. The piping was carrying the heated air, generated by the burning of compressed charcoal briquettes, called *Vontan*. Burned outside the building it channeled the heat underneath the floors to the chimney on the opposite side of the building. As the heat rose from the warm floor, a comfortable temperature was being felt just about everywhere, whether you were sitting, sleeping on the floor or walking barefoot.

As for refrigeration, the people in the rural areas, where the western culture had not quite reached them as yet, usually just kept items cool underground. This applies especially to the storage and further fermentation of *Kim-chi*. It is usually made from highly spiced pickled vegetables and Chinese cabbage for months at a time. Christine's visit to Korea prompted quite a few changes in my life, such as the custom of leaving your shoes outside, adherence to Feng shui, Tai Chi, oriental art and the oriental food, which all became part of our lives, mixing our German culture with that of the orient.

Christine enjoyed the visit with Kim, who was an excellent and charming hostess. Kim did have some difficulty showing her the ways of using the common restroom facilities. Pointing out the absence of the western style seats and running water in the toilet Kim did not need to apologize. We quickly explained to her that even we still had some backward areas with out-houses in the States just as one still finds in many countries in Eastern Europe.

After about four days of roaming around the countryside among historical landmarks and rice paddies watching the farmers work, we vacated the Commander's quarters and left for the capitol of Seoul. Perry dropped us off at the only western style Hotel, the Chosun. Only about eighteen years after the end of the war and armistice, Korea was still in the process of rebuilding the city. Since we always enjoyed walking, we decided to walk from one end of the city to the other. Stopping whenever we liked to check out unusual items and wares, we found a lot of Koreans closely looking at Christine, the tall blond, blue-eyed woman, who just did not fit into the surroundings.

Frequently we had several women come up to her just to touch her hair. It was not surprising, because neither Seoul nor the northern part of the Peninsula was on any calendar of the tourist agencies at that time.

We assumed that it was probably because there was not that much interest in visiting an area like Seoul.

The city was only a mere twenty-five miles from the DMZ and still being threatened by a hostile force from the North. After a visit to the 8th US Army Headquarters at Seoul we spent an interesting and thoroughly enjoyable evening at the Officers Club. Without a doubt, we had the best eight-course oriental dinner ever in the company of some charming fellow soldiers. Old timers in Korea, many of them gave us a lot of hints and recommendations of sights to see and places to visit in the southern part of South Korea.

Excited, we purchased a railroad ticket on the UN "Blue Train" to spend a day in the city of Pusan. Staying in a hotel along the sea coastline, we had a fantastic view of the Korea Strait, which connects with the East China Sea and the Sea of Japan. It was a very nice hotel, but something had us both very stymied. Looking out of the windows to enjoy the sights, we noticed the long window curtains stirring, as if the wind was moving them. To our surprise we also noticed a pair of underwear on the floor moving. Baffled, but Intrigued, I lifted up the pants and, to our astonishment, we found the largest and ugliest bug we had ever seen, similar to a huge cockroach, inside. After it was shaken out, it was dashing towards the curtains, where we found several more hiding in the folds.

Neither one of us could believe the size nor the power of these bugs. Accepting these creatures as a natural phenomenon in these parts of the country, we carefully got rid of them, making sure we did not have any more hiding among the bed sheets or the suitcase.

The rest of our stay in Pusan was interesting, but otherwise rather uneventful. We boarded our Blue Train the next day for our return trip to Seoul and found some very nice accommodations at the Visiting Officers Quarters, the VOQ at a Signal Site Post at Yong San, with an adjacent Club. Anybody seeking a brief R&R from the DMZ usually visited this place. Only about an hour from the Demarcation Line, it provided the visitor with a nearby PX, club facilities and a city with several entertainment spots. We had about three days left before our flight to Tokyo and the EXPO and found ample time to relax, visiting Seoul again for some more sightseeing.

One interesting and unusual thing happened to Christine while we were staying at the VOQ. Whenever we talked about Korea, this strange, unexplainable incident always came up in the conversation. Every time we left the room to go to the Officers Club, a little yellow bird sitting nearby in a tree, dove down on Christine with a shrill shriek, which sounded like "chosipseo", or the Korean "please". The bird actually hit Christine on top of the head several times, forcing her to cover her hair. As soon as we started to cross the open space, the same thing happened and the yellow bird was making its diving run, shrieking, no matter when or how fast we ran. Eventually it forced us to cover ourselves with a chair, which we took with us when going back and forth.

A friend of ours, Hans Sachs, a Major in the Signal Corps stationed there and living in the same quarters, told us he had never seen or heard anything like this before. We still wonder what may have caused the bird to behave like this. Could it have been her blond hair, maybe? On our last trip downtown to Seoul, we paid a visit to an old brass factory. Resembling a factory out of the middle ages, appearing rather primitive, it had the reputation to have the best brass articles and artisans well-known for their superb creations.

I had always liked works of art in brass and when we saw a sample of a beautiful landing eagle with a wingspan of about two and a half feet, weighing nearly seven pounds, I could not resist buying it. Admiring it,

I could already visualize this masterpiece hanging over my white stone fireplace, which I was still striving to own someday in the future. While in Korea, my baggage and goods were getting heavier and more sizeable from one day to the next.

Visiting Tokyo, Japan

At last, we left Seoul for Tokyo, Japan to visit one of the finest All-Services Transient Hotels, the Sanno, a renowned four-star hotel. It offered everything one desires, from the best food, the most elaborate rooms to first class entertainment. A daily double occupancy room for husband and wife was listed at a "whopping" $9.40. One of the highly recommended features was their Turkish Bath and complete massage for $1.60 an hour with different types of massages, depending on the individual's taste, which everyone strongly recommended. Orientals have a unique way of massaging, as I had found out in Viet-Nam, where I occasionally had a massage, never experienced anywhere else before.

The best massage I ever had, was done by an older, blind Viet-Namese, who seemed to be able to sense and find the sore areas, stimulating the affected muscles in such a way, that there was instant relief of any discomfort within minutes. Even his walks on my back were a pleasure rather than a discomfort.

When Christine suggested that I might as well live it up and take the best, I selected the extra special. Needless to say, after the Sauna-style sweatbox and the once-in-a-lifetime massage, with walking on my back, I returned weak but totally relaxed. Feeling absolutely no pain or aches I slept so well, that I was ready to have another sauna massage before departing.

Just like we did in Seoul, we armed ourselves with a city map and set out for another all day hike through Tokyo. It was definitely much more exciting than a Kamikaze taxi ride through the city, which we already had lived through. Visiting the Imperial Gardens was a must and we both enjoyed the architecture, the landscape and the tranquility, which incited both of us to envision our future garden's look.

During our walk through the city, we were continuously impressed by the neatness of people. Most of the men were wearing suits and ties, as if they all worked as corporate executives. The cleanliness of the buildings and streets in general, where even the street sweepers looked well dressed and presentable, were a sight not seen anywhere else during our travels.

Departing the Sanno Hotel a few days later, we boarded the "Bullet Train", a beautifully streamlined high-speed train for our trip to Osaka, Japan, the site for the 1970 World EXPO. A two-hundred-fifty-mile ride took us about two hours through a breathtaking countryside, changing between coastal areas, to mountainous as well as flat terrain.

Because of the speed of the train, we could only clearly see the landscape in the distance, while the close-up features were generally fuzzy and blurred. Both of us had never attended an EXPO, so it was an unusual experience visiting the various exhibitions of many countries showing off their progress and culture. The exposition also included a pavilion of the Soviet Union, which tried to put their best foot forward. To us, we found that most of the information was strictly propaganda and not truly representing the Russian way of life. We spent the entire day just taking in the sights and tasting the numerous ethnic foods offered by the different nations until late that evening, when we returned by Bullet Train to Tokyo.

On our last evening we went strolling through Tokyo we accidentally walked by an unusual restaurant. The sign outside said "*Bei Rudi*" or "At Rudi's". From the looks and sounds it was a German restaurant. Naturally we had to try it out. Its main attraction besides the advertised food was the Bavarian "Edelweis Band", as posted outside on a large flyer. It certainly looked like it had attracted a lot of Americans, probably because of the original German beer and music, which was certainly rare in these parts of the globe.

After entering, we noted that it was not only the Americans frequenting Rudi. We also noticed a lot of Japanese who seemed to enjoy the German atmosphere, its food and drinks. When he had heard the band and the songs before we went inside, we had wondered why Germans would be playing and working in Bangkok so far from their own culture and country. The answer was obvious. We were astonished to see the entire "Oompah" band dressed in typical Bavarian outfits, but each one of the band members were Japanese. Since they sang so well in German, even with a Bavarian dialect, I asked them for a particular song in German, only to look into blank faces and getting shaking heads.

The band leader signaled with a hand wave to a tall bald gentleman, who then approached the band. After a brief talk with the band leader, he turned to me to explain in a true Berlin dialect that, unfortunately, not a single member of the band spoke any German and all their songs had been memorized from Bavarian record and tapes. We had an interesting conversation with Rudi, who came from either Berlin or near Christine's home town after World War II to seek his fortune outside Germany. Somehow he ended up remaining in Tokyo after a visit, because he admired the people and figured that living in a dream world he could make a little fortune, while at the same time give traveling German visitors a home away from home. It was a strange and surprising encounter.

Our vacation, and with it our stay at the Sanno Hotel, was rapidly coming to a close. For an appropriate farewell we chose to enjoy a final dinner at the Mongolian Barbeque, where a very talented chef prepared an unforgettable dinner right in front of you. The Casino and countless slot machines invited us for some last pulls, making sure that we left all the loose change behind. Christine departed from Tokyo Airport after a heartfelt goodbye for her return flight to the US.

Returning from Tokyo to Seoul I still had another day of vacation left and decided to spend it in Seoul with my fried Hans. My driver Perry showed up at the prearranged time to pick me up. Not only Perry but also my staff had been anxiously waiting for my return. It was great to see some familiar faces again.

Ups and Downs in Korea

Back at the DMZ, I had plenty of work waiting for me. From various routine personnel actions, such as court-martials to special investigations concerning misappropriation of mail. There was also one unique matter, which involved an investigation to find out why and where the film "Bedazzled", starring Raquel Welsh in a nude scene, was modified by cutting out that specific scene. Complaints had been received from troops stationed within the 2nd Division area, who had seen the film before, but now found the good scenes removed from that the film. My initial investigation revealed that the film appeared to have been modified or censored.

Following a thorough check of all theatres within our Division, I determined that the changes must have been made outside our area between Japan and Korea. Submitting my findings to our command, it was strongly felt by 8th Army that this unusual, and possibly criminal act, needed to be further investigated and so I subsequently found myself returning to Japan again.

Assigned temporary duty by the 2nd Infantry Division, I took a military aircraft from Kimpo to Yokota Air Base in Japan to see Rachel Welsh, not in person but starring in an original complete version of her film, uncut, provided by the Army /Air Force Exchange. I was to follow the trail by viewing it in various military theatres to find out who might be tampering with the film. I watched the film repeatedly about ten times before I finally noticed the particular scene cut again on the second day. I found that a senior Air Force Sergeant, the projection manager, was the person who had, as previously done, cut scenes from the film. Evidently he had established his own personal film library of sexually explicit clippings. The suspected sergeant was promptly charged and brought before court-martial. With my investigation complete, I returned to my unit, glad to be able to resume my regular duties, which unexpectedly turned out to be rather unpleasant.

One evening, after a routine check of my outposts, I retired to my quarters only to be called down to the enlisted quarters, where shooting had been reported. Upon my arrival, I found the platoon sergeant and several men standing around a bunk, where a young soldier was laying on the bed, apparently dead, with blood running from underneath the mattress. His body showed several visible bullet holes all over his body and no sign of any pulse. After an unsuccessful attempt to contact the Battalion Commander, who was at Brigade Headquarters, I collected as much information as I could obtain from those present.

Questioning personnel in the quarters I found that the one soldier had a dispute with another soldier, who had reportedly smoked pot. In a rage provoked for an unknown reason the suspect grabbed his M-16 rifle, emptying an entire clip of ammunition into the resting soldier. Summoned to the scene, the Battalion surgeon declared the victim dead of multiple gunshot wounds, which were too many to count. The mattress underneath was in shreds, making it difficult to move him. It was a horrendous sight. Looking for the suspect, we found that the killer had run off.

Immediately contacting the bridge detail, we were informed that the suspect had already crossed the bridge proceeding South toward a small village, where I understood he had a Korean girlfriend. Properly armed, we pursued him with two jeeps and finally spotted a jeep at one of the huts. Surrounding the dwelling we then entered it with the help of a Korean woman, finding him inside, huddling in the corner of a room with a girl kneeling beside him. Unarmed and looking disoriented, we had no problem securing him, since he still seemed to be under the influence of drugs. After I was informed that his weapon had been found in the Battalion area, I had the detainee driven to Brigade Headquarters, where he was to be properly evaluated and confined to face military court-martial for murder.

It was a very sad moment for me. Never had I felt so bad to write a letter of condolence to a soldier's wife and his two young children back in the States. Not too long before this incident, I had written personal letters to all dependents and relatives of our Battalion members. In those letters I reiterated to them, that our unit is proud of its history and record, and assured them that we will make sure that their loved ones will return home safe and sound.

Following a thorough investigation by the CIC, the Criminal Investigation Corps, it was revealed that marijuana was easily accessible in many towns and villages, which some soldiers frequented when stationed South of the Imjin River. This fact made it a necessity to frequently and randomly test the soldiers for drugs. Stationed at the DMZ, our unit was in possession of Red Eye anti-aircraft missiles. It was a defensive weapon, to be used against North Korean planes attempting to cross into South Korea. The availability of this weapon made it even more critical that troops in charge of such weapons be alert and drug free.

Only a very few select personnel with the highest clearance, had access to them. The Army wanted to make sure, that this status is being maintained. Understandably, the Air Force had always been somewhat jittery, knowing that we had those missiles, particularly since they conducted some very essential reconnaissance flights close to and along the border.

Our Division routinely conducted helicopter reconnaissance flights along the DMZ to insure the North is not trying to penetrate or infiltrate the South. Strange as it may seem, occasionally, when I visited the outpost in the middle of the DMZ, it felt like the ground was slightly vibrating. It felt as if someone was tunneling underneath our position. Experiences in Viet Nam have shown that our enemy had done it quite frequently in the past. We all knew that the communists were constantly attempting to undermine our efforts. For many years they had successfully infiltrated their agents by land and by sea for the purposes of espionage and sabotage. Gen. Michaelis, the Division Commander had made it a point to visit our Battalion and troops out front often to impress upon us the importance of our vigilance.

The General's personal visits showed us his sincerity and determination to help maintain the freedom of the South Korean Republic. He was well liked and during his visits he always insisted on using my black jeep and Perry. To identify him, my jeep had a covered red plate with his silver stars permanently mounted on the fender. It would only be uncovered and displayed when the General drove in the jeep. Perry sometimes liked to show off, by removing the black cover at times to get some salutes, I guess.

We all knew our mission was critical and serious, but I always felt that troops could always use some humor. Mentioning to Christine in numerous letters that I miss her and dreaded sleeping alone, she and the kids had the audacity to send me a rubberized blow-up doll. Complete with dress and a blond wig it looked almost real, especially from the distance. After I had received it, I dressed it properly and layed it in my bed. When my houseboy spotted this full sized blond girl in my bed, he was obviously embarrassed to find her in my bed, and his face showed it. When I uncovered her whole 'body', he realized that it was only a rubber doll. He laughed for quite a while trying to shade his eyes. Calmed down at last, he suggested that I take her for a ride in the jeep into the DMZ to harass the communists, who were obviously watching every one of our moves.

The Commander and the troops thought it was a splendid idea and without any objection from the boss, I took her for a ride to the outposts, carefully holding "Betty" straight in the seat. It was a shame that I could never find out what the other side was saying about the crazy American taking a blond into the DMZ. It was a wonder I was not being fired upon. I did expect that a complaint would be filed with the Armistice Group complaining about taking a civilian into the DMZ. They didn't know it was just a rubber doll.

Plainly visible from the recently installed huge window of my quarters, I could see a small village just north of the DMZ. Named Ki-jong-dong, we called it Propaganda Village. It seemed to be occupied, with assorted laundry hanging outside, including children's clothes and women's dresses. Every once in awhile we could see just one person walking around the village, which had several newly built tall apartment buildings. It seemed very strange that we could never see a larger population or children. The whole scene looked very suspicious, suggesting to us that it was a convincing mock up and a façade for our benefit and our helicopter over-flights.

One late afternoon, an unknown high-flying aircraft passed along the DMZ, probably one of ours. I happened to be at one of our outposts in the DMZ, when I spotted some motion in the village. While I could not see one person walking, I instead noticed one of the roofs moving. It seemed to be sliding to the side, as if it was opening up. Wondering about the aircraft flying overhead and the changing of the roof, I became convinced, that the village buildings could have probably been a camouflage for a battery of anti-aircraft missiles or artillery inside. Our intelligence had neither any positive information nor clarification for this unusual action. Observations from the JSA nearby seemed to support the belief that the little town with several four-story buildings is vacant, with the exception of some maintenance personnel. It was a weird sight.

Not so in another small village next to Panmunjom in the western part of the DMZ. Following the armistice and establishment of the Zone, people from that village refused to be relocated. Willing to be cut off and isolated, they were permitted to remain. Called Taesong-dong, dubbed "Freedom Village", its villagers lived a fairly normal life, tending to fields and working. They were being supported by a Civil Affairs Platoon and received assistance from the UN Command. In contrast to the huge North Korean flag flying over the Propaganda Village on a 100 meters (approximately 333 feet) high steel tower, Freedom Village hoisted their oversized flag of the Republic of South Korea, over what appeared to be a 100 meters high "Eiffel Tower"-like structure.

General Michaelis's visits, even if he was only attending the meeting at Panmunjom, were always a pleasant and welcomed event, as the troops genuinely felt their mission to be important. Our Battalion Commander also appreciated the Division Commander's interest in our troops and their welfare. He was trying to find an appropriate souvenir our Battalion could present to the general, when he was leaving his assignment in Korea. I suggested an oil painting, depicting the Korean landscape of our area with an enlarged picture of our Distinctive Unit Insignia, a circular shaped dragon, as found on our belt buckle. He liked the suggestion and ran it by our staff to get their input.

Agreeing with the idea, they had apparently also found an artist to do the picture. Namely the guy, who came up with this idea. It was quite clear to me that, in their eyes, I had practically volunteered for the job. I considered it a privilege but actually had visualized a Korean artist doing the job. Everybody felt, that this then would not have been a personal gift.

It took me awhile to acquire the necessary paint and canvas, but Kim came through and procured all the material including a hand-carved frame, which is usually more intricate and expensive than the painting itself. All I had to do is give up my chess and playing billiard for a couple weeks of off duty time. It was actually more fun and enjoyable than I had imagined to play the Battalion's artist. To be honest, I had a ball picking up on an old hobby for a change. To my very own satisfaction, the painting turned out better than I had expected, even though I was working under some time pressure.

Over-committed and unable for us all to attend his farewell party at Division Headquarters down South, we surprised the General during his last visit at the DMZ. Our entire Camp Liberty Bell and I personally were extremely proud and gratified, when he expressed his sincere admiration accepting the painting as a special gift from the members of his command.

The continued reports and actual incidents, where South Korean troops detected and captured North Korean agents infiltrating either by sea or by land, motivated us at the DMZ to conduct more thorough patrols inside and just below the Demilitarized Zone. Checking just below the southern fence, we stumbled upon a small, neatly camouflaged tunnel opening, large enough to permit a small person to crawl through. The spot was just on the line, where our Battalion's area of responsibility bordered the adjacent Battalion's area. We were sure that the North Koreans knew exactly where the line was and that troops usually stopped just short of the adjacent unit's area.

Only about two feet inside the tunnel, we found a complete set of a North Korean Army uniform and a few articles of western style civilian clothing. For us it was proof positive that some northern agent had already infiltrated and was walking around somewhere in South Korea. Hopefully he was not working somewhere for the US Army being a mole for the North. After reporting the violation of the South Korean territory by a North Korean military a protest was lodged at the following combined meeting at Panmunjom. The communists naturally denied everything. I was hoping that the South Koreans would take advantage of this unique opportunity and send someone into the tunnel to go North to find the point of origin. It would have been quite interesting. Besides, it would have been concrete proof of their intent to violate the armistice agreement. Probably lacking a volunteer for this undertaking, which seemed like a suicide mission, it was instead decided to make this breach impassable and destroy the tunnel on the lower side of the demarcation line.

Goodbye Korea. Farewell My 'Manchus' !

After thirteen months of service in a hostile fire zone, in a land of ration cards, military script money and of course 'Kimchee', I had to prepare my-self to leave a country I had actually grown fond of, especially our Korean soldiers. An integral part of our Battalion, they were living with us in the same barracks, being totally assimilated into the unit. I also remembered the excellent combat record of the Korean "White Horse" Division in Viet-Nam. Both, the VC and the North Viet-Namese regulars, during their first contacts with the Koreans, had so many great losses, that they respected and feared the Korean troops to the point, that they rarely attacked them and always tried to avoid them.

They were loyal, disciplined and well trained, which made them a reliable member of our UN Forces and the 8th US Army. Upon my pend-ing departure I was proud to be asked to take back to the States the three flags which flew over the camp at the DMZ, the US, Korean and United Nations flag.

Before finally leaving however, I had to undergo a similar ritual that I had taken part in upon my arrival. Having watched other officers depart during my tour of duty, I was determined to be better prepared this time and leave the Club walking straight, rather than being carried out. Prior to the affair I had a serious meeting with my Mess Sergeant. I introduced him to an old German dish, essential for the survival of any hardcore alcoholic encounter. It was the genuine *"Strammer Max"*, or straight Max.

A traditional Berliner Hamburger, unlike a normal Hamburger, con-sisted of half a pound of raw beef, mixed with two raw eggs and onions. Saturated with olive oil, it is normally served on German sunflower seed bread. The latter of course unavailable, had to be substituted with regular bread. Prior to my drive over to the JSA Officers Club, the Monastery, also referred to as the *"Home of the Merry Mad Monks"* at the DMZ, I devoured the "Max" under the watchful eyes of the Mess Sergeant, who just kept shaking his head, especially when I refused to have the Hamburger fried. With most of the old officers, who had witnessed my own initiation gone and the new members remembering their own fiascos, I was not about to make the same mistake twice. To the contrary I was going to show them what I can take. And indeed I did.

When I was handed my name inscribed silver goblet in flames, I downed this perfect 151 proof Manchu elixir and followed it up by our traditional battle cry of "Keep up the Fire". As usual, my driver Perry, who was also preparing for his rotation home, was standing by the door after about three minutes, waiting to come to my aid. But while everybody was anxiously waiting for me to cave in, I was feeling so well, that I even started reminiscing and talking about my experiences with the CIDG and Montagnards in Viet-Nam and their rice wine rituals. After about an hour, I saw the driver sitting down and somebody whisper in the back of me, doubting that it was really a '151', which the adjutant confirmed. I turned around and stated to the doubter that I had overheard that and turning to the Adjutant, I told him to fill the goblet again. After my S-2 tasted the drink and confirmed the genuine content, I toasted again to everybody's applause.

Getting a little warm after about ten minutes, I realized that I had reached my absolute limit. I decided to quickly bid my farewell and slowly walked out of the club under my own power. I made it safely into the quarters, hoping that nobody would start a war that night. My replacement, a young major, had already arrived pulling duty officer, having no idea what was confronting him the following week during his initiation.

It took me almost two days to say goodbye to all my fellow officers, as I could never get them together at the same time, because of their duties. I had also made many good friends among the Korean troops, the Korean workers, close friends and the children of the "Love Orphanage". I wished I could have taken many of them with me to the States. The students of the school, which our Battalion supported, presented me with a traditional Korean suit, complete with the tall black hat and small opium pipe. The pipe remained clean of all tobacco traces to this date.

The evening before my personal property was to be packed for shipment home, I decided to use up some of my canned food I still had left. Since the club was already closed, and thanks to the pot-belly stove in our quarters, I quickly put a can of chili beans on the stove. Answering the telephone in the next room, I totally forgot about the dish on the stove until a loud explosion reminded me that my dinner must have been ready. Entering my room I could not believe the unique change of the interior decoration. What had previously been sitting on top of the stove, i.e. red Chili, was now dripping from the ceiling with the beans sliding down my walls and oil paintings. I could not believe that there were that many beans in just one can. The red food coloring could not be easily removed as I had expected. Lacking appropriate cleaning material, other than soap and water, it took me several hours, under the watchful eyes of "Betty", to clean up at least the items that were being shipped. To this day, every time I hold a can of chili in my hand, I think of Korea.

The distinctive
Unit insignia of the
"Manchu" Battalion

Observing the enemy in the north

Christine being chaufferured around the DMZ

The daily session between the North Koreans and the
United Nations Command personnel.

Entrance to the UN Neutral
Nations Camp at the DMZ

Christine dared to sit on the North side of the DMZ

After my final goodbye to my Battalion I took my last trip over the Freedom Bridge to reach my last stop in Korea, Kimpo Airbase. After a long flight and a rewarding sleep, I finally set foot on American soil again.

Chapter VIII

Europe Once More

An Assignment Which Was Not To Be.

My life as the Battalion Executive Officer in Korea was definitely educational, considering the various additional duties this job carried. From running the staff, presiding over court-martials, being the Equal Opportunity and Treatment Officer, Red Eye Control Officer, Investigative Officer, Member of the Enlisted Promotion Selection Board, Unit Fund Inspector, Assistant Adjutant, Member, Board of Inquiry, Logistical Readiness Officer to being a Counselor between the soldiers and their families, I had my hands full. What job could be more challenging?

It was certainly time to get back to the one job I enjoyed most. And that was to be in charge of my family and to look out for their welfare at home. I often felt I neglected them in favor of the military family. The greatest drawback of military life is also the fact, that we make so many genuine friendships and find solid comradeships, only to lose them again through transfers. You often wished that you could just take those good people along with you to the next assignment or even back to your hometown.

Unfortunately, it was not my time yet to return to my regular home, my residence in Fayetteville and Fort Bragg. I quickly found that out, when I picked up new marching orders from Division HQ. My orders read that I had been assigned to Central Army Group, SHAPE, The Supreme Headquarters Allied Powers Europe with its US Army Element located in Mannheim-Seckenheim, Germany, only 10 minutes from my former home, Heidelberg.

Granted the routine thirty-days leave of absence after my return to the States and a brief school attendance of the Junior Officer Preventive Maintenance Course at Fort Knox, KY, the birthplace of our son Dieter Jr., I could consider myself back home once more. The kids were glad to see me, I hoped. Being the authoritarian in the family I often wondered if the kids are rather happy when they see the old man gone again and again. Being at home, it gave the family and me a chance to get used to each other anew and for me to wind down, while getting packed for shipment to Germany. It certainly would have been nice to stay a little longer in the States and at home, which I rarely got to live in during those two years while serving in Viet Nam and Korea.

Both, our daughter Ines and Dieter had made a lot of buddies and, just like their parents, were now also getting used to making friends and soon there after losing them again. This seems to happen just about every three years as a result of my repeated rotations. Ines had developed a very good friendship with a lady living across the street, who worked for the Air Force at Pope Air Force Base. She was a genuine horse lover and maintained her very own horse. Her hobby naturally rubbed off on our daughter, who became so enthused about the horsemanship, that we had to get her a horse, too. Turned into an avid rider, both English and Western, she was able to bring home several impressive trophies, which she had earned during the tournaments and other competitive events.

Kept busy with her 'love of horses' she had hardly any time to get into trouble with some of the other wild kids. Living in an area close to a Base you can clearly tell that many children are missing the firm hand of a male, as many fathers were on an assignment outside the country, leaving the wife to raise the children alone. One thing, which had bothered me a lot, was the fact that Christine must have had the more difficult time bearing the responsibility of caring for the two kids and maintaining the household all by herself. Rejoined with the family it gave me that great feeling of being an actively participating member of the family. Being that involved with the military truly makes your family often take second place.

The end of November is not the most desirable month to move a family to Germany. Weather usually turns out to be on the cold and wet side. Pending winter and the holidays coming up, we expected some inconveniences, but since we were returning to the old home and parents, it made everything a little easier.

My parents were naturally ecstatic not only to see their oldest son and Christine, but I had the feeling they were especially looking forward to meeting the children. The kids had grown considerably since they saw them last, some five years back. Christine's father in Heidelberg and her mother in Karlsruhe were also looking forward to seeing our family. Fortunately, we had no problem to turn over our home in Fayetteville to a real estate agency to rent it out during our assignment in Germany.

We all left North Carolina by commercial air to Frankfurt, having taken our new Ford Fairlane 500 convertible to Charleston, SC for shipment by sea to Bremerhaven, Germany. Now old hands at this game we hoped, that after nearly fifteen years in the Army, that this would be the last time in our career to make a move to the old country. Considering our children were getting older, with Ines, the oldest, now approaching her eleventh birthday and young Dieter being almost ten years old, these constant changes in schools and friends must have been giving them a feeling of instability. Anytime they were away from home they urged us to return back home soon. But I never knew if they meant our stateside home in Fayetteville, my parent's home or even our temporary quarters, wherever they were.

Germany was at least not new or strange to the children. They seemed to quickly adjust to the German language, speaking freely not only to the grandparents, but also to us. Young Dieter surprised us in particular. I don't know why, but when we heard him the first time after departing the US speaking German, we were surprised and happy and had to laugh. For some unknown reason however, he must have misunderstood our laughter. Ever since then will he rarely, if ever, freely talk in German to us again. Strangely enough, when with grandparents or other strangers in Germany he does not mind speaking German.

Arriving in Frankfurt, Christine and the children naturally wanted to visit my parents in Heidelberg first, while I reported in to my new duty station in Mannheim-Seckenheim, using my father's car. Our car was not scheduled to arrive until a week or so later. I was very excited to be assigned to CENTAG, because this unique Headquarters was a combined staff of US, German, French, British and Canadian military personnel. It promised to be an outstanding General Staff experience.

Unknown to me though, my name and reputation must have preceded me. When I reported in I was informed that there had been an unexpected change in my assignment, and that the General, the US Commander, was looking forward to talk to me. I didn't know what to expect from the personal interview by the three-star general, but was soon to find out that politics, even in the military, often plays a big role when you are dealing with a mix of different national armies. The General did not beat around the bush and told me confidentially, that certain elements in his combined staff were not looking too favorably upon the idea, that a former German, who had previously been rejected by the German Army was about to become part of the General Staff as an American Officer.

It seemed that the German intelligence apparatus had my name on their list of undesirables. They appeared to fear another 'faux pas', which they experienced during my American Exchange Officer attendance at the German Army College. Without a doubt, they were quite embarrassed and did not want to repeat it. The CENTAG Commander regretted this unfortunate development, but hoped for my understanding. He assured me that I had an excellent record and he personally would have liked for me to serve at his staff, but understands some of the Germans' worries. German staffers would have had to be very careful in their personal discussions knowing that some outsider could understand every word they were saying. Americans in general could not understand the various German dialects, which some Germans often use if they want to make sure nobody else would understand their conversation.

Expressing my genuine disappointment to the commander, I also told him that I regretted having caused the embarrassing situation he was placed in. He promised me that I could have a pick of any other desirable higher staff assignment in the area, such as a position within the US Army Theater Support Command, USTASCOMEUR, which was short of German-speaking staff officers. Since field grade officer assignments generally come from Washington and an immediate opening was not available, I would have to be placed in a temporary position requiring immediate filling.

Willing to serve with troops, I was given a chance to be the Battalion Executive Officer of the 2nd Battalion, 13th Infantry for a brief period. I accepted, as long as did not have to move again for the next primary duty station. Family quarters, as usual being unavailable for immediate occupation, our family had to move into temporary quarters until an opening became available in permanent quarters.

New Experiences in a Changed Germany

I must honestly say, my wife and children were true troopers. This family was willing to accept whatever came along, as long as we could stay together. Temporary quarters were usually furnished, so that we did not have to use any of our own furniture. Besides our belongings were en route across the Atlantic. The kids loved the "temps" since they consisted of a converted attic which had previously been used as maid's quarters for the entire housing block. With twelve rooms along a long corridor, our kids had their own "bowling alley", but their unique playground was not to be theirs long. Permanent quarters became ready for occupancy shortly thereafter and we moved into the quarters, this time with our very own furniture.

After I had picked up our car at Bremerhaven once more, we were finally ready to settle down to a more normal life. The kids were already making new friends in the military housing complex and in the German neighborhood and I was getting acclimatized in my new unit. Although a "leg" outfit, I was satisfied to again serve in a unit with a proud and famous history, having been "First At Vicksburg", as the motto stated.

Being part of the 8th Infantry Division I was very familiar with it from my previous years with the 504th Airborne in Mainz, nearby. Familiar with their mission I did not have too much to get acquainted with. Our potential enemy still being the same, I was sure to visit the Fulda Gap anew, where the Russians were assumed to be attacking across, should it ever come to a war. We all doubted that very much, believing that they would not assault the Allies in an area, where we were concentrating our forces. Naturally, the war games had to go on and that included the families' preparedness for any and all eventualities during an open conflict.

Evacuation procedures for dependents, from the contemplated combat zone to the West through France, were regularly practiced. Even though France consistently disapproved any of our dependents retreating through France's national territory, especially since they were no longer members of NATO, we knew the French did not have the power to stop any such evacuation.

Exercises conducted by the command with the dependents were called NEO Exercises. They required that each family had at least one case of C-Rations in the trunk of their cars, together with a 5-gallon can of gasoline. This was to guarantee that they would make it to the next refueling point west of our location and to make sure they are all familiar with the routes to be taken. My only hope was that this day would never come. I could not envision all of our dependents simultaneously driving toward the West through France to make it off the continent. Occasionally an alarm was announced upon which the families jumped into their vehicles and proceeded to certain assembly points. To me, they were all exercises of futility, but apparently it made some people more confident in our abilities to provide security for our dependents.

To this day, I cannot understand why the French, at least the political arm of that country, disliked the Americans so much. After all the United States and their troops had saved their country twice, in WWI and WWII, giving their blood to keep the French free. Even later, we not only supported the French in Viet-Nam, but actually continued their lost fight and protected their precious rubber plantations along with other national interests there.

I could understand their age-old dislike for the Germans, which was mutual among the older generations but not among the younger generation, who was not so familiar with World War II. The older French people, who had experienced the war and the later liberation by American troops usually did remember and fostered a stronger American-French friendship. While in Germany, Christine and I had the chance to visit Paris twice and found the average French very hospitable. Hopefully this was not just because of our tourist money, but because some French still remembered the days when the United States saved their lives.

Back with the grunts, I was confronted with the usual responsibilities and the common special assignments. As a Battalion XO. I was again working as an Equal Opportunities Treatment Officer, Top Secret Control Officer, NEO Officer, Special Investigation Officer to mention just a few extra burdens. The Infantry Officers always seemed to be getting the unusual, but required details, while personnel of other technical branches only needed to concentrate on their particular branch material responsibilities.

The city of Mannheim had changed significantly over the past two decades since I had left. The drug scene being one of the more significant changes. On one unannounced inspection of the quarters and the basements of our unit, I had found several pounds of marijuana, hidden in the basement's boiler room. After reporting it to the Military Police, I was advised to pick it up and turn it in to the station. To my surprise, after all my careful retrieval efforts not to wipe off any fingerprints, the young MP sergeant was about to flush it down the toilet, after I had given my written statement. I was certain, a proper investigation would naturally follow but was told, that they were picking up so much of the drugs, that they could no longer investigate all the finds. They were advised by their command to just flush it down the drain to take it out of circulation, making sure though, that I was witnessing its destruction. I found that utterly disgusting, because it definitely did not help my unit to fight illegal drug use.

Not only the Army, but also the Germany which I used to know so well, had drastically changed. Returning to Germany, I was intent to promote and foster closer relations and improved cooperation between Americans and our host country. As expected, I was to get more involved in the weeks to come. The steady increases in criminal activities and incidents involving both Americans and Germans brought me closer together with members of the German Criminal Police.

I felt that working closer with their Vice Squad would be essential to stop the increased influx of drugs into our area, whether within the troop complexes or the military family housing area. It was also the first time in my entire Army career, other than my brother's, that I received a report of an AWOL, a soldier Absent Without Leave in my Battalion.

Living in a well-regulated society it was unusual in those days to hide without the authorities finding an individual on a short notice. I could not believe my eyes what I found, when I conducted another covert search of the barracks during normal duty hours. Diverting from the usual routine this time and being more thorough, I searched the normally locked and rarely used attic of the troops billets. Huddled in the corner, covered with blankets, I found my AWOL soldier, who had actually not been absent from the unit. He had, unknown to the commanders, stayed in the barracks for many days and only missing the roll calls at the formations. It appeared to me that this young soldier was truly scared but after I promised him to be lenient if he revealed the reason why he went AWOL, he spoke freely.

He stated that he had detected some pot in the basement and after telling someone about his discovery, he was later confronted by a gang of colored soldiers. They were from an outside unit, but using our barracks as a storage area. The gang threatened him with bodily harm unless he returned the missing pot. Since he did not take it and therefore could not produce it, he decided to hide until things cooled down. The missing pot, I realized immediately, was the same I had found and turned in to the MP's for their disposition. Rather than report the incident to his commander or me, he was afraid of the implications and decided to hide instead.

Some of his buddies, not realizing they are not really helping him, supplied him with food and drink during his hiding. He hoped it would last only a short time and, when the gang could no longer find him, would just give up. Persuaded to cooperate with my staff, we set up a trap with him and after a few days were able to arrest the gang members. Unbelievable as it seemed, they were not members of the active Army, but former members, who had decided to leave the military, stay in Germany and run a profitable drug and prostitution ring in the city.

As non-military personnel they were under the jurisdiction of the German law and when I turned them over to their local law enforcement authority, I was fortunate enough to meet a very respectable Vice Squad officer, *Kommissar "Graukopf"* (Gray Head). The Kommissar was a very jovial older police officer, who obviously got his name from his distinguished looking gray hair.

Graukopf was enormously informed and familiar with just about all the underground operations of drug dealers and prostitution rings of the city. Prostitution was not illegal, except for those unregistered persons controlled by gangs. Our CID people, the Army's Criminal Investigation Detachment was seriously understaffed and not quite as responsive, as witnessed by the destruction of pot I had found. Graukopf suggested to me that he would welcome a greater degree of cooperation from the commanders directly. Closer mutual support would definitely benefit the Army, as well as the German community.

To reduce drug trafficking, I received clearance from my command to provide as much assistance as possible, as long as it did not interfere with my normal duties. For several weeks I spent time with him and the vice squad off duty and was surprised how many former soldiers had found Germany to be a very profitable ground for their illegal trade. Those dealers quite often transacted business with Turks and other Mediterraneans living and working in Germany. Those suppliers provided them with inexpensive stashes of hashish and other narcotics to saturate the military community.

To get away from the sometimes stressful military duties and its obligations, I made sure I spent as much time as possible with Christine and the kids. Friends made during past tours of duty were always happy to see us and we took full advantage of our free time to visit them. When we met some old friends and close acquaintances of Christine from the East, who had also fled the "socialist camp", we were eager to renew those friendships. And so it happened that, when we were invited to join their Sailboat club on the Rhine River, we gladly accepted.

Although we did not have a boat, we became honorary members, partaking in their sailing trips on the Rhine River. In turn, we were only too happy to contribute and provide some of the greatest USDA approved steaks for our common picnics. Since most members had children of our kids's age, Ines and Dieter both had a blast on the water and playing with them in the Clubhouse.

During the Spring season and definitely the Summer, driving around in Germany in a big American convertible was a pleasure they fully enjoyed. But most of us Americans and Germans alike were still hooked and addicted to Nicotine. We smoked a lot in those days since they were so inexpensive and 'chic'. Our children on the other hand did not think much of this bad habit at all. Both kids were usually hiding behind the front seats on the floor while we were driving and smoking in an open convertible.

Little did we realize in those days how stupid smoking really was and how much smoke we exposed our children to. Being good kids, they did not dare to criticize their parents, let alone tell them openly how smoking affected them. We had to admitting to them later that it was indeed a bad habit. Whenever the subject of smoking came up in conversations, they made sure to remind us how much they hated our smoking.

Our Battalion traditionally had a good relationship with the German Army's Defense District Command 43 at Wiesbaden. Our commands conducted marksmanship exercises and competitions together on an annual basis, where they fired our weapons while the US personnel fired German weapons to qualify for the German Army *"Schützenschnur"*, a bronze marksmanship award with silver cord. Following the competition firing and qualifying for this unique award, we usually had a social get-together and award banquet, where serious male bonding took place.

During the Spring, Summer and Fall the Germans also held their popular *"Volksmarsch"*, where even family members could take part to win medals for their participation. I always enjoyed these events and was happy that our family was eager to participate in physical events. When Ines, missing her horse back riding in the States, asked me if Germans have riding stables, I remembered some friends, who did have stables at one time. Making a few contacts I found an Equestrian School and enrolled Ines in the school, with the proviso that she had to maintain her good grades at her regular school. Her mother naturally liked the idea, too, and made herself available to drive about ten miles to the stables whenever she had riding classes.

As fate wanted it, during a visit to Germany about thirty years later, Ines was to meet her old instructor again by accident, while we visited a stable near Heidelberg with her uncle Michael, also an avid rider.

Still waiting to get that promised General Staff assignment, my new long awaited orders finally came in, transferring me to Headquarters USTASCOMEUR, the United States Army Support Command, Europe at Worms on the Rhine. It was close to home, only about 20 minutes from Mannheim, permitting the family to remain in the quarters, while I traveled to the office daily on the *Autobahn*, the German interstate.

The primary mission of this Headquarters was to provide general support to all US Forces in Europe, including manpower, equipment and stationing or relocating units, if required. My new job as Chief, Force Structure Branch under the Force Development Division required me to conduct frequent manpower evaluations. It also entailed determinations to consequently either add or, if no longer required, eliminate positions, of which the latter was a rather unpopular task.

My boss, Lieutenant Colonel Ralph Zwicker, the Chief of the Force Development Division and I once had a rather unpleasant job. Determine if US Army facilities at the city of Kassel were still essential to our mission. Kassel, was a larger city located halfway to Bremerhaven, our Port of Embarkation and Debarkation. The Army maintained a garrison there with a missile battery and an airfield, as well as a brand new commissary and PX with a gas station. Both, Commissary, PX and gas station were operated as a rest stop to support military personnel traveling between the Atlantic and the US Zone in the South of Germany. Streamlining of our forces, it was suggested that we could easily live without the facilities there and thereby save on costs. We had the obligation to investigate and, if feasible, take the appropriate steps to close the post.

Our job was to meet with members of the German Treasury and Finance Department to discuss the closure of the US facilities at Kassel. Our talks were held in German, because the majority of participants did not sufficiently understand English. It therefore required me to interpret the discussions for clarity off and on, although Ralph had a fairly good knowledge of German, being married to Inge, an attractive Bavarian lady from Nürnberg. It was determined that the Army could do without the facilities without experiencing any hardships for our personnel.

It was a very uncomfortable position I felt myself placed in, especially when I had to tell the German employees, most of whom had loyally worked for the Americans for over 20 years, that we had to close the facilities. We certainly hoped that the German government would undoubtedly find appropriate jobs for them after our departure. With the German Army expanding, the local government could easily use our newly constructed buildings, since they would be perfect for the German Army with all employees already on board. Many Americans were certainly not pleased with the elimination of US support at Kassel, but for economical reasons, we had no other alternative.

We saw nothing but sad faces for the two days of our additional final coordination and were both glad to conclude our discussion to the satisfaction of both negotiation parties before we returned south. I had the distinct impression, talking to some German employees, that if given a choice, they preferred working for the US Army over an employment with the German Military.

Losing a Proud Family Member

It was in November of 1971, after our family had just visited my father and mother over the weekend, when my mother called and told us that my father had been in a bad accident. Crossing the streetcar tracks on foot on the way to a hardware store not too far from where they lived, he was struck by an oncoming streetcar and was seriously injured.

I had often tried to talk my father out of driving those few blocks and instead take a brisk walk for exercise, especially after taking medications. He had done that more frequently, only this time he had apparently taken some medication for his malaria, which made him oblivious of the approaching streetcar. Not hearing the bells, and the train unable to stop in time, he was caught and dragged for about one hundred yards before the streetcar came to a stop. Somehow, I felt responsible for his accident, because had he taken the car, it might not have happened.

When I arrived at the hospital, located just across the apartment where my parents lived, I found my father resting in bed with several tubes sticking out of his mouth, nose and chest. Bandages were covering his entire torso testifying to the severity of his injuries. It was a depressing sight, but the doctor spoke encouragingly and told me that he should recover, if he gets over the next eight to nine days. Inquiring about his personal belongings, which my mother asked me to bring home, I was told that there were no personal items on his body except for his German identity card. The ambulance personnel had not turned in anything else, such as his watch and rings.

Mother was very disappointed about this, but stated that this is not really unusual. Many workers covering accidents are foreign workers and low paid helpers. Since nobody pays any special attention at those accidents, some of these people are tempted to help themselves. Professional hospital personnel, not being at the scene, can only emphatically apologize for any loss of personal items.

I visited him almost daily, as did my brother Reiner, who at that time lived and worked as a professor at the Goethe University at Frankfurt. After a week it seemed that he would recuperate from the injuries, when my mother called again to tell me that he had just succumbed to pneumonia. According to my mother, my brother had visited him the day before and complained to the doctors that he found father lying in bed covered only by a bed sheet, without a blanket or cover but with the windows wide open.

It has always seemed strange to me that many elderly people, hospitalized for something minor like a slipped disk or broken bone, inadvertently died in hospitals from pneumonia. This almost lends credence to the belief of some Germans, that the government tends to save a lot of money in pensions from older people dying early. Our Father was well on his way to recovery, had it not been for the pneumonia, which strangely enough killed him.

I felt a great loss, especially because I never even imagined that he could die in what I believed to be his prime years. Enjoying traveling, hiking, and socializing with his comrades–in–war, he also frequently visited his former colleagues at the *Heidelberger Finanz Amt*, the city's Finance Office, from which he had retired as a First Secretary, the equivalent of a GS-11 in our Treasury Department.

Regretfully, my father never talked much about his experiences during World War I and II. While he was still alive I never felt like asking him until after I had joined the military myself. For some reason there never seemed to be the right time, or time enough to question him about his past experiences. We thought that we would have plenty of time later on, not realizing that life could be cut short at any moment. Discovering a few of his personal papers after his death, I finally took the time to go through some of his records and files to find out what a great and proud man he had been.

Among his papers I found trial records from the years, when former members of the Nazi-Party were tried after WWII for their participation in, or commission of, alleged atrocities. Both my mother and father were found not guilty and subsequently declared *"entnazifiziert"*, which is a certification that they were no longer considered Nazis. His innocence was established by his military records of both WWI and WWII, where he was highly decorated and wounded twice, while serving in France, Holland, Belgium, Russia, Africa as a member of the Afrika Korps and in Italy.

Captured by the Allies on 8 May 1945 he was confined in an Allied Internment Camp near Darmstadt, close to Frankfurt. Testimonies showed that, although he had been an outstanding charter member of the party and bearer of the rare golden party emblem, he had frequently and publicly criticized Hitler as well as Dr. Goebbels for tolerating actions by radical leaders such as Himmler and Heidrich. This placed him in disfavor with the political hierarchy in the late '30s. Recognizing his past accomplishments and loyalty during the years of struggle against the Bolsheviks, he was strongly "encouraged" simply to resign.

His refusal to resign and the party noting his increasing political unreliability and criticism of their activities prompted them to conduct a house search. There they found books, banned and forbidden to be kept by party members, such as Karl Marx's writings and some anti-war writings like *"Im Westen Nichts Neues"* (Nothing New in the West). Arrested and taken into custody for 6 weeks, he was eventually expelled from active rolls of the party, while my mother remained a member to protect his job.

Proud of his past achievements, and not discouraged, he still firmly believed in helping the nation regain prominence and recover from World War I. He started working for the new Air Transport Ministry, the *Luftfahrtministerium* in Berlin, as a federal government employee. Following the declaration of war, he volunteered for active duty in the German Air Force, where he served in the 6th Airborne Division as a First Lieutenant until the end of the war, when he was released as POW and *"Oberleutnant"*. Going through old photo albums and other records I also found out that he had participated in the 1936 Olympic Games as a marathon runner. Later he became a member of several Sports Clubs, where he received many awards not only in track but also in boxing, which resulted in numerous different injuries of a broken nose.

His funeral was a very small and private affair, conducted at the cemetery in Heidelberg by cremation, attended only by family, close friends and veterans, as he had desired. During all my later visits to Heidelberg I always took the time to visit his gravesite at a quaint little cemetery outside the city limits. I am determined to recover his urn and take it back to the United States once the lease on his grave has expired.

Reunion with Old Comrades and Happy Hours

Time permitting, I always tried to make and maintain contact with my former comrades and friends. After I had returned from my trip to Kassel and its unpleasant reduction of personnel there, I had to conduct another survey of a unit, which I had once served in. Never would I have dreamed as a previous German citizen, that I would some day, as American soldier, be required to validate the need of this unit, even its further existence. It was the last Labor Service unit I had been a member of as a LS Sergeant, before I immigrated to the States and it was scheduled for a manpower survey to find out if personnel increases or reductions were justified.

I had not had any contact with any of the members of my old unit since my emigration and felt both embarrassment and immense pride. Walking into the unit, not dressed in the gray LS uniform as a German, but as a Major of the United States Army was a slight shock to those still remembering me from my younger days. There I was, their old comrade, now with the responsibility and power to make vital changes to their organization and possibly their livelihood. Some of the Department of the Army civilians, who had made it a career to work for the Army in Germany and who had even given me Letters of Recommendation when I emigrated, could hardly believe their eyes. This situation was almost unbelievable.

Obviously they were very happy with my success and their previous genuine belief in my prospects for the future. It was a memorable, unplanned and unexpected reunion, even though the reason was not exactly a joyous one. It was hard to tell the new Chief of the Division that several positions were no longer justified and had to be reduced or consolidated. By sheer coincidence, and it almost sounded like a joke, among the positions to be eliminated was the one I once had occupied and previously considered very important.

With the survey completed, the Division Chief, an old Infantry Colonel shook my hand before my departure, expressing his pride in my accomplishments in the Army as a former member of the Labor Service.

Some of my old comrades and friends of twenty and more years service, were standing around, some smiling with tears in their eyes. Questioned as to why I had never paid them a visit before, since I had been in Germany for several years before, I was unable to come up with any excuse, but I had to promise them that I would make it a point to see them more often, but only socially and on neutral territory.

Most of them still met every Sunday morning in one of the many favorite sports club pubs, where we used to hang out. I made good on my promise only too well, as Christine can attest to. There were many Sunday mornings, when we met at different locations on a rotational basis, visiting all the old familiar places as soon as they opened early in the morning, while many of their grandkids were playing soccer nearby.

Quite understandably, most wives were not too happy with our newly established 'Stammtisch' rounds. Being regular customers in several pubs, we had our reserved table, the 'Stammtisch' waiting for us. Figuring that I was probably the driving force behind it, the wives also knew that it would not last too long, only until I had to return to the States. Then they could take sole possession of their husbands on Sundays again. Christine in a way benefited from my Sunday Happy Hours too. Because I used the car quite a bit more, especially driving from our family quarters to my Headquarters, we had to look for a second car.

When my Chief decided to sell his car to buy a Mercedes, I saw my chance to latch on to an almost new bronze colored Dodge Challenger Convertible. A beauty, with only about 9000 miles for a one year old car, we did not hesitate for a moment and Christine finally had a new car of her own.

The entire family always liked convertibles and as far as we could look back, these cars had always given us continued pleasure. It was so much nicer to cruise in an open car along the many rivers and across wide-open fields visiting unforgettable historical sites. Having clean, fresh air in your face and a clear view of the mountains surrounding you, it made traveling so much more enjoyable, especially during our vacations in the Bavarian, the Austrian and the Swiss Alps.

Stunningly gorgeous with apparent great power, this car was certainly not a racing car, as I was soon to recognize. Falsely believing that my eight-cylinder V8 could easily beat a R600 BMW motorcycle on the German interstate, the Autobahn, I was proven seriously wrong. Cruising on the highway one day, I was challenged by a young motorcycle rider and encouraged by my kids to accept his challenge. We felt sure to show him what a big American car can do. Well, I did pretty good for a short while until I reached about 120 miles per hour. When he was unexpectedly passing me I tried to keep up with him, when I suddenly heard a clacking sound coming from underneath my hood. This awful sound was, in no uncertain terms, telling me to slow down and stop to check and see what could have caused that noise. It almost sounded like one cylinder or a rod had gone bad.

I had never been an auto-mechanically inclined individual and felt at a loss. We decided to play it safe and wait for a patrol from the German Automobil Club, ADAC, of which I was a longtime member, to get some assistance. As they constantly patrolled the highways, we only had to wait about fifteen minutes before one stopped. After he listened to the engine noise and checked the engine, he determined that I must have thrown a rod, a problem he could not remedy on the road. He suggested that we turn around at the next exit and drive to the nearest Chrysler dealer in a small town about 20 miles from our location. He assured us that we could safely do it, if I drive no more than 10 miles an hour off the main road along the emergency strip.

After he gave me directions to the dealer, we started limping along the autobahn, with the kids hiding in the back, more embarrassed than I was and probably feeling guilty too to have encouraged me to race the car. The dealer confirmed the ADAC findings and stated that he needed to keep the car for a couple days until parts would come in. With no other choice available, we accepted after he offered to drop us off at home.

About a week later we received a phone call from the dealer informing us that the parts had come in, but he now had to order a new convertible top for the car. Questioning the replacement of a relatively new top he explained that while our car was parked inside the garage, someone had broken into the shop. Trying to get inside the convertible, he had resorted to slashing the top with the intent to take whatever was inside the car. He profusely apologized for this incident and promised to make good for the damage, of course, and any other loss I may have had. Neither Christine nor I could remember and if so, that it was nothing very valuable. He promised to repair it as fast as possible and before the *"Fasching"* Holiday, the German *"Karnival"* or Mardi Gras was coming up.

I really didn't have much other choice, but was completely flabbergasted, when he asked me for a favor. He was wondering if I could lend him the convertible for their big parade. It would be the prize car leading the parade with the Prince and Princess riding in it. I could not believe that this man had the guts to even ask me. Surprised about his unusual request I promised him that he could. He assured me that our convertible was going to be in top-notch shape, waxed and all, before and after the parade of course. He was to personally drive it and our whole family was invited to the festivities as his honored guests, which the kids naturally looked forward to.

On the day of the parade, we were all lined up with hundreds of people dressed in costumes, waiting for the parade to arrive at the center of the little town. We all smiled, when we watched our car being the first vehicle at the head of the parade with the prince and princess thoroughly thrilled and all smiles, sitting on top of the back seat. Ines was a bit anxious when the car went by and spontaneously ran forward to touch her car. A policeman escorting the car naturally stopped her from touching the car, which almost made her cry because, after all, it was her car. She was frantically trying to tell him that by pointing at the American license plates, but to no avail. It was hard for me to calm her down and explain.

Fasching was always an exciting time of frolicking, partying and poking fun at the government, its politicians and other liked or disliked personalities. The German carnival generally went on for months from 11 November, 11 o'clock, 11 minutes and 11 seconds each year, coincidentally falling on the same day and time as our Veterans Day, until sometimes the end of February or whatever day Ash Wednesday falls on. Spirits were high and moral attitudes usually low until the end of the season. Everybody then took their makeup off, dressed properly and returned to normal again, behaving as if nothing had happened during the past two to three months of wild weekends.

Husbands and wives talked to each other again, after they made up and mutually forgave each other for their Fasching affairs with other people. It was not considered unusual, that most of divorce proceedings were filed after Ash Wednesday. Courts were habitually being swamped with adultery cases, while for some reason Catholics were mostly forgiven for their extramarital sins. It seemed rather surprising to me that during this fun period hardly anybody was stopped or convicted for drunk driving. The only explanation for this could be because the law enforcement officers were generally inside the dance and festival halls to stay warm while they also insured order is maintained, leaving hardly anybody outside. A good reason for this could have been the fact that this period was usually extremely cold. This, however, did not seem to bother the celebrating, sparsely clad crowd.

American soldiers stationed in Germany were offered a lot of things to make them feel at home. Whether it was food and drink, US Postal services, American standard living quarters or purchasing their favorite goods through the PX and Commissaries. Of course troops also had access to US car dealerships and representatives of other enterprises such as real estate companies.

Military clubs and messes were the most popular places for commercial agents to set up shop and offer their respective financial opportunities. This included offers for insurance, stock, mutual funds and especially retirement properties for investment. Getting closer to the date when one retires, one thinks of Florida or the West coast with the idea of eventually living there after you leave the military. On one particular weekend, we ran across a group of representatives from Horizon Corporation offering those beautiful sites with 'enormous' investment profit potential. Offered dinners with persuasive propaganda, Christine and I were in no time hooked, purchasing a double lot in Florida near Melbourne, close to Patrick Air Force Base and Cape Canaveral.

It sounded really great, because as a military family you want to be close to medical support in the later years. Listening to the speakers, this area seemed to have it all. Some German friends of ours who we had invited for an evening out, became as enticed as we did and were considering owning a piece of America. It did not take long and they also purchased a lot, if for nothing else than an investment in the future. As usual companies generally had door prizes, including offers of a chance to win a trip or something else worthwhile. For being so cooperative and even bringing some other customers to buy land, we surprisingly pulled the lucky straw giving us an all-inclusive free trip over an extended weekend to the city of lights Paris, France.

I somehow felt that it was rigged, but then again, maybe not. At least Christine and I had a chance to see Paris again, which we had first visited shortly after our wedding. Since we never had a true honeymoon because of my duties at that time, we intended to make it one that time. Although relatively short, we took a weekend with a holiday on a Monday to give us three days. My mother was nice enough, as usual, to play baby sitter during our short absence.

As crowded and crammed as the traffic was in Paris, our customary walks took us away from the main avenues, where we enjoyed the river banks of the Seine, the Arc de Triomphe and the clean side streets and alleys with their hidden little cafés and bistros. It was a truly exciting and enjoyable short vacation. On the way home to Germany we made a stop at Epernay in the French wine country. There we tasted the finest wines and champagnes, made from grapes grown in one of France's best soils. Anxious to put my French language to a test again, I quickly realized that only practice makes perfect, and I was very far from that.

Keeping a Promise. Revisiting Bangkok, Thailand

Having accumulated a lot of leave time again, I decided to make good on the promise I had made to myself when I was in Thailand on R&R. I wanted to take Christine on a vacation to Thailand and show her this beautiful land of enchantment. Through American Express and the German Automobil Club we booked a trip to Bangkok and took up my mother's offer to come to our quarters in Mannheim to take care of our two kids. Both had to attend school while we were gone for two weeks, and they looked forward to her visit because Oma was always willing to do favors for them.

The tour's flight to Bangkok had about fifty percent Americans and the other half Germans taking the trip. Flying with Pan American non-stop from Frankfurt to Bangkok, it should have been a straight trip, except for an unscheduled interruption. To our disbelief it turned out to be, what I considered, a skyjacking. Instead of a normal non-stop flight, the aircraft was abruptly forced to land in Karachi, Pakistan. For reasons still unknown to all of us, we descended onto the airport and taxied to the tarmac. Shortly after the aircraft stopped, all of us passengers were escorted off the aircraft to the waiting room, flanked by a line-up of armed soldiers.

It was not exactly a plush area, but they had at least several coke machines with soft drinks available for purchase, of course. There was not much interest or willingness on the passengers' part to pay three dollars for a small bottle. Our questions directed to the Pakistani official regarding our landing there were left unanswered. Some people jokingly stated that they got the impression, they only got us there to sell us drinks. There seemed to be nothing wrong with the engines, which gave way to rumors, that we were actually forced to land by the Iraqi for reasons unknown to all. The flight crew only shrugged their shoulders.

The rest of the journey was uneventful, with the pilot apologizing for the delay, still without giving any explanation, only serving us additional drinks, which most of the passengers were more interested in anyway, especially the Germans. Since we had some seats empty, we could not even figure out whether someone had left or was added to the flight.

We arrived in Bangkok on a beautiful sunny day and a climate that reminded me instantly of Viet Nam again, but it had a much nicer smell of flowers in the air than I could remember from the days gone by. The tour that we had booked, put us into a beautiful three star hotel, the Chavalit Hotel, the same which had previously served our R&R personnel from Viet-Nam. It had a grand restaurant and outstanding swimming pool. Surrounded by a multitude of exotic flower gardens with beautiful little Buddhist prayer sites, which looked liked oversize birdhouses, we were continuously at awe. A miniature image of Buddha inside the little edifice was surrounded by tokens, fresh flowers and burning incense.

Still suffering from jet lag, we just took it easy the first evening, while I made contact with Nyom, my old Thai Special Forces buddy. He was genuinely surprised and happy to see us again and promised to be our guide during our vacation. I was quite sure I would not be able to find my former guide and her brother from my R&R days and accepted his offer. Nyom, I found out, was the Commander of the Royal Thai Guard, responsible for the protection of the Royal family in Bangkok.

Despite his duties, he promised us to take some time off to show us Thailand and sites not normally visited or seen by the tourist groups. I was indeed glad when we finally met Nyom again, because we felt the imperative need to separate from the travel group. Some of the German tourists had apparently given a bad impression in the past on the Thais as we found out from Nyom. We considered it better not to be associated with them, which was really a shame, because most of them were nice fellow travelers.

Talking to some Germans, we found out that although it was a combined tour, prices paid for the tour varied, as Americans put in a different class, paid more. It became obvious because the Americans were eating separately and were being offered a better menu, while the Germans ate a typical "continental" meal. From one of the Thai speaking Americans we had also found out that several Germans had been arrested the first day at the hotel. They had invited a few call girls into their rooms for parties, but refused to pay for their personal service. Another couple, not familiar with the Thai customs, had stepped on a twenty "Baht" bill, the Thai currency, which had fallen onto the ground and was about to blow away in the wind.

It was considered a serious insult and offense when someone steps on the images or pictures of the king or the queen. It was apparent that the Germans were not properly informed of the customs of the Thai people and their proud traditions. I was ashamed for the Germans, because a few uneducated, boisterous and obnoxious people, who believed to be better than the rest of the world, would tarnish the reputation not only of their fellow countrymen, but also their country. There were other embarrassing incidents one waiter told us about, which convinced us to refrain from speaking German, which we usually did not do anyway unless we talked to a German.

Nyom showed up the next day with a Thai military jeep and took us on a trip to the River Kwai and its famous bridge. Near the river, we spotted an idyllic area in the garden of a restaurant adjacent to the bridge. The bridge, of course, had been rebuilt more recently when the bridge became a tourist attraction after the war.

Eating a typical Thai dinner and drinking the customary national Singha beer, we watched small fishing boats and recreational boats with powerful engines race up and down the river, loaded with tourists. Nyom explained to us that many things that we observed were strictly for the tourist's benefit and not normally enjoyed by the local population, which we realized was usually the case for most travel spots. I was truly happy that Christine now also had the chance to enjoy some of the sights, which I had previously experienced and frequently talked about following my return from Viet-Nam.

Watching the expressions in her face, I could tell that she also admired the land and the people like I did. TIMLAND, the huge park that depicted Thailand in Miniature was certainly a must to visit, since it introduced the foreign visitor to some of its culture, traditions and life as you would find it throughout their nation. Through several demonstrations we were also shown the versatility of Elephants, which were naturally the workhorses of the Thai farmers. It was amazing to see what these fabulously trained animals could do under the guidance of a man sitting on their back behind the ears of the animal.

With Nyom accompanying us, he was able to give us an even better insight into the common people's lives and their faith and beliefs. With a personal friend at your side, you will not get the standard, official 'shtick', but receive an honest insight into their lives, their hard work and struggle for survival, as well as their various types of leisure activity, be it theatre, dancing, or food. Wearing fantastic colorful dresses and headgear, we watched for hours groups of Thai dancers perform their traditional dances with charm and exotic expressions.

Strolling through the enormous park I suddenly saw and fell in love with something extremely beautiful. Not a fad in the States at that time, I noticed many beautiful ponds and lagoons containing a wide variety of fish, including the Japanese Koi. While admiring those majestic fish, it gave me the idea to build my own pond with Koi once in retirement and after we had settled down and were able to enjoy it. Traveling a lot while in the Army, I was taking in a lot of new sights and experiences not only from the orient but also from other areas I had visited. With all those ideas in my mind, I could hardly wait to put those ideas into reality, but wondered if I would ever have enough time to accomplish them.

Nyom was without a doubt a perfect host and tried his very best to show us his country and all the impressive Buddhist temples with their huge sculptures of deities and animals guarding the temples and sanctuaries. We found him to be very experienced in Buddhism, especially since he had once served as a Buddhist monk, prior to his military service, as required before becoming an officer in the Royal Thai Army. He also introduced us to the many fine dishes of his country, many of them delicacies in the orient while, I am sure, quite objectionable to Americans. Among those dishes was "the only one", which is part of an animal's reproductive organ served in a soup. It was absolutely delicious tasting even after he told us what it was. We had this dish many times thereafter. Christine and I only felt we were missing out on one thing during our visit. Something we had been looking forward to was to meet Nyom's wife and children.

I remembered however, and realized it later, that in most oriental countries wives are by tradition working in the background and rarely show their faces to guests. We had the same experience in Korea every time we were invited to a home of a male Korean friend. We did not press him though, respecting their customs, but we still hoped that with time their customs would eventually change and permit us to meet them, too.

Before we left Bangkok, we visited the Floating Market, a 'must see' event. The river flowing through Bangkok was packed with thousands of small boats floating on the river side by side. They appeared almost so tight, as if they were interconnected, permitting a person to walk across the river or canal from one bank to other without touching the water. Each one of those little barges, usually manned by either a woman or man, carried a variety of wares from household items to clothing, to food and to other trinkets. It was a unique market on water.

Nyom finally had to return to his unit, but before saying farewell, we promised each other that, if we had even a slight chance to see each other again, we will make every effort to do so. Maybe we will some day, still.

Having thoroughly enjoyed Thailand together, Christine and I regretted that we had to prepare for our return to reality and Germany, but not without one last shopping spree. Since jewelry was among the most promising past times during my last visit, we figured on splurging and spending any extra vacation money we had left. Stopping by one of those stores I had visited years before, we sat down on the counter and as customary, had a drink and a soup while bargaining over prices of several beautiful pieces of jewelry. I remembered never to pay the asking price but to skillfully bargain, until we finally reached a price acceptable to all parties.

After several beers and the average piece of gold jewelry costing only thirty-four dollars an ounce, including labor and design. The customer could never go wrong even with the posted price, especially when the dealer throws in several extra trinkets and gifts. We were all happy with our purchases, until Christine noticed a tiger skin on the wall, which she was really attracted to. Having spent nearly all the money we had allocated for the trip the $750 it was marked for was quite high for us. Figuring on bargaining again, we felt that we might still be able to get it. Well, when we got down to about half the price and bargaining got very hard, we both knew that trying to get the price any lower would be insulting to the Thai. So we politely withdrew from this purchase and considering our other purchases, we left totally satisfied, happy and smiling.

Saying our goodbye by bowing our heads was promptly returned by our gracious merchants. We knew that we had a field day and had made sure that we brought back a lot of rings and other jewelry for family and close friends.

Attending C&GS College in Alpine Surroundings.

Flying home I mentally revisited Bangkok for a while until reality set in and started thinking about the tasks, which were facing me upon my return from vacation. Aside from my Force Structure branch duties I also recalled the strong recommendation I received from Infantry Branch. The Army has always been stressing additional military education such as the attendance of the Command and General Staff College. This was a definite requirement for retention and promotion to Lieutenant Colonel and more.

I had chosen to take the correspondence course classes in the past, because a regular attendance at the college by quota was very limited and primarily for regular Army officers. It leaves Reserve Officers on active duty the only other avenue, and that is to take the classes by correspondence. Studying for the past three years, I was required to attend the school for two weeks, which was usually difficult, depending upon the location of the officer and the school. Germany, as one of the major theaters in Europe which had established a branch of the Command and General Staff College from Fort Leavenworth, Kansas in Oberammergau, Bavaria. Qualified Officers were able to apply for and attend the two-week course on temporary duty status.

Waiting for notification to attend, I prepared myself to go sometime soon after my return from Thailand. I did not have to wait too long. Promptly after Christine and I arrived home we picked up our happy kids and I contacted my office to report back for duty. Among other messages, I was told that I had received my TDY orders for the US Army School at Oberammergau, which scheduled me to attend the college in about a month, which gave me adequate time to catch up. I had to make sure I did not leave too much work to my staff while going on another trip. Although I knew that this course was demanding I looked forward to spending some time in my most favorite vacation spot of Germany.

Although the course is very demanding and requires a lot of study time, I was sure I could take Christine and the kids with me, so that they could have a nice family vacation while I also had some time to be with them at least in the late evenings in the hotel. We made arrangements to stay at the 'Von Steuben Hotel', the military Visiting Officers Quarters, which was one of the nicest and oldest German Hotels in Garmisch-Partenkirchen nearby. The trip in ideal convertible weather was a pleasure for all of us and we tried to make the most of it, knowing that in about another year we would be returning to the States again. It would certainly be a long time until we had another chance to visit Germany and the Alps again.

During the school's weekend our family took advantage of the breathtaking scenery to climb and hike the mountains and even visit aunt Ilse, one of Christine's relatives, who was lucky enough to work and live in

Garmisch. My old Labor Service outfit, where I used to spend my first Bavarian vacation, was still there and reminded me of my youthful years and my embarrassing encounter with the manure pile. So much for the memories.

Christine and I had a much nicer experience one evening, when we visited a well-known old restaurant, *"Die Alte Waffenschmiede"*, or 'The Old Arms Blacksmith', where an equally well-known Bavarian zither player, singer and yodler Leni Dellacher entertained each afternoon. The restaurant was a favorite among American tourists and troops.

We had been there for about an hour, when several men, well dressed, wearing dark sunglasses entered the large dining room. They were going from table to table asking people politely to leave that room for another, just before Leni was to perform. I did not know what to make of it when they came to our table asking us in broken German to leave. I naturally refused to leave the seat, which was pretty close to the stage. Besides, I didn't like for some guys, apparently not employees, to push their weight around. When I questioned their authority in German, they asked me for my German ID Card, after they produced their Secret Service ID. Not carrying a German ID Card, I showed them my military ID. Two of them looked at each other, whereupon one said that I could stay. I still didn't know what to make of it.

Unknown to us and obviously the restaurant personnel, the US president had decided to make a brief visit accompanied by a general. After a while the room had filled up with a group of Americans, German dignitaries and an entourage of reporters and staff. We unfortunately did not even got a glimpse of the President. After Leni had played for about half an hour, the Nixon presidential group departed and the normal evening continued with a delightful group of musicians and singers. The presentation was so impressive that I tried and eventually succeeded in getting one of the little band's recordings and her signature.

Just like in the United States, where you have the Yankees and the Rebels, Germany has their Prussians in the Northern part and the Bavarians in the South. Being an old Prussian or so-called *"Sau-Preuss"*, I usually had my occasional run-ins with the *"Batzis"* as the Northerners call the Southerners from Bavaria. When those two "adversaries" meet, they often make fun of each other, but I never thought that I could create a ruckus all by myself. A Bavarian friend once told me that, if I ever wanted to have real fun visiting a pub, just climb on the table, he said, and tell the present crowd in German: "I am a Prussian! Do you know my colors?"

I did not realize how much the Bavarians love their traditional white and blue colors, while the Prussians' flag is black and white. We never really considered it important, until I actually felt like trying his advice after a few good Bavarian beers with a friend. Just stepping on my chair and lifting my mug I got the immediate attention of those Bavarians present. Before I even got to 'Do you know my colors', I noticed the men's faces change and heard some chairs sliding back. That got my attention. I immediately recognized that I had stepped into a hornet's nest and being outnumbered I briefly saluted and stepped down fast, putting on a broad smile, while raising my one-liter mug for a toast to Bavaria. I believe that I had probably averted a fistfight by appearing to be an American and not really knowing what I was saying or doing.

I remember how Germans, just for fun, often taught American GI's some 'nice things to say' while in reality they were teaching them rather offensive sayings getting them into unexpected trouble. It reminded me of my time in Karlsruhe when I taught my fellow GI's some German. Hearing the guys readjusting their chairs, my friend and I figured that a possible disaster had been averted. I really did not feel good being a coward, but my friend, who did not believe the stories about our two groups in Germany, was thoroughly convinced and glad he did not have to fight his way out of the pub.

The two-week residential college course was crammed with material, but not having to worry about any other duties made it possible for me to fully concentrate on my study material. Most of the officers attending the course were Reserve Officers like I was, on active duty for an indefinite time, trying to advance themselves in preparation for a continued career. Competition in the military was stiff, especially in a peacetime environment, when the military was being scaled down and even a lot of Regular Army Officers with mediocre efficiency reports could easily face the ax.

It was for that reason that I had to show a serious interest in furthering my education and that I was interested in an extended Army career. I had already jumped the first and most important hurdle from company grade to field grade officer, putting the "scrambled eggs" on the visor. However, I was not exactly the crème of the crop academically because I had never attended an American college or received a degree. Nevertheless, I had always managed to stay within the top half despite some earlier handicap, language-wise.

Completing the course in Oberammergau qualified me for attending the final four weeks to graduate from the C&GS College at Fort Leaven-worth KS, at that time a necessity for the next promotion. Before returning back to my unit from the college course and home, the entire family went sightseeing for two more days, saying goodbye to Christine's relatives and the Alps. Both, young Dieter and Ines had a blast and Christine and I were quite impressed with how well they used their German when talking to people. We were very glad that they understood German so well and that we did not have to translate anything to them. As parents, we always felt that we needed to give them a well-rounded education and I firmly believe that we did. Every chance we got we also tried to instill in them a sense of pride, good morals, courtesy and the respect for others.

Just like our parents gave us the right to choose our careers and religious beliefs, so did we by giving them a free choice. We just made sure to give them the proper guidance and be good role models. It was also my firm belief that a mother should not have to go to work if she has children to raise. Occasionally though, without depriving the children of any time with their mother, she worked at the Military Hospital as a Red Cross volunteer. It still gave Christine ample time to be there to raise them and help them with any problems. Thereafter, it was up to them to decide on their own life style to achieve happiness, as my wife and I did during our long marriage.

I was extremely fortunate to have found a truly free-spirited soul mate in my wife. We basically have the same good taste, a healthy outlook on life, remaining independent of any political and religious beliefs and strongly believing in what is correct and proper. I do not remember ever having had a serious argument or exchanged any bad words in our entire life together. I was hoping that our children had adopted our philosophies.

Following my return to TASCOMEUR I was confronted with another difficult task. Faced with cuts in military spending, the Army was compelled to initiate the closings of several favorite and beneficial institutions. I would have never imagined that cuts in military spending would force us, and my branch in particular, to plan to consolidate many unit functions and to relocate several facilities. Among the affected schools was not only the Non-Commissioned Officers Academy at Warner Barracks in Munich, which I had attended previously to become an NCO, but then also the C&GS College Extension Program at Ober-Ammergau from which I had just returned.

Some of the beautiful R&R hotels in Garmisch, which had served the military population for so many years, needed to be returned to the German owners. This action reduced our available recreational hotels and facilities by about fifty percent. To make up for the closings of some hotels, one charming hotel at Chiemsee, located along a huge lake, was not only retained, but also enlarged and doubled in size. Availability of recreational amenities for our troops and their dependents had always been our goal and was considered essential for the morale and welfare in the military. The US military always made sure that their troops were well cared for. They were not to be without those basic items they were accustomed to as citizens of the US, whether it was a Commissary, PX, movie theater or adequate living quarters.

A favorite of the US troops and also many Germans, was having American television and radio broadcast stations such as AFN and AFTV, the armed forces radio and television network. These services provided for the troops and their dependents unbiased information and entertainment, minus commercials. Ines and Dieter Jr., attended the American-operated Kindergartens and schools, giving them an education, which was second to none. Department of Defense schools maintained one of highest standards and were beyond the influence of any local government or any Board of Education.

Nearing the end of my overseas tour in Germany I had attained almost seventeen years of military service. After many exciting and some unbelievable occurrences, I was going to have a totally different, not so pleasant and totally unexpected event. Following the Viet Nam war, with the military being over strength, many Reserve Officers called to active duty were subsequently released from active service and returned to their Reserve Units. They had served their purpose and were no longer needed. Many of my fellow officers, who I had the pleasure of serving with, had already been released and returned home, while I was still retained in an active duty status.

My friends had considered this unusual, as I too began to believe that my luck was due to run out soon. And it did. The general draw-down must have finally caught up with me when I received an extremely nice sounding letter from the Department of Defense. The Secretary of Defense and the President of the United States were thanking me for my outstanding and exemplary service to our country, while at the same time they regretted to inform me, that my services as a Reserve Officer were no longer needed in an Active Duty status. Following the end of my tour in Germany and my return to the United States, I would be released from Active Duty and reassigned to a Reserve Control Group.

Naturally, I was very disappointed as were the other members of the staff. Several calls and communication with the appropriated offices at the Pentagon by my boss were to no avail. Congress felt no need for such a large military anymore and subsequently instituted the routine RIF, a Reduction in Force, releasing not only Reserve Personnel but also terminating those Regulars, who had been passed over for promotion.

Having spent most of my adult life in the military it was going to be difficult to find a new career, especially since all my training could hardly be applied to any civilian job. My best two options open were to either return to a Reserve Unit and complete my service obligation for retirement while working as a civilian, or remain on Active Duty by reenlisting in my initial Regular Army grade of Staff Sergeant, as permitted by law. The latter choice would require me to serve only another three years to be able to retire with my permanent commissioned rank. I decided to stay in the service. Needless to say, this choice demanded serious cutbacks on unnecessary expenditures. Being frugal in our overall lifestyle anyway, Christine and I decided to bite into the sour apple and remain on Active Duty until retirement.

Even though it was a somewhat demoralizing situation, replacing my officers uniform with that of an enlisted man, it was still the only sensible option offered to me in order to complete my service for the right to a well deserved retirement. The strangest part of course was the unusual spot I frequently found myself in. Returning to Fort Bragg, I might have to serve under an officer, who was formerly my subordinate or another senior enlisted soldier, who had previously served under my command. It was going to be something not too many people go through more than once, but I was determined to make the best of it.

We were lucky that we still had the small house in Fayetteville to which we could return to while assigned to Fort Bragg. I was willing to face some embarrassing and possibly humiliating situations. It definitely meant that we would have to tighten our belts and live on less than half the usual income. It was just another challenge our family was confronted with.

My Commander, the Division Chief and my staff all expressed their disappointment and hated to see me leave after this scheduled rotation. They had seriously been hoping that I would extend my assignment in Germany for a few more years. That was not to be, however, and so the family prepared to get ready for probably the last move in my career from good old Germany to our final destination in North Carolina, a move the kids did not mind at all.

Again, we found ourselves in the same position as many times before. Packing our belongings, saying farewell to even more friends than we had ever known before. Clearing the Post, we made sure of taking a few more small trips to visit our favorite places before we left. Christine was always shaking her head, when I told my friends that, once we return home to the United States and got settled, they were all welcome to visit us any time after my retirement at the ripe old age of forty-four years.

Evidently, my most heavy-hearted farewell was saying goodbye to my mother, who we had not only visited a lot, but also taken along with us on many trips. She was going to be left alone, except for a few good friends of mine. It was reassuring to know that they all promised they would take good care of her, including Christine's father, who lived only a few blocks from her. With my sister Ute in the States too, there was only my brother left, who rarely visited, possibly because I was still around. Considering his behavior in the past and the embarrassment he caused my parents and me, we naturally did not see eye to eye at all.

After my last *"Auf Wiedersehen"* at my favorite Sunday morning happy hour establishments, I made my final trip to Bremerhaven to turn in our favorite Dodge Convertible. Pending our final departure from Frankfurt Rhein-Main Airbase, we were hanging on to the other car, the white Ford Fairlane convertible, to be used until our actual departure. One of my Sergeants was just too happy to buy it, since it was in an excellent shape. The kids would have liked to keep that one too but they finally relented after I explained to them, that we could only take one vehicle back and we chose the Dodge, which was newer and held more pleasant memories for us.

Chapter IX

Back in the USA

Home Again at the Special Warfare Center

Arriving back in Fort Bragg, I immediately visited my old Headquarters and buddies from the John F. Kennedy Center for Special Warfare. Many of them were either still or again there and when I explained to my former bosses that I am being released from Active Duty, I got the immediate uniform reaction to reenlist once released and request assignment to the Special Warfare Center. Several vacancies requiring my specific Military Occupational Specialty, were urgently waiting to be filled, as the Center was seriously short of Officers. There were several highly qualified NCOs filling officers positions already and I could at least continue to be an asset.

The Literature Division had a Branch with a major's position and a Master Sergeant's slot, but no one to fill it. Accepting it, I would continue to have the responsibilities of an Officer and get rated as such, in accordance with regulations. I was overwhelmed with several offers and finally accepted the Literature Branch assignment, writing classified manuals and producing the necessary art and graphics for them. Still holding a Special Forces MOS, I was also back in a jump slot, drawing specialty pay. Not believing in buying things on credit or assuming unnecessary debts, the additional income was urgently needed.

Two weeks later, I was released from active duty and assigned to the Reserve Component as a Major. The following day, I reenlisted for three years, accepting my old grade of Staff Sergeant thereby becoming a so-called Dual Component Officer; a Commissioned Officer serving in an enlisted status. I continued to attend my classes and the correspondence course for the Command & General Staff College for future promotions should I be recalled to Active Duty as an Officer again, which frequently happens.

Not to lose touch with other military affairs I joined the ROA, the Reserve Officers Association Chapter at Ft Bragg, where I assumed the role of the Chapter Secretary. Strangely enough, during one of our meetings at the Officers Club one of the senior sergeants working at the club as bar tender, spotted me in my Major's uniform and was seemingly embarrassed. Not knowing that I was a Dual Component Officer, I had to explain my position to him, a situation, which he obviously was not familiar with. Remembering my old first sergeant in the engineers, who had an Officer's serial number as a Reserve Major, but was RIF'd after the Korean War, I relayed that story to him for a better explanation. Queried, as to why I would stay in as a Sergeant, I explained to him, that I was still a Major in the Reserves, only drawing Sergeant's pay until I retire. It was my choice, which some of my contemporaries in the Reserves could not easily make.

Assigned to the Headquarters Company of the Special Warfare Center, I was exempt from all other details since I worked directly for the General Staff on several special projects. Considering the breaks and benefits I was given, I was definitely content with my assignment. My family was quite delighted, because it was a generally seven to five workdays with free weekends. It seemed like I found a new niche, a very satisfying, and challenging job permitting me to dedicate plenty of time to the family. Another advantage my new job offered was that it also gave me the opportunity to be artistically creative, which included working with ceramics. It gave me a chance to make special souvenirs for fellow soldiers and other people retiring or departing for another assignment.

As our Nations 200th Birthday approached in 1976, I saw my chance to design and really create something unique. Similar to a small coffee table I once made displaying major German city coat of arms, I started working on a larger coffee table. The top showed an American eagle, centered, and the flags of all fifty States, hand painted on ceramics, with inset mosaic pieces surrounding the eagle and the flags. The entire table with its various colored inlaid mosaic pieces looked so impressive, that I was encouraged to enter it into an arts and crafts exhibit in honor of and celebration of this special anniversary. Apparently, it was good enough to earn a monetary award and special recognition for its beauty and originality.

Fortunately, my job was not filled with only routine office work. It also had some excitement built in. Constantly in need of volunteers, I found myself participating in a test conducted by the Marine Corps at Camp LeJeune one day. Looking for some parachutists to participate in a special parachute insertion technique, they apparently could not find volunteers crazy enough to try out the system. Maybe they did not trust their own dare devil pilots.

The system to be tested was the covert insertion of parachutists into a foreign territory by flying a Navy OV2, a small double-seated, dual fuselage aircraft below radar at tree top level to the target area. The aircraft had a separate compartment behind the cockpit, only big enough to cram in two jumpers with their equipment. Once they reached the selected Drop Zone, the pilot would pull straight up until the aircraft almost stalled, dropping the parachutists out of the back and then quickly dive down to below radar level again. It was supposed to be fun and exhilarating and I figured I might as well do something unusual before retiring.

Unfortunately, it did not turn out to be such a great fun thing to do after we got the green light and were dropped like a sack of unwanted baggage. My co-jumper and I cleared the aircraft and spotted the plane speed away underneath us, while we looked for the Drop Zone, which for some reason did not appear to be where we expected it to be according to information received during the briefing. All we could see were the typical and so familiar North Carolina pines, stretching for miles within our view. The small opening of the DZ, where we were supposed to be inserted, was nowhere to be seen. It became clear to me that the Marine pilots had either made a mistake and had gotten off course, or they just wanted to see what some Special Forces guys would do when dropped into nowhere.

Floating down we both signaled each other to point out the most feasible area in which to attempt a landing. With hardly an acceptable place in view, we were forced to make our own choices, while still trying to stay as close together as possible for any eventual support either one of us might require. My fellow jumper was a burley Sergeant, who had his share of jumps behind him and I was confident that we both would survive this landing.

Descending rapidly, there appeared to be nothing else to do except perform a tree landing. No matter how we slipped and maneuvered, there were no suitable openings to land in. With a total quiet surrounding us, we both hit the trees only about 30 meters apart. Dropping in between an array of trees I suddenly felt being yanked up by my parachute. Looking up I saw that the chute was draped over three trees with my body suspended in between about 20-30 feet from the ground. Hearing moaning nearby, I looked around for my buddy and spotted him in between some trees in about the same situation I was in. I was horrified to see his one upper leg impaled by a broken off branch, his wound bleeding.

With nobody else around to help, I quickly released my reserve chute and let it drop down. Using it to slide down on the lines I hoped to be able to reach the ground and to help him. Anxious to get to the ground, I completely disregarded the common precautions drilled into us during Ranger training. Improper handling of nylon ropes can cause severe burns. As a result, the lines of the parachute cut into my flesh while sliding downward. Extreme pain and the closeness to the ground prompted me to let go of the lines. Falling down into the reserve chute below, it made me flip over for some reason. Dangling upside down, still about 10 feet above the ground my boots were caught in some parachute lines. The only way I could free myself, was to reach my survival knife on my boot. After several unsuccessful attempts, I heard some voices approaching in the distance and to my surprise saw several Marines coming towards our location.

Embarrassed to have those guys find me in such a helpless position, with my buddy still "nailed" to the tree unable to free himself, I made another try for the knife. I finally succeeded in pulling it out of the sheath and cut the entangling lines, dropping to the ground without any other injuries, except hurting of my pride. The Marines could not believe what had happened to us, but immediately went about to get my partner off the tree. He was not that high above the ground, but it still took the troops to form a human pyramid and gently pull my comrade off the tree. Probably because of the loss of blood he had passed out before we could finish applying a tourniquet and bandage him for an ambulance to take us both back to the base.

Although the burns to my hands were not too bad, I was limited in the full use of my hands for several weeks. This mishap convinced me, that it was probably time for me to discontinue volunteering for those challenging tests so close to my retirement. It was, without a doubt, time for the younger generation to assume some of these challenges and risks. It dawned on me that my family is depending on me to stay alive and to support them.

My daily duties and responsibilities involving the writing, designing and illustrating technical manuals for SF operations provided me with plenty of challenges of a safer nature. Seeing my family every night was very gratifying. In contrast I reminded myself of those men and women, who were laying their lives on the line every day in so many theaters of the world, while I was fortunate to be spending some quality time with the children and Christine. I hoped that they could not be any happier without me around, even though I was by nature a very strict and authoritative father.

Finally home without an immediate threat of another overseas employment I seemed to be trying hard to make up for the lost time when I was separated from them. My daughter later admitted and confessed, that I could have been a lot tougher with them, but that she would not have resented it, as long as I was home with the family.

Graduating from C&GSC

Having completed most of my required correspondence course material for C&GSC, I received orders from the US Army Reserve Components Center in St. Louis Missouri. My instructions were to report to the US Army Command & General Staff College, Fort Leavenworth, Kansas to attend class 76-1 for the Final Phase of the course on 25 January 1976.

It was a rather strange thing I had to go through in order to attend the course. First, it involved my recall to Active Duty as a Major after my discharge from my Enlisted Status. Hanging up my Sergeant stripes, I changed in to my other uniform and the gold leaves. I vividly remember the day, on which I signed out from my unit to attend C&GSC.

As I passed my company assembled in formation for roll call, the Company Commander, a young Captain, called the entire company to attention rendering the customary salute to a Senior Officer, which I proudly returned. Suddenly recognizing me, he seemed surprised and I realized how uncomfortable he must have felt. Rarely visiting the company, I had totally neglected to keep my Company informed of my discharge and recall, which was done by the Personnel Office. I quickly made up for my oversight and apologized to him, putting myself into his position.

Fort Leavenworth's Staff College was a unique experience, especially finding many of my fellow Reserve Officers with combat service in Viet-Nam. Several of them, who had been serving with Army and National Guard units, had experiences quite similar to my own, serving as NCOs on Active Duty. They had also been called up just to attend the college.

We had a lot of unique stories to share. The tactical portion of the classes included some historical maneuvers executed during past wars in Europe. The majority of subjects taught involved war-gaming for a possible future military conflict with the Warsaw Pact countries, should it ever evolve out of the "cold war" situation..

It was apparent to me, that some of the planners were not quite up-to-date on the more recent developments in the Western part of Germany, especially along the critical areas of the Rhine River. It was obvious to me that the old plans, which they had presented for several years, needed to be brought up to date. After many serious discussions and possible considerations of several suggestions, I had the satisfying feeling to have contributed to the revision of some of the operational options, especially in light of the more recent developments on both sides.

Our class material was packed with overwhelming information about new weapons, our military capabilities and the requirements for in-depth studies of ever changing contingency plans. On the less serious side, we all had ample time to enjoy the sights, sounds and tastes of Kansas City, both in Kansas and Missouri. I had previously heard about the famous and unbelievable Kansas steaks and looked forward to experiencing the food myself. The students were definitely intrigued by special offers in some restaurants. Patrons were challenged through offers of 'no charge' for the dinner, if they could honestly finish their ordered steak meal by totally cleaning their plate.

Hungry as I was, I had to resist all the encouraging words of my classmates to accept the challenge. Seeing the huge steaks being served, I knew good and well that I could never win, especially after I already had finished a big plate of salad. The steak was not only the biggest, but also the best tasting I have ever had in my life. I was quite satisfied with just enjoying a truly great dinner without any pressure.

Graduating from the college, I received the only ring I was ever able to earn, as Germany did not have such a symbol or tradition. Following the two-week final phase of the college course and our graduation following a four-year correspondence program, I returned to Fort Bragg's Special Warfare Center and to the life of a dual personality. Subsequent to my return to the Company, I immediately sought out my Company Commander for an important act he had to perform. My orders stipulated that I would be authorized to reenlist again to complete my original tour, following my release from Active Duty as a Commissioned Officer. I wanted to be sure, that my Company Commander would swear me in again for the continu-ation of my Active Duty tour then again as a Non-Commissioned Officer until the date of my retirement. I was about to reach that date in only five more months.

Carrying two military identification cards, one recognizing me as an Officer, the other as a Non-Commissioned Officer, I could visit either the NCO Club or the Officers Club, which I usually preferred. Having been a member of the Officers Club for many years, I naturally continued to pay my membership as a Reserve Component member. I could sympathize with the Sergeants, most of whom disliked having an Officer observe their behavior while socializing in their very own club.

Strange situations and obvious conflicts encountered by the Dual Component Officers over decades had resulted in many recommendations to change this perceptibly archaic regulation. For a military individual serving in both a commissioned and non-commissioned status seemed to-tally illogical. Maybe some day it will be realized by those in power, that a change is in order. I never had any reason to complain about the treatment while in the service, but I felt bad for those in the Reserves, who had been called up several times during the Korean Conflict and later the Vietnam War, only to be discharged again, after the conflict ended. "Tommy" was good enough to serve during critical periods, but following the successful accomplishments and peacetime, they were liable to be quickly terminated again and again.

My Last "Hurrah"

On 31 July 1976, I finally approached the long-awaited important high-light not only in my life, but also in the life of my family. Having served my new and adopted country for over 20 years, the Active Army was offering me a retirement, which I could not refuse and gladly accepted. Witnessing a gradual change in the Armed Forces by shifting to an all-vol-unteer force, it also began liberalizing their traditional methods of opera-tion and conduct. Unfortunately, many time-honored traditions were either watered down or totally abolished which in my opinion visibly weakened its effectiveness.

Prior to leaving the Army I had to take part in one final out-process-ing, which included a rather thorough medical examination. Not expecting anything wrong anyway, I walked away with a clean bill of health and promising long life. Determined to continue adhering to a healthy life style, I had no intention to change what I knew was good for me.

It was a beautiful morning at Ft. Bragg, when the John F. Kennedy Center for Special Warfare held their traditional monthly retirement ceremony. Surrounded by hundreds of troops, I was getting ready to participate in my last official ceremonial. While I was proudly wearing my Class A Green uniform and the green beret moving into formation, I was honestly moved hearing the band playing of the Green Beret Anthem followed by traditional Army marches. Christine was standing next to me in the front line of retirees, when the Commanding General of the Center read the names of selected retirees and those troops who were receiving awards. I felt a slight push into my side, when one of the names was that of Major Dieter H.B. Protsch, United States Army, Infantry. But I was equally proud of those other comrade-in-arms standing in formation, who either received an award or were to retire after a 'lifetime of service' to our nation.

Not forgetting that behind each soldier always stands a great woman, the military services have always recognized the important role the wives play in their life. Naturally, I was extremely proud to see Christine standing next to me, receiving her Certificate of Appreciation for her service to this country. Faithfully supporting a husband and the family during often trying times, while he was apart from them. She certainly fulfilled her sworn obligation.

Following the ceremony, we briefly went to the Officers Club, toasting to the Commander-in-Chief and my last award for Meritorious Service. Bidding a final farewell to those remaining to hold down the Fort, we returned home to get ready for, hopefully, one last move in our military service. It was time to find a place to be our retirement residence.

Although we had purchased 'property unseen' while in the service, such as a double lot in Port Malabar, Florida, a double lot near Tombstone, Arizona and another five-acre lot close to Phoenix, Arizona, we had decided to move to Hagerstown, Maryland. From past visits there, we knew that we would find a climate and scenery close to that of Germany and be close to some old friends. Another consideration was also the fact that Fort Ritchie was located nearby, which would provide us with the essential medical service, Post Exchange and Commissary services. Promised by our government as one of our benefits for serving the nation until retirement, it was to many people one of the reasons for serving.

Having served in the military for such a long time without any close ties with other family members or relatives in the States, we had come to believe that the Army was our family. We learned that this big family was always ready to provide the support you could depend on. But before we could actually move our household goods and sell our house in Fayetteville, we had to find a home in Hagerstown or vicinity. And we had to do it fast. After a few contacts with friends in Hagerstown, we traveled to our future retirement area. Checking out about six or seven possibilities, we were impressed by a relatively new home, only four years old. It was owned by an airline pilot, who was forced to relocate to Chicago. A plain standard white split rock ranch home, situated on a large hill top surrounded by fields and farms, it looked beautiful and promising. The clean, fresh air and relative quiet of the area made our choice and final decision rather easy.

Chapter X

Permanent Retirement Not in My Cards

Finding a Permanent Home

Looking at the surrounding countryside, we knew we were at last looking at our first permanent residence. It was a great and rewarding feeling after living through twelve moves and relocations while in the Army. Our new home was located near Smithsburg, MD between Hagerstown and Ft Ritchie, with Camp David, the President's retreat only eight miles away. As a bonus for future hikers in the family, we were within sight and only two miles from the Appalachian trail, the renowned hiking route leading from Maine to Georgia for a length of 2,174 miles. The property was an Infantryman's dream, occupying high ground with a perfect view of the surrounding area and without any obstacles to block one's view. Everybody seemed totally content. At least so it seemed.

Considering the education of our two children, we were also told that the closest school was considered one of the best in the county for our son Dieter and daughter Ines. She was a senior in high school and already very particular about a school and her friends. Since she had made very close friends in the Fayetteville High School, she was not at all pleased to be uprooted and moved during her senior year, thereby loosing many of her friends. Another factor I had not considered, was the very close friendship or better called relationship, which Ines had developed with Chuck, a young Airborne Trooper of the 82nd Airborne Division, my old unit on Ft. Bragg.

Only a few weeks after we had moved to Maryland we were totally shocked and completely surprised when we found Ines missing during the day and the following night. This was highly unusual behavior on her part, since she always told us where she was going and also asking for permission to go. When Christine mentioned to me that Ines had written several love letters to Chuck, I could only deduct that she had probably run off to return to him and her school friends in North Carolina. A very good indication that she left on her own, was the fact that some of her clothes and a bag were found missing.

I was quite angry and disappointed in her behavior. Had she been of age eighteen, I would not have been worried too much about her running off. Her being only seventeen years old however, as parents we were still responsible for her well being and safety. I had to really restrain myself from notifying the local law enforcement after twenty-four hours. Gradually settling down, I decided to make a few phone calls to friends in our former neighborhood. Not really surprised, we heard that she had indeed returned to the Fayetteville area and had contacted several friends who confirmed that she had called them. Since she did not stay with any of them, we suspected that she had obviously returned to her boyfriend.

I contacted the Commanding General of the Division and advised him of the possibility, that one of his soldiers might be harboring a minor runaway, my daughter from Maryland. After giving him Chuck's last name, he promised to look into this matter. It was only after about an hour that we received a phone call from a Company Commander, who stated that he questioned Chuck. After talking to him, he freely admitted that Ines was indeed with him and that she intended to stay with him.

The Company Commander naturally asked me what action I preferred he should take against his trooper. After a brief discussion with Christine, we reached a consensus, that since she is close to her eighteenth birthday, we would agree that she could remain there, provided that they get married immediately, if that was both their firm desire, otherwise I would prefer charges against Chuck for illegally harboring a minor. The Company Commander ordered Chuck to promptly contact us to confirm his intention; otherwise he would have to face a court-martial. Chuck, I was sure, must have been scared and called to insure us that they would indeed try to get married within two weeks, which, to our surprise, they did. He also promised that she would continue her high school education there, as we had stipulated.

We did not quite believe, but sincerely hoped that they would carry out their intention. I was ready though to return to North Carolina and pick her up to bring her home. The only document Ines had to get properly married was her birth certificate from Germany. Eloping to South Carolina, where there were apparently no restrictions, it must have been accepted by the official and permitted them to get married. For all practical purposes, Ines was actually still a German citizen, who had neither a German passport with an immigration visa nor an American passport. We were quite certain nobody could read her German birth certificate and prohibit them to marry. To all our surprise, those two nevertheless succeeded.

It was a somewhat disturbing event, but Christine and I realized, that we really did not have much of a choice to prevent this young couple from possibly making their biggest mistake of their young lives. We just needed to make sure, that Ines was safe and sound and under the wings of a responsible young man. Several people disagreed with our decision and handling of the situation, but we both felt different. Looking at our very own past, when Christine was only seventeen and madly enough in love to get married, we did not want to deny my daughter the same right, even though she had a loving family, who would have done anything for her.

Although everything seemed to go their way initially, Chuck decided to leave the Army for a more liberated lifestyle, where after their life seemed to change for the worse. It looked like some of our previous feelings about their immaturity were substantiated. But then again, it was her life and she had to learn to take full responsibility for all her actions.

Retiring? Looking for a New Niche

Young Dieter meanwhile settled down in his new school and turned out to be a good student with great potential having found his own niche and good friends. As far as I was concerned, having settled in our new home, I found plenty of work to change things to our liking. Refurbishing the bare basement into an attractive recreational space, where we could relax with friends and enjoy retirement, was my first project.

The drastic changeover from a busy military life to a life without any serious responsibilities, made me suddenly feel like somebody put out on the pasture. It was a lifestyle, which I could not so easily get used to. Since Christine had played housewife and mother to two children during my service years, she now only had to worry about one older teenager. She was also left with a lot of time on her hands, which encouraged both of us to find ourselves some satisfying niches. The fact that military retirement pay was only about fifty percent of regular monthly income was another good reason to give us the proper incentive to continue actively in the workforce.

Christine, had always been challenged by statistics and bookkeeping, which she had learned in Germany and was earnestly considering working in that area again. Even before my retirement, she had decided to learn more about taxes and possibly work as an income tax consultant. I believe she had noticed me earlier getting frustrated doing our annual tax returns. She did quite well in her tax consultant job working seasonably for four months each year. She seemed happy to be able to do something constructive and to contribute to our income. Besides some bookkeeping for a well-known historic restaurant and later Bavarian restaurant, taxes were her main interest and more permanent involvement.

It was a little bit different for me. With a new house and about three acres of ground to maintain, I was not quite ready for a full time job. After many encouraging letters from the Veterans Administration to utilize my available funds from VA educational benefits, I found myself enticed to attend college, something I had never done before in the US, except for military schooling.

Enrolling at the Junior College in Hagerstown I found myself in the strange position sitting next to teens studying liberal arts. Gradually, I began to enjoy studying some subjects totally new to me, except for French and German, which I also had to take. It only took two classes of German, before the Ukrainian-born Professor asked me to skip the classes. I had inadvertently taken the liberty of correcting him in his German every once in a while. Assuring me that I would still receive an "A" in his class because of my excellent German language knowledge, I willingly skipped his class.

Not having spoken French for years though, and feeling somewhat rusty, I also took classes in French. This was actually a lot more fun than any of the other classes, which I had to take. My particular interest, of course, was art, and I was glad to be able to learn more about design and graphics than I expected. This special interest had led me to purchase a kiln, when we were still living in Fayetteville, enabling me to do ceramic work on my own and be able to fire it at home.

With a 4.0 average after three semesters, I was invited to join the college's honor society and shortly thereafter, I found myself elected the president of Phi Theta Kappa. Undoubtedly, it was due to my life experiences, my age and, I suppose, because I definitely had more time to spare than other students for required extracurricular activities.

After I graduated with an Associate Degree in Arts, I was determined to actually try out my newly gained knowledge. I picked up a job in a small printing establishment in Hagerstown as a graphic artist. They needed someone, who they thought was talented enough to work on designs, prepare layouts for printing and create logos for various companies looking for a new image. While the work was quite interesting and challenging, the promised income was not materializing as promised and as I had expected. At least I had my first taste of a civilian employment.

Our son, graduating from High School, also had a desire to enter into the graphic arts field. When he started looking for employment without finding the right company, I convinced my employer that my son could probably fill my job much better than I could. Since he was young and energetic and besides definitely needed the job more than I did, the employer seemed swayed. He agreed to hire Dieter for the same pay, giving me a graceful way out of his employment.

Many of my fellow retired military officers probably felt the same way I did, still being drawn to military type activities. The motto for our retirees had always been "Still Serving", which implied that we should use our experiences and knowledge to continue contributing to our community. I found many of them getting involved in veterans affairs as a substitute for active service. Realizing that our active troops always needed support from outside sources, I found that I could still do my part by volunteering for the many available positions, which could help in maintaining, protecting and promoting the welfare of the military members.

Living near Fort Ritchie, I was encouraged to become a member of the Officers Club Advisory Council. Once back in the system, it was not hard to subsequently be talked into the different memberships, like the Infantry Officers Ball committee. There, a group of about eight proud Infantry Officers felt that they had the need to carry on the old Infantry tradition. Namely holding an annual Infantry Ball. The need probably felt greater by those retired.

Stationed on an Army Post, where the host was the Signal Corps and most Officers assigned were Signal Officers, it presented a tremendous challenge to show the over three hundred Officers, what the Infantry, the "Queen of the Battle" is made of. After careful planning, we held our first Infantry Ball at Fort Ritchie. As the only one with some talent for visuals and graphics, my special "committee of one" was quite busy for several years. First I had to design and then continuously make emblems and patches symbolic of the Infantry, while others were doing the organizing.

For just one special evening, the Club was converted from a typical signal-orientated ceremonial site into a shrine for the "Infantry Grunts". Crossed rifles of the Infantry had temporarily replaced all mementos and signs of the proud Signal Corps. Naturally the Infantry respected and admired this corps because we knew and believed that in order to properly fight and shoot you have to be able communicate. But this day and evening was to be ours. Several years of continued improvements of the decorations, we found ourselves spending an entire day just decorating the beautiful historic Officers Club building.

From hand-carved oversize Infantry insignias, to Airborne wings, Ranger tabs, Air Assault badges to a multitude of other items, including unit patches; we displayed them all. Our displays became so well known within the military community, that we were even asked to lend the decorations to the Army War College at Carlisle occasionally for their ceremonies and special events.

Being the self-appointed caretaker of our mementos and decorations it took several vanloads to haul those items home after the affair. Our annual balls became the highlight of the Army life at Fort Ritchie and I will never forget those memorable evenings with all the Officers dressed in their blues while their ladies dressed in their formals. The club was always filled to the limit and the guests truly enjoyed the special performances by the Army's Old Guard from D.C. and the Soldiers Chorus; not to forget dancing to the sounds of the famous Blues Band of the well renowned 1st United States Army Band.

Ines called us frequently from North Carolina to keep us up-to-date. Not being a dependent of our family her status had drastically changed. She relayed to us just how frustrated she was to have to go to court each year to register as an alien, wondering how long she would have to wait to become an American citizen. Living together with your family, she never needed to prove her citizenship. I had totally forgotten after all these years, that although born in a US Army Hospital in Germany, she was not an American citizen, but still a German.

After contacting and talking to the INS, the Immigration and Naturalization Service, I was happy to tell her, that having been living in the US now for over five years, she was eligible to apply and become a US citizen.

Of course, after taking and successfully passing the citizenship test. We invited her to visit us and we would all go to Baltimore, where she could get her citizenship. I made all the necessary preparations with the Immigration and Naturalization Service for the particular date of swearing in. On the 27th of August 1981, our daughter after passing the citizenship test was proud to finally call herself an American.

Getting New and Varied Experiences

I had enjoyed college so much a few years earlier that I was determined to continue another two years picking Criminal Justice as my major this time, since I had always been interested in the American justice system. Shortly after I began my second two years for the other AA degree, I noticed that the college's Campus Security was seriously lacking. Whether it pertained to traffic control, incidents involving vandalism and an occasional flasher, it made the female populace of the college quite nervous. When I brought up the subject of security and policing of the campus, the professor recommended that I write a study about our college's safety and security, including certain recommendations.

In order to obtain a good perspective and accuracy it was even suggested that, with my prior military training and experience, I should play part-time cop, on the payroll, while attending the college. Finishing my two years and receiving my Associate Degree in Criminal Justice I was able to present to the college a comprehensive study with appropriate recommendations for an improved security infrastructure, which was adopted only after several years had passed. The usual shortages of funds to establish an effective campus law enforcement element prevented any immediate implementation, but the college finally had a professional and dedicated campus security force.

Remembering discussions I had with some of my fellow students attending the criminal justice classes, who were either studying to become Police Officers or Correctional Officers, finally persuaded me to consider actual work at the local prison system in Washington County. Only five years after my military retirement I chose to put on another uniform and try out for another stressful job by wearing a badge and be a State Employee. After taking and passing the necessary tests for State employment, I had to undergo special training conducted by the Maryland Correctional Training Academy.

This training lasted hardly more than four weeks and was a great disappointment to me in comparison with either the college or with other similar military training. It became clear to me later why most people refer to the employees as guards instead of Correctional Officers. Reason being, I could not find one individual, who either would or could correct any inmate. Being surrounded by convicted felons for eight hours a day had a depressing effect on any normal individual.

My first bad taste of the workings within the system was experienced when I attended the training course to qualify for the appointment as a Correctional Officer I. Studying for the upcoming exams and tests was a breeze and actually enjoyable until I was offered the test answers in advance by some fellow workers. I hated to call them officers, because the behavior displayed by many of them were just as despicable as that of the inmates. Fraud and cheating is something I have never tolerated in my life. The fact that I had to work with those individuals, and eventually depend on them for my safety, should a volatile situation ever occur inside the prison made me very suspicious and cautious. I often had to ask myself, why anybody with my previous background would even choose this type of work. I was determined, more than ever, to continue in order to find out what makes this system what it is. I knew full and well, that I could not really contribute anything worthwhile, except for locking and unlocking prison cells.

Unable to overlook this type of unacceptable and fraudulent behavior, I approached one of the instructors. Informing him of the compromised tests, suggesting they change them. I got the feeling that my comments were not well received by the staff at all. With the exception of a very few guards, I was considered an outsider, who would probably never conform to the rules of the inner circle.

I must admit that I had a very understanding and, I sensed, honorable man as a shift supervisor. He called me aside after my initial few weeks of work and bluntly told me, that the other guards and the warden suspected me of being a plant by the State and possibly the governor to spy on the operational personnel of the prison. My background would support their theory they believed. What was undoubtedly even more suspicious was my request, prior to my employment there, to be permitted to work in every position available to correctional officers, which was granted. Assuring the supervisor that I was not a plant or covert State mole, he responded with a broad smile, that he believed me but needed to warn me, that some of the other guards may not believe it, as I was soon to discover. Their suspicions even made my work actually more interesting. It almost felt like working in SF, incognito.

One particular incident, for example, was indicative of their mistrust toward me and showed a serious effort on their part to get rid of me. They apparently believed, that by making work miserable I would voluntarily quit or ask for a transfer. Assigned to a tier, which housed over twenty inmates, some of them had to be fed in their cells, requiring the guards to deliver the meals through their cell doors with only one piece of silverware, a spoon. Unbelievable as it may sound, spoons were critical items, which had to be properly accounted for because inmates have occasionally used spoons to manufacture knives. Following the meal, the spoons were collected and locked up in the tier's control box. Only accessible to guards on duty with the respective key, the exact number of spoons could later be returned to the dining room.

Unlocking my control box one day to turn the spoons in, I routinely took another count and to my surprise found two spoons missing. I questioned my tier partner who, not surprisingly, denied getting in to my box. I promptly notified my supervisor, as an immediate search of the missing silverware was required.

I had the distinct feeling that I had been set up. I felt it necessary to do a little investigating. I privately talked to one of the guards, who I always believed to be an honest young man. After assuring himself nobody else was nearby, he confidentially told me the name of the guard, whom he had observed opening my control box and removing some spoons without realizing that someone was watching him. After I had informed my supervisor of my findings, he questioned and searched the respective guard, who finally admitted taking my spoons, but only as a joke. It was not considered a joke in the minds of some of the staff and the guard was severely reprimanded.

It took several months for me to gain confidence in many of my coworkers as I moved through different posts within the complex. One rather humorous incident had many people in tears laughing, while I could only laugh about their apparent lack of proper English.

One day I was detailed to move inmates from their cells to the exercise area outside the building. I was told to take my inmates from the tier and to "leave them out" in the courtyard. I took the inmates to the exercise area in the yard and left them there, as told, expecting to be later told to return them.

Well, the inmates all enjoyed their time outside, but when a routine inspection was made of the tiers, they naturally found my cells empty. With the inmates missing, they turned to me to find out what happened to the prisoners. When I explained to the supervisor, that I was instructed to "leave" them outside, a quick check revealed they were indeed still outside enjoying themselves. Better educated, he had to laugh, when I tried to explain my understanding of "to let" and "to leave". Speaking proper English just did not work in the prison in certain circumstances. Apparently, the local education system left a lot to be desired as I found later. Trying to educate them or clarify certain wordage seemed futile, to say the least. Cautioned by this incident I learned to always ask people again if they mean "leave" or "let".

Their lack of a proper education was revealed many times, when some guards were required to write a report about incidents involving them, but were incapable to properly put their statement on paper. Warming up to me after a while, they frequently asked for help in writing their reports, which clearly showed that the system lacked the proper training and testing of qualifications of personnel.

I gradually gained the trust of many, who would otherwise have continued to consider me as 'untrustworthy' among the institution employees. Not that it mattered that much. Once I had 'mastered' all the various positions in the correctional institute, I was intent to leave, a lot wiser in the understanding of the penal system in Maryland. There were many other rather quaint and unique incidents during my two-year stint at the Correctional Institution, but some of them are too embarrassing to put on paper. Observing the guards it seemed to me that the inmate's habits and behavior seemed to rub off on the guards after the prolonged exposure to the prison environment.

During the last months of my employment the warden asked me for my help. Someone must have mentioned to him my passion for the art and design. He asked me, if I could help him come up with a new design of a shoulder patch for our uniforms and maybe even a sign for the new K-9 Department of the Maryland Correctional Institution. Even though it would not help me learn any more about the correctional system, I agreed because this was really in line of what I liked to do. At least I left some mark behind at the institution in form of a sign and a new uniform patch design, still being worn by the guards. Neither one of course would make

them more professional. Prison work was an experience I would not rec-
ommend trying to anybody.

Loss of the Last Close Family Member

It was January 1982 when our family was notified, that my mother, Margarete Protsch had passed away after a brief hospitalization in Heidelberg.
This unfortunate event required my sister Ute, as the executor and I to
return to Germany to arrange for the funeral and dissolve the household.
Christine unfortunately could not go with me because of her work, but I
had a chance to use a Space-Available flight with the Air Force from Dover, Delaware to Frankfurt, Germany.

Arriving in Germany, I found the countryside deep in snow, which
made driving to Heidelberg aggravating and hazardous. Germans, for
some reasons, do not clear the roads and their highways as we do. It
was not an ideal time to visit Heidelberg in the middle of Winter. Overwhelmed with all the stuff we had to dispose of, we turned to friends and
some charitable organizations to help us distribute some of the goods.
Several Russian refugees were extremely happy to accept several fur coats
my mother owned. We just could not imagine our women wearing them in
the States. Most of mother's possessions went to her friends. Searching for
some of the items my father had once promised me, I found them missing.
Questioning some close friends, who always took care of mother while we
were in the States, we were told that my brother had taken items from the
apartment before we arrived from the US.

Brother Reiner persistently denied having taken anything until confronted by neighbors, who witnessed him taking several valuable large
pieces from the apartment. He finally admitted taking some selected
valuable items and heirlooms, of which he only returned a few obvious
items. While Ute and I took several days to totally dissolve and remove
everything our family had owned. Our brother Reiner graced us with his
absence during our apartment clearing; obviously he had already taken
what he felt was valuable to him. I knew that I could never forgive him
for his actions.

From what I had learned from a very good friend of our family,
Annemarie, who took very good care of mother almost like a daughter,
Reiner rarely visited her. When she became ill and required more assis-
tance and support, he even suggested that our mother move to the United
States permanently, where my family could take care of her. Naturally

she refused. She always loved to visit us in the States, but had too many friends and her roots in Germany.

According to Annemarie, our mother was shocked hearing him suggest this. As she became sicker and was admitted to a hospital doctors even talked about removing one of her legs, because of a blood clot. Our mother could not bear the idea to eventually be placed in an "Old People's Home". Being a strong willed person, she apparently willed herself to death. Knowing my mother quite well considering everything we had gone through together, this was just what I would have expected her to do.

A little subdued over the loss, I was happy to be returning to the US again, after a small funeral and a little dinner following the cremation. Aside from my annual visits to Germany and my parent's gravesite, Annemarie would religiously take care of their grave every Sunday. My brother never bothered to visit. With both my parents gone and my sister in the States I felt that all my family ties with Germany were finally gone and buried. I was looking forward to closer ties with an ever-growing family in the States.

Never a Dull Day in Semi-Retirement

I had truly enjoyed my four years of college and the company and friendships of those who studied along with me. It gave me a different insight into the American school life and the aspirations of the young people facing an uncertain future.

Having finally graduated with my second Associate of Arts degree and a 4.0 grade average, I had the very good feeling of not having wasted a moment in furthering my education. I just hope that all my grandchildren will have the sincere drive to study and learn in their younger years. My occasional apprehension, that I was not going to be fully occupied following my adult college, was soon replaced by an important upcoming event and an unusual challenge.

The Ft Ritchie Post Commander called to tell me that he felt I was perfectly suited for a special project he was asked to participate in by the County. He asked me to represent our military community in fulfilling a request by the Washington County Commissioners for military assistance. The State of Maryland was approaching the 350th Anniversary of its founding and many counties decided to celebrate it with a grand birthday party. Washington County was determined to put on its own big bash and turned to the Fort for organizational and personnel support.

Always being short in personnel because of their commitments, the Post usually turned to its retired community to provide the needed help. It was strange though that the County could not find enough people among their own local people. They finally ended up selecting two recent immigrants, a Lebanese Dr. Farah and a German, a retired Army Major, to be tasked to organize and put on the celebration. For some reason my name apparently came up to be the overall coordinator of the whole event to help the County Committee chairman. Being a member of the Fort Ritchie Infantry Ball Committee, well known to the command, must have made me an easy target. A young active duty female MP soldier was furnished to be my secretary to maintain records and help with communications between myself and other military units.

Among supporting units were Fort Bragg's Golden Knights, Special Forces Parachutists, essential Aviation support and the National Guard Artillery unit for the musical performance of the 1812 Overture. The Anniversary Celebration was scheduled for the 22nd July 1984 at the Municipal Stadium. Following months of preparation, the grand celebration was held under brilliant sunshine. The Municipal Stadium was packed to capacity, which had not seen a crowd like this for decades. While I had a great relationship with all the celebration committee members, I could not say the same to hold true between the chairman and me. He was trying to bring the usual politics into play, which I could not tolerate and strongly objected to. He finally relented.

Considering all the good work the people on the Committee and in the field were putting in I was impressed by the dedication and drive of all involved. It was a proud moment when the moderator Lou Scally, a local radio announcer, credited the execution and success of the event to the two foreigners responsible for it, citing by name the Lebanese chairman and the German Coordinator. I personally was very proud of all those volunteers, who often met with an unbelievable assortment of frustrations but gave their best to eventually make this event a huge, truly memorable and successful event.

Restless as usual, I was always looking for more excitement. After several months, while attending college, I was approached by our local fire company, which was looking for volunteers, and decided to become an active member. Surprisingly, I found myself enjoying the training and subsequently answered numerous calls to some critical fires. Participating in a few serious fires, it made me realize pretty soon, that I should not unnecessarily be exposing myself to situations, which were better handled by younger people. I decided to help with their administrative and operational procedures instead, such as writing a new SOP, their Standard Operating Procedure.

Following graduation from college I was seriously considering entering into a new and less hazardous career field. Receiving retired pay, I had the leisure of being choosy. I chose to take time out from actively looking for work until I would come up with something more satisfying. Meanwhile, Christine and I took advantage of available military flights, taking a short, but well-deserved vacation in Germany on the occasion of our 25th wedding anniversary.

Those flights were always quite adventurous at times, because one could never tell in advance whether you get to your selected destination, as planned, or as it often happened, be delayed or rerouted for several more days. Contrary to my wife, I didn't mind changes at all. Departing from Dover Air Force Base, Delaware to get to Frankfurt, Germany, I often ended up in Torrejon, Spain for a layover of several days before continuing, or being stuck on Lajes, the Azores Islands of Portugal. Forced to survive on escargots for awhile before continuing the flight was alright with me. While she did not like the inherent waiting game, I decided to take advantage of various Space "A" opportunities frequently, visiting the old fatherland and friends I was missing off and on.

Since Christine did not like the uncertainties to be expected in military stand-by flights, we took several vacations together, going by commercial air. This, of course, had the advantage to be able to more properly plan our short visits to relatives. Christine's father and her brother living in close proximity to each other were our prime destination. When her father was placed on some medication preventing him to fly to the States, we made it a point to visit him in Germany every year if possible.

Not being tied down by a full time job, I was always available to volunteer for various projects and organizations. Utilizing my given talents I was able to fulfill several requests from other individuals and units. Among those requests were special services, such as the production of mementos for farewell gifts and various special awards, once people became aware of my talents. Once I became known as a freelance artist, I became swamped with requests for pen & ink drawings, designing heraldic coat of arms, diplomas and doing calligraphy. Quite often I was asked to provide woodcarvings of distinctive military unit crests and insignias for distinguished visitors and military and civilian personnel departing or retiring. I was quite happy being busy doing what I liked doing most.

When Fort Ritchie lost its director of the Community Center through a transfer, the Post Commander believed that I had the ability and talent to take over that job, even though only temporarily. For a period of six months, I was able to arrange for and provide the Fort Ritchie population with programs and special events such as performances by special military units, including the traditional Old Guard and the 1st US Army Band. When the former director lost her position as a result of cutbacks at her station, she returned to our post looking for a job. Explaining her dilemma and hardships, I felt bad of holding down her former job, which I really did not need. It was not hard for me to convince the Commander to hire her back offering my resignation.

This freed me again and also gave me the opportunity to enter several art competitions. When the town of Sharpsburg, adjacent to the Antietam Battlefield, a well-known site from the Civil War era, challenged local artists to design a town seal or coat of arms for their historical township, I took the challenge and immediately got immersed into its historical past. Researching all available data in archives and libraries I came up with a design, which I believed to be an appropriate and meaningful seal and coat of arms. Hoping for its approval but not really expecting it, I was still surprised when the town selected my design. It is always gratifying to see my work on road signs and on documents of the town of Sharpsburg, MD.

Sometimes I wondered, why it is so hard for some people to find a good and satisfying job, while I constantly seem to be falling from one into another more challenging employment. Not long after I had left the director's position at the Community Center, a man called me from a Stud Farm near Waterford, Virginia. He had heard about my background and offered me an interesting position in his security unit of the Catoctin Stud Farm, a corporation owned and operated by the Firestones. The head of the unit was a retired CIA agent, who was looking for reliable retired military personnel. They would receive proper training in armed private security services by the State. Provided with all the necessary equipment and vehicles to patrol the huge estate, including numerous barns, stables, a race track to include the residences for the employees and groomers, it sounded like an interesting assignment. It was so tempting and nearly too good to be true, that I agreed to visit the estate for a personal interview before making any decision.

Crossing the Potomac River and entering Virginia, I found myself in some of the most beautiful countryside of this area. It took me over an hour passing several horse farms and pastures, driving on asphalt and gravel roads, before I arrived at the estate. I could not believe the absolutely wonderful manicured fields, the old residences but in contrast modern facilities for the care of the racehorses, among which I found offsprings of Secretariat. Seeing the absolutely clean, beautiful stables with interior walnut and oak paneling and the built-in quarters of the caretakers, I felt like being in a horse paradise. Being part of this estate's armed security looked like a dream assignment and it did not take much convincing to consider taking this job.

Working there for over a year I enjoyed every day, including the daily drive to work in my little low profile historic Triumph Spitfire I had acquired. Battling snowstorms in winter on hardly trafficable country roads, which never saw a snowplow, was a true challenge. I could have continued working there indefinitely. Unfortunately, our son Dieter lost his job when the advertising company he was working for went bankrupt. Meeting with difficulties in finding a good company to work for and planning to get married, our family had to make a quick decision. I had no choice but to terminate my cushy employment at the horse farm.

Since Dieter had the talent for graphics and good communication skills, while I could also do graphics and typesetting, we all agreed to establish our own company. Based on our past experiences with other small businesses and the prospect to take over some accounts of his bankrupt company, 'DP Graphics and Advertisement' was born in late 1988. It was an expensive investment in typesetting equipment initially, but diligently working in a home based environment, with a lot of hard work, we both got it to work pretty well. Our clientele grew quite fast over the next two years. But so did my son's family, who had decided to get married and have children, without carefully considering the consequences of such move, especially when the family expects to have adequate health insurance.

This was something our small company could hardly afford. I never needed any private health coverage, as the Army was taking care of its own, including retirees. It was decision time again and Dieter Junior started looking for a company, which would provide adequate health coverage for a young family and children, which rapidly grew to six children. While Dieter had the luck to find a good company and left to work there, I continued working under DP Graphics, but had to scale down, only accepting assignments I could easily handle and at the time enjoy.

In enviable health in the past and after my retirement, but finding myself sitting more behind the desk and in front of the computer and typesetter, I was gradually being bothered by lower back pain. The pain increasingly worsened, forcing me to seek medical advice, resulting in taking prescription painkillers, which in turn resulted in higher blood pressure. Needless to say, I could not accept Ft Ritchie's medical determination that taking high blood pressure medication would be for life and that the lower back pain is rather common among older people. A visit to the Army's Walter Reed Medical Center in D.C, taking some thorough tests and further examinations, they found two severely herniated and one slipped disk.

Instead of any type of surgery, I opted for a more practical and natural solution. A young Captain, a neurosurgeon, suggested a possible restoration of my previous physical condition I had on Active Duty, which would not only remedy my back problem, but also lower my blood pressure. Hating any kind of handicap and medication I promised myself to change my lifestyle. I decided to return to a regimen of exercise, as recommended by the Army.

A follow-up MRI about a year later, found absolutely no trace of any previous problem in the spinal area. Doing regular exercises, mostly side by side with Christine, was the apparent solution to all my previous problems. By regularly visiting the Wellness Center at the Community College and participating in a Fit for Life program, I rebuilt my stamina and overall fitness to the point that I lowered my blood pressure. This recovery eliminated the need to take blood pressure medication many people have to take.

I believed to finally have found the happy medium between working inside and being active outside, while also adhering to a proper diet. Eating only real sunflower, linseed and 5-grain bread freshly shipped in from Canada became part of our diet. Returning to eating habits of my earlier years definitely helped. Never infatuated by any of the multitude of soft drinks and never frequenting fast food restaurants turned out to be a big benefit in my life.

Always interested in veteran's affairs, I had been a member of the American Legion Post and Life Member of the Veterans of Foreign Wars for over a quarter century. While discussing our past services over a few scotches and beers and the general apathy of most of our young generation in particular, we felt that we do more than just reminisce. Talks usually went back to the days of World War II, considering most WWI veterans completely gone. There were, however, quite a few Korea and Viet Nam veterans present, who remember their fathers, killed in both great wars. Some of those fallen veterans had their name inscribed at a memorial here or there, but many had never been personally memorialized anywhere.

While many cities and smaller towns held Veterans Day parades with floats in honor and memory of the fallen citizens. Hagerstown was lacking such an event. It only had the traditional Mummers Day Parade and to many it seemed that we should also have a Veterans Day Parade to show our pride and commitment to those who made the ultimate sacrifice. With over ten different veterans organizations in the County going their own way, it was decided to form a Joint Veterans Council in the County to coordinate veterans' efforts in our area.

Representatives of each organization were appointed to the Council to plan combined events and projects in the name of all veterans groups. As a delegate of the Viet-Nam Veterans Last Man Club of the American Legion Post 42, and its first president, I was elected as the first Secretary to the Council. I must admit I underestimated the drive and enthusiasm of my fellow veterans. I had my hands full. It did not take long, before we held the first of many annual Veterans Parades in Hagerstown. For five years thereafter, we conducted our parades with great success. The veterans units themselves had funded them until, to our dismay, the cost of holding them reached a point where we could no longer support this program.

We knew that we could not just stop there. During my ten-year tenure as the secretary and historian, the Council beginning in 1989 decided and was able to build a Veterans Memorial in a memorial park in Hagerstown to provide the community with a dedicated site to conduct our annual Memorial Day and Veterans Day services in lieu of a parade.

But we even went further than that. Designing small memorial markers, as I called them, for every Washington County serviceman who lost his life in combat, we paid a special tribute to them. The recognition included all GIs killed in action, those who died as the direct result of wounds received, others designated as missing in action and those servicemen taken prisoner, who never returned home. I was proud to have made over 250 of the 2 ½ by 12 inch two-sided black markers.

Prior to the wall being built in late 1961 Russian and American tanks face each other in a stand-off.

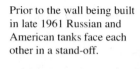

A 19-year old East German escapee, shot and killed by East German Police and troops is recovered and dragged back.

Check Point "Charlie" is being overrun by Berliners from both parts on 9 November 1989.

East and West Berliners on top of the wall at the Brandenburg Gate. There was a total absence of any uniformed person on this historic day. The wall had come down and Germany was finally re-united. I personally witnessed it, lived it and shall remember it all my life.

Each marker bore their name, rank, date born and killed, to include branch of service and a ribbon showing the war or conflict they became a casualty in.

This project lasted for over twelve years. A small team of uniformed veterans conducted a small dedication ceremony each Sunday morning at the sites where the individual had lived during their service. Granted permission by the City and County government, and armed with a ladder and a power drill, I spent hours riveting those memorial markers on top of street signs throughout Washington County. Very often relatives and dependents of the former member of the service attended the little ceremony.

During our research to find accurate records for our war dead we noted that neither the County Library nor the Newspaper had complete information of their background. Our twelve-year search finally produced adequate documentation to establish a reliable record, which we shared with the County Library, the County Court House and the State Archives at Annapolis, Maryland.

Witnessing the "Fall of the Berlin Wall".
A Historical Event

The year of 1989 turned out to be another exciting and memorable year. It was the beginning of November, when my old friend Dieter, the Police Officer from Berlin called me and strongly advised me to make a return visit to Berlin as soon as possible. Some historic event was about to take place within the next few weeks and he was sure that I would not want to miss it. He had received some reliable intelligence reports he could not discuss over the phone, but assured me that it will have an 'immense impact on the lives of all Berliners' and possibly the rest of Germany.

Christine did not have any particular desire to return to Berlin. So, on the 6th of November 1989, I took a Lufthansa Airline flight to Berlin, Germany, where I met with Dieter. Shortly after my arrival he took me to the old symbol of the city, the Brandenburg Gate, close to the Soviet Army Memorial. There, to my surprise, CNN had parked a flatbed open trailer. It was an ominous sign, according to Dieter, that something big was going to happen, because they always positioned themselves there, like during presidential visits, etc.

Patience was required, he stated. I stayed in his apartment for three days, when we were alerted that mobs were demonstrating on the eastern side of the Berlin Wall. Proceeding to the site, we arrived at the Brandenburg Gate and with the sun setting, we saw a large crowd also on the western side of the wall. We could not believe our own eyes when we noticed jubilant East Berliners standing next to the *VOPOs*, on top of the Wall. The dreaded People's Police or *Volkspolizei*, was commonly armed and patrolling the area, keeping the population from even getting close to the wall. Not so this time. On several sections of the wall in the West, we spotted people with hammers and pickaxes hammering away at the wall, attempting to take it down, piece-by-piece. Others could be seen and heard singing, while raising bottles of Champagne in an apparent toast to some unique happening.

The scene was unbelievable. We soon found out, that for all practical purposes, the Wall was being torn down. This was reminding me of President Ronald Reagan's visit to the wall not so long ago, calling on the Russian Premier Gorbachov to take the wall down. I was mesmerized, watching the uniformed border police of the East German Regime, without visible weapons, helplessly standing there, obviously joining the people in the celebration. Without any shots being fired, this was clearly the collapse of the Communist Regime in East Germany.

Enthused and taken in by this unbelievable event, I don't even remember how I ended up with a full bottle of wine in my hands, toasting with Dieter and the rest of the Berliners. I was just wondering what prompted the fall of the East German regime. How would that effect our military presence in Berlin and what changes this new and unbelievable event would bring to the general political situation? Like all the rest of the Berliners, I also scrambled to get a hold of a couple pieces of the wall chipped of the concrete fortification, as I wanted to remember this date, the 9th November 1989 forever.

For two days, I walked along the wall with thousands of other Berliners watching people drive through the wall at several points, where large cranes from the East had removed entire sections. It brought tears to my eyes, when I saw families being reunited again, embracing each other after all the years of separation. It only took about a day or so and I found several vendors already along the wall selling T-shirts imprinted with the slogans in English and German "I was there when the Wall came down" and "The last one leaving, turn the lights off". Some entrepreneurs must have been working all night to produce them. I could not resist buying several; to include one depicting an older version of a Berlin City Map as a divided city depicting the four allied sectors.

As I realized the importance of this historic event, I was looking for a large piece of the wall and found a concrete post of the first wall, from a site, where several people were killed climbing the old barbed wire fence. Without a hammer available anywhere, I was desperate to find any kind of tool to get me a larger piece to take home to the US. Dieter and I were in the British Sector alongside the wall, when we finally spotted a slow driving British MP jeep patrolling the area. We were both wondering what they thought about the new situation.

We approached the jeep and I asked the ranking corporal if they had any tool in the jeep, which could be helpful to remove a piece of the wall. Initially hesitating, I explained to him the reason why I desperately needed this piece of souvenir after which he finally nodded to his companion, who brought out a small pickax. It was good enough to remove a large chunk of the concrete wall, weighing nearly 30 pounds. I spent a couple more days celebrating with Dieter and friends, observing the radical change in Berlin, brought about by the reunification of Germany's capitol and as a matter of fact, all of Germany. This was something I did not expect to come about in my lifetime.

I finally had to leave Berlin. With the wall down, people of the former communist state, now defunct, were flooding West Berlin. The government of West Berlin and the Allies, apparently totally surprised were trying to cope with this unexpected new influx of people enjoying their newly found freedom. So much for the reliability of our allied intelligence.

What we took for granted in the West, such as tropical fruit, food from around the world, modern appliances and a strong currency made the East Germans feel like visiting paradise. Being able to see and touch, they were however not yet able to buy and enjoy those precious items. Their money was no longer worth anything actually, until the Federal Republic of Germany found a way to provide some kind of exchange rate. We could see many East Germans now even throwing their obviously worthless lightweight aluminum coins into the air. Everything seemed hilarious and almost unreal.

Changes Impacting on Europe and NATO

Returning home from Germany, lugging a heavy piece of history, I watched the news and tried to imagine the implications this drastic political change in Berlin would have for all of Germany and to Europe. Berlin especially, with its four-sector division and an Allied Command, would totally change. All of our troops stationed in an area formerly surrounded by a hostile force could now be returning to the West. Regaining freedom of movement, which we did not have when we were stationed in Berlin, was going to be a welcomed and tremendous change for the troops. Their special status and critical mission had suddenly disappeared over night. With Germany reunited, the hated Soviet Army occupation force was now in some areas experiencing open hostility from the general German civilian populace.

The Soviets, overwhelmed themselves by this drastic change were trying to slowly extricate themselves, leaving their communist German counterparts behind. The hardcore communists and their government now faced retribution from the population, as their friends, the Russians were departing from Germany, leaving them unprotected. But Germany was not going to be the only country affected by the fall of the wall and the dismantling of the so-called "iron curtain" running through Germany. All neighboring countries, such as Czechoslovakia, were subsequently apt to change, making the previous Warsaw Pact Alliance a thing of the past.

Politically, Germany was not the only country to undergo significant changes. Once the Soviet troops began withdrawing from the eastern part of Germany, the former DDR, adjoining countries such as Hungary and Poland, who had uprisings against the Soviet system before, now also appeared to gain new courage to liberate themselves. This in turn had a ripple effect throughout the Soviet controlled Eastern Europe, to include states that made up the Union of Soviet Socialist Republics. It was not to take long for the republics to obtain their freedom and independence, eventually leading to the collapse of the Soviet Union. This totally unexpected development was sure to have serious implications on the stability and security within the Eastern hemisphere in the future, which nobody had expected.

Great To Be Back Home. Making the Most of It

Glad to be back home again, I was getting back into my former element. In possession of several chunks of the Berlin Wall, I was busy making souvenirs for my friends by mounting pieces of the wall on small plaques of black walnut with an engraved personal inscription underneath each piece of the Berlin Wall.

Staring at this despicable wall for years, I would have never dreamed that parts of it would one day become a significant part of our history with traces of it displayed all over the world as a symbol of freedom over tyranny. Of course there were numerous other remnants of the former communist regime, now souvenirs, which found their way back to the US. An entire East German Army Major's uniform to insignias, huge flags and even to a Russian Space program memento celebrating the launching of their German/Russian rocket program, they all found a new home in my own little "museum". Settling down from this rather moving trip, and a dramatically changed Germany, I now turned my attention to designing again. Not to forget, I still had a small graphics company of one to run.

Eager to get back to a normal life, I immediately entered another type of competition, which was part of the Maryland State Senior Citizens Arts Competition under the title "Maryland You Are Beautiful". Having learned a few things and improving my talent in the area of woodcarving, I entered Washington County's Competition. Entering a unique carving I was proud to be declared the County's First Place winner in Woodcarving. Following its further submission to the committee established by the Governor in Baltimore, my artwork was additionally declared "Best in Show" by the State.

The woodcarving was a relief of the "Old Heidelberg" Castle, carved out of a large solid oak kitchen cabinet door I once received from a friend at Fort Ritchie, who felt it was too nice to throw away. He remembered me from previous carvings I made for their souvenirs and farewell gifts and was sure I could to do something with it. While I always visualize a piece of art to come out of something people might want to discard, my wife is more for cleaning up things and getting rid of old things. It is intriguing to me how I sometimes manage to surprise my wife with new things made from seemingly useless old items. The State's prize and recognition consisted of a truly beautiful long weekend including a tour of Annapolis, compliments of the State of Maryland, a lunch with Governor Schaeffer, presentation of a "Salute to Excellence" and a pin recognizing the wearer as a "Maryland Ambassador".

Daring to repeat this feat I competed again the following year. I thought to outdo myself by entering an even larger woodcarving, this time depicting all of the county's prominent historical sites. It was almost 20"x 26", made from solid oak again and really impressive looking. Since I had won the year before, I really thought of just entering without expecting to win again, which I did not. The recognition of the piece as being 'worth of mentioning' was reward enough for me.

As time went on, I was privileged to be guest speaker a few times such as at the Exchange Club Dinner and several High Schools in the area, speaking about my youth in Germany, my military career or relating my experiences during the Viet-Nam war. When Fort Ritchie was finally closed by the Army during one of their Base Closure projects, the civilians and troops and especially the military retirees who retired around the Base, were obviously heartbroken, to loose such a beautiful site.

Having been associated with the Post, for quite awhile, I was honored to be chosen as the Post's last guest speaker during a grand sit-in dinner for the last departing group of NCOs and Officers. As requested, I gave them my perspective of an immigrant seeking the service in the military, especially the Army, pointing out the excellent opportunity to serve my new country. Following my speech, which could have been a lot longer, many guests asked for more details. I suddenly realized that there was a need on my part, to actually sit down some day and put all my experiences in writing. Quite often my grandchildren had questions about me and my life when I was younger and my experiences during the war. Writing your memoirs, I was advised, would be the best way to satisfy the frequent questions from my children, their spouses and my eight grandchildren. I decided to do just that with this book.

I have no regrets for the things I have done in my life. I only wished that I could have done more to help those who needed a hand. I lived by my own code of ethics and my very own belief, strengthened through my service in Special Forces. Its motto "De Oppresso Liber", meaning 'Freedom to the Oppressed' from Latin has become my sincere conviction to pursue.

Hoping that in the eyes of my fellow man I was seen as being an unquestionably good and fair person, I am striving hard to do my best in serving my country, living by the principles of Duty, Honor, and Country.

Still serving!

De Oppresso Liber!

DATE DUE

ISBN 141203674-7